An Introduction to Psychological Assessment and Psychometrics

Keith Coaley

SAGE

Los Angeles | London | New Delhi
Singapore | Washington DC

First published 2009

SAGE Publications Ltd
1 Oliver's Yard
55 City Road
London EC1Y 1SP

SAGE Publications Inc.
2455 Teller Road
Thousand Oaks, California 91320

SAGE Publications India Pvt Ltd
B 1/I 1 Mohan Cooperative Industrial Area
Mathura Road
New Delhi 110 044

SAGE Publications Asia-Pacific Pte Ltd
33 Pekin Street #02-01
Far East Square
Singapore 048763

Library of Congress Control Number: 2009929038

British Library Cataloguing in Publication data

A catalogue record for this book is available from
the British Library

ISBN 978-1-84787-478-8
ISBN 978-1-84787-479-5 (pbk)

Typeset by C&M Digitals (P) Ltd, Chennai, India
Printed in Great Britain by TJ International Ltd, Padstow, Cornwall
Printed on paper from sustainable resources

TO
Rhys, Llywelyn, Megan and Lucas

Contents

Preface

I wrote this book for two reasons. First, because best practice in psychological assessment and testing is something which has preoccupied me for many years and, secondly, because there was a need for an easily readable and accessible introductory text. It is designed to be an interesting and enjoyable, practical approach to the most important of all applied psychological activities. This fascinating and exciting subject has been squeezed down to its essentials.

All the technicalities are there for you to grasp. It's always difficult to understand something when you don't know at the start what its purpose is. Technicalities (yawn) only make sense when you know 'why?' and 'what for?' and I have tried to remove the jargon, to put them in context and relate them to real life applications.

There was a need for an introductory text to help a range of people. These include both undergraduate and post-graduate students, as well as Human Resources and allied professionals doing the British Psychological Society's certificates of competence in testing. To begin with, I investigated the undergraduate syllabi of a number of universities, aiming to provide for these, as well as the elements of competence set for the Level A and B certificates.

For those of you who are undergraduates I cover the different professional areas of psychology, so that you can know what assessment issues are relevant to areas of practice. This will, I hope, help you to understand better the future career alternatives. For HR professionals I hope that I have provided you with a broader view of assessment and a better grasp of what is involved. The same applies to those of you who are doing Master's degrees.

This book is organized in six parts: Introduction: Foundations of Psychological Assessment; Part I: The Essential Tools of Psychological Measurement, Part II: The Essential Characteristics of Psychological Measurement; Part III: Applications of Assessment and Measurement; Part IV: Ethical and Professional Issues; and Part V: Constructing Your Own Test or Questionnaire. The differing sections can be taught separately as topic areas. Chapter 11 on constructing a test has been added to support both students and lecturers in a practical research activity, as well as other practition-ers who want to know how to go about it. Each chapter has been organized around key objectives which are listed at the beginning, and important themes are highlighted at the end.

I have aimed to provide a conceptual understanding of issues, including modern developments, and have linked them to an individual differences approach because many tests and questionnaires invariably measure differences between people. In addi-tion, I have sought to lay the groundwork of statistical foundations and the parameters of sound assessment, such as reliability and validity, first and then to use these in eval-uation of techniques. A key aspect is best practice, including the evaluation and selec-tion of tests and their fair and ethical use.

I also wanted to write a book which is reasonably comprehensive, interesting and accessible, based on the way in which I have taught the subject over a long time. I have had a lot of pleasure explaining difficult concepts in simple and sometimes silly ways, often using drawings and examples, and have attempted to transfer some to the book. Humour is often more memorable. I hope, too, that it will provide a useful reference and source book for you in the future.

Psychological assessment and testing has expanded considerably. The use of new technology has advanced, enabling development of new tests, inventories and scales, as well as new methods of administration, scoring and interpretation. But they have been the subject of criticism, with lay people frequently lacking understanding of their nature and technical foundations. When I discuss them with others I constantly find they are surprised by this. A prime need is, therefore, for well-trained practitioners who have sound understanding, who can 'carry the flag' and explain their benefits and advantages for modern society. Provision of good training is integral to this.

I would like to thank a number of people for their help and support in writing this book. They include the university lecturers who reviewed and commented on various chapters, as well as Dr Tanya Edmonds who also reviewed some chapters. Thanks go to Dr Barry Cripps for his help and to Liam Healy for his valuable encouragement. The Sage team of Michael Carmichael, my editor, and Sophie Hine also provided substan-tial help throughout. Any of the book's shortcomings should, however, be attributed to myself. I am grateful to Dr Laurence Paltiel for his kind permission to reproduce copy-right material. Thank you, too, to the people who matter most: my readers.

Keith
April 2009
Hertfordshire

About the Author

Dr Keith Coaley is a chartered occupational and clinical psychologist, having many years of experience as an applied psychologist, trainer and lecturer at both HE and university levels. After a first undergraduate degree, he did a second degree in psychology with the Open University before a Master's degree at Cardiff University and another later in forensic and legal psychology at Leicester University. He was awarded his PhD for his research in stress, health and job performance at Manchester. Having extensive experience of psychological assessment in practice, he has researched and published on topics relating to the fields of psychometrics and assessment. He has experience of work in Human Resources, in consultancy and in the National Health Service and prison settings, and has worked in the UK, Ireland, the Far East and Africa.

1

Introduction: Foundations of Psychological Assessment

Learning Objectives

By the end of this chapter you should be able to:

- Understand the basic principles underlying psychological assessment, how they contrast with common perceptions, and distinguish between its different forms.
- Identify the key figures in the historical development of assessment methods.
- Give an account of the core characteristics and issues relating to different approaches.
- Understand their use in the different areas of applied psychology.

What is This Chapter About?

Applied psychologists ply their trade in the real world. So we have to begin by introducing many of the core definitions, characteristics and foundations underlying modern approaches to assessment and psychometrics. It helps also to have an understanding of the historical tradition preceding modern practice, so we will review its development from its historical roots, identifying those explorers who have had a significant and enduring influence. We will also take a look at some key terms and issues, followed by discussion of common types of test and how these can be classified or grouped. The chapter will conclude with brief descriptions of how and why assessments are used in the different fields of applied psychology today.

What Do We Mean by Psychological Assessment and Psychometrics?

The common thread that unites all of the domains of applied psychology is measurement. Psychometrics are designed to do measurement; in fact, the term is an abbreviation for 'psychological measurement'. They form a branch of a wider field referred to as psychological assessment, which seeks to understand the psychology of the individual, whatever the circumstances, whether in clinical, forensic, educational, counselling, health, coaching or occupational settings. The complexity of the mind makes this a difficult task to achieve.

A proliferation of terms used over the years has tended to cause some confusion and so the word 'test' has been applied as a generic word for absolutely everything linked to assessment. It could mean a questionnaire or an inventory, and is interchangeable with equivalent terms such as tool, assessment, measure or instrument. But in practice there are distinctions. Let's say, for argument's sake, you feel a bit depressed and go to see a clinical or counselling psychologist. Your psychologist may firstly go through a detailed interview and make notes, and then ask you to complete a depression inventory. Or you have just been subjected to hospital treatment and feel a bit anxious about your state of health so you visit a health psychologist who goes through a similar process using an anxiety inventory. Or you apply for a new job and have to face an assessment centre which includes interviews, tests, questionnaires and work sample exercises. In all these cases you undertake an assessment which has different components. The whole process consists of a psychological assessment and is designed to describe, predict, explain, diagnose and make decisions about you. The actions required by social services to care for you, in some instances, may also be included. Therefore measurement, using quantitative inventories, tests or questionnaires, actually forms one or more parts of a broader thing called psychological assessment (see Figure 1.1).

A 'test' is a sub-component of measurement, being focussed on those tasks/questions (called items) which have right or wrong answers, and are mostly referred to as cognitive, ability or aptitude tests. That means that you cannot really describe a personality questionnaire as a 'personality test', even though it may make use of measurement. Many experienced psychologists who have written books like this one mix the two terms. People get worried when they encounter the term 'personality tests', so I think it is neither an accurate description nor good public relations to use it. Similarly, a 'questionnaire' is also a sub-component of measurement, although having items which do not have right or wrong answers. They may, for example, ask people to agree or disagree about a statement or to indicate whether a particular statement is true or false about them. A response to say a statement is false about me as an individual would, surely, not be a wrong answer. The term 'inventory' is sometimes also used for these instruments. Lastly, the term 'psychometric', as I said earlier, refers to those things which are based upon a measurement process, including tests and questionnaires which are not tests. An understanding of the statistics underlying tests and questionnaires is essential for good practice use of them. To confuse things further, I prefer to describe some components solely as 'assessments', for example

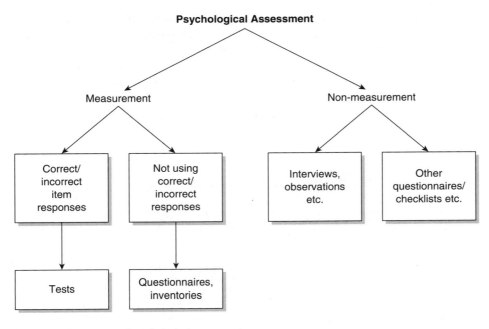

Figure 1.1   A taxonomy of psychological assessment

interviews, simple checklists and observations, to distinguish them from activities which do involve measurement. So psychological assessments are far more than tests. True assessment really is a more complex enterprise involving the integration of information from different sources to get a more comprehensive understanding of a person, using multiple sources including personal, social and medical history where relevant.

Measurement ultimately evolved from the study of individual differences in human psychology which has aimed to be more objective in its descriptions of people. The concern is to establish what exists rather than whether what exists is good or bad. Key questions are: What are the ways by which people differ and how can we objectively measure the differences? Over the last 100 years or so the discipline has become increasingly scientific in its approach, and the growth of empirical thinking has had enormous consequences in how we make assessments. Psychology is concerned to discover not just what characteristics are possessed by a person, but also the way these are organized to make the individual different from others. The aim is to be more precise, enabling the trained professional to make justifiable and verifiable predictions. In other words, we seek to use clearly agreed criteria to define psychological constructs and, where possible, to measure these through the use of scales and statistical techniques. Often scales can be standardized so as to compare a person with others, for example the general population or other people diagnosed as suffering depression or anxiety, or other managers in an occupational setting. Psychometric instruments are carefully constructed to ensure their measurements are both accurate and replicable.

The science of psychology operates on the basis of clear criteria and standardized measurement scales. We need to be explicit about what we mean and how we measure, whether in research or practice. Used well, measurement can give us accurate and relevant information which leads to more effective decision-making, providing insights not available through observations and interviews. These latter methods, anyway, are often influenced by personal factors relating to the person doing the assessment. So it is clear that to adopt a scientific approach we need to base our methods upon measurement (see Box 1.1 which discusses what we mean by measurement and its benefits).

Box 1.1   What is Measurement?

Measurement is the assignment of numbers to properties or attributes of people, objects or events using a set of rules, according to Stevens (1946, 1968). From this definition several characteristics of measurement may be derived (Aguinis, Henle and Ostroff, 2001):

1 It focuses on attributes of people, objects or events not on actual people, objects or events.
2 It uses a set of rules to quantify these. They must be standardized, clear, understandable and easy to apply.
3 It consists of scaling and classification. Scaling deals with assignment of numbers so as to quantify them, i.e. to determine how much of an attribute is present. Classification refers to defining whether people, objects or events fall into the same or different categories.

Aguinis et al. add that Stevens' definition relates to a process of measurement. This means that:

1 Its purpose should be determined, for example, in prediction, classification or decision-making.
2 The attribute should be identified and defined. A definition needs to be agreed before it is measured or different rules may be applied, resulting in varying numbers being assigned. The purpose of measurement should guide this definition.
3 A set of rules, based on the definition, should be determined to quantify the attribute.
4 Lastly, the rules are applied to translate the attribute into numerical terms.

Benefits of Measurement

1 The key benefit is objectivity, which minimises subjective judgement and allows theories to be tested (Aguinis, 1993).
2 Measurement results in quantification. This enables more detail to be gathered than through personal judgements.
3 More subtle effects can be observed and statistical analysis used to make precise statements about patterns of attributes and relationships (Pedhazur and Pedhazur Schmelkin, 1991).
4 Better communication is possible because standardized measures lead to a common language and understanding.

Surveys of public attitudes towards psychological assessment and measurement are comparatively rare. There has been a growing recognition of the value of psychological assessment among people at large and other health professionals, increasing demand in the US. Elsewhere data is based upon acceptance of test materials and methods in the workplace. In the UK one survey found that most employers, whilst still using traditional methods, such as application forms, references and interviews, are increasingly also using ability tests, personality questionnaires and assessment centres (Hodgkinson, Daley and Payne, 1996). There have been studies of the perceptions of graduates and managers about the use of psychometrics, especially for recruitment and selection, and these are generally positive, with some worries about, for example, the need for professionally qualified administrators (as shown in Box 1.2).

Box 1.2   Evaluating Perceptions of Testing

How people think about psychological assessment is important in applied psychology. In clinical settings studies of people's perceptions are focussed mainly on therapeutic methods and outcomes. In the workplace they have often been based upon perceptions of fairness and relevance to jobs. Increased use of unsupervised computer-based testing has been subject to evaluation because of concerns about lack of standardization and a potential for cheating. A study by Hughes and Tate (2007) demonstrates that many applicants feel that such testing is unfair.

Method

Participants completed an online questionnaire requesting their views and experiences regarding computer-based ability testing. The target population was made up of undergraduates and graduates who were considered more likely to have been exposed to this kind of testing.

Results and Discussion

A total of 46 per cent thought computer-based testing to be a fair selection method, 41 per cent felt it was not fair, 6 per cent felt it depended on circumstances and 7 per cent did not express a view. Comments of those who said that it depended on the circumstances of use tended to focus on:

- Its use alongside other selection measures
- The relevance of the test to the job
- The test's quality and provision of practice items and feedback
- Whether cheating could be controlled.

The authors say that the high proportion who did not feel the tests were fair demonstrates a need for employers to ensure tests are appropriate and the reasons for using them are explained. Their purpose and the process by which candidates are assessed should be made transparent in pre-test information. In other words, communication is a key issue in managing perceptions.

(Cont'd)

This is particularly important for selection methods. When there is high unemployment employers might feel they can ignore candidates' reactions, but in a labour shortage unpopular techniques could deter some from applying. One study even suggests that candidates who are uncomfortable with an organization's methods may react by not buying its products (Stinglhamber, Vandebberghe and Brancart, 1999). Some techniques are more popular. Interviews, work samples and assessment centres are preferred to peer assessment, personality questionnaires and abstract reasoning tests because they appear less job-related.

The picture is less clear among other European countries, with some national differences (Cook and Cripps, 2005). Assessment and measurement in occupational settings are most popular in Spain, Portugal and the Netherlands, whilst there is some resistance, notably in Germany and Turkey. There is not much information about other areas of the world – Australia and New Zealand appear to have a similar approach to the UK, and in some African countries, such as Nigeria and Ghana, there has been a move towards testing. Some evidence is available, based upon personal experience, the country's historical background and the introduction of test producers to China, that the Chinese are also using them.

Psychologists and others, such as HR professionals, using assessment instruments will need more than just technical skills to make their way in the world. These skills include knowing how to administer test materials relevant to their area of practice both accurately and ethically. But they also need a sound understanding of the theoretical and conceptual foundations of their science, combined with cultural awareness. And they will need the communication skills to be able to explain what they are doing and why.

Summary

The psychology of individual differences seeks to describe the ways in which people differ, and to understand how and why these arise, and because of this assessment instruments are used widely in applied psychology today. They are founded upon an objective, scientific and empirical approach to making justifiable and verifiable predictions about people, rather than being based on subjective opinion. Psychological assessment refers to the integration of information from multiple sources in order to describe, predict, explain, diagnose and make decisions. Psychometrics are those instruments which measure people's characteristics, having been subjected to standardization using scales which enable scores to be compared. In any form of assessment the tasks or questions are called items. Where an instrument has right/wrong items it is often referred to as a test; whilst others are better referred to as questionnaires or inventories. It is important for those who make use of these instruments to do so in an ethical way and to adhere to codes of practice.

Historical Background

The Chinese invented gunpowder and also psychological assessment, not that the two are connected. They used testing some 4000 years ago for job selection purposes and appeared to be a test-dominated society. A variety of assessments were used for civil service examinations designed to choose Mandarins and all of the Emperor's officials were examined every third year, including job sample tests to identify proficiency in arithmetic, archery, music, writing and ceremonial skills (Bowman, 1989; Doyle, 1974). Candidates were also assessed for their ability to memorize and understand the Confucian classics, as well as in essay and poem composition. Formal procedures were established, including independent assessments by at least two assessors and the standardization of test conditions, as is done often today. The Greek philosophers Plato and Aristotle also discussed individual differences in their works. Interest then declined during the Middle Ages until a new recognition of individualism came in the sixteenth century Renaissance.

By the seventeenth century post-Renaissance philosophers began to look at ideas, events and phenomena in more scientific ways, leading to a new way of thinking called 'empiricism'. This said that all factual or true knowledge comes from experience and was developed by John Locke into an organized school of thought. When Charles Darwin provided an account of the mechanisms of evolution between 1858 and 1877, he influenced early psychology. His principal thesis was that members of a species exhibit variability of characteristics and this variability results in some being better suited than others to any particular set of environmental conditions. His term 'characteristic' meant anything which could be attributed to an individual organism, for example agility or height. Those best adapted would reproduce more prolifically, possibly being the only ones to survive to maturity and reproduce. The significance of individual differences between those belonging to the same species was, therefore, a key factor which influenced early psychologists and statisticians, many of whom contributed to the development of a new science of mental measurement. Experimental psychologists such as Gustav Fechner, Wilhelm Wundt and Hermann Ebbinghaus, discovered that psychological phenomena could be described in rational and quantitative ways.

Especially important was the Englishman Francis Galton (1822–1911), whose career was similar to that of his cousin Darwin. You are in good company if you have felt close to a breakdown before exams because Galton studied maths at Trinity College, Cambridge, and suffered a breakdown before his finals so he didn't get a very good honours degree. But, like his cousin, Galton adopted the new scientific ideas which he thought could be proven only by careful enquiry and used his wealth to pursue this. Among many other interests, he became obsessed with making all kinds of measurements of people in his research laboratory. More than 17,000 people paid for the privilege of providing measurements, such as height, weight, strength, rate of movement and reaction times.

Galton was a prolific writer and a zealous scientist. He was the first to emphasize the importance of individual differences, created the first tests of mental ability and was the first to use questionnaires. He discovered a number of statistical procedures to analyse data, many still in use today, for example he found that a wide range of measures of human physiology and abilities produce what is still referred to as a 'normal curve', sometimes as the 'bell curve' or 'normal distribution'. He said this curve could be meaningfully summarized by its mean and standard deviation, and suggested the use of these to describe measures of human attributes. Galton also invented the scatter-plot to illustrate data. His application of exact quantitative methods resulted in the discovery of a numerical factor which he called correlation, specifying the degree of relationship between individuals or any two attributes. He was one of the first to realize the importance of posted questionnaires, which he accompanied with prizes! Outside of psychology, he was the discoverer of finger-printing and weather-reporting (Galton, 1865, 1869, 1874).

The Frenchman Alfred Binet (1857–1911) had a rather different background, being the child of a single mother who took him to Paris at the age of 15. He qualified in law but then switched to medicine, although his interest in psychology was more important. Working at the Sorbonne in 1891, he became assistant director of the laboratory of physiological psychology and in 1905 opened a Paris laboratory for child study and experimental teaching. Influenced by Galton's work, he was appointed to a ministerial commission to study the plight of retarded school children to ensure they would have an adequate education. A mechanism was needed to identify pupils in need of alternative education. So Binet set out to identify the differences that separate the abnormal child from the normal and to measure them.

He constructed a series of tests, including short, varied problems about daily life, as well as tests of cognitive processes such as memory. They were made up of a series of tasks thought to be representative of a typical child's abilities at different ages. Binet ranked the tests in accordance with age levels corresponding to performances by the average child. In doing so he distinguished between the mental age attained on the scale and the chronological age of a child. The outcomes, developed with his assistant Theodore Simon, were received throughout the world with wide acclaim. Binet and Simon published their last revision in 1911 (Binet and Simon, 1911; Binet, 1916; Binet and Simon, 1916). In the United States Lewis Terman (1877–1956) standardized the Binet–Simon scale using sampling methods, resulting in what has since been called the Stanford–Binet Intelligence Test (Terman, 1916, 1917).

Galton's works also influenced Karl Pearson (1857–1936), who was noted for saying: 'Have you ever attempted to conceive all there is in the world worth knowing – that not one subject in the universe is unworthy of study?' A thorough polymath (meaning he liked to study many different things), Pearson could lecture in different subjects. As a freethinker, too, he hated authoritarianism, forcing Cambridge University to drop compulsory church attendance. One of Galton's books played a major part in changing his career, and he became interested in finding mathematical ways of studying evolution and heredity. As a result he wrote papers which contributed to the development of regression analysis and the correlation coefficient (think of the Pearson Product–Moment Correlation Coefficient), and discovered the chi-square test of statistical significance.

One of the most productive scaling theorists was Louis Thurstone (1887–1955), a mechanical engineer, who made important contributions to psychology. Thurstone spent most of his career at the University of Chicago where he founded the

Psychometric Laboratory. He designed techniques for measurement scales, for the assessment of attitudes and developed test theory (Thurstone, 1919, 1953). His major contribution was in the creation of new methods of factor analysis to identify the nature and number of potential constructs within a set of observed variables.

Although a mathematician, Georg Rasch (1901–1980) is best known for his contribution to psychometrics through the development of a group of statistical models known as Rasch models (Rasch, 1980). His work has had an influence on later adaptive testing by computers which have been used for the administration of tailored tests. In these the selection of questions to give a precise estimate of ability is based upon a rigorous model. Where people interact with assessment questions or items in a way which enables comparisons between them, Rasch models have provided a quantitative means of measuring attributes which are on a continuum or scale.

One of the twentieth century's foremost contributors was Raymond Cattell (1905–1998), whose first degree was in chemistry and physics. He had a major influence on the theoretical development of personality as he sought to apply empirical techniques to understand its basic structure (Cattell, 1965). He extended existing methods of factor analysis and explored new approaches to assessment, and has been unrivalled in the creation of a unified theory of individual differences, combining research in intelligence with that of personality.

The first person to emphasize that different cultures have alternative concepts of what an 'intelligent person' is and that traditional tests measure only skills valued in academia and work in industrialized societies was sometimes referred to as 'the test guru.' Anne Anastasi (1908–2001) went to college at 15, completed a first degree in psychology at 19 and her doctorate in just two years. Anastasi undertook major studies of test construction, test misuse, misinterpretation and cultural bias, and was the author of the influential book *Psychological Testing* (1988), which has been the core text in this field since its first edition in 1954. The seventh edition was published in 1997 (Anastasi and Urbina, 1997).

Lastly, we should include the first professor of psychometrics in the UK, Paul Kline (1937–1999), whose two major interests were psychometrics and Freudian theory. He did much to explain what has become an increasingly complex field and provided evaluations of the most widely-used tests. In his last book *The New Psychometrics: Science, Psychology and Measurement* (1998), he argued that truly scientific forms of measurement could be developed to provide a new psychometrics which would transform psychology from a social to a pure science.

The development of diagnostic assessment in the clinical arena has a history all of its own, and has encountered problems because of its psychiatric background. Arguments have arisen between psychiatrists on the nature of mental illness and its scientific status, as well as through challenges by others. For example, the French thinker Michel Foucault wrote in his book *Madness and Civilization* that mental illness was a cultural construct rather than a natural fact and that the history of madness properly written would be about questions of freedom and control, knowledge and power (Foucault, 2001). The main emphasis of psychiatry has been upon the development of a scientific understanding of mental illness and of healing the mentally ill. Jean-Etienne Esquirol (1772–1840) transformed the classification and diagnosis of mental disorder so that diagnosticians could develop clearly defined profiles on the basis of symptoms. Jean-Martin Charcot (1825–1893) extended the classification and played a key role in beginning modern psychiatry. Emil Kraepelin (1856–1926) also contributed significantly to the concepts of mental disease and its classification. Influenced by experimental psychology, Kraepelin also pioneered psychological testing with psychiatric patients.

As a consequence of the work of Sigmund Freud (1856–1939) and others, classification was extended by the 1950s to include the complexes and neuroses of ordinary people, leading eventually to the depression, anxiety, eating and sexual disorders of the late twentieth century. The old rigid distinction between the mad and the sane no longer existed and many practitioners believed that most disorders were among the community at large rather than in hospitals. Most people were thought to experience some degree of mental ill-health at some time. On the shelf above me there is a postcard propped against the books – it says in large letters 'Who is normal? Anyone can experience mental distress. No one needs the stigma to go with it'.

All of this has resulted in a continuing commitment to the development of assessment classifications, extending them to include 'milder' and 'borderline' cases and many new conditions such as Post-Traumatic Stress Disorder (PTSD) and Attention-Deficit Hyperactivity Disorder (ADHD). The handbook for this is known as the *Diagnostic and Statistical Manual of Mental Disorders* (DSM), of the American Psychiatric Association, first published in 1952, which was based on the 'mental disorders' sections of the *International Classification of Diseases* (ICD) published by the World Health Organization. The ICD, the latest version of which is the ICD-10, classifies both mental and physical disorders, and is more widely used in Europe (World Health Organization, 2004). There is now a large degree of overlap between the two systems.

A revised edition of the manual, the *DSM-III*, was published in 1980 and a further edition, *DSM-IV*, in 1994, including collaboration with those developing the ICD equivalent (American Psychiatric Association, 1994). The contents have grown over the years, reflecting a large increase in the number of identified disorders. The manual has introduced detailed procedures which are widely accepted, although being subject to the criticism that they are not based upon any theory or quantitative approach and are, therefore, weak. For an enjoyable account and critique of the *DSM*, see Kutchins and Kirk (1997). As with all previous psychiatric classifications, it is accused of containing clinical observations which are treated as objective and independent of any theory, the classical reference being Szasz (1970).

The most recent version mentions 'traits' in descriptions and use of this term needs objective evidence on the basis of the statistical tool of factor analysis. An additional criticism concerns the overlap between diagnostic criteria for categories, being either identical or very similar in some cases. Indeed, research by Widiger and Costa (1994) found no evidence to support the *DSM-IV* classifications. There have also been arguments over its unnecessary 'medicalization' of typical characteristics of people, for example the addition of 'shyness' as a psychiatric disorder. Kline is damning: '…It would be possible to agree that, whenever a sigh of wind was heard in a chimney, a unicorn had passed overhead. With good training the judgement between wind and unicorn could be perfect' (2000: 377). Whether the unicorn exists is another matter!

However, the manual does state that it is used by a wide range of professionals from medical, psychological and social domains and can be applied across settings, and that the initial impetus for developing a classification was the need to collect statistical information. Many of the criticisms made are discussed in the introduction, which outlines the limitations of the categorical approach and its use in clinical decision-making.

Another traditional form of assessment widely used in health settings has involved projection, including the Rorschach inkblot test and the Thematic Apperception Test, which ask people to describe ambiguous visual stimuli. Although popular, these have also been subject to criticism, as we shall see in Chapter 9. The number of alternative clinically oriented assessments which are psychometrically sound has, however, grown in recent years.

Summary

Psychological assessment has had a long history, although the most rapid development was from the mid-nineteenth to the mid-twentieth centuries. A key focus has been upon empirical measurement and individual differences, culminating in modern psychometrics with its emphasis upon the normal distribution, standard deviation, correlation, sampling and standardization, measurement scales, factor analysis, statistical models, and more recently test construction, as well as issues of best-practice and culture. These terms, placed in more of an historical order rather than a conceptual one, are all commonplace today. To practise effectively in any form of applied psychology requires a good understanding of all of these. In addition, the *Diagnostic and Statistical Manual of Mental Disorders* (DSM) and the *International Classification of Diseases* (ICD) have worldwide use in assessment of mental disorders.

Core Characteristics of Assessment

All psychological assessments are made up of a collection of questions or tasks, known as items. In a questionnaire this may involve a multiple-choice response format such as an anxiety questionnaire:

Indicate how much you have been bothered by each symptom during the PAST WEEK, INCLUDING TODAY, by placing an X in the corresponding space in the column next to each symptom.

	NOT AT ALL	MILDLY	MODERATELY	SEVERELY
		It did not bother me a lot	It was very unpleasant but I could cope	I could hardly stand it
1 Stomach upsets				
2 Having dizzy spells				
3 Feeling scared				

Or a personality questionnaire:

Begin here

1   I would enjoy being an engineer more than being a primary school teacher.

   a.   True
   b.   Not sure
   c.   False

2   When something bothers me, I can often laugh it off.
   a.   True
   b.   Not sure
   c.   False

Or an ability test:

Q1. 1.08, 2.16, 3.24, 4.32, 5.4, 6.48 ...... What number comes next?

1	2	3	4	5	6
6.56	6.66	7.56	7.58	7.66	7.76

For the last two measures you would, of course, have a response sheet to mark your answers on. Only parts of possible ones are shown here for illustration purposes. How would you go about scoring these? For the anxiety questionnaire you might give a number of value 0, 1, 2 or 3 for each of the column headings and then sum the totals for all of the columns, as is actually done with the Beck Anxiety Inventory. With the ability test, you could just determine the number of correct responses by counting them to give a total score. Life gets a bit more complicated with personality question-naires because they often have more than one scale, sometimes as many as 30 or more. In these, all of the items relating to the scales are jumbled up in the questionnaire; otherwise the respondent might guess at what is being assessed by a particular group of them. They are separated either by scoring keys or software to give a total score for each of the scales. These then form the profile for a person.

The Technical Nature of Assessment

But what makes the difference between assessments like these and a questionnaire printed in a popular magazine which aims, say, to tell you how attractive you might be to others? The answer is centred upon technical information about the instruments themselves and often the procedures by which they are administered:

- Standardized administration is required for many tests so that the administration and instructions are the same for everyone who takes them.
- Tests and questionnaires often have normative information, i.e. about how different groups have responded as part of a process of standardization. Their results are measured on scales and items are specifically related to measurement on these scales. This information about different groups is usually available within a technical

manual. It helps administrators to identify the difference between high, average and low scores for a group of people.
- Test publishers also provide information on the accuracy/consistency of scores (known as reliability).
- They also give evidence of validity, which provides the basis for making valid inferences about people from their scores.

The basis of psychometrics lies in these things – standardization, reliability and validity. Put simply, the differences between an acceptable psychological measurement and that set of questions in a magazine lie in:

- A scientific rationale for what is being measured
- An explanation of construction
- Standardized administration procedures in many cases
- Use of a large sample to establish norms or a process for comparison with others
- Accuracy and error measures
- Evidence for validity
- Guidance on interpretation

These sorts of things should be available, either in a test manual or some other format, for any type of assessment provided by a publisher. It is important for purchasers who are unfamiliar with a particular assessment to study the manual carefully before using it. The dangers of not doing so could include:

- Purchasing an assessment which is inappropriate for the purpose required
- Purchasing one which is of poor quality
- Not understanding how to use the assessment properly and, therefore, affecting important factors such as its accuracy
- Not administering or scoring the assessment effectively and thus having a detrimental impact upon accuracy and whether you can interpret any scores appropriately
- Misusing the test and the interpretation of its outcomes in feedback to individuals.

A second factor relates to the question: What do tests and questionnaires really measure? It might be easier to answer this question when we consider other sciences, for example in physics we measure such things as mass or volume, in chemistry we might measure temperature or concentration of a solution, in biology metabolic rate or response level to a stimulus. In engineering we might look at the length and height of materials, the velocity of moving components, rate of electrical flow or voltage, and so on.

All of these appear more substantial than factors such as verbal reasoning, spatial reasoning, levels of emotional stability or social confidence, or of depression or psychopathology, or the whole host of things measured by psychologists. We seem to be dealing with concepts which are more abstract. Can we put a hand on a specimen of, say, anxiety or a form of reasoning or of emotional stability, etc? No, of course not. To assess them we need to undertake an inferential process, i.e. we need to make an inference about the level of something based upon observations. That something may be described as a hypothetical concept, and we are restricted to identifying how we can compare individuals in terms of this. Mind you, the same is true for many things also measured in other sciences and technology. What about forces? We can observe their outcomes but can we see them directly? Some forces are based upon more of an inference than others, for example the nuclear binding force holding together an atomic nucleus. We can't really see electrical current, i.e. the electrons thought to be flowing along a cable, or even voltage. There are many things measured in physical sciences which are also based on inferential processes, just like in psychology. However, some people prefer to cope with things which are easily observable and understandable. They may prefer dealing with the physical world, disliking concepts which are less concrete or visible. But you can't escape them.

So psychology focuses upon assessment of concepts which are based on inference, and this lies at the heart of what we mean by validity which is explored in Chapter 6. To illustrate this process, consider the question: 'Where would you rather go – to a social event with your friends or a quiet evening alone following your own interests?' If you reply that you would rather go to the social event then I might infer that you are more extraverted than introverted; if you choose the solitary evening then I might infer the opposite. Obviously, that is not enough information to make a decision about you; it just illustrates an inferential process. Evidence of validity is, therefore, important because it provides a justification of the inferences you can make from an assessment. Put simply, validity is about what any assessment actually measures. By means of different techniques we ask about a person's responses, behaviour or mental states and use these as indicators of underlying characteristics.

All of this means that competence in using any assessment lies in looking past its superficial characteristics, such as the items and how they are written, to its underlying technical properties. That is why it is important to discourage people from seeking to discuss items in terms of their structure, the way they are phrased or even their punctuation. Reliability and validity are constructed on the basis of all of the items operating together as a unity; although this doesn't mean to say that designers don't look at these factors when they construct them. They do, it's just that they have to make a decision about the format of items and, once having done so, then establish its technical properties. Once items have been constructed we need to be more concerned with the technicalities of the instrument. Competence in using assessment lies not in dealing with what might be called its surface content, but rather with a body of information and statistics.

To make assessments of people is, frankly, a dangerous thing. If we do it badly and the assessed person dislikes the outcomes, then we may encounter rejection, hostility and in some instances complaints. There are good forms of assessment and bad ones – and there is bad use of good ones. We need to ensure we are using appropriate and relevant methods and that we do so in a way which is fair and acceptable. The important point is that we do not provide qualitative unverifiable judgements, which everyone, whether non-psychologists or psychologists, is capable of making, but should instead aim to provide quantitative and verifiable evidence. This is particularly important when we are dealing with the lives and careers of people.

Stable and Changing Characteristics

Traits are defined as relatively constant, long-lasting tendencies or characteristics of individuals, being predictable and indicating underlying potential (Allport and Odbert, 1936; Allport, 1961). They remain relatively stable throughout the life span, especially after adulthood. Mike Smith and his wife Pam (Smith and Smith, 2005) say a trait is a 'posh name' for a characteristic and quote the definition of a trait as 'a dimension of individual differences in tendencies to show consistent patterns of thoughts, feelings and actions'. They also add that trait theory is based upon two self-evident ideas that:

- People's thoughts, feelings and actions differ on a number of dimensions, and
- These dimensions can be measured.

Trait measures try to assess people in terms of how they usually are. However, it is important to note that people can change, sometimes dramatically through unusual circumstances or gradually through life experience – hence the use of the word 'relatively'. We can't measure traits directly, and our principal aim is to compare a person's position on a trait scale to that of others, for example I might demonstrate the trait of aggressiveness but just how aggressive am I? Am I more or less aggressive than others or am I at a level which is typical for most people? On this basis traits can provide useful descriptions of how people typically behave.

Traits can be grouped into three classes – attainments, ability traits and personality traits. Measures of attainment indicate how well a person performs in a particular field following a course of instruction, for example school exams. They tend to be retrospective, looking backwards to knowledge or skills learned, and are influenced by factors such as teaching ability and resources. Ability traits relate to a person's level of cognitive performance in some area, referring to thinking skills which can predict future potential, rather than just knowledge. Personality traits indicate an individual's style of behaviour. Many theorists have attempted to develop a descriptive classification of people in terms of trait characteristics, such as being introverted, emotionally stable, dominant, impulsive and shy, and which relate to objectively observable behaviours. Psychometric evidence has led many psychologists to view individual differences in terms of such things. Many personality measures, such as the 16PF, the 15FQ and the Occupational Personality Questionnaire (OPQ), are therefore trait measures. Despite situational influences at the time of assessment, personality traits may be a useful tool in predicting how individuals are likely to behave most of the time.

Traits should be distinguished from states, which are transient or temporary aspects of the person, such as moods, happiness, anger, fear, displeasure and even surprise, and which tend to be shown physiologically. They can result from the effects of situational circumstances or feelings, for example through fatigue, anger, boredom or just having a hangover, lasting hopefully for quite short durations. To complicate things, consider a possible exception: motivation. You may not be motivated now because you don't like the author of this book although you have to read it, but tomorrow will be doing something you love and will be strongly motivated by it (suggesting motivation is a state characteristic). However, there are people who seem to go through life being always motivated – whatever they do they are always doing their best and putting in a lot of energy (suggesting motivation is a trait). Another exception concerns anxiety, which can be split into trait and state anxiety. Trait anxiety is the general level of anxiety each person has, assuming nothing has happened recently to increase it. State anxiety, however, reflects that caused by some thought or event, and tends to be situational.

In general, mood states can influence behaviour regardless of traits, as when sadness impairs the interpersonal skills of someone who is normally well-liked. Assessment of states is more common in therapeutic settings through the use of measures of depression, anxiety, helplessness and suicidal ideation. It has also been suggested that moods should be distinguished from motivational forces which direct behaviour temporarily, for example the basic biological drives of food, sex, aggression or social contact (Cattell, 1957). These, too, are states because they decline after having been met. Traits help us to understand long-term behaviour, although states are important if we are trying to predict how a person will behave at a certain time. A few measures are made up of assessments of both, for example the Spielberger State-Trait Anxiety Inventory.

Summary

Competence in psychological assessment and measurement relies on the understanding of technical information so that quantitative and verifiable evidence is gained. The basis of psychometrics lies in standardization, reliability and validity. Standardization provides information about how groups have responded to assessment and enables users to identify high, average and low scores. Reliability provides information on the accuracy of scores and validity about what an instrument measures. A publisher's manual is often provided to give information about these. Assessment materials mostly measure abstract concepts and interpretation involves a process of inference. Both trait and state-based assessment instruments are available today. Traits represent relatively constant and stable, enduring characteristics of individuals, whilst states are defined as being made up of more transient characteristics.

Types of Measurement

There appears to be many ways in which tests can be classified or categorized, and this doesn't help the newcomer. First, they may be classified in terms of the method of measurement they use. The broadest of these approaches distinguishes between how people perform in seeking to do their best and how they react to items. They can then be grouped into two areas:

- Measures of maximum performance, and
- Measures of typical performance

Maximum Performance Measures

Measures of maximum performance include tests of ability, aptitude and attainment. As suggested, attainment measures indicate how well a person performs in a particular field following instruction or teaching. They are retrospective and are influenced by external factors. They are, therefore, outside the scope of psychological measurement, although the distinction between attainment and aptitude is not necessarily always clear-cut. Ability tests, aptitude tests and other objective tests are maximum performance measures because they are about how well people do things, how well they have learned skills or how great their potential is. They aim to identify what we can do when we try our hardest. They range from abstract concepts for example:

- Abstract reasoning
- Spatial orientation or relations
- Numerical reasoning
- Inductive reasoning
- Ideational fluency
- Musical sensitivity

to the rather practical, for example:

- Clerical speed and aptitude
- Programming aptitude
- Spelling and grammar
- Manual dexterity
- Hand tool dexterity

In this case there are right or wrong, good or bad answers, and the tests are usually timed so that response speed is involved. They provide raw scores, which is the total number of correct answers, and these are then converted to more usable scores such as percentiles. Aptitude scores may sometimes be influenced by attainment, for example a certain level of reading ability may be needed to understand items. Those with relatively easy items with a strict time limit are called speed tests. They have items of similar difficulty and measure how many can be completed accurately within a set time. True speed tests consist of items which, if given without the time limit, would be correctly answered by almost everyone and are mostly useful in assessing aptitudes such as clerical skill or perceptual speed tasks. In one instance a speed test was devised for the selection of traders and dealers working for an international bank, and was designed to check on their ability to accurately work out currency conversions whilst under high pressure.

If the score depends solely on the ability to answer questions, rather than speed, although this remains a factor involved, then we have a power test which measures the ability to do something. Having a time limit ensures a maximum score is set. Power tests tend to get harder as a candidate progresses through items; the time limit enables norms to be provided for comparison of someone's score with others and sets the top level of ability achieved.

Typical Performance Measures

Measures of typical performance include assessments of personality, belief, values and interests (i.e. what we typically are, what we would normally do), and so are more 'user friendly'. Personality dispositions are preferred or typical ways of thinking and behaving, being referred to as underlying characteristics or traits. They are often assessed by self-report measures having multiple scales, including scales for such things as assertiveness, anxiety or ambition. There is no right or wrong in terms of the responses given (which is why I prefer to call them 'questionnaires' or 'inventories' rather than 'tests') and there is usually no set time limit. They will encourage individuals to be as honest as possible in their responses. I can hear you saying that because they are self-report instruments 'they can be faked'. As we shall see in Chapter 8, their designers try to identify any level of this or other forms of sabotage. Examples of personality questionnaires include:

- The 16 Personality Factor questionnaire (16PF)
- The Personality Assessment Inventory (PAI)
- The Occupational Personality Profile (OPP)
- The 15 Factor Questionnaire (15FQ)
- The California Personality Inventory (CPI)
- The Myers-Briggs Type Indicator (MBTI)
- The Minnesota Multiphasic Personality Inventory (MMPI)
- The Jung Type Indicator (JTI)
- The Millon Adolescent Personality Inventory
- The Occupational Personality Questionnaire (OPQ)
- The Criterion Attribution Library (CAL)

An alternative way of classifying assessment lies in terms of a distinction between standardized and non-standardized techniques. A standardized instrument has been administered to a representative sample of people from a group or population, whose converted scale scores, or norms, serve as a basis for interpreting the scores of others. These contrast with non-standardized measures, for example learning tests used informally by teachers or questionnaires to identify your preferred team role. Lacking standardization means that you cannot compare the scores of individuals with typical scores.

Another way of classifying measures is on the basis of group or individual administration. Many of those used in health, forensic or educational settings are individually administered, including the Wechsler Adult Intelligence Scale (WAIS) or the Wechsler Intelligence Scale for Children (WISC). Others, for example Raven's Progressive Matrices, the 15FQ and the Critical Reasoning Test Battery, can be administered to a group and because of this are useful as part of job selection or development programmes. Group assessments mostly use pencil-and-paper measures, with booklets and answer forms. They can also be distinguished from apparatus tests which are often linked to sensory-motor abilities or sensory acuity. An example is the Movement Assessment Battery for Children, which includes equipment for manual dexterity and ball skills. Similarly, some tests contain only verbal materials, compared to those needing the manipulation of objects like the soldering of components, which are called performance tests. Yet another approach to classification is based upon the method of scoring responses. Objective tests use precise scoring procedures, for example through counting correct answers. In contrast, elicitation questionnaires, like essays, need a more subjective approach to marking and are seen as non-objective.

A broader view again might be to see a distinction between assessments in terms of cognitive versus affective methods. Those which are cognitive tests aim to quantify a form of mental activity, for example reasoning ability or an aptitude of some kind, whilst affective measures may assess aspects of personality, as well as interests, values, motives and attitudes. And lastly, yet another approach to classification concerns the level of qualification possessed by people who wish to buy and use them, which we will consider in Chapter 10.

Quality and Measurement

In general terms what might be the quality criteria when we come to consider any form of psychological assessment? The following is not an exhaustive list, but provides us with something to think about if we are preparing to buy or construct a measure:

- The scope – including the range of attributes covered, of norm groups or of people who can potentially be assessed (its breadth).
- Reliability or accuracy of the test. See Chapter 5.
- Validity of the test. See Chapter 6.
- Acceptability – can its purposes be explained and feedback offered?
- Practicality – including the cost, equipment and facilities needed for its use.
- Fairness, in terms of any legal issues involved, for example where this might relate to discrimination relating to sex, race, disability or age. Where tests are used to compare people, they are designed to discriminate between them, although in a fair and ethical way. This is discussed in Chapter 10.
- Utility – the costs and benefits in any applied domain of using an assessment and the alternatives available.

So What Are They Used For?

To conclude this first chapter, it might be helpful to set the scene for what is to come by considering briefly some of the uses of assessment methods and tests in different fields of applied psychology. They are used throughout psychology, whether research-based or applied, allied disciplines. You just can't get away from them. There are now hundreds of assessment materials being produced and distributed commercially. It's helpful if you can see how they are being used in different domains, especially those you might be considering for a future career.

Assessment tools are often used in clinical psychology as a means of diagnosing mental health problems, for assessing change in a patient's mental state in response to therapy, for conducting audits of treatment outcomes, and for distinguishing between clinical groups.

For example, a psychologist might want to track change in the mental state of a patient by regularly administering a depression inventory to see if there has been improvement. In working with children the psychologist might want to know whether a young person has behaviours which are, say, autistic in nature or indicate a learning disability. Those working with older people may be concerned to identify whether someone is suffering from depression using a geriatric depression scale. These are just a few illustrative examples. Similar measures will also be used by psychologists specializing in counselling psychology.

This kind of programme can also be used in forensic psychology in working therapeutically with offenders, as well as in conducting assessments requested by courts of law to help in decision-making. For example, a court may want to know the level of intellectual functioning of an offender, the person's suggestibility and compliance before sentencing, or competency to stand trial. It may want to know more about an offender's mental state, including such things as high levels of depression or anxiety, or psychosis, Attention-Deficit Hyperactivity Disorder or Post-Traumatic Stress Disorder. In clinical neuropsychology practitioners use many assessment tools in diagnosing brain damage resulting from accidents, strokes or dementia and in helping people suffering epilepsy. The consequences of an accident or stroke may result in poorer attention span, weaker memory and poorer use of language, as shown in Box 1.3. A neuropsychologist may want to assess these using specific tests, as well as the effect of events on a person's visual perception, bodily senses and motor functions. Neuropsychological tests can identify the localization in the brain of damage, its nature and effect upon bodily or social functioning and emotional state, and how best to conduct rehabilitation.

Box 1.3   Understanding Brain Injury

Mrs Smith could remember travelling along in the car and the moment when it was in collision with a lorry. Her next memory was of waking in hospital four days later. Life up until then had seemed normal. Her children had grown up; she was happily married and still working. She had many interests. But after treatment, things were no longer the same. She would have sudden angry outbursts, which were 'out of character'. She couldn't do the cooking any more. Her memory was poor and she couldn't concentrate.

In the UK some 50 per cent of serious head injuries are caused by road accidents. Most of these are closed head injuries involving major primary brain damage. This might be centred in one area or in a number of areas or even be spread throughout a large part. It can occur in areas different from the location of the original impact. It is not surprising that many accident victims experience impairments which make daily functioning more difficult.

Mrs Smith (not her real name) was referred to a clinical neuropsychologist because of dizziness, poor memory and an inability to concentrate. Assessment began with a structured interview. Despite appearing alert, Mrs Smith had experienced post-traumatic amnesia over a four-day period, suggesting she may have sustained a moderately severe head injury. This was followed by administration of a number of tests:

The National Adult Reading Test version 2 (NART-2) provided an estimate of pre-morbid intellectual ability, i.e. of ability before any injury or trauma.

The Wechsler Adult Intelligence Scale (WAIS-III) measured aspects of intellectual functioning.

The Wechsler Memory Scale (WMS-III) was used and the Controlled Oral Word Association Test.

The Rey-Osterrieth Complex Figure Test assessed visual–spatial ability and visual memory.

The Trail-Making Test (TMT) measured visual conceptual and visuomotor tracking/attentional switching.

The Hayling Test measured basic task initiation speed.

The Tower of Hanoi Puzzle assessed planning, response inhibition, information-processing speed and working memory.

Analysis showed Mrs Smith had sustained a moderately severe head injury, suffering impairments in general and working memory, learning, retrieval of new information and attention, as well as slower cognitive processing and impairment in higher-level functioning. A plan was drawn up to help her, including attendance at a head injury group providing education sessions, advice on memory aids and strategies, occupational therapy to help with household activities and vocational rehabilitation.

Where a child has problems in learning at school the practice of educational psychology enables the identification of potential learning difficulties and how these might best be remedied. Assessment materials are available today to look at overall achievement or specific areas of potential difficulty such as reading comprehension, speed and accuracy of reading, auditory processing of language, memory skills, general reasoning and writing skills. Tests can be used to identify problems like dyslexia. The outcomes will help a psychologist to decide what intervention will best support the child and what advice to give teachers and parents.

In health psychology practitioners may help people to cope with a wide range of problems, possibly being based in a hospital or community service. The psychologist might identify how best to support someone who has experienced a major heart operation or a diagnosis of cancer and provide guidance to carers and families. Where an individual is suffering high levels of depression or anxiety, assessment materials can aid diagnosis. There are instruments designed to identify health problems, to assess opinions and beliefs about health, to measure pain perception and control, and to assess stress and ways of coping with it.

Ability, aptitude and personality assessments are used widely in occupational psychology. They can be used for selection, for promotion, coaching, development and training purposes and in career counselling by occupational psychologists and other professionals. An employer may be interested in finding the best person available for a senior managerial position. This could involve design of an assessment centre including work samples, structured interviews, ability tests and personality questionnaires. Outputs are then combined to give an overall view of individual strengths.

Summary

In this section we have considered a number of ways of classifying psychological measures. The main approach is to divide them into those which distinguish between how people perform in trying to do their best (maximum performance measures) and those which distinguish in terms of how they react to items (typical performance measures). Among other classifications discussed is the level of qualification which might be needed to use them effectively. We have also looked at issues concerning quality criteria in evaluating assessment tools, and briefly at how they might be used in different fields of applied psychology.

What Have We Discovered About the Foundations of Psychological Assessment?

This chapter was designed to provide an introduction to psychological assessment, which involves the integration of information from multiple sources in order to understand people. We have seen that measurement techniques form a major part of assessment throughout psychology. Lack of regard for these techniques will mean that assessments do not have an objective and scientific basis, and any critical evaluation needs to be focussed on identifying measurement issues. We have learned:

- About the nature of psychological assessment, the need for measurement, standardization and for codes of practice and ethics.
- To distinguish between different forms of assessment and how they can be categorized.
- The key figures in historical development, including Galton, Binet, Cattell, Anastasi and Kline.
- About core characteristics and issues relating to different approaches, including reliability, validity and the differences between states and traits.
- About some of the ways in which applied psychologists make use of measures.

PART I

The Essential Tools of Psychological Measurement

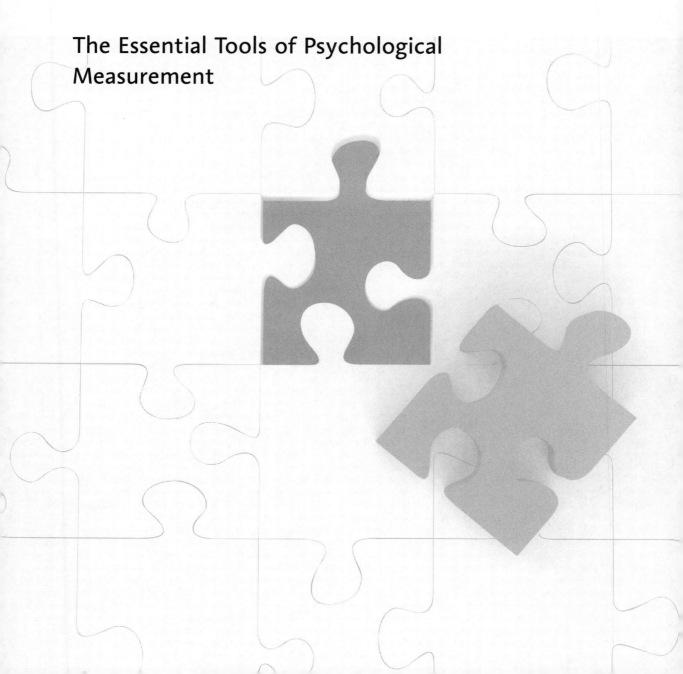

PART I

The Essential Topics of Psychological
Measurement

2

The Basic Components – Scales and Items

Learning Objectives

By the end of this chapter you should be able to:

- Give an account of the different types of scale and items available for psychological assessment and discuss their advantages and limitations.
- Explain and critically evaluate the principal approaches to item analysis using Classical Item Analysis, Item Response Theory and Rasch modelling.
- Understand scientific thinking about the nature of attitudes and their key characteristics.
- Identify the different approaches to scaling and measurement of attitudes.

What is This Chapter About?

This chapter deals with the basic underlying components of assessment – scales and items. Getting them right is crucial. Scales enable us to transform the responses of people into scores which provide a quantitative means of measuring characteristics – and measurement lies at the heart of accurate assessment. There are different types of scale available, not just in their level of precision but also in terms of their use. The second component – the items – could effectively form the units of measurement on the scale and provides the motor for measurement by generating responses. Their quantity and quality are also basic requirements for good testing. Items and scales need to work in an effective manner if we are to have acceptable methods. We will consider contrasting approaches to item analysis. Lastly, we will explore how different scales and methods have been applied to attitude measurement. At the end you should be able to draw a line between measures based on good scales and sufficient items from those which are flawed. Measurement is the foundation stone of assessment.

What Kinds of Scales are Available?

People differ in so many ways, whether in physical or psychological characteristics. These attributes, varying from person to person, are called variables (unlike constants which are fixed, such as the number of legs or ears we usually have), although a person can have only one value of a variable at any time. Variables are made up of intervals and are continuous, making it possible to measure them on scales. Some individual differences can be measured more precisely than others, depending upon the kind of scale used.

But measuring psychological concepts raises a fundamental problem. There isn't any external scale against which our scales can be judged. For example, in measuring height there are things like measuring tapes or sticks marked in standard units. Ultimately, these can be calibrated against an external standard measure kept in a laboratory at fixed temperature. The same thing can happen for some other kinds of measurement like weight/mass. But no similar external standard exists for psychological characteristics. There is not one perfect ability or personality measure sitting in splendid isolation in a laboratory somewhere. Yet there is a need for commonly agreed standards.

Psychology has coped with this in a number of ways and there has been much thought about measurement (Michell, 1990; Kline, 1998). By far the most common method is through the use of a reference population or norm group. An individual is regarded as a member of the group and the score obtained can be compared to a mean score for all of the other members. In the case of some measures, such as cognitive or reasoning tests, all of the correct items are counted to give just one raw scale score (sometimes referred to simply as the raw score for a person). In this case the maximum possible response sets the limit of the raw score scale. For an ability test having 40 items, a person might have a raw score anywhere from 0 to 40. For other instruments, the items may be separated into two or more groups, each with its own raw score scale:

- Specific ability or aptitude tests tend to keep their items separate, with a score for each test. Raw scores can then be summed to give an overall measure of general ability.
- General ability or reasoning measures will mix different types of item together and create a single score for the overall test.
- Personality and interest inventories will often mix all of the items together. Scoring keys or computer software separate the items belonging to different scales and give one score for each.

It is important to note that the raw score, however it is calculated, is an absolute score because it doesn't depend on or relate to the scores of others. In most instances this is transformed into another score, for example a standard based upon 10 (sten scores) or a percentile (the level below which others in the norm group have scored) or even a grade (usually A to E, a purely arbitrary scale) which does relate the individual's performance to responses in the reference population so as to provide a meaningful interpretation. In this way a score could be linked, say, to a population of people who have been diagnosed as suffering from depression, enabling us to determine a person's comparable level. Scores related to how others perform are called relative scores. When it comes to the scales used, there are four kinds available: nominal, ordinal, interval and ratio scales:

Nominal Scales

This is the most basic scale available. It is used for naming or describing things, for example by describing occupation, ethnic group, country of origin or sex (male = 1, female = 2) in terms of numbers, although it can't be used to indicate the order or magnitude of them. Nominal scales simply classify people into categories by labelling and are a convenient method of describing them as individuals or groups. Here are some examples of scales used to determine whether people belong in the same or different categories based on a particular attribute:

1 The number of people having each of the following eye colours: blue, hazel, brown, green, black.
2 The number of people who have: bought this book, loaned it from a library, borrowed it from a friend, found it somewhere, or stolen it.

The problem with nominal scales is that only a limited number of transformations and statistics can be conducted on data. The categories are not ordered in any way and, therefore, they are different but cannot be compared quantitatively. Any amount of difference between them may not be known and the only calculations possible are based upon the number of people in each category (their frequencies) and proportions. The Chi-square test may also be used to understand any association between categories.

Ordinal Scales

These provide a more precise level of measurement than nominal scales and place people in some kind of hierarchical order by assigning numbers or rank ordering. They indicate an individual's position regarding some variable where this can be ordered, for example from low to high or from first to last as in a competition. This can help decide whether one person is equal to, greater than, or less than another person based on the attribute concerned. If there are 20 people taking part in a 100m sprint, then the winner is number 1, the second person number 2, down to the last person who is number 20. If there are two people who are in joint third place, then they are both awarded the number 3. The scale is relative to the set of people being measured.

To put it another way, where ordinal scales are used people are placed in rank order with regard to a variable. The problems with this are that the scale does not indicate the absolute position of individuals on what is being measured and that there is no way of knowing the actual difference between them, and so the scale provides little useful quantitative information. This explains why world records in athletics keep changing, i.e. are getting faster, longer or shorter and higher etc., for there is no absolute standard set for how fast an athlete can run in a 100m race. We have no idea of their actual performance or of the differences in it. Statistical analyses available for ordinal data include the median and the mode. The middle rank on such a scale is the median. The median person is 50 per cent of the way up the scale, whilst the mode represents the most common score.

Scalar Variables

Scalar variables do provide a form of measurement which is independent of the person being measured. They are continuous and there is a clear indication of size or magnitude. Scalar processes are based on counting, such as a number of centimetres or seconds. Ability test scores would thus be counts of the number of items answered correctly and are scalar variables. There are two types of scale available:

1   *Interval scales* do not have a true zero, for example a person's level of anxiety, intelligence or of psychopathy. (Can you be sure anyone has a zero level of anxiety or even of psychopathy?) Like ordinal scales, interval scales assign numbers to indicate whether individuals are less than, greater than or equal to each other, but also represent the difference between them. On these scales, often going from 1 to 10, equal numerical differences are assumed to represent equal differences in what is being measured, like the Celsius temperature scale. Thus interval scales use constant units of measurement so that differences on a characteristic can be stated and compared.

  Scores on intelligence tests are generally considered to be measurements on an interval scale. The lack of a true 0, however, means that we do not know the absolute level of what is being measured. Calculating norms through a process of standardization helps to overcome this. Means, variance, standard deviation (the mean of all the sample means) and Pearson product-moment correlations can be calculated on interval scale data.

2   *Ratio scales*, the highest or ideal level of measurement, have a 'true' value of 0, indicating a complete absence of what is measured and also possess the characteristics of an interval scale (Nunnally, 1978). On this basis measurement can be interpreted in a meaningful way since the ratio scale is an interval scale in which people's distances are given relative to a rational zero. Examples might be people's income level, their reaction time to a particular stimulus or on performance tests. Although many physical characteristics are measured on ratio scales, most psychological ones are not. In general, assessment scores involve measurement on ordinal scales which enable comparison of an individual with other relevant people, whilst there are some measures using interval scales.

Test and questionnaire scores are scalar variables. They depend only on the number of items a person gets right or has marked in the case of, say, a questionnaire of self-esteem or personality. But they are not ratio scales. The person who scores 20 is not necessarily twice as able as the individual who scores 10. We can't make this conclusion. However, assessments effectively have their own measurement based on differing numbers of items, meaning that we cannot make direct comparisons between different measures and that there is no single independent standard to which we can relate scores. It is always important to know the type of scale we are using if we intend to use it as the basis for any calculations. For example, because of their nature, mathematical calculations cannot be carried out where an ordinal variable has been used as this does not represent natural numbers. If Ahmed gets percentile 40 in one test and then percentile 60 in another, these cannot be added and divided by two to give an average percentile of 50. Ratio scale scores can be subjected to mathematical analysis and so, too, to some extent, can scores on interval scales. The kind of measurement scale used limits the statistical analyses which can be applied.

Summary

Simple summation of numbers relating to item responses in assessment measures will provide a raw score which is a value on a raw score scale. This type of score is referred to as an absolute score because it does not relate a person's performance on the measure to that of other people. Scores which are related to how others perform are said to be relative scores. The type of scale we use, its precision, will determine the extent to which we can apply statistical analyses and make interpretations about scores, and four types are available: nominal, ordinal, interval and ratio scales. In making assessments practitioners will commonly make use of ordinal and, sometimes, interval scales. In rarer instances a ratio scale can be used.

 Construction and Analysis of Items

For any assessment to be a good measure it needs enough appropriate items and a scale which measures only the attribute and nothing else, a principle known as unidimensionality (Nunnally, 1978). Well-designed items are more likely to measure the intended attribute and to distinguish effectively between people. So the more care is taken in constructing items, the better we can make predictions from scores. To put it another way: although test scores are more often used to make decisions, they are only as good as the components which work to create them, i.e. the items. It is generally thought that at least 30 are needed for good accuracy, although it is difficult to predict how many and, since some will be discarded or revised by analysis, twice this number is often written. The number of items needed to measure something reliably will mostly depend on the nature of the characteristic involved. Test designers will often compose a large number of items and try to choose the best through a process of item analysis.

For ability or reasoning tests each item will need to be certain of having only one possible true answer. It should be constructed in a simple and clear way, without being vague or ambiguous. It should have a level of complexity appropriate for its target population and, obviously, not contain any form of language which might be thought offensive. Double negatives should also be avoided. Items in a personality questionnaire need similar properties and aim for specific rather than general behaviours. Different approaches have been proposed as a means of identifying the kinds of items possible for different measures. The best guide probably involves knowing where the different types of item are mostly used:

Intelligence Test Items

These generally seek to assess basic reasoning ability and a capacity to associate and to perceive relationships. The most common type, because of its flexibility and ease of manipulation of its difficulty, involves analogies, for example:

Sailor is to sail as Pilot is to?
1. run, 2. fly, 3. swim, 4. fight, 5. help, 6. play

Listen is to Radio as Read is to?
1. television, 2. telephone, 3. time, 4. picture, 5. book, 6. computer

Another popular type of item is based on the odd-one-out question:

Which of the following is the odd one out?
1. Germany, 2. Italy, 3. India, 4. China, 5. Asia, 6. Australia

Then there are sequences or series, such as:

1, 2, 4, 7, 11, 16 ... What number comes next?

Performance Tests

Also called objective tests (see Chapter 9), these are assessments which ask people to construct, make or demonstrate a capability in some way. There are often multiple ways of assessing them. Examples include the insertion of shaped objects into corresponding apertures, creating patterns using blocks, assembling physical objects, completing stories based upon card pictures or drawing people.

Ability and Aptitude Tests

These come in a range of measures. Ability tests can include tests of verbal, numerical, abstract and spatial abilities. Special ability measures can include mechanical, perceptual speed and creativity tests. They should not be confused with tests of attainment, which are based on assessment of knowledge (see Chapter 1). Items relating to ability tests can overlap with those used for measurement of intelligence, such as the examples given above relating to analogies (for verbal reasoning ability) and sequences (for numerical reasoning ability). Spatial ability relates to the capacity for visualising figures when they are rotated or oriented differently, for example:

[[+]] =   (i) []][(ii)]][]   (iii) [[[]   (iv) [[][

Those where respondents are offered more than two choices for their response, such as the analogies, odd-one-out and the example given immediately above, are commonly called multiple-choice items. The statement which presents the question is known as the stem, while the possible responses are the options. Incorrect options are referred to as distractors. Increasing their number reduces the probability of guessing correctly, although there are rarely more than five options. Such items are usually easy to administer or score, although they need time and skill in creation. Where an item uses only two options the chance of guessing the correct response rises to 50 per cent.

Person-based and Personality Questionnaires

The items written for questionnaires encounter some unique problems which we will discuss in more detail in Chapter 8. When it comes to person-based assessments, such as of mental health problems, or of personality, mood and attitudes, there are no right or wrong answers. A vast range of questionnaires has been developed over the years and it would be impossible to capture and demonstrate all of the kinds of items used, although the following shows some of the main ones:

Yes – No items
An example of one of these might be:

'I have often cried whilst watching sad films'. Yes – No.

This kind of item was used in the Eysenck Personality Questionnaire. It is a generally useful format because the items are simple to write, easy to understand and can apply to a wide range of thoughts, feelings or behaviour. A 'gut reaction' tends to work best with them, rather than an over-long and too analytical reaction, but they might on occasion be viewed as simplistic. Over-simplicity, in fact, could be seen as intellectually insulting and create a poor attitude among test-takers. Respondents may also complain that 'it all depends' and, therefore, they want an alternative response category made available. Such responses may also reflect an opinion that items like these cannot capture effectively the full complexity of personality and behaviour. A possible variation is to insert a middle question mark or 'uncertain' category between the two options, thus creating Yes – ? – No items, as a way of trying to overcome the issues raised by forcing respondents to choose between extremes.

The middle category, however, is often too attractive for some respondents, especially those wishing to respond defensively. In one instance a potential production director completed the 15 Factor Questionnaire. He said he was happy to undertake it and, when asked to use the 'uncertain' category sparingly, showed he understood the need for this. It was explained that if he over-used this category less knowledge would be gained about whether he might fit the job-role and the resulting profile would have little validity. Afterwards it was discovered that of the eight columns provided on the answer sheet he had completed five wholly by marking the ? category. So the middle category provides an option which, if marked, tells us nothing about people, except perhaps that they do not wish to give personal information. The problem persists where the 'yes' and 'no' format is varied to include the options: usually true – ? – usually false; true, it doesn't – ? – false, it does; hardly ever – ? – often; or even constructions like this:

I would rather work:

a. in a business office, supervising people
b. ?
c. in a library, on my own

Using this approach enables the item writer to capture a range of concepts. Other examples might include use of the terms: yes – uncertain – false; generally – sometimes – never; agree – uncertain – disagree. Potential options could probably go on for a long time, and I am sure you could think of a few, for example what about this…?

I would rather read:

a. a romantic novel
b. ?
c. a real-life crime story

True – False items
For example:

'People in authority frighten me'. True – False

Often written in the first person, these items include statements which respondents mark as being either true or false for them. Some questionnaires have modified this by simply listing adjectives or phrases as alternatives and then asking people to mark the one which is 'true' or best describes them. The True – False approach was used for the Minnesota Multiphasic Personality Inventory, widely used in the clinical field. It is similar to the Yes – No approach, apart from the fact that the language used in statements may often need to be different.

Like – Dislike items
For example:

'Spiders'. Like – Dislike

As demonstrated, this type of item normally consists of a single word or phrase to which respondents indicate their 'like' or 'dislike' and it may be appropriate for identification of clinical conditions such as phobias or obsessionality where only relevant terms need be provided. The choice of words should be based on some theoretical justification. Questionnaires can sometimes mix approaches to item construction, for example the Myers–Briggs Type Indicator Form G asks respondents in Part II which word in each pair listed appeals to them more than the other.

The straightforward 'Yes – No' and 'True – False' items, which might be classified as alternate choice approaches, have benefits in trying to assess knowledge of facts or verbal comprehension in a quick and easy way, although the risk of guessing correctly is high.

Items Having Rating Scales

Rating scales are used in the measurement of attitudes. They are based upon possible responses being seen to lie along a continuum of up to five or seven options, which are therefore ranked, in contrast to multiple-choice options which are independent of each other. A number of types are available, depending on language usage, with the most obvious ones being the first three in this list:

Strongly agree, agree, in-between, disagree, strongly disagree
Never, very rarely, rarely, occasionally, fairly frequently, very frequently
Never, rarely, occasionally, sometimes, often, usually
Nobody, one or two people, a few people, some people, many people, most people

Participants often seem to like these because they can respond more flexibly and, perhaps, more precisely when compared to the dichotomous approach of, say, yes versus no. Dichotomous ones have statistical problems when you try to correlate them. However, respondents can sometimes approach the scales with a 'mind set,' in other words they may consistently mark an extreme response to many items or choose the middle option in the case of an uneven number. Another problem is that people may also understand or interpret the language used differently, for example 'fairly frequently' may be viewed by someone as meaning the same as 'rarely'. The Jung Type Indicator uses the strongly agree to strongly disagree scale.

Forced-choice Items

These are primarily used in making personality questionnaires and involve asking respondents to choose one of a set of competing phrases, for example

When you are working, do you ...

a. enjoy times when you have to work hard to meet a deadline, or
b. dislike working under undue stress, or
c. try to plan ahead so that you don't work under pressure?

In these cases the number of choices can range from two to five, or even more. However, it is important to know that when individual choices gain scores on different scales, the resulting scores are intercorrelated. They are usually known as ipsative or self-referenced scores, discussed in Chapter 3. They are also associated with the relative rank on each scale for each person taking the test, rather than a ranking based on one scale for all individuals who do it. This means that it is not possible to compare one person with others, and thus no comparison can meaningfully be made between them (Johnson, Wood, and Blinkhorn, 1988; Kline, 2000). Norm groups which enable comparisons cannot be constructed. The nature of the scales also means that they cannot meaningfully be subjected to correlational analysis. For these reasons the items are best used for counselling, personal development or other forms of guidance, and it would be unwise to use them for situations where decisions about a person are made compared to others, for example in selection. The problem can be overcome by providing scores for the individual options, say 0, 1 and 2, on the same scale using a forced-choice format.

Item Analysis

Item analysis is a crucial first step in test development, involving different kinds of evaluation procedures. Once developed, the items will need to undergo a review which relates them to the characteristic assessed and an intended target population. Sometimes there will be a review by people called 'experts' who have knowledge of the subject matter and are able to suggest improvements. This is partly how the Concept Model of the Occupational Personality Questionnaire was constructed.

The most common method used is to trial the items on a representative sample of people of the target population including appropriate numbers of minority populations and containing a balance of genders, ages, ability levels and other relevant characteristics. At this stage the items are evaluated without any time limit being set. The sample should be sufficiently large enough to enable a satisfactory evaluation, with five times as many participants as the number of items. Feedback from them is important to establish the clarity of items, the adequacy of any time limit and to gain information about administration.

Box 2.1 demonstrates how one psychologist set about the important step of developing and evaluating items needed for measuring the attributions of care staff in homes for people suffering from dementia. Following earlier work in this area, she used the help of 'experts,' i.e. care staff, in a qualitative study to design items relevant to the UK before trialling them with an appropriate group.

Box 2.1   Helping Care Staff

How do you help people suffering from dementia when they behave in difficult ways? This is a problem for carers. Some behaviour might be considered aggressive, whilst others represent distress or need. Carers' responses will depend on what they think are the causes (attributions) and what they think is the best way to help. Training for them would need to evaluate attributions and ways of modifying them.

Shirley (2005) saw the need for a measure which would assess attributions and their consequences, leading to more effective training. The development of appropriate items was an important step.

Any relationship between understanding behaviour and the manner in which people act is influenced by emotional responses (Weiner, 1980). Attributions about the probability that behaviour will change over time are also significant in deciding on responses (Dagnan, Trower and Smith, 1998; Stanley and Standen, 2000). Care staff may be more likely to help, too, if they have high expectations of success (Sharrock, Day, Qazi and Brewin, 1990).

The Formal Caregiver Attribution Inventory (FCAI), developed in the US (Fopma-Loy, 1991), presented behaviour in a dementia setting using vignettes and measured carers' attributions for the behaviour, their feelings, expectations and responses. It was potentially a valid tool, although the items were culturally bound or difficult to interpret (Shirley, 2003). Study suggested its vignettes are familiar to carers and user friendly. Their essence was, therefore, retained, and the new measure would have similar sections. New items would be developed to reflect each aspect.

Items for two sections of the measure were developed from qualitative data. Carers were asked what they thought were the causes of behaviour and what kinds of help should be provided. Content analysis resulted in a number of attributional and helping categories. These were:

Perceived causes of behaviours:	Help-giving categories:
Dementia/disease process	Systematic/planned care
Emotional state	Decrease immediate threat
Interactions/relationships	Responding to individual needs
Physical cause	Personal contact
Environmental	Reassurance giving
Individual characteristics	Meal orientated
	Authoritative
	Let things run their course

A number of statements were developed to reflect each category. They formed an item pool for the sections which evaluated attributions and helping behaviour. Procedures were then established to check for their appropriateness and ease of understanding, as well as to conduct analysis in a large-scale study to identify the principal underlying variables. Another scale concerning emotional responses (Mitchell and Hastings, 1998) would also be evaluated in the same way.

To understand the effectiveness and functioning of items, two broad approaches are available, both having advantages and disadvantages, although some research has begun to combine them:

Classical Item Analysis

This is based on Classical Test Theory (CCT), which has been evolving ever since Binet constructed his intelligence test. It has enabled the development of many psychometrically sound measures over a long period of time, and is regarded as a simple, robust model. It is sometimes known as 'classical psychometrics' and modern approaches are labelled 'modern psychometric theory'. Its focus is primarily upon test level information, although it also provides useful information about the items used. The use of this approach in developing a modern test can be seen in Box 2.2.

Box 2.2   Test Construction in Action

The Jung Type Indicator (JTI) is a measure which was constructed using modern psychometric test theory. It aims to provide a reliable and valid assessment of the personality types created by Carl Jung, outlined in Chapter 8. Pioneering work in this field was conducted by Elizabeth Myers and Catherine Briggs which led to the development of the Myers Briggs Type Indicator® or MBTI. The JTI incorporates modifications to Jung's theory suggested by Myers (1962) although having important differences resulting from developments in Classical Test Theory.

The most significant difference is that the makers of the JTI viewed psychological types as being best described by a scale continuum rather than through discrete categories, as also did Jung (1921) and Eysenck (1960). So it was developed to assess bipolar continuous constructs, with each type being defined by the traits clustering at the ends of dimensions and having the type boundaries set in the middle of the scale.

Item Construction

Items were developed by psychologists experienced in type theory. Referring to Jung's original work and recent research, each one independently generated a set of items designed to assess the core characteristics of each type. They then agreed on the wording of each item and eliminated those on which there was no consensus.

Item Trialling

Items were trialled on three samples, two of which also completed the MBTI®. They were chosen for inclusion in the measure if they met certain criteria:

- Each item correlated substantially, 0.3 or greater, with the equivalent MBTI scales.
- Each item did not correlate substantially, 0.2 or less, with non-equivalent MBTI scales.
- The items combined to form homogeneous sets across each of the three samples, having corrected item-total correlations exceeding 0.3.
- Removing any item did not reduce the scale's alpha reliability coefficient (see Chapter 5).
- When more than 15 items met these criteria, those with the lowest item-total correlations were removed.

The resulting scales were found to have both good reliability and validity.

The foundation stone for the theory came from the physical sciences, i.e. that any measurement involves some error and thus any test result has two components: a 'true' score and error, each being independent of the other. One of its assumptions is that the true scores and the error values are uncorrelated. An individual's true score on a test can never be directly known and can only be inferred from the consistency of performance. We will never be able to specify exactly the performance on the unobservable trait.

The 'true' score is the ideal or perfectly accurate score but, because of a wide variety of other factors, it is unlikely that the measure will establish it accurately – it will produce instead an 'observed' score (Ferguson, 1981; Thompson, 1994). Thus the theory says that every score is fallible in practice. The actual true score is affected by the person's amount of the attribute being measured as well as by other incidental factors, which act in an unsystematic and random fashion, although the true score itself always stays constant. Where the error comes from will be discussed in Chapter 5. It prevents direct measurement and we have to rely on the observed score as an estimate of the true score. The relationship between the three components is often expressed by the equation:

Observed Score = True Score + Error

or

$$X \quad = \quad T \quad + \quad E$$

The true score (T) of a person can be found by taking the mean score that the person would get on the same measure if that individual were daft enough to complete it an infinite number of times. However, because no one is willing to do this and, besides, we could never do an infinite number of sessions, the true score is regarded as a hypothetical construct which is key to the theory. The principal concern is to deal effectively with the random error part (E). The less the random error when using the measure, the more the observed score (X) reflects the true score.

There is a range of helpful information in determining the usefulness of an item and to understand how it performs compared to others. Classical test analysis makes use of both traditional item and sample statistics, including item difficulty and discrimination estimates, distractor analysis and item-test intercorrelations, which can be modified to the construction of most forms of measure (Cooper, 1983). The criteria for the final item selection are often based on the intercorrelations, looking at associations between items involving internal consistency checks, although each one is best judged on a range of different parameters. These also typically include a measure for the overall consistency or reliability of scores.

Descriptive statistical analysis
This provides the most common means of evaluating items. It involves consideration of the item mean and its variability. In general, the more the mean is at the centre of the distribution of item scores and the higher its variability, the more effective an item will be.

Distractor analysis
This helps us to evaluate multiple-choice items by considering distractors, which are the incorrect responses forming part of them. The frequency by which participants

choose each of these, rather than the correct response, should be about the same. If one is selected less often it may be too obvious that it is a wrong answer and needs to be replaced. If a distractor is chosen more often, this may suggest the item is misleading or the distractor itself is connected in some way with the correct choice.

Item difficulty analysis

As its name suggests, this considers how difficult items are and how difficult it is to get them right. It is sometimes also referred to as 'item facility' in item response theory, which looks at the same thing but from the opposite view, i.e. item easiness. The difficulty indicator, known as the p value, represents the percentage of participants who have answered an item correctly and is calculated by dividing the number of people getting it right by the total number who attempted it. Clearly, if everyone got it right then the p value comes out as value 1.0, while if no one got it right then the p value is 0, so that the p values for all of the items will range from 0 to 1. A high value suggests most people answered correctly and, therefore, the item may be too easy. If everyone gets it right, then it simply increases all scores by 1. In this case, where an interval scale is used, the item will have no effect. On the other hand, a very low value suggests few got it right and that the item may be too difficult. If everyone gets an item wrong it will not make any contribution to the total scores and is redundant.

If all is well, the mean item p value is about 0.50, indicating a moderate difficulty level. Very high or low values tend not to discriminate effectively between people so items having extreme values need discarding or re-designing. This approach provides useful information for the design of ability, aptitude or achievement measures. But it does not mean that a mean p value of 0.50 is always appropriate because a high level assessment of cognitive ability may need more difficult items and, therefore, a lower mean value. It also does not work well when the items are all highly inter-correlated, because in this case the same 50 per cent of candidates will pass all of the items and just one item will suffice to differentiate groups. The way out of this is to create items of varying difficulty, providing a balance between easy and more difficult ones, and ensuring an average p value of 0.50. In some instances tests are designed to start with easy items and to get progressively more difficult. This is useful in assessment of individuals, such as for clinical measures, so that an assessor can identify where the person's cut-off is for successful responses and does not have to administer the whole test. The WAIS tells you how to do this by stating a discontinue rule, for example to stop after three consecutive scores of 0.

Analysis of difficulty can also be used to check whether any item exhibits bias or unfairness. If there is a different pattern of responses for one group compared to another, this may suggest the items concerned are not measuring the same construct for both groups and may unfairly discriminate. For example, we might give a test having just eight items to two groups and then rank the items in terms of the percentage of correct responses made by each group (the percentage ranks decreasing from 1 to 8), as shown in Figure 2.1. Seven of the items tend to show a generally similar pattern for both groups and the differences vary only by random fluctuations of one or two points. But item 3 appears to be rather harder for the second group, with a much smaller percentage of people answering correctly. Therefore, it appears harder for

	Item 1	Item 2	Item 3	Item 4	Item 5	Item 6	Item 7	Item 8
Group 1 Rank	1	2	3	4	5	6	7	8
Group 2 Rank	2	1	8	3	6	4	5	7
Difference	−1	1	−5	1	−1	2	2	1

Figure 2.1 An item difficulty approach to identifying unfairness

members of group 2 than for group 1. It may have inappropriate language or meaning for group 2 or it requires knowledge which its members are less likely to possess.

Item discrimination analysis

This evaluates whether a response to any one item is related to responses on all of the others. It identifies which are most effectively measuring the characteristic under investigation and whether they are distinguishing between those people who do well and those who don't. It checks that those who perform well on the measure overall are likely to get a particular item right, while those doing poorly overall are going to get it wrong. Imagine the case of an item which turns out to be answered wrongly by people who get a high total score but correctly by those gaining low scores overall. There is something clearly odd here because it seems to have a negative discrimination. More often it is found that an item has zero discrimination, suggesting that people having low scores overall are as likely to answer correctly as those who do much better. Therefore, the item is, perhaps, measuring something completely different from all of the others.

One way of investigating discrimination involves comparing high scorers and low scorers. The discrimination index d then compares the number of high scorers who answered an item correctly with the number of low scorers who also got it right. If the item is discriminating effectively between these groups, then more of the high scorers should get it right compared to the low scorers. The groups can be fixed by comparing the top and bottom quarters or thirds – the most appropriate percentage recommended for creating these is the top and bottom 27 per cent of the distribution of scores. If Ph and Pl are the numbers of people getting the item right in the higher and lower scoring groups, and Nh and Nl are the number of people in these groups, then d is calculated using the equation:

$$d = \frac{Ph}{Nh} - \frac{Pl}{Nl}$$

Items which discriminate well, being harder for the lower scoring group and easier for the higher group, have large, positive values of d. Those having a negative value are going to be easier for those who do less well, and are candidates for removal.

Analysis of item – total correlations

A popular method for evaluating how well an item can discriminate lies in calculating the correlation between it and a total score on the measure, which is used in test construction as we shall see in Chapter 3. The relationships between how individuals responded to each item are correlated with the corrected total score on the measure (Guilford and Fruchter, 1978). The correction is made to ensure that the total score does not include the response to the item being evaluated as total scores containing that item will have a spuriously higher relationship than total scores made up of only the others. This correction is important when there are only a few items. The underlying question addressed by each correlation coefficient is: How do responses to an item relate to the total test score?

Those items having high positive item-total score correlations are more clearly related to the characteristic being measured. They also have greater variability than other items with low correlations, suggesting they will discriminate more between high and low values. A negative value will indicate that an item is negatively related to other items. These are not useful because most measures try to assess a single construct and, therefore, you would expect them to have a positive correlation. Those having low correlations indicate that they do not fit in and need to be improved, omitted or replaced (Nunnally, 1978). Publishers sometimes show tables of these correlations in their manuals.

Item Response Theory (IRT)

This is the name given to a range of models designed to investigate the relationship between a person's response to an item and the attribute being measured, often described as an underlying 'latent trait'. In fact, the theory has also been called 'latent trait theory' (Birnbaum, 1968; Hattie, 1985). Whatever we call it, the theory can provide a wide-ranging analysis of items. It was originally developed to overcome problems with CTT. All of its models have in common the use of a mathematical function to specify the relationship between observable test performance and an unobservable trait. Because of this the approach has become highly mathematical, provoking debate about its focus upon this and its effectiveness in actually helping to make psychological measures.

Basically, it aims to analyse the relationship between responses to items and the associated trait, explaining how individual differences influence the behaviour of the person responding. Imagine someone taking a test of, say, diagrammatic reasoning, then it would make sense that a person who has a high capacity for this is more likely to get a difficult question right and, the opposite also, that a person of low ability would be more likely to get it wrong. So how someone responds to items is linked to the amount of attribute possessed by the person. This can be demonstrated graphically, as shown in Figure 2.2, which has the level of the attribute (or the total test scores obtained) along the horizontal x-axis and the probability of getting an item right on the vertical or y-axis. Different test items will usually have different difficulty levels, as shown by the curves for three items.

IRT is based on this form of graph which relates the probability of answering correctly, for each item, to a respondent's ability. Each item has its own curve. If what we have said above does make sense about items then, if an item is assessing the attribute, the probability of getting the correct answer should increase as the level of the attribute

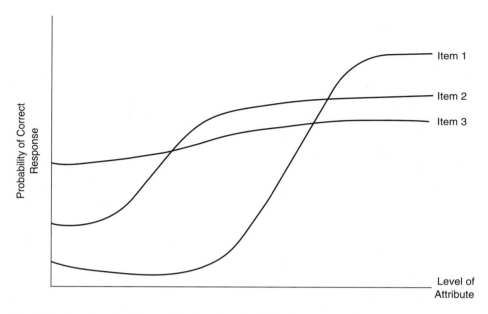

Figure 2.2   Item-characteristic curves for three hypothetical items

increases, so the graph needs to rise on the right-hand side. If it doesn't, there must be something wrong. Mind you, if an item is not actually measuring what it is intended to measure, i.e. is not valid, then even high-level individuals may not answer it correctly and so a probability of 1.0 or 100 per cent may not be achieved.

Even good values of the difficulty and discrimination indices can provide no certainty that any one item is working effectively. As the level of the underlying attribute increases, the probability of answering correctly should increase. For an item to be difficult it needs a large amount of the attribute to be able to get it right. A slightly different way of plotting this graph would be to plot the total test scores of individuals (as a measure of performance) along the x-axis against the proportion of people who gave correct responses to a particular item on the y-axis, meaning that we are looking at correct performance on this item relative to ability. The same sort of graph should result, all being well, of course. This kind of graph enables us to determine whether an item is behaving in the right kind of way, and is known as an item characteristic curve (ICC) (Lord, 1974, 1980). By looking at it we can work out item difficulty, discrimination and even the probability of responding correctly by guessing.

Item difficulty can be seen by examining the curve. With a difficult item, the curve needs to start to rise on the right-hand side. Easy items will have the curve beginning to rise on the left-hand side. If an item crosses the 0.5 probability level well to the left, then it is easy and respondents of moderate ability have a high probability of getting it right. But if the curve crosses the 0.5 probability point further over to the right, then it must represent a more difficult item. The difficulty level is the score at which

50 per cent of respondents give the correct answer. Item discrimination can be evaluated by inspecting the slope of the curve. The flatter the curve, the less it will discriminate between people – those with lowest discrimination will be flat. The discrimination index is the slope or gradient of the curve at the 50 per cent point. A small value suggests that people with a broad range of abilities have a reasonable chance of getting the item right. A high value will tend to make the curve become more upright.

However, someone who is low on the attribute may try to guess the answer rather than attempt to work it out. If the item is easy to guess then more people of low ability are likely to get it right (when they shouldn't), and the graph hits the y-axis higher up, i.e. the higher the curve starts on the y-axis the higher the chance of guessing correctly. In Figure 2.2 items 2 and 3 are easier than item 1 because their curves begin to increase further left. Item 3 is the least discriminating because its curve is flatter. Item 3 is also most vulnerable to guessing because it starts from a position higher on the y-axis. The two indexes of item difficulty and discrimination are similar to those obtained by classical analysis, although the ICC gives a more detailed understanding of how items function. When items vary only in terms of their difficulty, the curves run parallel to each other, with the more difficult items closer to the right-hand side, and this is referred to as a one-parameter model, only involving the difficulty variable. The assumptions made in using the curves are, firstly, that the probability of an individual answering an item correctly depends upon ability and the difficulty of the item, and is not associated with responses to other items and, secondly, that all of the items included measure only one attribute.

The ICC graphs can be described by a mathematical equation known as the logistic function (Weiss and Yoes, 1991) which ensures that the probability of a person answering correctly cannot have values outside of the range from 0 to 1.0 and that the curve moves upwards at a point set by the level of difficulty. The one-parameter logistic function described enables a test designer to determine the probability of any individual passing any item based upon knowledge of the person's ability and item difficulty (Rasch, 1980; Mislevy, 1982). Other models are based upon increasing the number of parameters involved. When both difficulty and discrimination factors are taken into account, unsurprisingly, the formula for a two-parameter function is needed. Introducing an allowance for guessing results in a three-parameter function.

Employing computer programmes to do the calculations, IRT aims to determine the most likely values for these parameters and the person's performance on the attribute independently of the actual difficulty of items and of the sample (Hambleton and Swaminathan, 1985). This is different to classical theory, where an individual's score is seen as the measure of the attribute and is linked to the difficulty of items. To do this IRT evaluates the fundamental algebraic characteristics of the ICC curves so as to extract equations which can predict the curve from basic data. Computer programs have been designed such that their estimates of these parameters are close to their true values for the one- and two-parameter models, provided that the number of items and individuals are large.

An example of a one-parameter model for analysis, using item difficulty only, is known as the Rasch model, based upon the name of its original designer (Rasch, 1960,

1966), and some researchers have developed this as an alternative approach to IRT known as Rasch Scaling. The mathematically oriented Rasch model assumes that indices for guessing and item discrimination are negligible. It also assumes, quite obviously, that the higher the individual is on the latent trait and the easier the item concerned, then the more likely it is that the person will answer correctly. Items in a particular data set are thought internally consistent and homogeneous if they conform to the model.

Being mathematically similar to IRT, it is designed to help with the construction of stable linear measures, while IRT is used to find the statistical model which best accounts for observed data. A relevant domain for the use of the Rasch model might be in assessment situations involving large populations. Its problems, however, are complex and have been the subject of much debate (Levy, 1973; Barrett and Kline, 1981; Roskam, 1985) including the suggestion that some of its assumptions are wrong. The two- and three-parameter models have been less subject to criticism and, with the development of computer sophistication, have gained in usefulness.

Comparing Classical Test Theory and Item Response Theory

Item analysis literature suggests that each of the theories has its own devotees, although both have advantages and disadvantages. Being the most longstanding approach, CTT is often referred to as a 'weak model' because its assumptions are easily met by traditional procedures (Kline, 2000). Although its focus is on test-level information, item statistics including difficulty and discrimination are also important. At this level the theory is relatively simple, since there are no complex models to understand. Major benefits include that fact that analyses can be carried out using smaller representative samples, that it makes use of relatively simpler mathematical procedures and that the estimations of parameters are more straightforward. Its theoretical assumptions make CTT easy to apply in many testing situations. However, it has several important limitations, including the problem of the item difficulty and discrimination parameters being both sample dependent. Another concerns the assumption that errors of measurement are the same for all respondents and are, therefore, constant across the trait range.

In contrast IRT models are generally referred to as 'strong', since the associated assumptions may be difficult to meet with test data. IRT is more precise than classical theory and its precision can develop more accurate methods of selecting items. Because of these benefits the theory has gained increasing attention in test design, item selection, in dealing with bias and in evaluating scores. But beware: the literature on IRT is highly technical. Its models are mostly designed to assess intellectual functioning and need large samples. Despite its advantages, many of its models assume that constructs are unidimensional and this is a problem in assessing personality as some of its constructs are inherently multidimensional (Wood, 1976). IRT should result in sample-free measurements and publishers would like this because having fewer samples to collect means a less expensive validation process! Empirical comparisons of the two approaches have suggested, funnily enough, that their outcomes are not much different, especially when large data samples have been used (Fan, 1998). Integration of both approaches is probably key to the future development of assessment methods.

Summary

How items are constructed depends upon the kind of psychological assessment intended and a range of different methods are available for this. A unidimensional measure focuses upon the assessment of only one attribute. Two principal approaches have been applied to understand the effectiveness of items: Classical Item Analysis, based upon Classical Test Theory (CTT), and Item Response Theory (IRT). CTT's principal focus is upon both test-level information and item statistics, and it is viewed as a 'weak model' because its assumptions can be easily met by traditional psychometric procedures. Based upon Item Characteristic Curves, IRT employs mathematical models to understand the behaviour of items, and is a 'strong model' in that its assumptions may be more difficult to meet in analysis of test data. Mathematical equations have been applied for one-, two- and three-parameter logistic functions.

 **Measuring Attitudes**

One area of psychological practice which involves the development and use of measurement scales is the study of attitudes. Attitudes are abstract hypothetical constructs which represent underlying tendencies of individuals to respond in certain ways, and they can't be measured directly. The term 'attitudes' is useful in two ways: first, when we want to explain someone's past or present behaviour towards others, or an issue, object or event, and secondly when we try to predict how the person will behave in the future. If we observe that an individual avoids certain other people, frequently makes disparaging remarks about them, and visibly bristles when someone enters the room, then we attribute to the person a particular form of negative attitude. An attitude is, therefore, an attribution made towards something, someone or some event. We identify it when an individual behaves consistently across many situations, encouraging us to make the attribution. Other factors may be associated in order to characterize it, for example its importance, focus, intensity or magnitude, and the person's feelings which contribute to these may be positive or negative. In seeking to measure an attitude we are concerned with its magnitude and direction.

There have been many attempts to define the term. The most well-known is that of the social psychologist Gordon Allport who said, 'An attitude is a mental and neural state of readiness, organised through experience, exerting a directive or dynamic influence upon the individual's response to all objects and situations with which it is related' (cited in Gahagan, 1987). Others have viewed it as a tendency to evaluate a stimulus (whatever that is) with some degree of favour or disfavour, being expressed in cognitive, emotional or behavioural responses (Ajzen and Fishbein, 2000). The common view is that an attitude is a predisposition to behave in a particular way and its 'object' may be anything a person distinguishes from others or holds in mind, whether concrete or abstract. Attitudes change as people learn to associate them with pleasant or unpleasant circumstances or outcomes.

Measurement of attitudes is an important part of applied psychology because it is so widely used, for example a clinical neuropsychologist may want to assess the attitudes of a patient's family towards rehabilitation and support services offered, just as a clinical psychologist might want to know the views of carers about their service, too. Similarly, a forensic psychologist might be interested in understanding the attitudes of other prison service employees. An occupational psychologist might be interested in knowing the attitudes of employees towards proposed changes in the workplace. Attitudes influence how people behave and, therefore, may deter or ensure support for services at many professional levels, whether individual, group or community. Disregarding people's attitudes can hinder collaborative working in many settings, whilst knowledge about them can guide service development and facilitate planning and change.

Attitude Measurement

To make inferences about the attitudes of any group we need data from its members. One way of doing this might be to make direct observations. This might be possible in some situations, for example in dealing with small groups or with children, although the accumulation of data will often be time-consuming and possibly expensive. Another approach might be to ask people directly what their attitudes are, although the trouble with this again is that it would be rather unscientific and have no means of accurate measurement.

A number of measurement techniques, mostly using questionnaires, have been developed for the analysis of attitudes. Different scales have also been developed. Construction of attitude questionnaires shares similar characteristics to those we have discussed in relation to other psychological attributes: we must firstly design items which are relevant and appropriate and then make use of a scale representing different numerical values. The most common method used has been to develop a scale made up of a set of positive and negative statements.

Thurstone's Scales

Thurstone and his colleagues used two approaches to the development of attitude scales in 1929: pair comparisons and equal-appearing intervals (Thurstone and Chave, 1929; Thurstone, 1938). First, they collected a large number of items indicating both positive and negative thoughts about a particular topic. The pair comparisons method was more difficult and time-consuming because it involved asking many people referred to as 'judges' to compare the items with each other and to identify which one in each pair indicated the more positive attitude.

The method of equal-appearing intervals has been more widely used because, instead, the judges are asked to independently sort items into 11 categories on a continuum ranging from most favourable, through neutral, to the most unfavourable attitude. In some instances the favourable to unfavourable dimension may not apply and an alternative dimension based on a degree of attitude may be needed. The 11 sets of items are designed to be placed at equal intervals along this continuum, so that the difference between any two adjacent points is identical to that between any other two points. Positions on the scale of the different items are then identified solely on the basis of how favourable or unfavourable they are. One way of doing this might be for each item to be written on a card so that they can be more easily sorted into 11 groups. A frequency distribution (see Chapter 4) can be constructed for each item based on the number of experts who located the item in each category, enabling the scale value or median to be determined. Scale values could then be used to rank order items and to determine the items selected (usually about 20 to 40 in number). This means that, when complete, every item in the Thurstone scale has a pre-determined numerical value. Any individual's score on the scale is the mean of the values of the items chosen.

One problem with this method of attitude measurement involves the fact that two respondents could end up with the same score from quite different patterns of responses. A second is that the sorting of items by the judges may be associated with their own subjective opinions, rather than being neutral (Bruvold, 1975), although Thurstone thought they would sort objectively and not be affected by personal views. It was thought possible to instruct the judges to limit any judgemental bias. Lastly, although Thurstone had tried to construct a technique leading to an objective equal-interval scale, it seems that in reality the scale is an ordinal one. Objections raised to this approach have concerned both practical and theoretical issues. The practical disadvantage suggests that for the scales to have accuracy 100 judges are needed and that these should be representative of the population for which the test is intended (Edwards, 1957). Theoretical objections involve the view that Thurstone scales are not consistent with the structure of attitudes and on these grounds their use is not recommended (Nunnally, 1978).

Likert Scales

If you want to design an attitude scale quickly, then the Likert scale approach is the one for you, because it has the advantage of not needing the judges (Selltiz, Wrightsman and Cook, 1976). This is based on the work of Rensis Likert (1932) and many researchers prefer his method. To construct Likert scales a large number of favourable and unfavourable items need to be developed. This time, however, they are administered to a large trial group of respondents who rate them on a continuum, often from 1 through to 5, sometimes from 1 to 7.

In the use of the five-point scale the numbers are given meaning, usually 1 = strongly agree, 2 = agree, 3 = not certain or undecided, 4 = disagree and 5 = strongly disagree. Total scores on this initial set of statements are determined by summing the scores for all of the items. From the total scores a discrimination index can be calculated, enabling selection for the final questionnaire of positively and negatively phrased items which discriminate significantly between respondents. Only those statements, therefore, are used which best differentiate between high and low scorers. Item analysis is also conducted to establish whether they are all measuring the same attitude. However, people sometimes make questionnaires which look like a Likert scale but have not subjected their statements to item analysis like this, as he suggested. It is not always possible to tell whether something is really a scale which has been designed using the Likert method.

The scale is also referred to as the scale of summated ratings because any individual's attitude score is the sum of all of the ratings for the different items in the questionnaire. Compared to the Thurstone scale, it does not involve a panel of judges and respondents indicate a level of agreement or disagreement towards items. But it, too, is ordinal and so can only order the attitudes of individuals on a continuous dimension, being unable to determine the magnitude of differences between scores. It is also similar to the Thurstone scale in that different patterns of responses may provide the same total score.

The major advantages are that the scale is easier and quicker to construct, it allows the use of a diverse range of items provided they are significantly correlated with total scores, and it tends to have greater accuracy than the same number of items in the Thurstone scale (Cronbach, 1946; Selltiz et al., 1976). This has led to the existence of many modern attitude scales based on the Likert model. But the approach assumes a linear model, i.e. that the sum of item scores has a linear relationship with the attribute measured, and it should, therefore, be considered with measures constructed on the basis of Classical Test Theory. This means Likert scales have all of the psychometric advantages of CTT measures, for example the more steps there are in a rating scale, the more reliable it is (see Chapter 5 for discussion of reliability). With Likert scales reliability increases up to the point of seven steps and then becomes level.

Guttman's Scalogram

Unidimensionality was mentioned earlier. We said that for any assessment to be a good measure of an attribute it needs appropriate items to match and a scale which measures only that and nothing else. Louis Guttman sought in the 1940s to develop a method which would identify whether responses on an attitude questionnaire represent a single dimension and thus reflect unidimensional attitudes (Guttman, 1944). His method is less well-known than those of Thurstone and Likert.

Using his scalogram analysis Guttman arranged his items in increasing order of difficulty of being accepted by respondents so that if an individual agrees with an item which states a higher level of acceptance then that person must agree with all the other items at a lower level. This would work only if all of the items in the scale are representative of the same attitude in the same way as cognitive test items which are measuring the same construct. The aim of the scalogram is, therefore, the design of a cumulative ordinal scale. Guttman thought that, despite the difficulty of establishing a true interval scale, his approach could make an approximation to this. A factor called the reproducibility coefficient could be determined to indicate the degree to which a true unidimensional scale is derived and this is determined by calculating the proportion of respondents whose responses fit into a perfect arrangement having an increasing degree of acceptance.

Construction of the scalogram involves the collection and arrangement of items in such an order that people would accept the first and, proceeding through the list, reducing numbers of people would endorse subsequent ones. They are presented to a large sample of people to determine the increasing degree of acceptance. The statements are then modified, arranged and administered again, with the process being repeated until a set of items is developed which demonstrates the increasing acceptance. The final outcome is the scalogram, having items identified by empirical analysis which can then be used to measure the attitudes of others. Any individual's score on the questionnaire is the total number of successive or nearly successive items endorsed. The difficulty in practice, however, is that often people will omit items, indicating the complexity of human attitudes, and that a perfectly unidimensional scale is not easy to construct.

The perfect ordering of items suggested by Guttman appears to have an intuitive appeal (Nunnally, 1978), especially in view of the fact that length, volume and weight can form perfect Guttman scales. However, modern psychometric analyses have shown also that, like one-parameter Rasch scaling, the underlying model of Guttman scaling does not fit well with psychological theories and it is unlikely that items could correlate perfectly with total scores on any particular measure (Kline, 2000). This means that perfect unidimensionality can't be achieved. And the scales are based on ordinal measurement only.

The Semantic Differential

The Semantic Differential, also a type of numerical rating scale, was developed by Osgood, Suci and Tannenbaum (1957) following studies in a range of cultures. It has been used extensively in research in the fields of personality and social psychology. Their research suggested that people give meaning to terms and concepts with regard to three dominant aspects, known as semantic dimensions. These are:

- The Evaluative Dimension: Good – Bad
- The Potency Dimension: Strong – Weak
- The Activity Dimension: Active – Passive

Their semantic differential was designed to provide a measurement based upon the meanings people attribute to terms or concepts connected with attitudes. This uses a questionnaire which lists bipolar adjectives such as good–bad, valuable–worthless, enjoyable–unenjoyable or friendly–unfriendly. Each bipolar pair is linked to a dimension or scale having seven points with the two ends represented by the contrasting adjectives, and the mid-point being a neutral position, like this:

Good	1	2	3	4	5	6	7	Bad
Valuable	1	2	3	4	5	6	7	Worthless
Enjoyable	1	2	3	4	5	6	7	Unenjoyable
Friendly	1	2	3	4	5	6	7	Unfriendly

Osgood et al. devised scales like these in order to study the connotative (personal) meanings that concepts such as 'sickness', 'sin', 'hatred' and 'love' generate among people. These concepts could then be extended to others which generate attitudes, for example 'sport', 'politics', 'television' and so on. Obviously, the choice of bipolar adjectives depends on the concept being investigated. Many of these will be evaluative and will principally indicate a person's feelings about it. The number of points across the scales can also be varied.

Respondents asked to complete the measure will simply be asked to make a mark on the scale points which indicate their attitude. It has been found that even young children, who would have difficulty with Thurstone or Likert scales, are able to respond to the semantic differential (Gahagan, 1987). A person's overall attitude score is represented by the sum, or possibly the mean, of the scores marked on all the dimensions. The responses to each concept may also be scored on the semantic dimensions (evaluative, potency and activity) and, by comparing these for one construct or more, to gain understanding of what is called the person's 'semantic space'.

However, responses which fall at the centre of the scale may be difficult to interpret, possibly representing either indifference or ignorance, and further investigation may then be needed to establish the person's view. In some instances it may also be possible that the individual responds by marking the extreme ends of the scale throughout the measure, regardless of any attitude adopted. This might not become clear unless a number of measures are administered.

Limitations of Attitude Measures

One problem common to all of these attitude measures is that of social desirability. This means that people may respond to them in a manner which has been influenced by the investigator or to preserve their self-image in some way. People could also feel apprehensive about disclosing their true attitudes towards an issue. Some may adopt what is called a 'response set', that is, they may adopt a consistent tendency to agree or disagree with statements, regardless of their meaning. Tactics have been adopted by designers to overcome these problems, for example in trying to make a measure's purpose less obvious by including irrelevant items and by giving assurances about anonymity and confidentiality. An individual's response set may also be disrupted by the inclusion of both positively and negatively expressed items. A multi-indicator approach to attitude measurement, involving administration of a number of instruments, is probably the best way of providing more reliable and valid assessments, and acknowledges that people's attitudes are more complex than previously thought. Attitudes were once perceived to be simple in nature and more straightforward to measure. Today this has changed to reflect the view that they are more interconnected and multifaceted than once thought.

Summary

In this section we have explored attitudes, how they are defined and how they can be measured. Key factors are that they tend to be consistent, are related to a person's feelings, and have importance, focus and intensity for the individual. Although they have been defined in different ways, they are thought to represent predispositions to behave in particular ways towards some stimulus. A number of measurement techniques and scales have been developed for their assessment including Thurstone's and Likert's scales, Guttman's Scalogram and the Semantic Differential.

What Have We Discovered About Scales and Items in Psychological Assessment?

This chapter has focussed upon the two things said to be the basic components of psychological assessment and measurement, i.e. scales and items. We have seen how different types of item can be constructed and that, through the use of scaling, the responses of individuals can be transformed into quantitative measurements. We have also seen how analysis can be made of the effectiveness of the items which go to make up a measure, including such aspects as their difficulty and their discrimination between responses. Analytical approaches have advanced substantially over the years, especially through development of computer technology and mathematical modelling. The specific applications of measurement techniques to the study of attitudes have also been examined. We have learned:

- The different types of scale and items available for scientific measurement and how they may be most effectively applied to assessment.
- The key principles of approaches to item analysis, such as Classical Test Theory and Item Response Theory, and their advantages and limitations.
- About the nature of attitudes and their measurement, including the different approaches of Thurstone, Likert and Guttman, and the Semantic Differential.

3

How Assessment Measures are Made

Learning Objectives

By the end of this chapter you should be able to:

- Understand how publishers go about designing a psychological measure.
- Distinguish between different types of construction, including the use of criterion-keying, factor analysis, CTT, IRT and Rasch scaling.
- Give an account of the principles of test standardization and percentile norms.
- Explain the differences between norm-referenced, criterion-referenced and self-referenced data.

What is This Chapter About?

If you want to become a millionaire by making a test and then selling it to a publisher or becoming a test publisher yourself, you have to begin with getting your materials right. If you think what I have just written is a little sensational, then I can tell you that it has been done. To do it you need to be able to spot a gap in the market, to be highly original and get things right at the right time and in the right place. Constructing measures in the right way means understanding what you're doing and why. Here we are concerned with understanding the steps involved in planning and design, then the different types of construction available, their applications and limitations. We also look at the differences between standardized and non-standardized assessments, and what is involved in creating a standardized measure. There's a lot you need to know just to be able to understand, evaluate and use measures properly in an applied field, let alone trying to make pots of money out of constructing them.

 Planning and Designing Assessment

Before beginning it is important to give careful thought to what the aims and purpose of any measure might be. The kinds of item and the construction used depend very much on the type of test planned. These will be different, for example, for ability and aptitude tests, intelligence tests, clinical or personality questionnaires. So construction begins with careful thought in identifying the type of measure, what kinds of attributes or constructs are relevant, what will be its purpose and content. Therefore, test planning and design involves preparation of a detailed outline of the steps needed (Bethell-Fox, 1989; Smith and Robertson, 1993; Guion, 1998). The greater the care taken at this stage, the fewer revisions might be needed down the track.

1   *Step 1: Set clear aims*
    Without clear aims, a test designer is sunk. Very specific answers are required to questions such as:

    - What precisely will this measure?
    - What is the intended target group?
    - What will be its purpose?

2   *Step 2: Define the attribute(s)*
    Failure to clarify exactly what is to be measured could mean that the designer ends up with an assessment which is muddled. It might result in the measurement of associated attributes rather than the one really intended. Having a good understanding of relevant psychological theory and research can help, enabling the designer to state what should and should not be included. A detailed description will help also in fixing the nature of the measure and its items.

3   *Step 3: Write a plan*
    Based upon the outcomes of steps 1 and 2, a detailed plan now needs to be written for the way ahead. This should include proposed specifications for the following:

    - Test content
    - Target population
    - The kinds of items needed and their number
    - Administration instructions
    - Any time limits or the time required for completion
    - How scores should be calculated and interpreted.

4   *Step 4: Writing items*
    After doing this the next step is to design and construct items, and to consider the most appropriate response format for people taking the test. This will lead also to

construction of a response or answer sheet in many instances. For any test the items form a set which is thought to be a random sample selected from a universe of all possible relevant ones. You can't imagine the thousands of items which make up the universe or domain of all the possible numerical reasoning items, for example. Locked in a room night and day for three months, we might generate thousands of acceptable ones. Obviously, you couldn't include the entire universe because you are unlikely to know them all and, if you did, this would make it so big that it takes a long time to design them and then test people. So you need a sufficient set which is representative of all the many possible items. A reasonably sufficient number, chosen well, can effectively measure someone's ability. The same applies to any attribute, whether level of confidence or abstract reasoning, for example. We could go on forever but we don't need to do this to capture its breadth and depth.

Some publishers employ people as item writers based upon their knowledge of the subject matter, so it is often helpful to inspect published tests to identify the nature of items which might work. They will construct what are known as item banks. These are made up of a collection of items designed to represent a specific domain and which are evaluated to estimate their parameters, such as difficulty and discrimination levels, as a means of understanding their quality (Nunnally, 1978). On the basis of this trial designers may make some improvements or add new ones, resulting in a constantly growing set of items. Although such item banks can be made homogeneous, the problem may sometimes be that they are not necessarily validly measuring any characteristic because item content is not a good guide to validity (Murphy and Davidshofer, 1998). Another problem also lies in the difficulty of deciding which ones are best for making effective tests of the right length.

5   *Step 5: Selecting items and standardizing*

A designer needs now to administer the items to a trial sample of people, including an appropriate balance of different minority groups and genders. A time limit may not be imposed at this stage, even when it is intended to impose one after development. In this case participants in the trial sample might be asked to indicate where they have reached among the items after different time intervals. The data gained from this process, including participant feedback, then undergo analysis in order to create an accurate and valid measure of one or more attributes. This analysis will be based upon one or more of the methods of test construction outlined in the next section. At this point, too, thought will be given to standardization of the measure, and more on this procedure also follows.

6   *Step 6: Final preparation*

Lastly, other important properties of the measure will be determined for inclusion in a manual, including information on reliability, validity and fairness. Done well, a good test will have high reliability, evidence of validity, discrimination and useful norms. There will also be the need for preparation of answer/response sheets and means of scoring, and guidance on score interpretation. In the case of personality questionnaires some form of profile construction is often needed.

Methods of Test Construction

Criterion-keyed Construction

Let's say that, given data bank containing all sorts of items, you need a test which will identify people who like eating chocolates. The aim is to discriminate this group from others who don't like eating chocolates so it is referred to as the 'criterion group'. Why you want to do this doesn't matter for purposes of illustration, although you might prefer to have friends, perhaps, who don't like chocolates so that you can always eat them without having to share. Perhaps you might be interested in doing it if you work for a chocolate manufacturer so that you can focus sales and marketing on people who matter. Items in the list would usefully be based upon a true or false approach and could include questions like:

I like watching football	True	False
I spend a lot of money on chocolates	True	False
I feel sad when I am alone	True	False
I prefer eating sweet foods	True	False
I prefer the circus to the theatre	True	False
Having lots of chocolate is important to me	True	False

To check out which items will discriminate chocolate-eaters from others you get a large group of people to answer them all. Among the group are people who tell us that they do like eating chocolate and others who say they don't. You might think you need to write items which are directly relevant to chocolate-eating, but that may not be the case at all. Many items will not appear to have any connection with this activity – you are interested purely in identifying items which can discriminate the criterion group, regardless of what they contain. To do this is to take a purely 'empirical' approach. When the test has been taken you can then identify which ones do discriminate the chocolate-eaters from the others and this could include one or more of the example items above. In this case you identify items which will discriminate the criterion group even though in some instances you don't understand why. Therefore, there is no theory or conceptual approach to doing this; you are being purely pragmatic about what will discriminate and in using this process to choose items for the test. The process is known as criterion-keying and in criterion-keyed test construction items are chosen if they can discriminate one or more criterion groups from controls. A number of tests have been made this way including the California Personality Inventory (Gough, 1975), the Minnesota Multiphasic Personality Inventory (MMPI) and some vocational interest tests. A range of clinical measures, like the MMPI (Hathaway and McKinley, 1951), were similarly made, where the items were designed based on knowing the typical symptoms exhibited by people having mental health problems. Obviously, only true–false or yes–no items associated with behaviour and feelings among clinical populations can be used and this means the items which do discriminate the groups are likely to appear appropriate. (I wonder what we would get if we did manage to produce a test to identify chocolate-eaters!)

Doing this with psychiatric symptoms would enable test users to distinguish between people who have, for example, symptoms of psychosis from those who do not and from other clinical groups. The MMPI includes scales, among others, for:

- hypochondriacs
- depressives
- psychopaths
- paranoiacs
- hysterics
- schizophrenics
- social introverts

The principal problem with these scales is that they were originally based upon traditional psychiatric classifications which have been subject to criticism, as we saw in Chapter 1.

An alternative use might be for the selection of people capable of doing special jobs such as pilots, air crew or air traffic controllers where scores on items are correlated with training performance scores. In the case of the California Psychological Inventory assessment of leadership potential is based on the ways in which students distinguished between leaders and followers, and items which failed to distinguish the two groups were rejected. It is the only occupational personality inventory based on this approach. With career guidance tests, the designers could argue that it doesn't matter why items discriminate or why people endorse them. It is more important that individual scores match those of the criterion group (Crowley, 1981). The most common method of statistical analysis correlates each item with membership of the two groups, selecting significant ones regardless of content. Other possibilities include the use of a simple Student's t test to compare the mean score of the groups to identify items which show a significant difference. Alternatively, each one can be correlated with the total criterion score using the point biserial correlation. The test should then include the most successful items and have its reliability checked, as well as being cross-validated on new criterion groups or with a criterion score for yet another group. This process may have to be repeated sufficiently to ensure effective discrimination and cross-validation.

However, this construction method is not normally recommended because it has problems, some of them rather obvious (see Kline (2000) for a detailed discussion). First, it does not provide any understanding of why such a test actually works because there is no theoretical basis. All we know is the extent to which the test does or does not discriminate between groups, and so it is best used where there is classification into groups. It can only be used for simple screening. Secondly, it is likely to produce scales which have poor reliability because criterion keying using large samples of disparate items would create scales measuring a mixture of different possible attributes. Lastly, the test would be specific only to the group used in construction and where jobs change or vary in some way it would be unhelpful. Because of these problems, criterion-keyed construction is not a good idea.

Construction Using Factor Analysis

In the real world people have difficulty remembering large quantities of data, let alone trying to summarize it in some useful way at the same time, so they might focus upon what they think are the most important factors or trends just to simplify and make sense of it. Factor analysis does this objectively and mathematically. It is a multivariate data reduction tool which enables us to simplify correlations between sets of variables (Nunnally, 1978). In constructing tests it is used with the aim of generating assessments which measure only one factor. Field (2005) provides an understandable account of factor analysis.

Factor analysis has become an important weapon in our statistical armoury. It has been the principal method used for the construction of many personality questionnaires, including some of the most well-known ones like the 16PF and the Eysenck Personality Inventory. Our focus is upon its use in test construction, although it has also been used to discover basic personality and ability dimensions and in understanding the number of traits measured by a group of tests together (Cattell, 1978; Child, 1991). It is primarily designed to summarize information, telling us which items go together and which don't, enabling us to make broad generalizations from large and complex data sets. Its strength is that it can analyse scores on a number of variables in such a way that they can be reduced to a yet smaller number of constructs called factors. Statistically speaking, a factor is a linear combination of variables obtained by applying weightings. The mathematics calculates the combinations and weightings, and describes data in terms of the fewest possible number of factors. Psychologists define a factor as a construct which is determined operationally by the correlations of variables (known as their loadings). For some aspects of personality, for example extraversion, this means that a factor is defined in terms of the variables which correlate significantly with it rather than in the loose fashion used by non-psychologists (Eysenck and Eysenck, 1985).

In test construction factor analysis is used to check whether items relate to a common theme or factor. It can also generate information about the conceptual structure of a test and on types of possible bias. Analysis begins by correlating every variable with every other one to generate a matrix. This is simply a set of numbers arranged in rows and columns, being the correlations between item scores. Once this has been done a specially designed piece of maths (or, thank goodness, a computer program) can be used to explore it with the aim of simplifying data through either identification of any trends present or by confirming a number of underlying factors. Exploration is the most common method. The process identifies the major factors or trends which account for most of the variance within scores (see Figures 3.1 and 3.2). A unidimensional scale, of course, will need only one factor to describe it. If other factors exist they are described as the second, third, fourth, etc. In large data sets it is unlikely that the variance can be described by just one factor and often a number of others need to be extracted. The number of these will depend on their loadings.

In test construction the aim is to examine items to clarify the number of distinct dimensions, which items relate to particular scales where more than one scale is involved, and which need to be eliminated. Analysis of scores obtained by a large sample on a group of items includes extraction of the factors which adequately

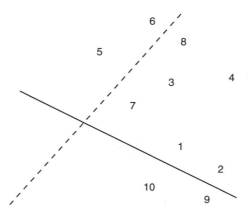

Figure 3.1 Factor analysis shows the trends among data (trend lines at 90° means they are orthogonal)

explain correlations and their interpretation. The sample needs to be large enough to reduce error to a low level, estimated at about 200 individuals per scale. Once this process has been used the items which don't relate to an attribute the test maker wishes to measure are rejected. Where oblique analysis, based upon fewer assumptions, is used the factors are correlated, whilst orthogonal analysis results in factors not related by correlation. In the case of an orthogonal process, all of the correlations between the factors are zero and they are independent. One of the earliest uses of this was by Raymond Cattell (1978) who identified 16 factors using oblique analysis of his data set, resulting in the well-known 16PF. He regarded the factors as determinants, fitting psychological theory better, and thought that in the field of personality the major factors would be correlated given their genetic and environmental basis. In contrast, Eysenck used orthogonal analysis to create his personality questionnaire, the EPQ (Eysenck and Eysenck, 1975). More on their methods is in Chapter 8.

With the development of computers, this kind of analysis has the double advantage of being both cheaper and quicker to do. But it needs large samples and has complex technical problems. For these reasons, it should be used with caution and with a good knowledge of its procedures (Child, 1990; Kline, 1994). Correctly used, it can provide good information about the structure and construction of a test (Carroll, 1993). However, even when a test comes out as being unidimensional it will still be necessary to determine what the factor is and to provide evidence of reliability and validity. This is probably an ideal and multi-factorial ones, such as motivational measures having more than one dimension, should not be rejected because they can still provide useful information about people.

Construction Using Classical Test Theory

Using CTT, the aim is to generate a test from a pilot sample which measures only one factor in a homogeneous way, suggesting each item should be measuring what the

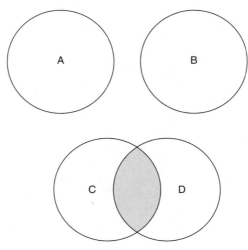

Figure 3.2 Venn diagrams illustrating sharing of variance – Factors A and B do not share variance whilst C and D have common variance

overall test measures. The way of checking this is to correlate each item with total scores. Some psychologists refer to this as item-whole correlation, while others call it item-total correlation, which was described in Chapter 2 in discussing classical item analysis. Those items which don't correlate sufficiently are candidates for removal or revision. In addition, items should discriminate effectively between people in terms of their difficulty. The end result is the creation of a pool of items of varying difficulty and which are all measuring the same thing. A pilot sample size should be as large as possible for this method, with a minimum of 100+.

Item homogeneity
For the first criterion of homogeneity, the most common approach is to use software to rank order items based on their item-total score correlations from highest to lowest (Nunnally and Bernstein, 1994). A measurement of reliability (we shall see this in Chapter 5 as 'alpha') can be calculated using, say, the top 30 items and if this is at a satisfactory level the test can then be made up of them. But if the reliability is not satisfactory, then more items can be added and it is again checked for the new set. This may need repeating a number of times until a desired reliability level is achieved.

Items having low item-total score correlations, below 0.2, would be removed as they do not improve reliability and could be measuring something different. Negative correlations would suggest the scoring process is the wrong way round and needs correcting. At each stage a decision is made on which to remove, followed by recalculation of the total scores and the remaining item-total correlations, and then of the reliability. When the latter is no longer increasing or starts to decrease, the process stops. We have discussed one problem of doing this before in discussing classical item analysis in Chapter 2: unless we do something, each item will contribute to the calculation because it is involved in calculating the total and is, partially, being correlated with itself. Correction methods have been devised to overcome this.

The difficulty indicator

The second criterion for each item is the difficulty indicator or p value, which we also met in Chapter 2. Items having p values between 0.2 and 0.8, i.e. discriminating ones, are best selected. If items are successively removed on the basis of the reliability and their difficulty levels, a short and well-balanced assessment can be the end-product (Guilford and Fruchter, 1978). This will now mean that it measures a specific variable clearly, is discriminating in terms of difficulty and is reliable. As with measures made using factor analysis, it will be important to validate it, i.e. to demonstrate what exactly it is measuring and to undertake standardization. It might also be useful to do a factor analysis to verify that only one factor is being measured. Using both methods together appears to be a sound way of generating tests and the evidence suggests there is good agreement between their results (Kline, 2000).

Construction Using Item Response Theory and Rasch Scaling

Item Response Theory (IRT) was discussed in Chapter 2, where we said the aim is to create a group of items which could be used with any sample regardless of participants' positions on the trait measured. It is said to be 'population free' and to have 'item-free' scores. The one-parameter logistic function, known as Rasch scaling, enables a test-maker to determine the probability of any individual passing any item based upon knowledge of the ability level and item difficulty. The simplest version involves just these parameters. It assumes that all of the items measure a single trait and, therefore, an initial factor analysis is needed to ensure this is the case. Any items which do not load substantially on the principal factor need to be removed before analysis by IRT software. A very large sample of people is required for adequate scaling.

Based upon the development of an ability test, computation of the Rasch parameters needs the sample data to be split into groups of high and low scorers, providing different levels of the difficulty value. In the classical approach a person's score is dependent on the difficulty level, whereas here the one parameter, performance on the underlying trait, is independent of the other, the facility level. In IRT the facility each item has for eliciting the trait among all subjects corresponds to the difficulty level in classical theory. If the facility of an item for eliciting the trait is the same for both groups, taking account of error, then it is seen as conforming to the model and is chosen for the scale. If not enough items achieve this criterion, new or improved ones need to be provided and the scaling re-run. On completion this should generate a group of items which demonstrate the same facility for both groups and so fit the Rasch model. Item-free measurement of all individuals is now needed. This is checked by assessing whether sub-groups of items generate the same scores for each person. To do this the items are divided into two tests, one having the most difficult items and the other containing the easiest.

Where items fit the model, each individual will obtain the same score on both tests. If this does not happen, items need to be discarded or revised. When two groups of items do this and, therefore, fit the model, cross-validation on a new, and smaller, sample needs to be conducted. The scaling is concluded when item groups persist in working on new samples. Where model fit is poor the estimates of ability level and item facilities are likely to be meaningless, as well as being inter-dependent. In the case of lack of fit, options include replacing items or the use of a more complex approach such as a two-parameter model.

A number of software packages are available to carry out the procedures, as well as for more complex models. The technique is useful for some ability tests provided large samples are available, which is one problem. Another concerns the influence of guessing by participants; where this has occurred it is likely that items will not fit the model. It has been subject to extensive criticism – it assumes items are equally discriminating, which can hardly ever be the case, and that there is no guessing (Kline, 2000). There has also been disagreement over the best approach to measurement of fitness. Even random data might fit the Rasch model (Wood, 1978).

To Standardize or Not to Standardize?

Standardized Measures

Many assessments are standardized and have norms. This part of the design process involves what is widely known as standardization. Some people generally place the emphasis on the creation of standard procedures for administration and scoring, whilst others emphasize development of norms. These are all outcomes of it, although the core aim is to establish the psychological meaning and, therefore, the interpretation of scores (Smith and Smith, 2005).

Standardization enables interpretation by creating norms (an abbreviation for normative data), based on mean scores for specific samples of people belonging to the target population. A set of norms can be defined effectively as a list of raw scores for a measure and their corresponding percentile ranks or other standard scores for a group of people (Angoff, 1971). This means that they can be used to convert raw scores into scores on more meaningful scales. The creation of standardized measures, providing accurate normative information, gives them considerable value compared to other forms of assessment like interviews or graphology which can't be standardized.

Standardization is also related to creation of a controlled environment in which some tests are taken, especially those of abilities, aptitudes and intelligence. This refers to the conditions which apply during administration, the instructions given and the time set, and publishers emphasize that changes can invalidate norms, meaning that comparisons cannot be made between scores. For example, the normative data for many tests assume a time limit has been imposed and are not valid if this has been altered. Poor and inconsistent administration results in inaccurate scores. Test administrators are trained to ensure every session follows a standard format, which is explained in Chapter 10.

Sampling

How good the norms are, and their usefulness, depends upon the samples on which they are based, particularly their size and how well they represent populations. Samples should adequately represent a population and be big enough to allow the calculation of accurate norms, although both of these factors are independent of each other. This means that while an adequate sample usually has more than 500 participants, it still may not genuinely reflect the population (Kline, 2000; Kozlowski and Klein, 2000). Sample sizes representing a country's general population would, obviously, have to be very large, of the order of 10,000 or more, although it can be difficult to obtain an adequate representative cross-section. For smaller specialized and homogeneous groups, sizes could be much smaller, for example research engineers in the telecoms industry or nuclear physicists. If there are estimated to be, say, about 500 of these potentially available, then a minimum sample size of above 50 may be enough.

The way in which a standardization sample is chosen from its population can range from simple random sampling to more complex forms such as stratified sampling. A sample is random if there is an equal chance for any individual to be chosen. Selection can be based upon tables of random numbers, although randomness doesn't necessarily ensure representativeness. It is only effective when the population concerned can be defined and listed, so that in many instances publishers use stratified sampling. This means categorization of the population into homogeneous groups based upon relevant variables which correlate with the attribute measured. Sex, age, social class or professional levels are often useful. Stratified random sampling minimizes the chances of selection of a biased sample, and the norms obtained are often considered to be superior (Cattell, Eber and Tatsuoka, 1970).

An alternative approach is to sample items as well as people. Varying samples of items can be administered to different randomly selected groups, so that whilst one group responds to one set of items, others respond to other sets. This takes less time and the norms obtained are closer to those from a larger sample. Some publishers 'grow' the sample by asking test purchasers to complete data forms about the people they test. As the forms are returned they contribute to development of more accurate norms. Standardization through the use of internet-acquired samples has been proposed, although this could result in an over-representation of males and professionals, as well as of more computer-literate and better educated individuals (Nicholson, White and Duncan, 1998; Stanton, 1998).

Standardization enables scores to be converted to relative scores, such as percentiles, so that the user can compare one individual's raw score with those of others. This process gives meaning to scores, known as interpretation. There are three ways in which meaning can be given – norm referencing, criterion referencing and self referencing.

Norm Referencing

The overwhelming majority of psychological measures are norm referenced. A person's score is norm referenced when it is converted into a statement of how the person compares to others who have done the same assessment. This makes use of a norm group which is a set of scores obtained by a group of comparable people who fit some specification, for example being graduates, sales managers, people aged between 20 and 30 years old, call centre staff or those diagnosed as suffering depression. An example of a norm-referenced statement might be 'Alan's suggestibility level is at the 60th percentile' or 'Sophie is in the top 5 per cent of people in terms of numerical reasoning'.

Having only an individual's raw score will generally tell us little. For example, imagine someone gets a score of 28 on a measure having 46 items. We have no idea, based on this information alone, whether the person is high or low on the scale. If most people get a higher score, then it must be low. If most get a lower score then it must be high. A raw score gives us no indication of this. What if someone gets a score of 32 on an assessment of depression? Just how depressed is this person compared to others also described as suffering depression? In applied psychology we need to know what the raw score represents and normative data tells us this through providing comparative information. The one place where norms are less applicable is in psychological research where raw scores are better suited to statistical analysis.

So norm-referencing enables us to compare a person's performance with those of others. A statement that someone is psychopathic must surely be based upon knowledge of how that person compares to others known to kill! Lacking information or having inaccurate data could result in injustice or complaint. Many neuropsychological tests are used to assess cognitive deficits as a result of brain damage, and these can involve norms for patients having different types of brain injury. The diagnosis of the location of damage depends partly on the quality of the norms available (Crawford, 2004). Assessment can be conducted well where normative data shows clear differences between conditions. Where tests have not been developed with good norms, they will be less effective in diagnosis. Criterion-keyed tests and symptom checklists are less effective than normative assessments.

Norms should be appropriate. In educational psychology a child might be assessed to identify a learning disability and its extent, meaning a comparison needs to be made with children of the same age. Many comparisons are made with people at large, i.e. the general population, and in this case we need information on how much a typical person demonstrates a particular characteristic. Similarly, in understanding personality, standardization using large groups of people enables us to say whether individuals are above or below average on an attribute. Standardization is, therefore, essential, especially when assessments are used to make decisions. We can speak of above average, average and below average scores. Norms are an essential prerequisite for understanding scores because, as indicated in Chapter 2, most scales do not have a true zero.

A set of norms should always include a statement of the mean and standard deviation for each group. The mean score $\bar{X}$ is given by

$$\bar{X} = \frac{\sum X}{N}$$

The mean is a hypothetical value and summarizes the scores obtained in the data set. It is calculated by summing the individual scores and then dividing the result by the number of them. X is each of the scores obtained, N is the number of people in the sample, and Σ means 'the sum of'.

The standard deviation, SD, is given by:

$$SD = \frac{\sqrt{\Sigma\,(X-\bar{x})^2}}{\sqrt{N-1}}$$

This is an indicator of how adequately the mean represents the data set. A small value suggests that all of the individual scores are close to the mean, while a large value indicates they are far away from it.

Test manuals

Many manuals contain norm tables which enable the user to convert from raw score to normative score. These, therefore, act as a frame of reference for interpretation and indicate performance relative to the distribution of scores obtained by others having the same age, sex, occupation, professional level or other relevant characteristics. The independence of the scales in normative measures also enables them to be used in many statistical tests. Wherever possible, scores should be linked to performance on some type of activity or work. Someone may have a score within the top 5 per cent on a test, but this doesn't indicate what the person is capable of. Norm groups chosen for any activity, especially where comparison is needed for decision-making, should always be relevant to the purpose, for example to a job and to the culture in which they are used. They shouldn't be used with people of another culture for which they were not designed and should be appropriate for the person. Manuals sometimes include tables of norms, with relevance to different countries, both sexes, and for different age groups. A good example of the provision of norms for different cultures is shown by the Wechsler Adult Intelligence Scale, which has been standardized in both the US and the UK.

General norms concern large populations, for example the general population of a particular country, its adult males, school-leavers, and so on. Regions around a country are representatively sampled so there is no bias and the sample used reflects the normal balance of males and females. Thousands of people are tested to ensure the structure of the sample represents the population at large.

Specific norms are linked to smaller populations or groups, for example IT workers in certain companies, clerical workers in one industry or a group of individuals who have been referred by law courts for assessment. The smaller size of a sample can sometimes impose a limitation on usefulness.

Local norms are used occasionally by commercial or public organizations in the assessment of candidates for employment. They are seen as being local to the organization concerned which builds up its own database and norms on an on-going basis, providing a useful comparison. The result is that new applicants will be compared against the mean scores of those already working for the organization.

Criterion Referencing

A test can sometimes be usefully related directly to some external factor or criterion, such as job performance or an aspect of it in the outside world, and it can therefore make statements about other standards. It can be linked to job competencies or behavioural elements of a job, which is its principal advantage. For example, a work-sample test is said to be criterion-referenced. Another example is criterion-referenced interviewing which is based upon assessment of a person's answers to questions against criteria obtained through job analysis (see Chapter 9). A typical criterion-referenced statement might be that 'a person with a score of above 75 will work well within a customer-facing environment'. Scores obtained this way can be used to distinguish between those who have or have not developed the knowledge, skills and abilities required for a specific activity (Anastasi, 1988). This approach is obviously linked to the field of occupational psychology, although it is also used in education where standards determine students' achievements as being satisfactory or unsatisfactory. In the occupational field some raw scores can be both norm and criterion-referenced.

But how good are the external standards set? This is the big question when it comes to criterion referencing. It is most obvious in measuring job performance, often through the use of appraisal by managers. Appraisal can be notoriously lacking in objectivity. To make a test criterion-referenced it has to be given to a sample of employees, while their managers decide which people are good or not so good at the job. It is unlikely they will admit having recruited people who are totally incapable. They might set a score value which reflects the line above which future applicants will be seen as capable. But the process may not be very objective. Common practice is to ask for the guidance of 'experts' who decide appropriate standards. Another disadvantage is that standards may change over time so that measures need to be readjusted.

Self Referencing

Not all assessments enable us to compare individuals. What about a test having the following items?

> In this question you are presented with pairs of adjectives. For each pair indicate which one best describes you:
>
> | | |
> |---|---|
> | Active | Sedentary |
> | Unambitious | Ambitious |
> | Competitive | Uncompetitive |
> | Sizzling | Sozzled |
> | Energetic | Laid back |

Where people are asked to choose options like this, being presented with forced choices, the process is called ipsative scaling and the questionnaires are said to be ipsative measures. Many use this format. Sometimes more options may be available than illustrated here. The essential point about the items is that any scores are solely self-referenced, i.e. they tell us only about the person completing the questionnaire and nothing about comparison with others. Any information obtained is about the relationship between aspects of one person. Thus ipsative questionnaires purely reflect variance within individuals and cannot tell us about variance between them. Any norms offered, therefore, are likely to have no psychological meaning. Questionnaires which ask people to rank items are also mostly ipsative. The only possible norms in such cases are of rank orders for, say, different interests, although the differences in distance between ranks cannot be calculated and, therefore, any psychological meaning is still doubtful. It might be argued that the only 'norm' possible is one within or about the person. Another problem is that, because of the nature of the correlations derived from items it is not possible to interpret meaningfully any factor analysis (Johnson et al., 1988; Kline, 1988).

Self-referencing is demonstrated through the use of statements like 'Jane's need for other people is less than her level of interest in sports'. That is an ipsative statement. In contrast, the statement 'Jane's need for other people and for achievement are both below average' is normative or norm-referenced. In ipsative questionnaires the scores on each scale are dependent upon each other to some extent, sometimes being negatively correlated. For example, in the example items given above it seems there are two scales: one about how much of a high achiever you are and the other about how much you like to stay at home and get drunk. So you get a score on one scale and one on the other. Because of the format, if you get a high score on one scale you also get a low score on the other, i.e. they are negatively correlated. All we can say is that you are higher on one than the other.

In many ipsative measures the score on one scale fixes the score on another. Mind you, this might not tell us much because it is possible that when you are at work you like to achieve and get a lot done, but when you go home you prefer to put your feet up and drink. It is worth noting that having forced-choice items does not necessarily make a questionnaire ipsative. For example, an item could have three choices labelled as having values 0, 1 and 2 on the same scale depending on the response. Responses could then be subject to statistical analysis and comparison with other scores.

The good news for a publisher making an ipsative questionnaire is that all the hard work of creating norms isn't needed. But the bad news is that comparison with others is meaningless (Johnson et al., 1988). Some provide tables which suggest scores have been converted to normative ones, although these are considered misleading and should be used only rarely. However, all is not lost. Firstly, vocational interest inventories are mostly ipsative in nature (see Chapter 9). Often they encourage a person to state preferences in terms of work areas (e.g. artistic versus scientific) and of self-presentation (e.g. extraverted versus introverted). Other ipsative questionnaires can be used in situations where discussion with the participant is of value. For example, in training, development, counselling, coaching or appraisal scenarios the information gained can be useful. Their strength is that they force people to identify characteristics as being more or less important to them than others.

Summary

We have outlined the basic steps needed for planning and design of assessment measures. Four methods of construction have been discussed: criterion-keying, factor analysis,

Classical Item Theory and Item Response Theory, each having its advantages and disadvantages. Standardization and the development of norms are important to measures which are norm referenced. General norms will compare individuals with others in the general population, whilst specific norms will be linked to particular groups of people. Organization-specific norms are referred to as local norms. When linked to external criteria, tests are said to be criterion referenced. Some measures are self referenced and are most suitable for discussion activities.

Percentile Norms

The simplest way of understanding percentiles is through imagining that an assessment has been given to exactly 100 people. These are then lined up from the person having the lowest score (whatever its value) standing at position 1 in the line through to the person having the average score (whatever its value again) standing at position 50 and upwards to the person having the highest score standing at the end of the line at position 100. Thinking this way demonstrates that percentiles are based on a rank ordering process. Because of their ordinal nature, percentiles are expressed only in whole numbers by convention. Be careful to avoid confusing percentiles with percentages as they are not the same, even if they are linked.

Percentiles allow us to compare someone's score with those of others making up a norm group. They provide a relative scale enabling comparison with the average defined as percentile 50. Someone achieving a percentile of, say, 75 is above average, whilst another at percentile 30 is below average. The proportion of people scoring less than a particular score is called its percentile rank and is often referred to simply as its percentile. To calculate it knowledge is needed of the proportion of people who did less well than that value.

Box 3.1   Measuring Suggestibility

People who falsely confess to crimes present a problem to the police and to courts. There are a number of reasons for this behaviour, for example in seeking publicity or wrongly believing during interrogation that they did commit a crime. The nature of the interrogation is one potential causal factor, although there are others such as stress and an individual's suggestibility. This last factor has been linked to poor memory, low intelligence and anxiety.

Gudjonsson (1989, 1997) has conducted much research into suggestibility and his Suggestibility Scales (GSS) are often used where there is doubt about someone's confession. Raw scores on the measure are converted into percentiles so that courts can compare any level of suggestibility to that of the general population and also to other people referred by the courts.

Mr Brown (not his real name) was said to have made admissions during interview and had later retracted them, and a psychological report was requested concerning his suggestibility. To do this a psychologist administered the GSS1.

Assessment began with the reading out of a short story and Mr Brown was asked to recall as much of this as possible immediately afterwards. A delay of 50 minutes then ensued whilst he was interviewed. After 50 minutes he was again asked to recall as much as he could of the story (delayed recall). He was then asked questions about it. Of the 20 questions, 15 contained different types of suggestive message, being misleading, seeking agreement or implying information not given. After initial answers were given, he was told he had made errors, had to answer them again and should be more accurate. All responses were recorded. The first response set indicates any yield to the questions, whilst the second indicates any shift in answering.

Raw scores were thus obtained for Mr Brown's immediate and delayed memory recall, as well as for his yield and shift in response to questions. These were combined to give a measure of his total suggestibility. Using norm tables provided and taking error into account, Mr Brown's immediate and delayed memory recall were in the bottom 20 per cent compared to the general population and at an average level compared to other court referrals. His total suggestibility was at percentile 95 compared to general population norms and at percentile 75 compared to court referrals. The results indicated a high level of suggestibility.

Calculating Percentiles from Raw Scores

Let's say that a publisher has administered a test having 20 items to a large standardization group involving 1000 participants. The following table shows the process used to convert raw scores into their percentile equivalents. The scores obtained by individuals would naturally go from 0 (those getting nothing right) through to 20 (those who get everything correct). But to make things simpler the table has been reduced to show the operations conducted to transform only the raw scores of 0 to 10; in practice, this would be extended as far as a raw score of 20 in the first column.

1	2	3	4	5	6	7
Raw Score	Number obtaining each score	Cumulative frequency	Cumulative number getting a lower score	Column 4 as a percentage	Final percentile ranks	Final percentile
0	2	2	0	0	0.1	1
1	4	6	2	0.2	0.4	1
2	12	18	6	0.6	1.2	1
3	21	39	18	1.8	2.85	3
4	29	68	39	3.9	5.35	5
5	44	112	68	6.8	9.0	9
6	62	174	112	11.2	14.3	14
7	81	255	174	17.4	21.45	21
8	116	371	255	25.5	31.3	31
9	138	509	371	37.1	44.0	44
10	144	653	509	50.9	–	–

As you can see, column 4 is an important column because it gives us the total number of people who have performed less well for each score, for example 39 people got scores below 4, while 255 got less than score 8. Column 5 transforms this into a percentage of 1000 people in total, i.e. it gives the proportion of people who did less well for each score listed in column 1.

To obtain the percentile rank of a score we have to carry out a process of 'interpolating' between the percentile ranks of its lower and upper limits. For example, for the raw score of 7 the lower limit of its percentile rank is 17.4 (that is 17.4 per cent of the sample of 1000 get 6 or less, the 174 in column 4 divided by 1000 to give the percentage of people scoring less than 7). The upper limit is 25.5 (that is, 25.5 per cent got 7 or less). Assuming, as canny statisticians tell us, that all of the people who actually got 7 can be thought of as being evenly spread throughout this interval, then our percentile rank is best represented by the mid-point between the lower and upper limits, i.e. half-way between 17.4 and 25.5. Half-way is at 21.45, so this is the figure in column 6, the final percentile rank for the score of 7. (To get this figure of 21.45 you can either calculate half of the distance between 17.4 and 25.5 by doing 25.5 − 17.4 = 8.1 ÷ 2 which gives 4.05 and then add this to 17.4, which gives 21.45. Or, the simplest way, you can add 17.4 to 25.5 to give 42.9 and then to divide this by 2 to give 21.45 again. Whatever method turns you on.)

Obviously, we can't calculate the percentile rank for the raw score value of 10 as the upper limit for this is set by the data for raw score 11 and we do not have the rest of the table. But this makes the point that we will not be able to calculate the final percentile rank for a raw score of 20, the highest possible and, therefore, percentile 100 doesn't really exist. Notice that column 7 is added to give the final percentile figure for each raw score by rounding to the nearest whole number.

In practice you do not have to do this calculation, it is done for you by the publisher and given as a table in the manual, like the one shown below. These make it easy to interpret a person's test score by just reading across each row. You might have to do the calculation if you ever work for a publisher, although it is easy to design a software program to do it. A typical norm table looks like:

Raw Score	Percentile	Raw Score	Percentile
0–3	1	16	55
4–5	2	17	60
6	4	18	65
7	5	19	70
8–9	9	20	75
10	13	21	80
11	18	22	85
12	25	23	87
	30	24	90
13	35	25	92
14	40	26	95
–	45	27	97
15	50	28–30	99

It is then simple to read off percentile ranks for each of the raw score totals obtained by different people. For example, if this conversion table is for an ability test, what is the percentile of someone who scored 29? What about someone who got 15 items correct? Someone who got just six items right? The answers are percentiles 99, 50 and 4, obtained by finding the item score and then reading across the table. Notice that the person with 15 items correct is at the average level (percentile 50). Personality questionnaires rarely use percentile scales. Neuropsychologists make great use of them. Box 3.1 provided an example of their use in assessment by a forensic psychologist.

With ability tests, interpretation of scores like this is required to give feedback to both candidate and line manager in job selection procedures. There are a number of ways in which this can be done, although it might be wise to state firstly that to give percentile figures to untrained people, like candidates and managers, is often not a good idea because they confuse them with percentages. Having a score of percentile 75 does not mean that a person has got 75 per cent of items correct. For this reason some publishers use interpretation systems such as:

A five-point grading system
This makes use of the link between percentages and percentiles, for example, the top 10 per cent becomes Grade A (percentiles 90 to 100); the next 20 per cent becomes Grade B (percentiles 70–90); the next 40 per cent becomes Grade C (percentiles 30–70, sometimes split into C+ and C-); the next 20 per cent becomes Grade D (percentiles 10–30); the bottom 10 per cent becomes Grade E (percentiles 1–10).

Quartiles
The raw scores are separated into four categories, each comprising 25 per cent of the distribution, i.e. the bottom quartile (percentiles 1 to 25), the second quartile (25–50), third quartile (50–75) and the top quartile (75–100).

Deciles
Here raw scores are separated into 10 categories, each containing 10 per cent of the distribution. Being similar to percentiles, they relate individual scores to their position in a representative sample of 10 people rather than 100. This would involve explaining the person's position in a line of 10 people from the lowest performance to the highest.

Interpreting Percentiles

There are three other ways of explaining percentiles to those who have been assessed or to others. The first of these transforms percentiles into words, for example:

Percentiles		
	90–100	Well above average
	70–90	Above average
	60–70	Slightly above average
	40–60	Average (taking account of error)
	30–40	Slightly below average
	20–30	Below average
	1–20	Well below average

The descriptions above enable feedback to people who are unlikely to understand percentiles or who might misinterpret them. Only words are used to describe performance.

Some people, such as managers involved in a selection or development exercise, would prefer to have a form of objective understanding involving numbers. In this case reporting back could be done in the following way:

Percentiles		
	95–100	The top 5 per cent
	90–100	The top 10 per cent
	85–100	The top 15 per cent
	80–100	The top 20 per cent
	75–100	The top 25 per cent (the top quartile)
	60–70	Slightly above average
	40–60	Average
	30–40	Slightly below average
	1–25	The bottom 25 per cent (the bottom quartile)
	1–20	The bottom 20 per cent
	1–15	The bottom 15 per cent
	1–10	The bottom 10 per cent
	1–5	The bottom 5 per cent

The third method is to use the approach in which percentiles were described in terms of a line of people. It involves saying: 'If 100 people who have done this test were lined up from the person having the lowest score (whatever its value) standing at position 1 in the line to the person having the average score standing at position 50 and onwards to the person having the highest score at position 100, then you would be person number … in the line'. Where someone has done particularly well, this is sure to bring a smile.

The main disadvantage of using percentile norms is that they are based on an ordinal scale. This means the units are not equal on all parts of the scale – they are closer together at the middle and further apart at its extremes. Therefore, the difference between an individual at percentile 10 and another at percentile 20 is not the same at that between people having percentiles 50 and 60 because the unit of measurement is greater for the first difference. In the middle range, a small difference in raw scores will correspond to a big difference in percentiles. Differences at the ends will have greater weight than those closer to the middle. Therefore, an equivalent difference between two percentile rankings may result in different clinical conclusions when the two scores occur at the extremes than if they are both near the centre of the distribution. Another disadvantage is that percentiles cannot be subjected to parametric statistical analysis. Their big advantage is that they can be explained easily to non-psychologists who understand percentages, although it should be made clear that performance is *not* based on calculation of the percentage of items answered correctly. They are also relatively easy to calculate and are more well-known.

Summary

Percentile norms provide a common method of interpreting assessment scores. To create them we need to know what proportion of people do less well. They can be interpreted using grading systems, quartiles, deciles or other formats such as word descriptions or links to percentages. Care should be taken to ensure people do not mis-interpret them.

What Have We Discovered About How Assessment Measures Are Made?

We have trekked many light years across the galaxy of different methods used to construct assessment measures. We have seen the commonality of life forms in that test publishers need to plan and design the process, establish clear aims and purposes, before writing a detailed plan of what they aim to achieve. You may have wanted to be beamed back up when we got to the different methods of item choice, including criterion-keyed, factor analytic, classical and item response theory methods. We reached firmer ground in considering standardization and norm referencing, although the passing inter-galactic comets of criterion referencing and self-referencing may have taken you by surprise. Ipsative measures are widely marketed, sparking a lot of debate. Percentiles, however, are common life-forms, being used as a simple means of comparing people with others. It is important, however, to understand their nature and disadvantages. We have learned:

- About the process of planning and design required for creating different kinds of measure.
- How to distinguish between different methods of item analysis used in test construction.
- How a process of standardization is conducted.
- About the differences between norm-referenced, criterion-referenced and self-referenced assessments.
- About percentiles, how they are calculated and interpreted.

4

Statistics for Psychological Measurement

Learning Objectives

By the end of this chapter you should be able to:

- Understand the graphical representation of frequency distributions of test scores and the properties of the normal curve.
- Determine measures of central tendency, including the standard deviation of distributions.
- Explain how sampling affects error around mean scores and how we can use confidence limits to estimate this error.
- Understand the different types of standard scores such as z scores, T scores, sten and stanine scores, how they are calculated and can be converted.

What is This Chapter About?

In Chapter 3 we looked at the construction of assessment measures, beginning with setting aims and concluding with creating percentile norms and interpretation systems. You might think this is a lot, but it is not the end of the story for there are still things to do. A publisher will want to see a graphical representation of scores in the standardization sample, to understand their distribution by portraying them in some way and calculating an indicator of their spread, and to compare the results with what is known as the normal curve. There will also be a need to check whether the mean score provided for a norm group is sufficiently accurate. Finally other scores may be needed for instances where the use of percentiles is not appropriate. A good understanding of basic stats is important in understanding and evaluating any assessment.

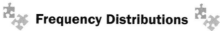

Frequency Distributions

Statistics enables us to summarize lots of information about people, for example after standardization when a lot of people have been measured on some variable and their scores collated. Another source to help you understand this terrifying subject is Field (2005). The test-maker needs to understand the distribution of raw scores among the standardization sample. Every person will have a score and the overall data set should be investigated in a meaningful way. The best way of doing this is to work out how often a score is obtained by different people, giving us what is called its frequency, and then to draw a graph summarizing all of the frequencies. For example, I might ask a group of students how many cups of coffee they drink each day and the data obtained could be:

```
1  1  2  2  2  2  3  3  3  3  3  3  4  4  4  4  4  4  4  5
5  5  5  5  5  5  5  5  5  6  6  6  6  6  6  6  6  7  7  7
7  7  7  8  8  8  8  9  9
```

Investigation of the data suggests that two people drank one cup a day, four drank two cups, six drank three cups, seven drank four, and so on. We can then plot a graph having the scores (the varying number of cups of coffee consumed) across the horizontal axis and the number of people swallowing the contents of each of the differing numbers of cups (called the frequency) on the vertical axis. To put it another way, the vertical axis indicates the number of people having a particular value on the horizontal one, i.e. it gives a frequency count. The result is called a pictogram, and it looks like Figure 4.1. Pictograms use a motif or symbol to represent a number of items and this type of display is often used in advertising.

The score distribution can be constructed using a variety of means including histograms and frequency polygons. This pictogram can be transformed into a histogram by replacing the pictures with bars of the same height, shown in Figure 4.2. Histograms often have their bars clustered together with the height on the vertical axis representing the number of people with scores between the intervals marked on the horizontal axis. Where test scores are used as the values it is often possible to summarize them by having the bars of the histogram representing scores in intervals, for example from 0 to 5. Each interval then represents the number of scores within a range, as shown in Figure 4.3. This figure summarizes data gained by giving a test to a group of people and indicates that there was only one person who got a test score having a value between 1 and 9, three people gaining scores between 10 and 19 and so on, making 23 scores in total.

Frequency distributions like this can be used to tell us how many people obtain each of the possible raw scores obtained from a test. They also help us to determine aspects of the distribution. The tallest bar, for example, indicates the most common score in the data set. The frequencies of different score intervals are mostly determined today using software, although you may have learned how to do this manually as a child at school through 'tallying'. This means listing all of the possible scores and then going through it, making a mark for each person against the row for that score. You learned tallying by using four strokes like this | | | | to represent the number four and then

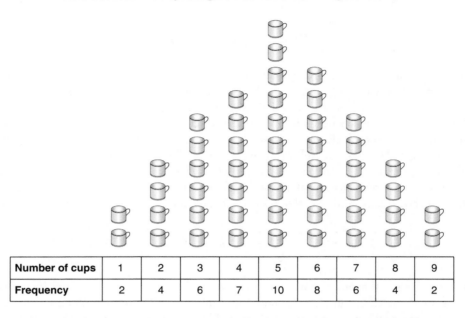

Number of cups	1	2	3	4	5	6	7	8	9
Frequency	2	4	6	7	10	8	6	4	2

Figure 4.1   A pictogram showing the frequency count of the numbers of cups of coffee consumed each day

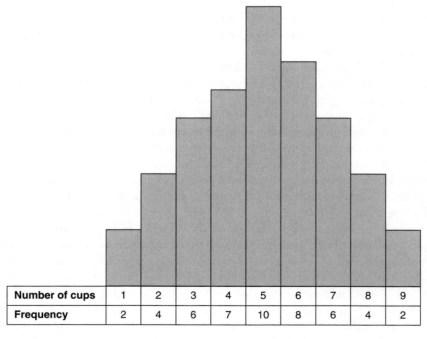

Number of cups	1	2	3	4	5	6	7	8	9
Frequency	2	4	6	7	10	8	6	4	2

Figure 4.2   A histogram, or frequency distribution, having bars indicating how many times each value occurs in the data set

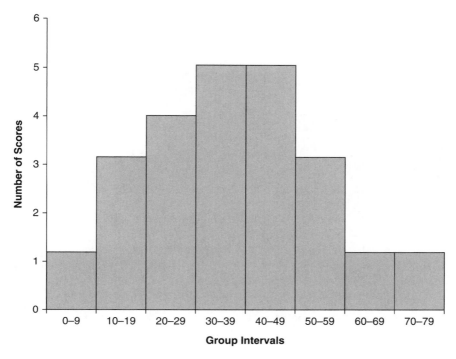

Figure 4.3   A frequency distribution in which the bars represent the number of test scores within a range

added one line through it as a diagonal (the five-bar gate) to represent the number five. From the resulting distribution we can identify three important aspects. These are:

- *The Mode*   This is the interval with the greatest number of people. It is the most common or frequent score. It defines the highest point in a frequency distribution.
- *The Median*   This is the middle score, i.e. it falls in the middle of the group and lies at the 50th percentile. Equal numbers of scores lie either side.
- *The Mean*   This indicates the position of the distribution on the measurement scale and is the average of scores.

The second way in which we can graphically illustrate the distribution is to draw a frequency polygon. This has the same basis as the histogram above. A cross (x) is drawn at the mid-point (the centres of the intervals) of the top of the bars and these are joined up to look more like a graph, as shown in Figure 4.4.

The Normal Curve

We have used just small samples of data in these illustrations. However, as more and more people are added to make the information greater, the shape of the distribution

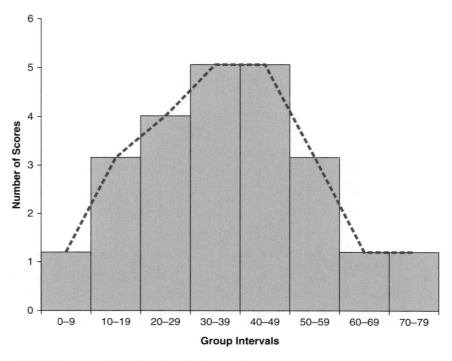

Figure 4.4   A frequency polygon showing a distribution of test scores

gradually changes to make the curve look smoother. It tends to become smoother overall and forms the bell-shape curve known as the normal frequency distribution curve
or just simply the normal curve (Figure 4.5). This distribution is found to occur for a
wide variety of both physical and psychological traits, and is sometimes called the
Gaussian distribution by mathematicians. The percentage of cases, i.e. the number of
people having a value on the scale measured (the horizontal axis), is mapped on the
vertical axis. The vertical axis can thus be referred to as the frequency of people or just
simply the frequency.

To understand this distribution, just think of the height of people – most are around
average height, which is at the centre, with progressively fewer people having greater
or lesser heights around it. Mathematically, the height at any point is called the ordinate. In this way the normal curve can be seen as having most of the scores lying at
its centre and then spreading outwards, demonstrating progressively lower frequencies for scores of lower and higher values. No one has suggested a good reason why so
many variables fit a normal curve: they just do. One might be that it seems to make
intuitive sense, although it also appears to be a natural consequence of probability
theory.

The normal distribution has its mean at the highest point (the mode, i.e. the distribution of test data has more people having average scores) and is symmetrical

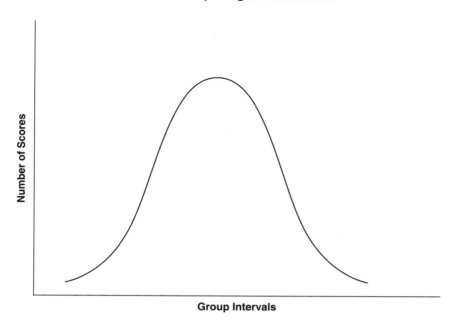

Figure 4.5 The normal curve

about the mean (making the median also coincide with the mean). So the mean, mode and median coincide at the centre. Many psychometric procedures assume that the measures they are dealing with are taken from an underlying normal distribution. It provides a standard reference distribution for measuring attributes and has known properties, including the fact that it is symmetrical with the mean, median and mode all being at the same place. The centre of the distribution is:

- the point about which variance is minimized,
- the point which divides the bottom 50 per cent of scores from the top 50 per cent, and
- the value with highest probability of occurrence.

The curve is perfectly symmetrical and asymptotic at the extremes, meaning that the line of the horizontal axis continually approaches the curve but doesn't meet it at a finite distance. The ordinate of the curve at any point along the test score axis (the x-axis) gives the proportion of people in the sample who have achieved a given score. The ordinates or heights representing a range of scores along the axis can also be added to determine the proportion of people who have a score within a range. Where the curve accurately represents a population distribution, the ordinate values also represent the probability of finding a given score or set of scores when they are randomly sampled from the population. So the whole graph can be viewed as a probability distribution. The mathematical equation defining the curve is:

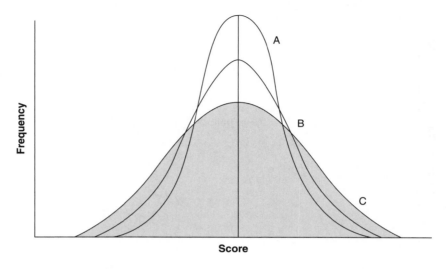

Figure 4.6   Three frequency distributions with the same average but with different variation

$$f(x) = \frac{1}{\sqrt{2\pi\sigma^2}} \, e - (x - \bar{x})^2$$

where:

f(x) = the ordinate of the curve for any particular test score,
x = the measurement values of scores on the horizontal axis,
$\bar{x}$ = the mean score,
σ = the distribution's standard deviation, and
e = the base of natural logarithms (the button marked 'e' on a scientific calculator shows this has a value of approximately 2.71).

Figure 4.6 shows three normal distributions having the same average, but with different variations along the score scale. The people represented by curve C have scores with greater spread or variance. In contrast, Figure 4.7 shows three normal curves which are identical in shape but with different averages. This might represent, for example, the scores of differing groups on a test – curve A could be for school-leavers (having the lowest mean), B for junior managers and C for senior managers or professionals (with the highest mean).

Skewed Distributions

Distributions can differ from normality by being skewed (leaning over) to the left or the right, or by making the top of the distribution more flattened or pointed. These may happen when there is a sampling bias, for example there may be too many good performers or too many easy items in a test. The result is what is called a skewed raw score distribution. Scores tend to be bunched at one end of the scale, with a tail of low frequencies. The distribution of income is often skewed, with average pay level being much higher than the median, which is higher again than the mode. Many people often

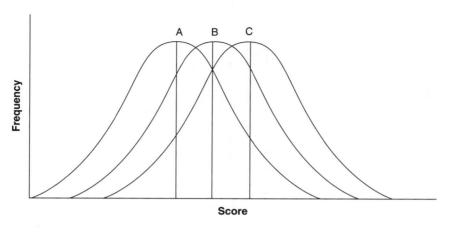

Figure 4.7   Three frequency distributions identical in shape but with different averages

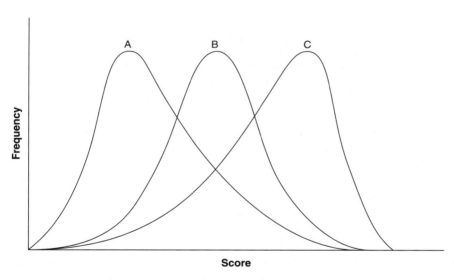

Figure 4.8   Three frequency distributions differing in skewness

think of national average pay as being the mode. The distributions shown in Figure 4.8 have different skewness – A is said to be positively skewed while C is negatively skewed. Distribution C could have too many easy items, giving most people high scores; while the opposite occurs for curve A.

Skew reflects the amount of asymmetry in a distribution. Negative values suggest the left tail is heavier and usually longer than the right tail which may be truncated (shortened). Positive values have the opposite pattern. A large skew value suggests that the distribution is truncated, with the score range being restricted on one side only.

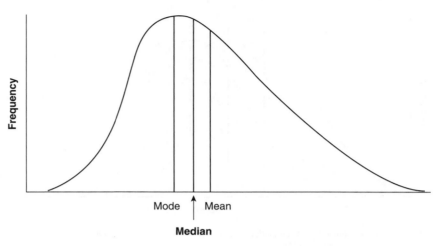

Figure 4.9   Relation between the mean, median and mode in a positively skewed frequency distribution

This happens often in measures of reaction time because there is a limit to the measurement of very small times, whilst it is possible to record and measure much larger reaction times. As a result distributions of reaction time measurements are often positively skewed. The presence of truncated tails also causes 'floor' and 'ceiling' effects in relation to item difficulty. A test has a high floor whenever a large percentage of people get raw scores at or close to the lowest possible, suggesting that it does not contain a satisfactory number and range of easier items. In other words, not many people do well. On the other hand, the test has a low ceiling if the opposite occurs, i.e. when a high percentage gain raw scores at or close to the highest possible, meaning that too many do too well. These effects may have a significant impact on future use of the test because one with a high floor may be inappropriate for individuals of lower abilities.

The mean, median and mode coincide at the centre of a truly normal distribution, which is rarely seen in practice. This is purely an ideal. They separate out once a distribution is skewed. For example, look at what happens in a positively skewed frequency distribution in Figure 4.9. This shows that the mode is still at the highest point, having the highest frequency. The mean occurs to the right of the median. A good question is why this should be referred to as a positively skewed distribution – many people seem to think that, being skewed to the left, it should intuitively be negatively skewed. The reason is that, because of the long 'tail' to the right, more people in the data set have scores higher than the mean. When a distribution has a tail at the upper end, then it is positively skewed. Figure 4.10 shows the opposite case, when a normal curve leans to the right and is said to be negatively skewed. Notice the relative positions of the mean, mode and median in the two distributions. Where there is a negative skew the mean is lower than the mode or median; where there is positive skew the mean is higher than the other two. In many instances the data obtained by a test-maker have a skewed distribution when illustrated graphically. Variations like these can be subjected to statistical correction in many instances.

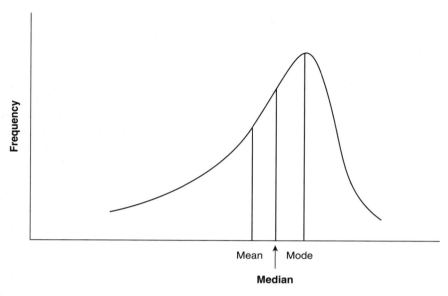

Figure 4.10   Relation between the mean, median and mode in a negatively skewed frequency distribution

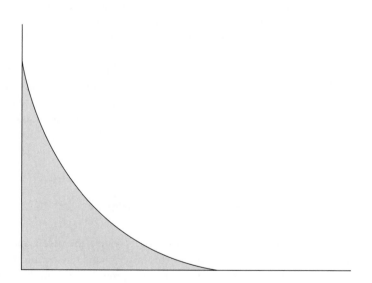

Figure 4.11   A Poisson distribution

As we have suggested, most human characteristics are usually normally distributed. But other kinds of distribution can, rarely, appear. For example, there is the Poisson distribution, shown in Figure 4.11. This occurs with certain types of event, such as accidents. Only small numbers of people have lots of accidents in one year, thankfully, meaning that the graph is higher at the low end of the horizontal axis, whilst most of the people in a population have just one or two accidents a year, making the curve lower at the high end.

Non-normality can be adjusted by changing items and continuously re-sampling. A positively skewed distribution may be corrected by introducing more easy items with the result that more lie in the centre instead of at the lower extreme. Done adequately, a greater number of people will get about 50 per cent of the items right. The adjusted level of difficulty will then give sufficient differentiation between people. However, it is important to recognize that an assessment showing a normal distribution of scores for the general population may demonstrate extreme skew or some other variation when it is given to a group differing substantially from the typical population. For example, this happens when a test designed for the general population is administered to a group having a substantially higher educational level in an ability, resulting in a negatively skewed curve having a low 'ceiling' (most people having scores at the high end). Conversely, if we administered it to people from a recent immigrant population having poor language skills we would obtain a positively skewed curve with a high floor. As a result the measure will not be able to discriminate effectively between members of either group because of the ceiling and floor effects, although it will still be useful for a general population. So we should always take into account the test's distribution, and its floor and ceiling effects, when we administer it to people who do not conform to a standardization sample. This will happen when we use high-level tests of verbal reasoning with people having a much lower degree of exposure to the English language. Therefore the generation of a normal distribution without negative or positive skewing forms a major factor in the evaluation of test bias.

But there are times when a normal curve may not be possible or even desirable, depending on what attribute is being tested. What if a characteristic is not normally distributed in the population at large? We might want to assess people when they are likely to be at the extreme end of an ability spectrum, for example in assessing those having learning disability or those children said to be highly gifted. Instances of this are rare.

Measures of Central Tendency

Key attributes of the normal curve are the position of its centre, the mean, and how much spread out it is. The term 'dispersion' refers to this latter characteristic and the standard deviation is the most common measure of it. The mean, median and mode are said to be measures of central tendency. The most important of these is the mean value. The three distributions of Figure 4.7 have different mean values. Simply put, it is the arithmetic average of a set of numbers and indicates where a distribution is situated on the measurement scale. The median and the mode provide less information. In the case of a nominal scale the mode is the only useful measure of central tendency. Indicating the most common score, this is of limited value because it can't be used with continuous variables or rank measures. The median, representing the middle value of a score set, is the measure of central tendency for an ordinal scale only and can sometimes be misleading because the numbers to one side may be more extreme than those on the other side. The values of the mean, mode and median are more stable for larger samples of data.

Normal curves can vary, especially in how fat or thin they are. Figure 4.6 demonstrates this by illustrating three distributions centred around the same mean value but having different amounts of dispersion. Distribution A has the smallest dispersion, clinging more tightly to the centre, whilst Distribution C has the largest dispersion, being fatter and more spread out. The standard deviation is the most commonly known indicator of the extent to which scores are spread out.

If we subtract the mean from each of the scores in turn we can calculate how far they are spread out around the mean. This gives us the deviation of each score. Averaging them would always give a result of zero because of positive and negative values. So we square them and then add the squared values. The result is the sum of squares, which represents the total dispersion existing in the data set. It is frequently quoted in published research and is a valuable first stage in many statistical procedures. However, the big disadvantage of the sum of squares is that its value is linked directly to the number of measurements, i.e. the sample size. Increasing the sample set will generally increase the sum of squares. So it has a purely random value which is dependent only on the size of the sample used.

The easiest way out of this predicament is to divide the sum of squares by the number of scores (the sample size N) to obtain the average sum of squares for all of the scores. Doing this provides the mean square or sample variance, often referred to simply as the variance, which is a measure of the amount of variation between scores within a sample. The bigger the variance, the more scores differ from each other. If N is fairly large the variance will not change drastically if the sample size changes because it forms part of the calculation. However, in cases where N is small the sum of squares is normally divided by N − 1.

Variance is an important statistic in many areas of psychology, for example in seeking to identify the percentage of the variance in criminality which is explained by different social and other factors or in attempting to discover how much of the variance among intelligence scores can be explained by heredity or environment. Serious stuff, indeed. So variance is useful in research. But it is not much help in dealing with practical issues in psychometrics because it does not link directly with the measurements made, basically because the differences between scores and the mean were squared. Undoing this, by square rooting the variance, converts it back to a distance on the scale used. The outcome is called the standard deviation.

We can use this procedure as a recipe for calculating the mean, sum of squares, variance and the standard deviation. The headings are:

score	mean	d	d squared

We can write our scores into the table under the first heading and then follow this recipe:

1   Calculate the mean by adding up all of the scores and dividing by the number of them.
2   Write the number obtained for the mean down the second column against each of the scores.
3   Subtract the mean from each score to give the distance between them (d for distance or dispersion) and list these in the column headed d. You could instead subtract each score from the mean and get the same result in the end.
4   The trouble with the last set of figures in step 3 is that some may have negative values. This is a nuisance because we want to calculate the average dispersion and calculating the average in the usual way doesn't work if we have negative numbers. To get rid of the minus signs, square the values of d in turn to get d squared and list these values in the final column.
5   Now total up the final column. This total value is the sum of squares.
6   To calculate the average dispersion of scores, divide the sum of squares by the number of scores (N). Remember that we divide by N − 1 in the case of small data sets. The value obtained is the variance.
7   Lastly, square root the value for the variance. What you get is the standard deviation.

The following shows the calculation for just a few scores as a simple demonstration:

score	mean	d	d squared
7	6.75	−0.25	0.063
9	6.75	−2.25	5.063
5	6.75	1.75	3.063
4	6.75	2.25	5.063
1	6.75	5.75	33.063
8	6.75	−1.25	1.563
9	6.75	−2.25	5.063
11	6.75	−4.25	18.063

Total   54   Sum of Squares =   71.004

Mean = 54 ÷ 8 = 6.75   Variance = 71.004 ÷ 7 (N − 1) = 10.14

So the Standard Deviation = $\sqrt{10.14}$ = 3.19

The similarity of the numbers in the d squared column is just a coincidence of the scores I arbitrarily chose for the calculation. The question is: Do you get the idea?

It is important to remember that the standard deviation, which I will occasionally abbreviate to SD, is a distance along the scale, whilst variance is a measure of the amount of dispersion of scores. This means that on a distribution graph we can mark the position of the mean and also the positions of one standard deviation above and below this, and the positions of two standard deviations above and below the mean also.

For the numbers given, the mean is 6.75 so one SD below this for these scores occurs at 6.75 − 3.19, i.e. at 3.56 on the scale. One SD above the mean occurs at 6.75 + 3.19 which is at value 9.94. If you calculate the values for both two SDs below the mean and two above the mean, you get 0.37 and 13.13. In the case of a much larger sample we would be able to calculate the points for plus and minus 2½ SDs around the mean. On the horizontal axis of both a histogram and a frequency polygon it is possible to mark the position of the mean of a set of scores and also the positions of where one SD above and one SD below this mean are on the scale.

The Normal Curve and Probability

The normal distribution can also be translated into percentiles. Information about the percentile scale can then be used to define the probability of any score occurring, for example the probability that a person will get a score at or below the 70th percentile is 0.7, which could also be thought of as a 7 out of 10 or 70 per cent chance. Each percentile can be considered as describing the likelihood of a person getting a score at least as good as that percentile value.

Any frequency distribution can be converted into a probability distribution by dividing each frequency (the number of people at each point) by the total number of people in the distribution. Then the sum of all the probabilities will be 1. This means there will be a probability that a person's score is somewhere along the scale, provided they take the test. This is easier, perhaps, to think of in the case of a histogram. For a histogram the total sum of the vertical bars represents the total number of people in the sample (think about it – the height of each bar signifies the number of people who got scores in that interval so adding them up will give the total sample size). If we then add together the heights of any set of bars and divide by the total number of people, we end up with the probability of a score being in the set of bars chosen. So the total area of a histogram represents the total number of people in the sample. In the same way, the total area of a probability distribution represents the total probability of any score being on the scale, which is 1.

The conclusion is that we can think of the normal curve as having an area of 1 and being divided into smaller areas which indicate the chances of scores occurring along the scale. Take a look at Figure 4.12 which shows the percentage distribution of cases in a normal curve. The lower-case Greek letter σ (sigma) is used in this figure to be an abbreviation for the term standard deviation. So +1σ, +2σ, and +3σ represent respectively one, two and three standard deviations above the mean. Similarly, we have −1σ, −2σ and −3σ to the left of the mean. Statisticians have calculated that 68.26 per cent of people get scores on the distribution between plus and minus one standard deviation around the mean. Similarly, 95.44 per cent get scores between plus and minus two standard deviations around it, while 99.72 per cent are covered by the range of plus and minus three standard deviations. In the last case that means almost effectively 100 per cent of everybody in a sample. Converted into a probability distribution, this means that you have about a 68 per cent chance of getting your score on any assessment in the plus/minus one standard deviation range. Thus most people are around the average. You have approximately a 95 per cent chance of getting a score in the plus/minus two range. Only about 2½ per cent of people will get scores at either extreme, and an individual has about a 2½ per cent chance of getting a score at one extreme.

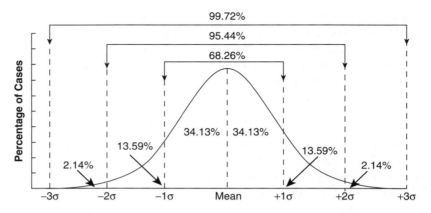

Figure 4.12   Percentage distribution of cases in a normal curve

Working on this basis, the normal curve has been suggested as one approach to identifying abnormality i.e. behaviours viewed as unique, rare or extreme. Typical behaviours can be seen as those which fall within the middle range, with those at the extremes defined as abnormal. We could estimate the 'normality' or 'abnormality' of any test score or range of scores, depending on whether they lie near the mean or at the extremes. However, we need to be aware there are likely to be many very large or small measurements, compared to the typical, which might not be described as abnormal, such as rare talents in sports, the arts or science. This approach could potentially classify rare behaviours as being negative or unwanted, which may well not be the case. But the normal curve still forms the basis of many common psychometric models, including Classical Test Theory, and is assumed to be the principal distribution for many measurements.

Sampling and Standard Error of the Mean

So a publisher tests a sample group of people and then calculates the mean, mode, median and standard deviation (SD) of the resulting distribution, as well as graphically representing it. Information on the sample and its mean will provide us with the norms mentioned in Chapter 3. As we said, in designing a test for the first time this sample is chosen to represent a much larger 'population'. As long as a sample is reasonably large and chosen to be representative of the population as a whole, the distribution can be similar to that of the whole population. Buyers will be concerned about having norms which are of good quality and accuracy. How can you check this out and avoid buying a 'dodgy' test?

Sampling Error

Only one sample of a certain size has been chosen from the set of all possible samples which together must make up any population. Imagine that a publisher starts with a small sample, but then goes on to choose another out of the population, a bit bigger than the first one, and calculates the parameters again. Then the publisher does it again using a different but larger still sample. And yet again, and again, each time taking a different but larger sample. Obviously, as the sample size gets larger and larger still, each one must become more representative of the overall population. As sample size continues to increase, the means and SDs of samples will inevitably differ less from each other. The biggest difference will be between the means and SDs of the smallest and largest possible samples. Samples of slightly different sizes will have slightly different mean values, owing to what is known as sampling error.

The Standard Error of the Mean

Eventually all of the possible samples taken together as a whole should be the same as the population. (Adding every possible sample size will surely give us the total population size.) So any frequency distribution of the means for the different samples will indicate that the mean of all the possible sample means has the same value as the true population mean, while the SD of the distribution of means will show how much they tend to vary around the population mean. This SD is referred to as the standard error of the mean and is written as SEmean for short.

Confidence Limits

It makes sense that as we increase the size of the sample taken, so each one will become more representative of the overall population, and the samples will vary less and less from each other (because they will all be whoppers in size). Variance of the sample means decreases at the same time because they will be clustering around the true mean. Thus as the sample size gets bigger, getting closer to the size of the population, we can be more confident that the sample mean is a good estimate of the overall population mean. The variance of the means can be used to give an actual measure of this confidence.

Based on what we said about the normal distribution and probability, then one SD of the sample means, the SEmean, either side of a particular sample mean, will have a 68 per cent chance of containing the true population mean. Two SEmeans plotted either side of any sample mean will have a 95 per cent chance of containing the true mean. We may never know what the true mean value is for everyone in a large unknown population, but we can specify a range in which it will lie with 68 per cent or even 95 per cent confidence. Going back to our question above about a 'dodgy' test, this means that if the confidence range turns out to be enormous we might as well bin the marketing information. Any enormous confidence range would mean we can't have much certainty where the true mean lies and any value given will contain a lot of error. So there is method in the madness. But we are not quite there yet, because we do need to be able to calculate how big the range is or, to put it a different way, we need to calculate the limits of the range as a distance on the scale. Keeping our thinking caps on suggests:

The sum of all of the possible samples from the population must equal the population itself.

The variation of the entire sample means combined must equal the population variation.

So: the Variance of the Sample Means × Sample Size = Population Variance giving us:

$$\text{Variance of the Sample Means} = \frac{\text{Population Variance}}{\text{Sample Size (N)}}$$

We got the SD earlier by square rooting the variance, so this means we can square root both sides to get:

$$\text{The SD of the Sample Means} = \frac{\text{Population SD}}{\sqrt{N}}$$

The SD of the Sample Means is the Standard Error of the Mean (SEmean), defined above, and we get the formula:

$$\text{SEmean} = \frac{\text{SD}}{\sqrt{N}}$$

Thus the stability of measures increases as a function of the square root of the sample size. The error also decreases as a function of the square root of the sample size, which makes sense because the bigger N is the smaller will be the Standard Error. The same thing applies to the sample SD, because this will underestimate, similarly, the population SD. With bigger samples the degree of under-estimation gets smaller. As you might expect, the more people included the less error will be made in assuming the sample characteristics represent those of the population. Therefore, this allows us to specify the degree of error likely to occur whenever we estimate a population value from a sample value. Using the above equation we can determine the Standard Error of the Mean for any sample and can calculate the limits of the error range.

For example, if a sample of size (N) of 400 people has a standard deviation of 42.5 and a calculated (observed) mean of value 55.0 on the raw score scale, then

$$\text{SEmean} = \frac{\text{SD}}{\sqrt{N}} = \frac{42.5}{\sqrt{400}} = \frac{42.5}{20} = 2.13$$

Because the Standard Error of the Mean is the SD of the sample means we can look at the range from one SEmean below the raw score mean to one SEmean above. This range is 55.0 ± 2.13 in this case, i.e. the range goes from 52.87 to 57.13 on the scale. Statistics tells us that 68 per cent of the possible true values of the sample mean lie within this range – from one SEmean below to one SEmean above the observed mean.

We can be 68 per cent sure that our true mean for the sample lies within this range. Put another way, the 68 per cent confidence limits go from 52.87 to 57.13. If we calculate the range covered by two SEmeans, i.e. the observed mean ± two SEmeans, then we have a 95 per cent confidence interval. This suggests we have a 95 per cent certainty of finding the true value of the sample mean within this range around the observed mean. This time the limits go from 50.74 to 59.26.

So when we use a sample of people to establish a normative mean for any measure, we can have an understanding of the error range involved. As the size of the sample increases (N), then the error decreases (SEmean) and the calculated observed mean gets closer to the true mean for a population. Any statistic based on a small sample is likely to be unstable, especially when the people involved differ widely. We can now see that the greater the size of a sample taken from a population, the better we are able to estimate the mean and the SD of scores. Bartram and Lindley (1994) suggest that sample sizes should be evaluated on the following criteria:

- Larger than 2000 – excellent
- 1000 to 1999 – good
- 500 to 999 – reasonable
- 200 to 499 – adequate
- under 200 – inadequate

The degree to which a sample distribution resembles the population normal curve increases as the number of scores (N) grows, and becomes less accurate as N gets smaller. A larger sample will have a more normal distribution, depending on whether the population distribution is actually normal itself. Having a large sample will not necessarily, therefore, always ensure that the underlying population distribution is normal. For example, some tests, such as the Wisconsin Card Sorting Test, have distributions which are non-normal, even though samples are large. It would not be possible, however, to assume that a population distribution is non-normal if the small sample representing it has non-normal properties. A number of factors can cause non-normal distributions, including the presence of distinct sub-populations having different capabilities.

Summary

Frequency distributions, such as histograms, enable scores obtained by standardization samples to be evaluated. As sample size increases the results begin to approximate the normal curve, which provides a standard reference distribution having known properties and can be seen as a probability distribution. Distributions differing from normality may be skewed, resulting in a significant impact on test use. Key attributes of the normal curve include its variance and standard deviation. Sampling error depends upon sample size and variations in test scores. We can calculate confidence intervals for the Standard Error of the Mean to estimate the score mean of a population.

The Normal Curve and Standard Scores

As we saw in Chapter 3, percentiles are widely used although they have limitations, being based on an ordinal scale, with units not being equal on all parts of the scale, and they can't be subjected to parametric statistical analysis. So we often have to use something else. Unlike percentiles, standard scores involve measurement on an interval scale and their norms represent scores having means and standard deviations chosen for their usefulness. Strictly defined, they are scores gained from a measure which can be referenced to the normal distribution, and are then said to be normalized. The principal types include z scores, T scores, sten and stanine scores. Norms are usually expressed in terms of either these or percentiles.

z scores

The z score, or z value, is the most basic of all standard scores and we can use it to calculate others. It is based on the assumption of a standard normal curve from which the properties of all other normal curves can be calculated. By definition, the standard curve has a mean of zero and a standard deviation of one whenever we use z scores. Any score along this scale is then said to be a z score. Why the name z, you ask? Apparently, this is because it is an abbreviation for 'zero mean plus or minus 1'. Because of the values chosen, it becomes easy to convert from any other normal curve to the standard z curve – we subtract the mean and divide by the SD. Doing this suggests that the mean becomes 0 and that one SD converts to value 1, two SDs convert to value 2 and so on. At one SD to the left of the mean the value becomes −1 and two SDs to the left become −2.

As Figure 4.13 shows, at three SDs below the mean we have −3, at two SDs below we have −2, at one below we have −1, at the centre of the curve we have 0, then at one SD above we have +1, at two above we have +2 and at three above we have +3. Values in-between the whole numbers can occur so that a person's score could be at 1.55 or −2.14 or 0.57, for example. The new values are the z scores. In accordance with its definition, for example, a z score of +1.5 is 1.5 SDs above the mean.

Conversion of raw scores to z scores is simple. If someone has a raw score of 36 and the scale has a mean of 25 and an SD of 8, then:

a) Subtract the mean from the score, so 36 − 25 = 11.
b) Divide this value by the standard deviation, so 11 ÷ 8 = 1.375, which is the z score.

It is also possible to go the other way – to convert from the z scores to a raw scale score by reversing the calculation. This means multiplying the z score by the scale's SD and then adding the mean. If a person had a z score of −1.5, the raw score would be obtained by:

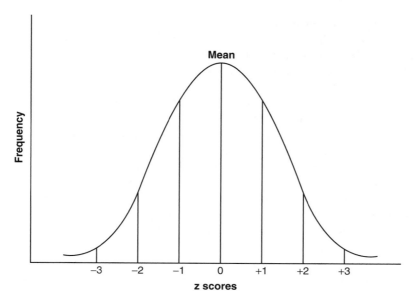

Figure 4.13   The distribution based upon z scores

a) Multiplying the z score by the SD, so $-1.5 \times 8 = -12$, and
b) Adding the mean to the result, $25 - 12 = 13$

Formulas for the two operations above of calculating score equivalents would be:

$$z\ score\ = \frac{test\ score - \bar{x}}{\sigma}\quad and\ Test\ raw\ score = (z\ score \times \sigma) + \bar{x}$$

where σ is the standard deviation (SD) and $\bar{x}$ is the mean.

This process provides a simple linear transformation of raw scores to their equivalent z scores and the result is that the mean and SD of the z scores are different from the original, although the shapes of the two distributions are the same. It is important to note that if the distribution of the raw scores is skewed in any way, then the z score distribution may be just as skewed.

We discussed earlier that the normal curve can be viewed as a probability distribution, and so the area under the curve between any two points gives us the probability of obtaining scores between them. Do you remember that the normal distribution can be translated into percentiles which may then be used to define the probability of any raw score occurring? For example, the area to the left of $z = 1$ contains 84 per cent of the area under the curve (and percentile 84 means that 84 per cent of people do less well) and so a z value of 1 corresponds to the 84th percentile. We can tabulate the correspondence between any z score and its related percentile, and manuals often give tables of these conversions.

Tables of areas under the normal curve relating to z scores, as shown in Appendix A, are also useful because of this link. In this table percentile ranks have been converted from proportions of 100 to proportions of 1 by dividing by 100, so that 72.91 becomes 0.7291. To use the table to identify the proportion of the area lying below a specific z score, find the z score in the first column (which indicates the value to one decimal place) and the first row of the table (indicating the second decimal place of the z score). Thus to find the area below a z score of value −0.23 find the intersection of −0.2 in the first column and .03 in the first row at the top. The value you get is 0.4090, so 40.9 per cent of the area under the curve lies below a z score of −0.23, suggesting that this value lies at approximately percentile 41. Similarly, a z score of 1.64 has an area under the curve below it of 94.95 per cent, near enough to percentile 95. On the other hand, to find the value of z below which a particular proportion of the area of the curve lies, start by locating that proportion somewhere in the body of the table by scanning rows and columns. Then find the z score in the corresponding row and column. So to discover the value of z below which 2.5 per cent of the area of the curve lies, start by finding 0.0250 in the table. This value is at the intersection of the row labelled −1.9 and the column headed 0.06, and therefore the corresponding z value is −1.96. Only 2.5 per cent of people will have scores below this.

Normalizing Scores

By calculating z scores from percentiles in this way, rather than from raw scores, we can ensure the resulting scores are normally distributed even if the test's raw scores are not. Therefore, if a manual contains raw score to percentile conversion tables, we can always produce what are known as normalized standard scores from the percentiles using Appendix A. Normalized scores provide a common standard scale for different tests. They are distributed along an equal interval scale and arithmetic operations can be carried out. Because they are normalized, a particular z score then always means the same thing in percentile terms. But there is no direct correspondence between z scores and percentiles for non-normalized standard scores. An underlying trait measured may actually be normally distributed in the general population, and so distortions in the raw score distribution could arise from a bias in the scaling used.

So z scores are useful, showing how many SDs away from the mean a score is. A positive value suggests that someone is above average, while a negative value is below average. As they are interval measures, scores can be added together or subtracted. They provide a common scale across tests which may have different scales. The simplest of scoring systems, they form the basis of other measurement procedures and are important in theoretical terms. But they have some distinct disadvantages. Going predominantly from −2 to +2, they don't discriminate effectively between people unless we use lots of decimal values, such as a z score of 1.282 which appears to be clumsy as an indicator of performance. It seems to be quite a narrow range: two-thirds of z scores lie between −1 and +1. Secondly, negative values can sometimes have their minus signs omitted accidentally, resulting in inaccurate records. Then there is the issue of z scores having both negative and positive numbers, meaning that people sometimes have difficulty in doing calculations. Lastly, people have a right to know what records are kept about them and may be unhappy during feedback to discover they have obtained a negative test value even when it is close to the mean and they have performed at a typical level. Imagine being told that you had a score of –0.5 on a particular test! We need more user-friendly systems. These disadvantages have led to other scoring systems which are still based on the normal curve and are calculated from z scores. The result is standard score norms which can have any preferred mean and SD.

T Scores

These provide a scale having a mean of 50 and a standard deviation of 10 (hence the name). T scores have a range from about 20 to 80, within the range of three SDs either sides of the mean. One SD down lies at value 40, two down at 30; one SD above the mean is at T score 60 and two up is at 70. They can be calculated using the formula:

$$T = 50 + \left(\frac{10 \times \text{test score} - \bar{x}}{\sigma} \right)$$

With T scores often being rounded to the nearest whole number, they form quite a simple scale which is widely used. It seems to be the best scale for most purposes.

Sten Scores

Standard Ten, or just sten, scores are widely used, especially in personality assessment because they provided the scale most preferred by Cattell in designing the original 16PF. Because they go from 1 to 10, the mid-point of 5.5 is the mean value on the scale, although scores of 0.5 and 10.5 can occasionally be obtained in constructing profiles and need to be marked as 1 and 10 on the scale. Dividing the normal curve into 10 scores, the sten scale is simple and seems to have an appropriate level of sensitivity in discriminating between trait scores. It has an SD of 2.0 so a range of two SDs below the mean occurs at value 1.5 and two above at 9.5. Stens are useful in giving feedback to people because they seem comfortable with a simple 1 to 10 scale.

Stanine Scores

Stanine scores, or 'standard of nine', form a scale (as you may have guessed) which goes from 1 to 9. They are a variation on the sten, dividing the normal curve into nine scores and having an SD of 2.0, although the mean this time is set at 5 on the scale. Once again, scores off the ends can be obtained sometimes in constructing profiles. A range of two SDs below the mean occurs at 1 on the scale and two above at 9. This scale has been widely used in the past, although it has declined over the years.

Converting Raw Scores to Standard Scores

So there are a number of different standard scores which are useful for different purposes. Percentiles remain more popular because they are easy to compute and to understand. But it is worth knowing that other scales exist, for example the WAIS-III subtests use scales having a mean of 10 and an SD of 3, whilst its scales for Verbal, Performance and Full Scale IQ scores have a mean of 100 and an SD of 15 in line with other intelligence tests. Norm tables also vary, depending on a publisher's approach. Some provide tables enabling just a conversion from raw score to percentile, whilst others give tables which also include translation to z, T and sten scores. As Chapter 3 demonstrated, it is mostly a simple matter of reading across from the raw score to other scores made available and occasionally to the grading system of A to E.

Norms obtained from percentiles can be converted to z scores using the normal curve table (Appendix A) and then converting them to the other standard scores. The benefit of doing this is that the standard scores are normally distributed. Its downside is that each can vary depending upon sample size, creating a significant disadvantage if it is small. Some test-makers appear to have a preference for normalized standardized scores. This seems to be sensible in the case of intelligence tests as intelligence is thought to be normally distributed among people at large. But they should only be used when there is a large sample and there is a reasonable theoretical prospect of a representative distribution.

Assessments which have a variety of norms available tend to be more useful. Regular updating of them will increase costs and be reflected in prices. What matters most is the rate of change in the population of an attribute. If it is fast, then more regular revision is required; if it is slow, there is less need. Performance on assessments such as Raven's Progressive Matrices has improved substantially since the 1940s and the use of old norm tables is not recommended.

Conversions between the standard scores are relatively easy to understand so long as we remember that z scores are the centre of the system and to convert from one to another we have to go via the z score.

To convert a z to a sten score we do the following:

- Multiply the z score by 2
- Add 5.5
- Round to the nearest whole number
- Values greater than 10 are given as 10; values less than 1 are given as 1

To convert a sten back to a z score we reverse this process:

- Subtract 5.5 from the sten score
- Divide the result by 2

To convert a z to a T score we:

- Multiply the z score by 10
- Add 50
- Round to the nearest whole number
- Values greater than 100 are given as 100; values less than 1 are given as 1

Lastly, to convert a T to a z score:

- Subtract 50 from the T score
- Divide by 10

Standard Scores in Practice

In some areas of practice, especially the clinical field, it is important to have a good understanding of the properties of the normal curve and of standard scores so as to take care when interpreting extremely low or high assessment scores. Clinical interpretation will depend on the characteristics of standardization samples used – they need to be large, well-constructed and have an approximate normal distribution, especially at extremes. Interpretation of a patient's score may not be legitimate if the standardization sample is skewed. While it may suggest the patient is suffering impairment, the value may give the clinician a false sense of accuracy and of comparison with others.

We have discussed forms of non-normality, such as skewness, earlier, although other types can also occur, such as multi-modality or a uniform or near-uniform distribution. Multi-modality happens when there is more than one 'peak' in a distribution (like a mountain range), having two modes. Measuring the same attribute in two clearly distinct groups might account for this. The other two forms occur where there is a curve having no or just a slight peak, together with a similar frequency across all of the scores. In these cases standard scores may be inaccurate and cannot be adequately interpreted. It would be wiser to base interpretation on percentile scores only. In these circumstances it is advisable for users to seek a description of any non-normality from the publisher, as well as of any techniques used to create standardized scores and their justification.

A neat summary of standard scores would be:

Name	Mean	SD	
z score	0	1	the basis of other scales
T score	50	10	usually limited to a range from 20 to 80
stens	5.5	2	standard ten i.e. 1 to 10 scale
stanines	5	2	standard nine i.e. 1 to 9 scale
IQ	100	15	the common intelligence scale

Another useful summary is given in Figure 4.14 which shows how the normal curve is linked to z scores, T scores, percentiles, stens and stanines.

Summary

Standard scores, such as z scores, T, sten or stanine scores, involve measurement on interval scales and norms based upon them are chosen for their usefulness. When they are calculated from test scores they may be as skewed as the original distribution. But if the test scores are converted to z scores using percentiles through inspection of

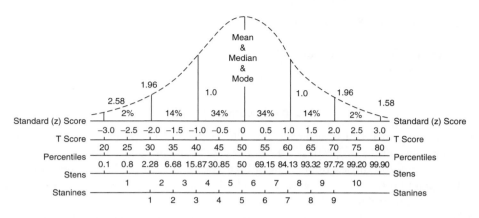

Figure 4.14   The normal curve, percentiles and the standard scores

normal curve tables they will become normalized scores. Z scores form the basis of other measurement scores, although not being so user-friendly. Sten and stanine scores have mostly been used for personality assessment. Extreme scores will need careful consideration in clinical practice, especially when the standardization sample has a non-normal distribution.

 ## What Have We Discovered About the Statistics Which Underpin Psychological Assessment?

We have seen how graphical representation of scores in standardization samples enables publishers to understand and evaluate their distribution, and to link this with the normal distribution curve. Where there is non-normality or skewness they can correct for this. Investigation of distributions includes calculation of central tendency parameters, such as their standard deviation. We have also seen how sample size is an important criterion for any standardization and how to calculate confidence intervals for the error affecting mean scores, so as to estimate a true population mean. We began with just raw score scales and percentile scales, but have moved on to standard scores such as z scores, T scores, sten and stanine scores, including the use of normal curve tables to produce normalized scores. We have learned:

- About the different ways in which test scores can be represented graphically.
- About the properties of the normal curve, including measures of central tendency, and how it can be viewed as a probability distribution.
- How sampling affects error around mean scores and that confidence limits enable us to estimate this error.
- About the different forms of standard score, including z scores, T scores, stens and stanines, and their conversions and practical applications.

PART II

The Essential Characteristics of Psychological Measurement

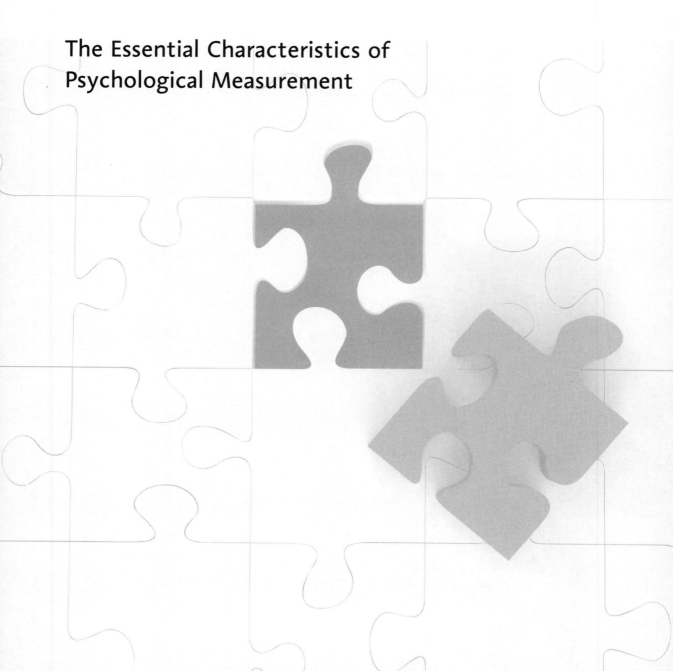

5

The Importance of Reliability

Learning Objectives

By the end of this chapter you should be able to:

- Understand the significance of reliability and the basic principles of correlation.
- Describe how test error arises, the different kinds of reliability coefficient and generalizability theory.
- Calculate Standard Error and determine confidence intervals around test scores.
- Evaluate differences between scores using the Standard Error of difference.

What is This Chapter About?

Having survived the statistics, understanding correlation is now an essential prerequisite for getting to grips with the key attributes of psychological measures, so we begin with what it means and its mathematical foundations. We then move on to identifying how test error arises and the different types of reliability coefficients. Afterwards we fall into the deep well of the Standard Error of Measurement and learn about the significance of confidence limits. The final nightmare before we escape lies in comparing scores and means using the Standard Error of difference.

 **Why Reliability?**

Consistency and Accuracy

The concept of reliability is very much tied up with the repeatability or reproducibility of any assessment. For any measure to be useful, it needs to have consistency so that it produces

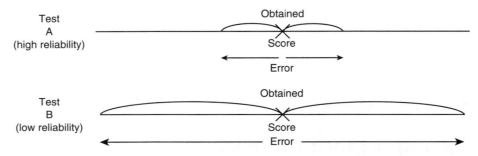

Figure 5.1   Visualizing the error range around two test scores – one of high reliability, the other having low reliability

more or less the same result for a person each time it is used. High reliability means that a measure gives similar results on different occasions. But no measure is completely accurate – there is always some degree of error. Knowing about reliability enables us to calculate that margin of error. It makes sense that the error in a test with high reliability is smaller than that for one of low reliability. Put simply, high reliability means low error and low reliability means enormous amounts of it in some instances. I think it is wise to try to visualize what this means, as in Figure 5.1 which pictures two scales, one having low amounts of error around a score (Test A) and the other having lots of it (Test B).

In the case of low reliability you can see that the error range around the score is so large that it is hardly worthwhile using that assessment. If you did, the score for someone could be meaningless and might be interpreted in a potentially harmful way. The error range around the score on Test A is much smaller. This idea of the 'margin of error' around scores applies to all forms of scientific measurement. No measurement is ever totally exact. Even the speedometer in your car is not wholly accurate – I was once told that the average error range for a speedometer is about two miles an hour. So if you think you are doing 40mph, you are really driving at a speed somewhere between 38 and 42 miles an hour. Similarly, if the margin of error is two points around a test score of 40, then this means the true score lies somewhere between 38 and 42. We shall see later that we can calculate these error margins.

Error can have consequences for a number of areas of applied psychology. Suppose, for example, we gave three people a test and their T scores, based on general population norms, were 48, 60 and 71. There is error around all three scores. The question is whether the highest score is really above average (50) and whether it is genuinely different from the others. In therapeutic assessment this might have implications for treatment or support. In the workplace the question could be whether the highest score is superior to the others. But all of them involve error and we need to take account of this.

Issues of reliability and validity are concerned with the nature of the relationship between an obtained test score, which reflects error, and a 'true' score in any assessment. This is a fundamental concept of Classical Test Theory. The two basic questions confronting us in using any assessment are:

1   How accurately does it measure?
2   What exactly does it measure?

These are obviously important. The first relates to reliability, whether a person's score on one occasion is linked to that on another; the second to validity, whether a score on one measure is similar to that on a different measure of the same attribute, which we shall deal with in Chapter 6. Both issues are quantified in terms of correlation – on the relationships between variables. Consistency, for example, will mean that to estimate test accuracy we must compare people's scores on different occasions. This is the heart of reliability. The degree to which they correlate is expressed by a statistic known as a correlation coefficient, and so we need to begin by understanding correlation.

Summary

We have seen that for any assessment to be of value it must be consistent, providing a similar outcome for any person each time it is used. Like any measurement, psychological assessment involves an error range around scores. Using a test means that we get an obtained score, although because of this error it is likely that it will not be the same as an ideal true score. Reliability establishes the accuracy and repeatability of any assessment, and involves the degree to which scores correlate with each other.

The Concept of Correlation

Scattergrams

One method of illustrating correlation between variables is through the use of scattergrams, where the coordinates of points indicate an association between an individual's score on one test and that on another. This is the simplest way of understanding correlation. They are called scatterplots by statisticians, although in the field of psychometrics they are commonly referred to as scattergrams. On the scattergram each cross or dot represents a person. Figure 5.2 shows scattergrams of different types of correlation between variables. The scores of individuals on variable X (test X) are allocated using the horizontal axis and their scores on variable Y (test Y) on the vertical axis. You may remember plotting coordinates at school such as the position (1, 1) or (1, 2) and so on. On this basis, the coordinates for one person, say (5, 8) represent a score of 5 on test X and of 8 on Y. The stronger the relationship represented, the more the scattergram appears as an elongated ellipse. A good indication of the correlation between variables would involve drawing a trend line through the centre of the points; accurate calculation of this gives what is called the regression line, enabling us to predict scores on one test from the other. Given a value for test X on the horizontal or x-axis, we could draw a vertical line up to the regression line and then horizontally across to the value for test Y on the vertical axis (the y-axis). This can be reversed to predict a person's score on test X from that on Y.

   As shown in Figure 5.2, high positive correlations form a long diagonal ellipse or oval shape, having points clustering generally together to make it thinner, and with few

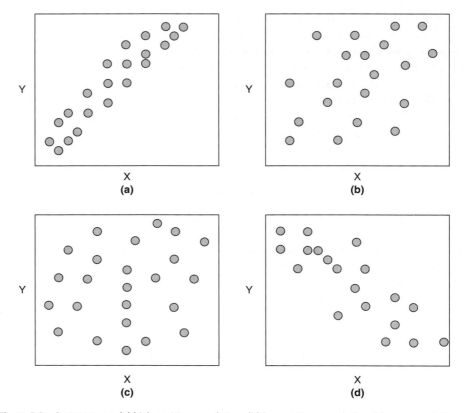

Figure 5.2 Scattergtams: (a) high positive correlation; (b) low positive correlation; (c) zero correlation; (d) negative correlation

moderate outliers. Low positive correlations enable the trend still to be seen, despite having more outliers and points being more spread out. For correlations of 0 there appears to be a random spread of points in what looks like a large circle with no clearly seen pattern or trend. Negative correlations concern variables which have the relationship that as one goes up the other goes down. How about the number of items you get right in a test and the number you get wrong? The more you answer correctly the fewer you are likely to get wrong. Scattergrams showing negative correlations have the same properties as positive ones, except that the slope of the trend line is going to descend from top left to bottom right on the x-axis. It is also possible to make predictions from these.

Positive and negative correlations can be shown graphically using straight-line graphs based on the regression line, as shown in Figure 5.3. To make predictions from one variable to another we have to use regression analysis. This enables us to draw a best-fitting line through the points on a scattergram. The mathematical equation for such a straight-line graph is given by

$$y = mx + c$$

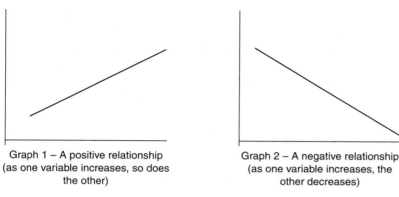

Graph 1 – A positive relationship
(as one variable increases, so does
the other)

Graph 2 – A negative relationship
(as one variable increases, the
other decreases)

Figure 5.3   Graphical representation of positive and negative relationships

You may remember this equation from school maths. It links the variables x (horizontal axis) and y (vertical axis) and allows us to calculate one from another, sometimes called the least squares regression line. The value of m is the gradient (or slope) of the line and the constant c is the value of where it hits the y-axis (the intersection). Knowing these, we can calculate the value of y for any value of x. For example, if m = 0.5 and c = 3, then we can use the equation

$y = 0.5x + 3$

so that when the value of x is 4:

$y = (0.5 \times 4) + 3$

$y = 2 + 3$

and $y = 5$

which gives us the coordinates (4, 5) on a scattergram or graph.

Graphs like these help us to estimate whether and what kind of correlation exists between variables, and to make predictions. But covariance and the correlation coefficient provide a more accurate evaluation of the relationship.

Covariance

The variance, as we saw in Chapter 4, tells us how much scores may vary about a mean, i.e. how much variation there is in a distribution of scores for one variable. It is linked with covariance which indicates how much variance is shared between two distributions of scores, for example scores on one test and those on another, or between test scores at one time and at another time, or between test scores and some other criterion variable outside testing. Sharing variance means that as one variable increases the other also does or, to put it another way, as one variable deviates from its mean then the other variable is expected to do so also in a similar way. Examples of this could include age and height variables, size of home and income.

Covariance is determined by multiplying the differences of one variable by the corresponding differences for the other to give the cross-product deviations and then dividing by the number of them to produce an averaged sum of combined differences. A positive value suggests that as one variable deviates from its mean, the other deviates in the same direction. A negative value suggests that as one deviates from the mean by increasing, the other deviates also but by decreasing. The problem of the covariance, however, is that it depends on the measurement scale used, meaning that we cannot compare values for different data sets unless they are measured in the same units. The covariance is, therefore, a crude measure of the relationship. So we convert it into a correlation coefficient by dividing the observed deviations by the standard deviation to give what is effectively a standardized covariance.

Correlation Coefficients

The more accurately we can predict one variable from another, the stronger will be the relationship between them. This relationship is quantified by the correlation coefficient. It can only be based on continuous variables, which excludes nominal and ordinal measures. The most commonly used version is the Pearson product-moment correlation. The correlation between two variables then suggests we can make a prediction, but does not mean one causes the other. You can't assume causation because two variables are correlated. This is because there may be other variables influencing the outcomes, whether measured or, in fact, unmeasured and possibly unknown. Any correlation is greater when there are few others of these 'confounding variables', which are related to either of the two principal variables. For example, the cognitive abilities of children during infancy may be correlated positively with physical characteristics and this may be the result of an intervening variable we call maturation or physical development. Apart from this, correlation coefficients do not tell us which variable causes the other to change.

Pearson developed his product-moment correlation coefficient 'r' for just this purpose, identifying both the magnitude and direction of a relationship. His coefficient is based upon calculation of the average cross-product of test scores given as z scores, providing a standardized form of covariance, and the correlation coefficients then have numerical values between −1 and +1. A value of zero means there is no correlation between variables, that there is no degree of association:

- +1 or −1 means there is a perfect correlation (an ideal which is never reached)
- +1 is a perfect positive correlation
- 0 means there is no correlation between variables and they are, therefore, independent and unrelated, for example how much I earn and the volume of traffic on any road you care to choose. In statistics we say they are orthogonal.
- −1 means a perfect negative correlation

By convention we use the letter 'r' to denote a correlation coefficient between variables. It indicates the degree of association, regardless of whether this is positive or negative.

Most relationships actually fall somewhere between the extremes of −1 and +1 and any value indicates how weak or strong the association is. Some examples are:

r = 0.10 means a weak (positive) relationship

r = 0.30 means a moderate relationship

r = 0.50 means there is quite a strong relationship

The value of r has an impact on the reliability of a test. The square of the correlation indicates the proportion of variance which the two variables share. In practice this can be a little idealistic and the correlations obtained are not a good representation of a relationship, often underestimating it. Values can be distorted by factors including:

- *Restriction of the range* of a variable, i.e. use of a data set which includes mostly information provided by people who have higher (or lower) scores. Statistical corrections can sometimes be used to fix this.
- Use of *non-linear variables*, whilst assuming that the direction of relationship between them is always consistently the same.
- *Variability* (or variance) in the variables.
- *Errors* in the measurement of some variables, such as imperfect measures of work performance when it is subjectively assessed.

Correlations will be maximized when error is reduced and the variables represent broader ranges of data. From a statistical point of view, you can't average correlation coefficients directly in the usual way because they don't form a uniform scale. Those based on samples of less than about 60 people are too small to have value, whilst those based on about 200 or more are good. Kline (2000) recommends a minimum of 100.

Summary

Correlation can be evaluated through the use of scattergrams and graphs which represent the association between a person's score on one test and that on another. Using these, regression lines enable us to predict one score from another. A more mathematical approach is to determine the covariance which indicates how much variance is shared by the distributions of variables. Correlation coefficients are based upon standardized covariance and the most common is the Pearson product-moment correlation. They identify both the magnitude and direction of relationships between variables.

 Identifying and Evaluating Error

The Fallibility of Scores

Classical Test Theory relates true scores and obtained scores on any measure. The items contained within it are thought to consist of a random sample taken from an infinite universe of all of the relevant ones, as described in Chapter 2. Good well-chosen items will make a good test. A person's true score is the ideal or perfectly accurate score which that person would have on the measure. But because of a variety of other factors it is unlikely that it will accurately establish the true score – it will produce instead an 'obtained' or 'observed' score, which is an estimate only of the true score. The theory says every measurement is fallible in practice and includes some amount of error (Nunnally, 1978). The actual true score is affected by someone's ability as well as other incidental factors acting in an unsystematic and random fashion. If a person were daft enough to do a test lots of times, we would end up with a normal distribution having a mean and standard deviation (SD). The SD of this distribution represents the degree to which there is error in the process, although the true score always remains constant. The SD of the errors of measurement is known as the Standard Error of Measurement, or SEM for short. This is an important concept in test theory. It is a measure of the amount of error likely to be associated with any score on a test. But where does the error come from?

Sources of Error

To increase the reliability of a measure, errors should be minimized and in an ideal situation they would be eliminated. Reducing error will make it more likely that the score obtained reflects a true score. One way of considering error variance is based on whether it is either:

1 *Systematic*, having a predictable effect on scores by introducing a consistently measurable bias every time a test is used, for example if there are ethnic group differences. A clock which gains three minutes every 12 hours will measure time with a systematic error. In tests a similar systematic bias is produced which damages validity. Causes include:

   - Bias against certain groups of people, such as age and cultural biases, as well as against those who lack relevant technical knowledge or experience;
   - Factors in test design, such as lack of standardized administration, low reliability and poor validity, item ambiguity and print quality of materials;
   - The response styles adopted by people such as in giving socially desirable answers or in over-using 'uncertain' response answers.

2 *Random*, in which case the effect is unpredictable. Sometimes unsystematic errors make scores bigger, sometimes they make them smaller, and thus reduce reliability.

Basically, these errors are made up of factors which differ every time a test is used, including non-standardized administration, environmental factors and inadequate scoring (Thompson, 1994). Longer-term developmental or historical factors can also affect performance, including education and schooling, people's socialization and upbringing. These sources of error may have a small impact on scores of some people, but a bigger impact on others.

Another way of considering error sources is to categorize them in terms of their relationships with test-takers, the measure being used, the procedures involved, as well as the surrounding environment and context. A detailed evaluation of sources of error variance is provided by Jensen (1980).

Candidate-related sources

The state of mind of test-takers can vary widely. This can include such aspects as:

- feelings
- anxiety
- motivation
- general well-being
- fatigue
- other preoccupations

In general, measures need to be short and interesting, but reliable and valid at the same time (Kline, 1992). You can't control for unpredictable variations in moods which can also influence responses. In clinical contexts fatigue might be an extra factor which needs exploring. Differences between people in terms of their backgrounds could mean they attribute different meanings to words or expressions. Another factor is test sophistication. Familiarity and practice may sometimes influence students' scores because they do so many tests for different employers. Yet another concerns guessing by candidates, especially when ability or reasoning tests are used.

Test-related sources

The items in a test are just a small sample of all those that could be asked. Where a measurement domain is very large, we need to ensure they are sampled from all areas of it to create a representative package; otherwise the test suffers from sampling error. Item construction can also be poor. Factors affecting performance can include any ambiguity, more than one right answer to a question, and so on. Physical construction, legibility, clarity of instructions and the design of response procedures may all influence performance.

Procedural sources

These involve ergonomic factors involved in the administration. They include, for example:

- Whether there are any interruptions, the comfort of test-takers at the time, noise level and any copying or cheating.
- The understanding by people of what is needed, keeping to conditions such as time limits, and completing answer sheets correctly. In one instance an administrator gave a test for an hour when it should have been 30 minutes.
- Accurate use of scoring keys and clerical errors in managing data. If you incorrectly score a response sheet, you are introducing error.

Environmental sources

Some factors which influence a person's test score can also be re-classified as 'environmental' in nature. These include the ambient temperature and lighting, any disruptive noise, the facilities available and seating comfort. They can all make scores less of a true reflection of the potential ability of people by reducing their capacity to concentrate.

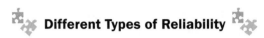

Different Types of Reliability

If reliability represents test accuracy, then as it goes up the amount of error will decrease and, conversely, as it goes down the error will increase. They are inversely related (Nunnally, 1978; Kline, 1986). But the determination of measurement error depends on both the SD of obtained scores and their reliability. Reliability has to be estimated because we can never directly measure the variance of true scores. Methods of estimating it are based on an assumption that correlations between items are linked to reliability. However, different methods tend to produce different estimates because each approach is sensitive to alternative error sources. The principal approaches used are:

1   *Test-retest reliability*
    This is the most obvious method as repeatability is at the heart of things – we use the test on two occasions and calculate a correlation between the results at time 1 and time 2. Sometimes it is called the retest method. It checks whether scores remain constant over time as we would expect with many traits. The underlying characteristic is believed to remain stable. But the method cannot be used for all measures because not all traits are perfectly stable over time. When it is calculated, the result is called the test-retest reliability coefficient or coefficient of stability which assesses the amount of error due to random fluctuations over time. If the time interval is fairly short then it is a coefficient of dependability. The time lapse has a significant importance and could be about one month or eight weeks or even three months, depending on publishers. Reliability tends to decrease with longer time intervals. An interval of a few days or weeks gives higher estimates compared to longer delays. However, if it is too short then exposure to items on the first occasion affects a person's responses during repeated assessment, especially in the case of reasoning, intelligence and performance measures. The process can also be regarded as inconvenient because test-makers need to contact participants to remind them to come back and be tested again. Often, a number of them don't return.

2   *Alternate and parallel-forms reliability*
    In Chapter 4 we discussed how publishers develop large item 'banks'. Sometimes they find they have too many to make just one test and have enough to make alternate versions. These can be useful in a number of situations, for example to monitor

the benefits of therapy over sessions we might want to assess a person's anxiety level using alternative measures at regular intervals. In this method of evaluating reliability two independent versions of a measure are used. People do both consecutively and a correlation coefficient, known as the alternate-form reliability coefficient, is calculated between the two data sets to give a measure of consistency. Often Version A might be administered initially to half the group and Version B to the other half, then, on second administration, the first group takes Version B and the second group Version A. Alternate forms occur in work psychology, for example the Graduate and Managerial Assessment forms A and B measure the same abilities although containing different items.

A similar process is carried out to create parallel forms, which are tests developed to have items of similar difficulty and distributions. Two tests are said to be parallel when each individual has the same true score on both forms and their error variances are identical. They are administered firstly to a large sample so that pairs of items with similar content and difficulty are obtained before being assigned to the different tests. The outcome is known as the parallel-form reliability coefficient. This method reduces the effects of memory as each version uses different items. It is particularly useful for tests which will be administered repeatedly, such as achievement measures. But it is difficult to set up because it is often time-consuming and arduous to generate enough items for two or more versions, meaning that it is rarely used. The test-maker needs to be certain that the measures are really parallel, i.e. measuring the same attribute, as well as being equivalent in terms of items, difficulty levels, and their means and standard deviations. The testing may also be long, resulting in tiredness and so reducing the coefficient.

3   *Measures of test homogeneity*
In this case people are given a score for the first half and then the second half of a measure, effectively using the two halves as parallel forms. A correlation can be calculated between them, although it is not possible to do this if the items get more difficult as people progress through it or if they are not sufficiently completed. An alternative would be to correlate odd and even items and, in fact, we could split a test in many ways, dividing it into any number of equal parts. An odd-even split-half approach is more common, although a publisher can arbitrarily decide on how to do it. The error here is defined as representing differences between items, their heterogeneity, and it is reduced where there is more homogeneity. The reliability calculated is known as the split-half correlation coefficient, and is based on the assumption that items or groups of them are equivalent.

The method's advantage is that it doesn't suffer from fatigue or memory effects and overcomes the time factor involved in retesting. One problem is that reliability depends to some extent upon test length i.e. the number of items. You might expect that longer tests have more of this reliability and, conversely, that shorter tests have less. In general, the more items in a test the more reliable it is until it gets so long that people feel tired and bored. This makes sense because the more questions we ask the more information we obtain, up to a point. Thus reliability decreases as tests get shorter, which happens whenever we make two tests out of just one, and we need to correct for this. A device known as the Spearman-Brown correction can be used to overcome the problem. The coefficient obtained is a measure of how consistent or homogeneous items are in a test, but is based on a single administration and thus doesn't consider errors occurring over time.

Another development is to calculate the average of all of the possible split-half coefficients. This would be a nightmare to do manually, although computer software makes it much easier. A stats package can do it very quickly and it is a common measure of reliability. The average of all possible split-half correlations is closely related to the average of all the possible inter-item correlations. For the mathematically minded:

If k = the number of items and R = the average of all the inter-item correlations, then the split-half reliability is given by:

$$\text{Reliability} = (k \times R) / (1 + (k - 1) \times R)$$

The most common method of calculating internal consistency is to use a formula based upon the ratio of the sum of the item variances to the score scale variance. The result is known as Cronbach's Alpha Coefficient of Reliability (Cronbach, 1951, 1976) or just simply Alpha, and is calculated using

$$\text{Coefficient Alpha} = k / k - 1 (1 - \Sigma\sigma i^2/\sigma t^2)$$

where σi^2 = the item variance and σt^2 = the test variance.

Alpha is often given in publishers' manuals as an indication of reliability and for any assessment should be between 0.7 and 0.9. Because it can be obtained by giving the test to a large sample of people, inputting the data to a spreadsheet and using software to do the calculation, it is the most usual figure given. It assumes that:

1 Items all measure a single factor trait,
2 Inter-item correlations would all be equal with a large sample of data, and
3 Items have equal variances with a large sample.

4 *Inter-rater reliability*
The forms of reliability above are relevant mainly to assessments having objective methods of scoring. Inter-rater reliability, in contrast, is a kind of internal-consistency reliability which differs from the others, but is often referred to alongside them. It is mainly used where subjective or inconsistent assessments are made, for example in conducting interviews and behavioural observations. Individuals are assessed independently by observers or interviewers who make use of rating scales agreed beforehand. Inter-rater reliability is also used with some rare forms of assessment where there is increased risk of subjectivity, for example, the Sociomoral Reflection Measure (Gibbs, Basinger and Fuller, 1992). Assessors undergo a detailed training to ensure consistency and high reliability. Different ratings can be correlated to establish the consistency among assessors and whether their characteristics are having too great an influence. A number of indices are available to evaluate how and to what extent raters make assessments, including percentage agreement, product-moment correlation and intra-class correlation.

Evaluation of Coefficients

It is important to note that reliability is a matter of degree and that we are concerned here with positive correlation coefficients. Publishers will often simply quote the figure obtained, such as 0.70. But estimates of it, too, are subject to error and to the effects of range restriction on the attribute measured, for example when data do not include lower scores. The most important issue is the size of the measurement error linked with it. The correlation also depends on the SD of scores and we shall shortly see that the bigger the SD the smaller the error will be. We should also place more reliance on reliabilities based upon large samples. A sample of people taking the test of less than 30 is inadequate, having an error margin of about 0.20. With a sample of 500 people we can be 95 per cent confident that reliability is at least 0.62 (Nunnally, 1978). So we should always look to see the sample size used: those less than 100 are inadequate for giving good reliability estimates (Kline, 2000). In addition, the coefficient will be increased through the use of a more heterogeneous sample having larger test-score variance. Publishers will sometimes report coefficients for age, gender and other groups.

You should always expect to see a test-retest value for ability and reasoning measures, although some publishers go just for the alpha because it is easier to compute. Alpha may be suitable for ability tests, but for speed tests it tends to overestimate reliability and is distorted. IQ tests usually have reliabilities greater than 0.9, while personality and interest inventories have lower values (0.70 to 0.90) because scales have broader but relatively fewer items (Bartram, 1995a). Projective assessments like the Rorschach inkblot test have very low reliabilities (Kline, 2000).

Reliability may also be expressed instead as the percentage of systematic variance, which is determined by multiplying the coefficient by 100. The lower limit for acceptability is, therefore, a correlation of 0.7 or 70 per cent in terms of the percentage of systematic variance (Anastasi, 1988; Bartram, 1995a), although lower coefficients may be suitable for research.

There are two significant things to remember. The first is that when someone tries to sell you an assessment measure you should always ask for a reliability coefficient and its value, and the size of the sample used to calculate it. Without a reliability coefficient, you will have no idea of the amount of error involved and in cases where none is provided the actual reliability may be as low as 0.1 or 0.2, which means the error is substantial. Remember:

- Never buy any assessment where there is no reliability coefficient or where it is below 0.7 (Kline, 1993).
- Personality and similar measures usually have coefficients between 0.6 and 0.8, although above 0.7 is often recommended as a minimum.
- Ability, aptitude, IQ and other forms of reasoning tests should have coefficients above 0.8. Above 0.85 has been recommended as an excellent value (Bartram, 1995a). Where the intention is to compare people's scores, values above 0.85 should be the aim.
- The sample size used for calculation of reliability should never be below 100.

Clinical Reliabilities

Sampling is a particular problem in the development of measures for clinical use because many groups, such as those having personality or psychotic disorders, tend to be difficult to test. Reliabilities will inevitably be low and practitioners need to be aware of the problem. It would be misleading to use a reliability coefficient gained from normal samples in a clinical situation (Crawford, 2004). The use of any assessment which lacks reliability in a health-related setting could result in misinterpretation of the results. A number of problems concerning reliability can arise, for example with the very young and older people, with tests involving response speed or of neurological disorders (Anastasi and Urbina, 1997). Therefore, it is recommended that clinically related reliability estimates should be provided for both normal and clinical populations, and characteristics of samples should be fully stated by publishers.

Generalizability Theory

It might seem odd to say this now, but any measure in itself is neither reliable nor unreliable. Reliability is not a property of a test itself; it is really a function of the scores we get when the measure is administered to a group on a particular date and in certain conditions. Taking this view has a number of implications, for example that having the property of consistency may not mean a test is accurate after all.

Generalizability theory or G *theory*, developed by Cronbach and his colleagues as an alternative approach to that of Classical Theory (Cronbach, Gleser, Nanda and Rajaratnan, 1972; Cronbach 1994), views each score as one sample which belongs to a universe of possible scores and its reliability as the accuracy in which it estimates the more generalized universal value or true score. Their technique seeks to identify all of the error sources arising during an assessment, to evaluate them independently and to correct each person's score for their influence.

Using statistical models of multivariate analysis, the technique computes 'generalizability coefficients', similar to reliability coefficients, based upon the ratio of the expected variance of scores in the universe to the variance of scores in a sample. To achieve this, information is gathered from people who have been tested under differing circumstances, and the coefficients have appeared in some manuals, especially for large clinical batteries. Cronbach also demonstrated that traditional techniques of construction and use of a test can be considered as multi-level models. This has led to the estimation of a universal value of a score corresponding to the true score of classical theory. The theory views the generalizability, or dependability, of scores as a function of the conditions in which the test is taken, its scoring processes and the possible item samples within it. It assesses the circumstances in which inferences made from a measure can be applied and, in so doing, evaluates how well a measure assesses any characteristic. While classical theory considers such issues in a limited way, generalizability theory explores experimentally many sources of error simultaneously rather than one at a time and indicates how much total variance comes from different sources.

This approach, like Item Response Theory, depends on developments in software technology and has advanced ideas about the nature of error, although its applications have not been much used because of its complexity. It has enhanced awareness of the potential sources of bias involved in test development. One of these relates to the administration procedure developed by publishers which was used with standardization and reliability samples. My point is: You can't change this admin script in any way. If you do, error variance will be added to scores and the reliability will no longer apply. Even small changes in test administration can reduce reliability, so it is important to conform to the published script. Any changes could mean that it is impossible to deduce how well people have performed compared to the norms provided.

Summary

Test error originates from a number of sources, some systematic, others random. They include factors relating to the people being tested, the design, construction and administration of tests, as well as other environmental aspects. Reliability coefficients evaluate their impact on test accuracy. Measures of reliability include test-retest, alternate and parallel-form, split-half and Cronbach alpha coefficients, as well as inter-rater coefficients. An alternative approach, generalizability theory uses statistical analysis to compute coefficients which can evaluate the effectiveness of assessment of any characteristic. Its key message is that changes in test administration can damage reliability.

Measuring Error and Making Decisions

If we can quantify error we will be in a better position to interpret test results. Every time a person takes a test a random amount of error is added to or subtracted from the score. Classical theory defines reliability as the proportion of variance which is not caused by random error because of the basic rule that:

The Obtained Score = The True Score $\pm$ Measurement Error

Errors will vary randomly each time a test is taken successively by a person. In the long run positive and negative errors cancel each other out, giving an average error of zero. Again there is going to be a normal distribution of scores – its mean is the true score because this is at the point at which errors cancel out. If the obtained score equals the true score, then the errors must have zero value. Because of this we can compare the distribution of true scores and the distribution of the errors of measurement:

1   The first distribution has a mean equal to the true score and no variance.
2   The second is a normal distribution with a mean of zero and a standard deviation representing the variation in obtained scores due to error.

We could ask many people to do a test hundreds of times each – a fanciful proposition! The distributions would all have the same error distribution with a mean of zero and an SD equal to the Standard Error of Measurement (SEM), but would have each person's true score located at the appropriate point on the scale. In theory, for a given test, the measurement error is the same for everybody: what will differ between people are their true scores. The error distributions, being normal, will lie on top of each other while the true scores may differ. If we were able to take everyone's true scores and produce a distribution, its mean would be the average true score for the population and the SD would show how dispersed people's scores are. But, in practice, we get a distribution of the obtained scores.

For an enormous population the average of the errors tends towards zero, as we saw in Chapter 3 in discussing the Standard Error of a mean. If the average of the errors of measurement is zero, there will be no difference between the average of the obtained scores and that of the true scores. They will be the same provided a big sample is used. However, although the errors can cancel each other out, they do not disappear. Their distribution must still be there and its variance reflects their average size. Deviations from the mean can be squared, totalled, and the square root of the result gives the SD of the errors, in the same way as we calculated SD in Chapter 4. This SD of all the errors provides a good indication of how much error is involved each time we make a measurement. This is the Standard Error of Measurement.

If we compare the distribution of obtained scores with that of the true scores we will see that the first will be more spread out because error variance adds to the true score variance to produce the obtained score variance – whether errors are positive or negative. As the error distribution always has a mean of zero, when we add the error distribution to the true score distribution, the mean doesn't change. But when we add error variance to the true score variance (being zero), the variance is increased by this amount. Adding error variance to true scores, therefore, simply increases the overall spread of scores without changing their mean. So, on average, errors of measurement affect the variance of scores and not their average, and the more error there is in the process the more the obtained scores will vary compared to true ones.

Put simply, reliability represents the accuracy with which a test can measure true scores. No errors would mean a perfectly reliable measure. It makes sense that if scores are due only to error then the test will have no reliability. Thus:

- If reliability is large, then the SEM is low. Obtained scores will have little error and be close to true scores.
- If reliability is small, then the SEM is high. Obtained scores will have a lot of error.

Reliability was defined as the ratio of the true and obtained score variances. Where these are the same it will have a perfect ideal value of 1. Obtained score variance will always be larger, however, making the reliability have a value of less than 1.

$$\text{reliability} = \frac{\text{true score variance}}{\text{obtained score variance}}$$

But, as suggested, the obtained score variance amounts to the sum of true score variance and error score variance, therefore:

$$\text{reliability} = \frac{\text{true score variance}}{(\text{true score variance} + \text{error variance})}$$

Whenever we calculate standard deviation we square root the variance, so variance is the SD squared. We can simply add variances together because they are amounts of variation. The equation we then get is:

$$\text{SEM} = \text{SD} \times \sqrt{(1 - \text{reliability})}$$

or more simply:

$$\text{SEM} = \text{SD} \times \sqrt{(1 - r)}$$

where SD is the standard deviation for the scale. This enables us to convert the reliability coefficient to the SEM, which provides an actual measurement along the scale used (because it is a standard deviation). The SEM is on the same scale as the test and is in the same units of measurement as the scale's SD, either raw or standard scores. It will be directly related to scores and enables us to calculate the error margin around them. Reliability, r, is always a positive correlation coefficient between 0 and 1. When a score is plotted on a scale and the distance covered by one standard error each side is marked then, based upon the probability properties of the normal curve, we can be about 68 per cent sure that the true score lies within that range. Doubling the SEM each side of a score gives us 95 per cent confidence of finding the true score. Used in this way, the SEM can help us to make a variety of decisions.

If a measure has a raw score SD of 8.6 and a reliability of 0.66 we can find the SEM by substituting the values:

$$\text{SEM} = 8.6 \times \sqrt{(1 - 0.66)}$$
$$= 8.6 \times 0.583$$
$$= 5.0$$

Notice it is wise to start from the right-hand side of the equation, subtracting 0.66 from 1 and then to square root the result before multiplying by 8.6. If you are uncertain, try out the example this way on your calculator. The result is that one amount of the error margin around a score on this scale is ±5 points.

Connecting SEM and Reliability

I sometimes say to students, let's have a bit of fun with these two characters. OK, you might think I have a warped sense of humour. But doing what I propose now helps to make sense of things. Think back to the section above about reliability and let's say we have a very good measure, say an r of 0.9. Let's calculate the SEM for it. We start by writing the equation, then pop in some figures and come up with the SEM. To make things easier, let's work on a T score scale which has an SD of 10.

1   *A very good measure*
    Here we go: the equation is $SEM = SD \times \sqrt{(1 - r)}$
    Insert the figures: $= 10 \times \sqrt{(1 - 0.9)}$
    Calculate the SEM $= 3.16$ to 2 decimal places
    So, on a T score scale, for a very good measure one SEM around a score amounts to approximately 3 to 4 points. That was painless, wasn't it? Don't forget to do the $1 - 0.9$ first and press = and then square root the result before multiplying by 10. So let's do it again.

2   *A good measure*, having a reliability, say, of 0.8.
    Here we go again: the equation is $SEM = SD \times \sqrt{(1 - r)}$
    Insert the figures: $= 10 \times \sqrt{(1 - 0.8)}$
    Calculate the SEM $= 4.47$ to 2 decimal places
    Can you see that as reliability has gone down, the error (SEM) has increased? It makes sense.

3   Let's do it again. Let's use *a rather poor measure* with a reliability of 0.5.
    The equation is $SEM = SD \times \sqrt{(1 - r)}$
    Insert the figures: $= 10 \times \sqrt{(1 - 0.5)}$
    Calculate the SEM $= 7.07$
    Once again we have reduced the reliability and error has increased.

4   Let's do this for a last time, using *a lousy measure*, one you would never now choose to use with a reliability of 0.2. Here we go:
    The equation is $SEM = SD \times \sqrt{(1 - r)}$
    Insert the figures: $= 10 \times \sqrt{(1 - 0.2)}$
    So the SEM is $= 8.94$
    The error margin this time is very large, making it pointless to use the measure because you are approaching 10 points around the score. A true score could lie anywhere within this range. If you think this is bad, which it is, it gets even worse when I say in a little while that one SEM around a score is an inadequate measure of the error and that we mostly need to use two of them for a 95 per cent confidence interval. This means the error margin is close to 20 points around the score on a T score scale. You might as well bin the test!

To do something different, we could take the example of the Wechsler Intelligence Scale for Children (WISC) which has a reliability of approximately 0.9 and a standard deviation of 15. Then:

The equation is	$SEM = SD \times \sqrt{(1 - r)}$
Insert the figures	$= 15 \times \sqrt{(1 - 0.9)}$
So the SEM is	$= 4.7$

So for an obtained score of 100 and, using a 95 per cent confidence interval, the true score lies between 100 plus or minus 4.7 × 2, between about 91 and 109. This is a fair-sized range and explains why reporting of clinical scales should include the extent of the 95 per cent confidence interval.

Effects of Range Restriction

We need now to consider the influence on the standard error and reliability of what was earlier called range restriction. Imagine one group of people take a test and a wide score range is produced, including low, average and high ones. Yet another group give only high scores. In this case the two samples have different variances. The first has the variance expected from a random representative sample, while the second has lower variance because everyone was a high scorer. The range is said to have been restricted. Whenever we introduce some form of bias into a method of assessment, we are likely to reduce the variance similarly through range restriction (Ree, 1995). For example, people offered jobs tend to have less variance than the candidate group originally tested. Any sample chosen on the basis of a narrow criterion, like university students, will have reliabilities lower than that of the general population. The expected reliability will be higher where the SD is larger. So any change in sample variance affects the reliability of a test. In fact, alpha for high scorers is less than that for a wider range of people, although any change in reliability might be cancelled out by a change in SD, making the SEM stay the same when we use its equation.

But the SEM will tend to vary from sample to sample owing to sampling error. These variations will be random and their amounts will depend on sample size (the smaller the samples the more the variation between samples). Reliability estimates obtained will vary systematically with changes in SD. This relationship between variance and reliability provides a means of estimating the reliability for the full range of scores when we have only a restricted range. It is possible to use a formula to estimate the unrestricted reliability for a test. But in practice the SEM is more important than reliability. SEM is considered to be unaffected by changes in sample variance while measures of reliability are.

We now can use the equation:

$SEM = SD \times \sqrt{(1 - reliability)}$

which enables us to calculate the Standard Error of Measurement as a measure of the error for any test.

It can be manipulated to give:

$$1 \quad SD = \frac{SEM}{\sqrt{(1 - reliability)}}$$

so we can calculate the standard deviation if we know the standard error.

2. Reliability $= \dfrac{(SD^2 - SEM^2)}{SD^2}$

which can be manipulated again to give:

3. Reliability, $r = 1 - \dfrac{SEM^2}{SD^2}$

which means that as the SD gets bigger, then reliability r also gets bigger and closer to 1. So there is the evidence for the prediction we made about reliability depending on the standard deviation of a distribution, as well as the standard error. This equation also enables us to calculate the reliability from a given value of SEM.

SEM and Standard Scale Scores

Do you remember learning about standard scores in Chapter 4? Just to recap quickly:

* Z scores have a mean of 0 and SD of 1
* T scores have a mean of 50 and SD of 10
* Sten scores have a mean of 5.5 and SD of 2
* Stanines have a mean of 5 and SD of 2

Thus we can use our equation with each of these:

$$SEM = SD \times \sqrt{(1 - reliability)}$$

by inserting the value of the SD for each scale, i.e. 1 for z scores, 10 for T scores, 2 for sten scores or stanines. The square root part of the equation gives the SEM of the z score scale since, by definition, its SD is 1.

Confidence Limits

We met these in Chapter 3 when we were discussing standard error around a mean. They are a product of the properties of the normal curve and its standard deviation. As you now know, the Standard Error of Measurement (SEM) is the standard deviation of the distribution of errors of measurement around an obtained score. Again the properties of the normal curve apply. One of these is that 95 per cent of the distribution lies within a range of ± 1.96 SDs around the mean. Being a core characteristic, it means that 95 per cent of scores on any test are found in the range from two SDs below the mean to two SDs above it (Field, 2005). The figure of 1.96 is usually rounded to 2 for convenience.

To make things perfectly clear let's review two points. An obtained score is that determined by the test. The same person's true score represents his/her true ability on it if there were no error. Thus if a person's true score is 30 and the SEM is 4 we can say with

95 per cent confidence that any score obtained is 30 plus or minus 8 on the scale, i.e. it lies in the range 22–38. In practice we know the SEM from test information and the obtained score, but not the true score. The size of the confidence interval is the same. If the obtained score lies in the interval around the true score, then the true score must lie in the same interval around the obtained score. Therefore, we can be 95 per cent confident that the true score lies somewhere in the interval which is ± two standard errors around an obtained score. Another way of saying this is that the interval of two SEMs around an obtained score sets the limits for where we can find the true score with 95 per cent confidence.

If we use 95 per cent confidence limits there is a 1 in 20 chance we could be wrong and that the true score is outside the limits. We get this 1 in 20 because there is a 5 per cent chance of being wrong, which is $5 \div 100$ which cancels to 1 over 20, and if we key this into a calculator we get the decimal value of 0.05, so this is the statistical significance level written as $p < 0.05$. There is a 68 per cent chance of a true score lying within one standard error either side of the obtained score. In general, a 1 in 20 chance of being wrong is considered acceptable. This is a convention in the social sciences where it is impossible to be exact about many figures. For 99 per cent confidence we need an interval of about 2.6 SEMs either side, as the percentage figure for three standard deviations either side of the mean would have to be rounded up to 100 per cent (see Figure 4.12 in Chapter 4 which gives the precise figure of 99.72 per cent for the area below three standard deviations). OK, so 95 per cent is not 100 per cent, but remember that everything measurable is subject to error and in the social sciences it is impossible to be 100 per cent about the most complex organism known to humankind, i.e. humankind. Whenever we report test scores we should *always state the limits*. Why? Because all assessments are fallible and they enable us to quantify and stress this fallibility to others.

Confidence intervals vary depending on the amount of certainty needed. If we wanted to risk being wrong just 1 time in 1000, then we would need a 99.9 per cent interval. At a much lower certainty, we can say that ± the value of one SEM around an obtained score provides a range in which we have a 68 per cent chance of finding a true score. Calculating the end points of this range by subtraction and addition of the SEM gives us 68 per cent limits. Plus and minus the value of two SEMs around an obtained score gives a range in which we have a 95 per cent chance of finding the true score. The end points of this range are called the 95 per cent confidence limits. Plus and minus 2.6 times the value of the SEM around a score gives a range where we have a 99 per cent chance of finding the true score. Again, the end points of the range provide the 99 per cent confidence limits. Limits of 95 per cent and above are preferred because we have a 5 per cent or less chance of being wrong. A limit of 68 per cent would have an enormous 32 per cent chance of being wrong, meaning we could be wrong more often than is acceptable, so 1 in 20 at 95 per cent or 1 in 100 at 99 per cent are better options.

Standard error of estimation
SEM, therefore, enables us to construct confidence intervals around scores and acts as a measure of accuracy. It is possible similarly to estimate confidence limits for estimated true scores, in other words the possible range of true scores around an estimated true score. This is calculated by multiplying the obtained score, in deviation form, by the reliability:

Estimated true score $= r (X - \bar{x}) + \bar{x}$

where r is the reliability, X is the obtained score and $\bar{x}$ is the mean. In this case the Standard Error of estimation (SEe) is used, given by:

$$SEe = SD \times \sqrt{r (1 - r)}$$

where SD is the standard deviation of the variable measured. This is another measure of precision, like the SEM, providing confidence limits around estimated true scores. It enables the calculation of 68 per cent and 95 per cent confidence intervals for an individual's true score based upon administration of a large number of randomly parallel versions of a test. For measures of high reliability the limits will be much the same.

Standard error of prediction

In addition, where alternate forms are being used and the SD of obtained scores for one of them is known, it is possible to determine the possible range of scores anticipated during retesting with the other. Another standard error, the Standard Error of prediction (SEp), can be used to construct confidence limits, given by:

$$SEp = SD \times \sqrt{(1 - r^2)}$$

where r is the reliability of the form used in the first assessment and SD is the standard deviation of the parallel form administered during retesting. Confidence limits for 68 per cent and 95 per cent can be obtained by multiplying the result by the SD of the scale being used. One problem is the assumption that there are no effects caused by prior testing.

Standard Error of Difference

Now I want to add something in order to prepare you for the future – the next section, in fact. Visualizing things helps a lot, so I have drawn Figure 5.4 to show three things:

(a) The first is a scale having test scores 1 and 2 marked on it with two amounts of the SEM, one lot drawn to the left and the other to the right of both, therefore referring to 95 per cent limits each side of the scores. Some of my students have referred to them as 'Keith's humps and bumps'. Of course, the error doesn't look like this; it's just a convenient way to illustrate the error range in SEMs. My point is that to compare two scores we need to combine errors around both.

(b) If two scores have associated error, we must combine their SEMs to produce a composite called the Standard Error of difference (written SEdiff for short). This can be plotted around one score, whilst the other can then be treated effectively as having no error around it (as shown in the second illustration in Figure 5.4). The error around score 2 has gone: you could say it has disappeared into the SEdiff. If score 2 is outside the complete error range, i.e. twice the SEdiff, then we can say that the scores are *statistically significantly different* with 95 per cent confidence. Or, putting it another way, the score higher up the scale is statistically significantly greater than the

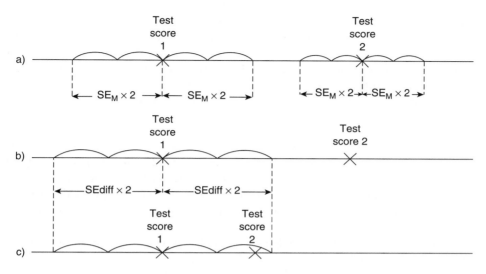

Figure 5.4 Comparing scores: (a) both have error around them; (b) errors have been combined in the SEdiff and score 2 lies outside the 95 per cent confidence limits; (c) the score lies within the 95 per cent confidence limits

other. We could say that score 1 can have a true score only up to both the minimum and maximum of the range. Therefore, it cannot have a true score with the value of the other score (at 95 per cent confidence) because that value lies outside the range. To state the obvious: I plotted the SEdiff around both sides of score 1, although I could have plotted it around score 2 and said score 1 is then statistically significantly lower with 95 per cent confidence, the conclusion being just the same. Secondly, although I have drawn the SEdiff range around both sides of one score, only the error pointing towards the other is really relevant. The error on the other side is there but not relevant. In some instances one of the scores could be a mean so we would have to calculate the Standard Error of the mean and combine this with the SEM to make the Standard Error of difference. This is important in all areas of applied psychology.

(c) In the lowest part of Figure 5.4 a higher score is shown which does not fall outside the range of double the SEdiff. In this case score 1, having the error range centred around it, could have a true value identical to the other score, so they cannot be statistically significantly different with 95 per cent confidence. I have marked the higher score in a place where the two scores could be different with 68 per cent confidence, although conventionally this is not sufficient for decision-making. It is important that you understand all of this to cope with the next section.

Comparing and Combining Scores

We often compare scores. We may say that someone has a higher score than another or that some people did better on one assessment than they did on another. But what is the difference between a score of 55 and another of 60 on a T-score scale? If we take error into account can we truly say one is higher than the other? Are we making a fair distinction? If we compare a score on a clinical assessment to a mean score, can we justifiably say this person's psychopathology is significantly different from others in a norm group? Clinical assessment may often need to evaluate differences. If we set a cut-off score of 40 on a test, and someone gets 38, can we be OK to reject the person in a selection process? Our decisions in such cases can have an enormous impact in many ways.

Differences between two obtained scores

Errors are always assumed to be unsystematic, uncorrelated and independent of each other. Consequently sources of error variation can be added. When they are added, we do so by summing the variances not the standard deviations, like the Standard Error of Measurement, of the mean, and of difference, because variance represents the amount of variation. Any SD is the square root of the variance and so we square them to obtain the variance in each case.

The Standard Error of difference for a score on test A and a score on a different test B (SEdiffAB) is given by:

$$\text{SEdiffAB} \quad = \quad \sqrt{(\text{SEMA}^2 + \text{SEMB}^2)}$$

where SEdiffAB is the Standard Error of difference between scores on measures A and B. Both SEMs must apply to the same scale, e.g. T scores.

Evaluating scores on different tests

For example, Mary Jones has T scores of 45 on one test and 60 on another. The first test A has a reliability of 0.80 and the second B of 0.90. Was her score on test B statistically significantly better than her score on test A? The scale SD is 10 on both tests because both are T scores. To answer this question we use four steps:

1. *First calculate the SEMs*:
   We use the equation for calculating SEM from the SD and the reliability:

   $$\text{SEM} \quad = \quad \text{SD} \times \sqrt{(1 - r)}$$

   For test A the SEM is $10 \times \sqrt{(1 - 0.80)} = 4.47$
   For test B the SEM is $10 \times \sqrt{(1 - 0.90)} = 3.16$

2. *Now calculate the SEdiff*:
   We use the equation given above:

   $$\text{SEdiffAB} \quad = \quad \sqrt{(\text{SEMA}^2 + \text{SEMB}^2)}$$

   Thus SEdiffAB $\quad = \quad \sqrt{(4.47^2 + 3.16^2)} \quad = \quad 5.47$

3. *Evaluate the difference (or distance) between scores and see if this is greater or less than two SEdiffs*:
   One score is 45 and the other is 60. So the difference between the two scores is 60–45. This is a distance of 15 points – which is greater than two SEdiffs (twice 5.47). Another method is to divide the distance by the SEdiffAB to see if the answer comes out bigger than 2:

15 ÷ 5.47 = 2.74 SEdiffs

So the two scores are 2.74 SEdiffs apart.

4. *Decide on the confidence level*:
   If two scores differ by one SEdiff we can be 68 per cent confident only that the true scores are different. If they differ by 2 or more SEdiffs we can be 95 per cent confident the true scores really differ. In this case they have a difference of 2.74 SEdiffs which is greater than the 95 per cent confidence interval. So if the difference is 2.74 SEdiffs we can be sure that the two scores are significantly different with 95 per cent confidence.

Therefore, Mary really is better on test B than on test A.

A further question might be: How big a difference in T scores would we need on the two tests before we concluded with 95 per cent confidence that someone was better at one than the other?

One SEdiff is 5.47. Confidence of 95 per cent is based on 2 SEdiffs. Thus any difference greater than 2 x 5.47 would indicate a statistically significant difference between scores. *So the answer is any value above 10.94.*

Evaluating scores on the same test
The formula simplifies in this case to:

SEdiffA = 1.41 × SEMA

This is because

SEdiffAB	=	$\sqrt{(SEMA^2 + SEMB^2)}$
becomes SEdiffA	=	$\sqrt{(SEMA^2 + SEMA^2)}$
which is SEdiffA	=	$\sqrt{(2SEMA^2)}$
which is SEdiffA	=	$\sqrt{2} \times \sqrt{SEMA^2}$

If you square root the number 2 in your calculator, you get the value 1.41 and so:

SEdiffA   =   1.41 x SEMA

For example: Fred Thomas obtained a T score of 57 on a test while Jack Harris obtained a score of 49. The test has a reliability of 0.75. Can we decide that Fred is better on the test?

Remember that the T-score mean is always 50 and the SD 10. We learned this earlier and I deliberately keep on repeating it. Similar steps apply as in the first example concerning Mary Jones.

1. *First calculate the SEM:*
   Using $SEM = SD \times (1 - r)$
   Then $SEM = 10 \times (1 - 0.75)$
              $= 5$
2. *Calculate the SEdiff:*
   This time we use $SEdiffA = 1.41 \times SEMA$
   So: $SEdiff = 1.41 \times 5$
              $= 7.05$

3. *Evaluate the difference between scores:*

The scores differ by 8 points (57 − 49). This is only 8 ÷ 7.05 i.e. 1.13 SEdiffs. The distance is smaller than 2 SEdiffs. Therefore, the difference between the scores is not large enough for us to be 95 per cent confident their true scores are significantly different. Practical use of this procedure is described in Box 5.1.

Box 5.1   Making Selection Decisions

Understanding reliability and knowing how to use it play an important part in testing. This was demonstrated when an organization asked for help in screening potential candidates for a senior appointment. Having a large number of applicants for the post the chief executive wished to reduce the number to a suitable size and to do this in an objective way. On paper all of their CVs looked satisfactory, but the list was too long for interviews and other assessments to be conducted with everyone. After reviewing the options, he chose to use a high-level test to screen candidates.

Choice of the test was based on information provided by the person specification for the job. After the process of testing, a range of scores for the different applicants needed to be evaluated. The 16 highest scores were:

CANDIDATE NUMBER	RAW SCORES
1	44
2	46
3	49
4	49
5	52
6	53
7	53
8	57
9	62
10	72
11	73
12	73
13	73
14	74
15	75
16	77

Based on these outcomes, the question was whether candidates 10 to 17 could go through to the next stage because the difference between candidates 9 and 10 appeared to be large. This meant answering the question: Was candidate 10's score statistically significantly higher than that of candidate 9? It meant doing a calculation. The reliability of the scale was 0.88 and its standard deviation 9.23.

$$\text{In this case SEM} = \text{SD} \times \sqrt{(1 - r)}$$
$$= 9.23 \times \sqrt{(1 - 0.88)}$$
$$= 3.2$$

Then the Standard Error of difference in the case of one test could be determined:

$$SEdiffA = 1.41 \times SEMA$$
$$= 1.41 \times 3.2$$
$$= 4.51$$

So for 95 per cent confidence there would have to be a gap between the scores of greater than 2×4.51, i.e. 9.02 points. The actual gap was 10 points, so that candidate number 10 had a score which was statistically significantly greater.

The conclusion was that candidates 10 to 16 should go through to the next stage of assessment for the appointment.

Comparing scores with sample means

Here we are looking to see if a score is better than the average for a group of people and is a common practice in clinical assessment. For the individual score the error is given by the SEM. For the group mean it is the SEmean. We looked at this in Chapter 3. We need to take account of the fact that the sample mean is only an estimate of the true population mean. We learned that:

$$SEMean = \frac{SD}{\sqrt{N}}$$

where N is the size of the sample used for calculation of the mean and SD is the standard deviation of the sample distribution. If we know these, we can calculate confidence limits for the sample alone. We can again add the two error sources as variances to get a measure to determine differences, making a small amendment to the usual formula for the SEdiff so that:

$$\text{SEdiff between sample mean and obtained score} = \sqrt{\{SEmean^2 + SEM^2\}}$$

If the sample is large, the effect of the Standard Error of the mean on the overall Standard Error of difference is small. If you need to compare a score with the mean of an extremely large sample, you could treat the mean as a fixed value having no error. As in previous examples, you evaluate the distance between a person's score and the mean to determine whether it is greater or less than two Standard Errors of difference.

Using cut-off scores

These are used widely in practice and are sometimes called cutting scores. For example, a specific score may be set to distinguish those experiencing severe levels of depression or anxiety from others, or to reject candidates in job selection. Cut-off scores are arbitrary, having a predefined value, and are often subjectively set. They become fixed points which are defined in an absolute manner. Hence there is no error associated with them, but this does not mean it cannot be taken into account.

People having scores above the cut-off will be treated differently in some way to those whose scores are lower. There will always be people whose true scores are above the cut-off, but their obtained scores fall below. These are known as false negatives. There will also be others whose true scores fall below but whose obtained scores are passes, called false positives. So when we know the SEM for the test we can make accurate predictions of how many of these we will get in different score bands around the cut-off. Lowering the cut-off will obviously let in more people.

Combining scores – the standard error of a sum

When people do more than one test or a battery made up of sub-tests we may need an overall measure of performance. All measures must be on the same scale so we can add scores. To make inferences we need the Standard Error of the sum. In this case it only makes sense to use the SEsum for combining two scores for the same person. The Standard Error of the sum of scores on test A and test B is given by:

$$\text{SEsum}(A + B) \quad \sqrt{\{\text{SEMA}^2 + \text{SEMB}^2\}}$$

which is the same formula as that for the Standard Error of difference.

This would apply with, for example, a general ability or aptitude test battery, where each sub-test has its own score. However, score sums can sometimes appear misleading, containing different obtained scores for different tests. If we add scores for tests which are correlated then the reliability of the new scale is increased. But if we look at the reliability of a scale created by calculating the difference between them it is found to be reduced.

Summary

Classical theory suggests that random amounts of error variance are added to test score variance and that the error distribution has a standard deviation called the Standard Error of measurement (SEM). The greater the SEM, the greater the error margin around scores. Range restriction and other forms of bias will enhance the SEM and reduce test reliability. As a standard deviation the SEM provides a process for determining the error margin as a distance along scales, called a confidence interval, enabling us to determine 68 per cent, 95 per cent and other confidence limits for true scores. Similar limits can also be obtained for the Standard Error of difference, which is calculated by combining error variance. Both types of standard error help us to interpret score differences and to determine whether any difference is at a level of acceptable statistical significance. Other forms of standard error, such as the Standard Error of estimation and of prediction, also help in understanding a measure's level of precision.

What Have We Discovered About Reliability?

This has been an important chapter which should keep us out of trouble by ensuring that we never use unreliable measures. We have discovered that consistency and repeatability are key factors in evaluation of any test. Psychological measures are subject to error arising from a number of sources. The consistency, or accuracy, is indicated by a reliability coefficient and this can come in different forms, including retest, alternate and parallel-form, split-half and alpha coefficients. Each has its own properties and needs careful evaluation. Generalizability theory is an alternative approach which explores many error sources using complex statistical models. Although reliability is useful in determining test acceptability, it does not directly estimate error ranges around scores. We need to convert them to the Standard Error of measurement (SEM) which can provide 68 per cent, 95 per cent and other confidence intervals. SEMs can be combined to evaluate score differences at different levels of statistical significance through conversion to a Standard Error of difference. This enables us to interpret and make decisions about assessment outcomes. We have learned:

- About correlation, how this is used to determine the reliability of measures and their potential sources of error.
- About the classical model of test error and the more complex approach of generalizability theory.
- How reliability coefficients can be converted into the Standard Error of measurement as a means of identifying limits containing true scores at different levels of confidence.
- About the Standard Error of difference and its use in making decisions about scores at appropriate levels of statistical significance.

6

The Significance of Validity

Learning Objectives

By the end of this chapter you should be able to:

- Understand the significance of validity and what it means, and explain the different models, including content, criterion-related and construct validity.
- Outline what is meant by 'spurious validity' and give an account of its different forms.
- Explain the nature and purpose of validation.
- Evaluate validity coefficients and identify the factors which influence them.

What is This Chapter About?

Validity and validation are crucial to understanding psychological assessment. We explain the different models of validity and their application to forms of assessment. If you are going to buy and use them in the future you will need to know what is involved in validation and how to evaluate this, so we look at how it should be conducted and what it contains. In doing so we encounter 'spurious' forms of validity which attract the interest of non-psychologists and learn how to deal with these in applied situations. And we learn how to evaluate validity coefficients and the range of factors affecting them.

 **Why Validity?**

From being a small matter many years ago, validity has exploded in the face of psychologists. Reliability and validity go hand in hand, you might think. But psychologists have realized that validity is more important than reliability, and many see reliability as being either a factor within validity or, at best, a junior partner. As we said in Chapter 5, reliability concerns the accuracy of a test, while validity concerns the nature of the construct measured. Any test must surely need to be measuring 'something' accurately for it to be validly measuring it. On this basis, validity can't exist without reliability and, therefore, a measure can't be valid unless it is reliable. But this doesn't apply the other way round – a test can have reliability without necessarily being valid. In other words it is measuring something accurately and consistently, although we don't know what on earth it is.

In considering the importance of validity a few examples might help. Think of the 'lie detector', or polygraph, which monitors heart rate, respiration and electrical conductivity of the skin caused by sweating. Imagine being accused of murder and clamped to the machine. It wouldn't be surprising if your heart beats faster, your breathing rate goes up and you sweat more. People in favour of using it will say you are telling lies. But anyone in this situation is going to feel anxious and anxiety notoriously gives you heart palpitations, causes faster breathing and makes you sweat. So the supposed lie detector doesn't validly measure deception; it actually measures anxiety level which is different. It might have validity as a measure of anxiety, but not of lying or deception. The use of tests having poor validity can be seriously misleading.

Think of the traditional Rorschach inkblot test as another example. Having low validity, despite the best efforts of some, it would be far from adequate as the sole instrument to make a decision on whether someone is suffering schizophrenia. Imagine a measure of self-esteem having, say, just eight items. Self-esteem is a broad concept and such a small number of items could never validly assess it. Lastly, what about a measure designed to identify corporate leadership? Just how well does it identify leaders? Evidence is needed to support this. Such questions make us realize the significance of the concept. Invalid tests can be misleading. An organization could choose a senior manager who is, in fact, a poor manager. Bad advice could be given to people seeking career guidance. Our approach in psychometrics is to conduct assessment of many attributes, including personality traits, through the use of measures proven to have validity. Now we can see why it is so important.

Defining Validity

Despite the fact that we have been trying hard to be rigorously scientific in approaching assessment, validity remains a slippery customer and exists in a number of different ways. Its definition has evolved over the years along with changing requirements. What doesn't help is that many people will muddle it with an everyday unscientific use of the word. But we are seeking to be scientific and need clear definitions. The simplest definition might seem rather banal: a test is considered to be valid if it measures what it is claimed to measure. Put another way, it concerns the extent to which a test measures what it claims or purports to measure (Anastasi, 1988). Both definitions do not do justice to the term and lack clarity and precision. They are also misleading because they suggest that any measure possesses just one validity, which we will see to be untrue.

A more rigorous view was taken in 1989 when the British Psychological Society's Steering Committee on Test Standards said: 'Validity is the extent to which a test measures what it claims to be measuring, the extent to which it is possible to make appropriate inferences from the test score'. This links the concept with the ability to make decisions through inferences. Validity ultimately concerns these inferences and scores and this view has changed the focus from the measure itself to the uses made of scores. Another approach states that validity relates to the 'correctness' of the inferences made from scores (Landy, 1980) and a yet more refined view is that psychological measures do not intrinsically possess validity, rather it is the inferences made which have validities depending upon their use in appropriate circumstances. A test may be valid for a special purpose or group, for example one could be valid for selection of engineers but not for librarians. Another way of saying this is that a measure cannot just be categorized as either valid or invalid because validity needs always to be determined in relation to a purpose, as Vernon (1960) suggested.

So validity is about the use of tests in practical circumstances and users need to be able to discriminate between where these are appropriate and where inappropriate. Competent users know the difference. This places responsibility on both the test publisher and the user. We should be able to decide when measures are appropriate for our purposes and when they are not. Tests may have many differing validities based upon the objectives of their construction and their target groups, so the number of validities should match the range of potential inferences.

We also need a good understanding of the different approaches to validation and how to evaluate these in applied settings. We can't assume that a measure is valid just because it was provided by a highly regarded publisher, even if the standardization process is sound and reliability looks good. Validity should indicate what any measure is really assessing, not what the test-maker has set out to assess. These two may not be the same. Similarly, even when a collection of items looks as if they are measuring one thing on a scale, it may not be possible to identify what that is purely by inspection. This has to be identified on an empirical basis through a process of validation.

What Does Validation Mean?

Whilst reliability can be recorded and assessed through the use of a single value, this is not the case for validity. There cannot be one single statistic for validity. Any measure will demonstrate different kinds and levels of it across a range of alternative uses and population groups. As we have said, validity is not an attribute possessed by the measure itself: it is an attribute of the interpretation given to any score. It is meaningful, therefore, only in terms of applied contexts. Consequently, validation is a process of building up evidence about what we can and cannot infer from scores. The real issue is about scores and whether we can make justifiable and correct inferences each time a test is used.

To do this we need empirical or 'hard' evidence, just like detectives who gather evidence to identify and convict an offender. Theoretical justifications also need to be available to endorse the acceptability of interpretations made about test scores. Validation thus requires both theoretical and empirical support. On this basis a collection of different types of evidence needs to be gathered by any publisher to back up any measure. The evidence needs to be sufficient, as in any kind of detective work, although not every type of validity is necessarily important. The process is time-consuming, difficult to do

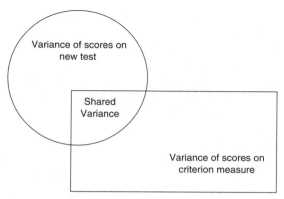

Figure 6.1   Illustrating the variance shared between a new test and a criterion measure

and of crucial significance. Information needs to be provided sometimes on the validity of a measure for a wide spectrum of potential applications.

In practice this means that test scores should be associated with any other means we have available of measuring the same attribute, often referred to as a criterion variable or just as the criterion. For example, the prediction of performance in a particular job is often the aim of occupational measures and so people's scores on the measure are correlated with performance appraisal ratings. For sales people the criterion could be the amount of revenue they generate. If people who generate a lot are more likely to get high scores and vice versa, then we could say this is evidence of validity. Elsewhere in psychology, the aim has been to identify whether offenders can be distinguished from non-offenders through the use of personality measures and the Jessness Inventory was designed for this purpose. It has been shown by a number of investigations to be able to discriminate between delinquent and non-delinquent groups, as well as between different types of delinquent. The criterion in this case might be the recorded number of offences committed. A significant correlation between the number of offences and test scores provides evidence of validity.

In both cases, the more accurate the inferences made, the greater will be the correlation between a score and the criterion. Therefore we may define validity in terms of the extent to which the *variance of any form of assessment is associated with the variance of its criterion*. Whatever kind of validity we consider, it comes down to this: we assemble scores on the test as well as on a relevant criterion, and then measure the association between their variances through correlation to see if it is sufficient to justify inferences (see Figure 6.1). Different types of validity exist ultimately on this basis, although they use alternative means of collecting the data.

Perfect validity studies, however, are impossible to achieve because it is impossible to have a perfect criterion, and because of other problems. Correlation coefficients can often be just good estimations of validity. Doing the same investigation again with a different sample and another suitable criterion can often lead to different results. This finding has led to the view that measures need to be continually checked for their validity as situations of use differ and change, known as the principle of situational specificity. Just how high a correlation has to be to indicate a test is valid is not an easy question to answer.

Different models have been constructed to guide this process, generally including evidence relating to a test's content and internal structure, relating to its associations with external criteria and other variables, and sometimes with unrelated variables. Models vary depending upon the different applied fields of use of the measure concerned (Barrett, Phillips and Alexander, 1981; Guion and Cranny, 1982). In some fields, for example therapeutic uses, theoretical rationales become more significant, as does generalizability across differing settings and groups. The most common model divides validity into three parts: content validity, criterion-related validity and construct validity. Most other types are included as subsets of one of these three. But the different titles are not thought nowadays to represent different forms of validity, as in the past, rather they are perceived as being different forms of evidence for validity. Messick (1989) provides a good overview of them. From this point of view, validation can never actually be concluded because it needs to be continually revised in the light of ever-changing circumstances and populations.

A Catalogue of Validity

The three main categories are:

1   Content-related validity
2   Criterion-related validity
3   Construct-related validity

These are not alternatives but, rather, complementary forms and represent different types of evidence of validity, not different types of validity. There are also some more specialized forms which we shall defer until later.

Content Validity

Content validity is an attribute of a measure itself and how well it has been constructed, being a key task in construction. It indicates how effectively inferences can be drawn from a test score to a larger domain of items similar to those actually being used. It has also been called 'content relevance'. The content of any form of assessment is drawn from a domain of all the knowledge, skills and behaviour of possible relevance to it. For example, an assessment of computer programming ability would need to measure as closely as possible the complete range of skills relevant to it. Thus content validity concerns *the degree to which a test samples the domain* and elicits responses in a representative way, and is more concerned with the method of construction used (Messick, 1975, 1980). In some assessments, such as attainment and ability tests, the domain of items is fairly clear, although it is less so in others. Many non-psychologists are often more concerned about content validity than any other kind because they appear focussed on what is in a test, the nature of its questions or tasks, rather than what it might measure. It is also worth noting that a measure having content validity alone might still not be valid in other respects, so it is not sufficient on its own and there is a need for evidence of other forms.

Content validity originated in educational testing where it was focussed on whether any assessment applied effectively to a particular curriculum. It has been emphasized also in relation to work-sample exercises and tests of job-related knowledge attainment. In these fields, therefore, it is concerned with measuring in the right proportions what people need to know. Anything that does not reflect this is a potential cause of bias. The more a measure matches the content domain, the stronger is the evidence of content validity. It is relevant also to other assessments, for example any intelligence test must represent all the different aspects of 'intelligence,' including language, memory and problem-solving, while any measure of the trait of impulsiveness needs to contain items assessing all aspects of it. Some measures designed for clinical and forensic applications have poor content validity (Kline, 2000), making it harder for them to meet other criteria.

Because of its nature, content validity will depend on the judgements of potential users and experts on the domain being represented. For an ideal investigation the publisher should:

- Where appropriate, conduct a job analysis or provide a theoretical rationale for the domain being measured, together with a literature review.
- Ensure the item sample is sufficient to be representative and has an appropriate range of difficulty, where this is applicable.
- Provide a description of scales measured.
- Report on an evaluation of items by independent experts or judges, selected according to specific criteria, who know the relevant area of application. The experts might be researchers. They should evaluate the accuracy and relevance of items and identify the scale to which each belongs.
- The content validity ratio (CVR) is a measure of the degree to which experts agree. This is determined by asking experts to rate whether each item is essential, useful although not essential, or unnecessary. If n is the number of experts who gave ratings of essential for an item and N is the total number of experts, then:

$$CVR = \frac{n - N/2}{N/2}$$

For example, if 20 experts rate a particular item and 15 regard it as essential, then:

$$CVR = \frac{15 - 20/2}{20/2} = .5$$

Values can range from −1 to +1 and those closer to +1 suggest that a majority of experts agree there is an association between the item and the domain. Values for items can be averaged to provide evidence of expert views regarding the association between the overall measure and the relevant domain.

Criterion-related Validity

This kind of evidence is especially helpful in evaluating whether a measure can be used to make predictions and/or decisions about people. It refers to correlations between scale scores (the predictor) and other criteria or sources (the criterion), such as job competence or ratings of children's behaviour by teachers, to identify whether accurate predictions can be made. It can also be seen in terms of an ability to predict differences in average test scores between criterion groups, such as people working at different levels. Good evidence will suggest a test can be used to make sound decisions.

Predictive validity

Predictive validation is aimed at predicting future behaviour. A measure is said to possess predictive validity if it can predict scores on a criterion. An example might be to give potential students tests of verbal and numerical reasoning before they begin studies and then correlating their scores with final exam results. If the tests are any good they should indicate that people having high scores get better results and that those who do badly also perform less well academically. Predictive validity is often regarded as the most important form of validity in occupational assessment, where selection measures try to predict job performance, although it has relevance also in other contexts.

Finding a clear criterion for prediction is not often easy and even where it is possible there are problems. Time lags present a formidable obstacle because people take a test and then later on, perhaps after 12 months, are given ratings, such as in appraisal or educational assessment. Correlations between test scores and performance at a later stage will also be different because of increased maturity, more experience, because poor performers will have left, and because at the second stage people will have seen the test before. The method of conducting appraisal, i.e. criterion measurement, may also be poor. Similarly, in the educational domain, an issue might be the adequacy of academic measurement. Another problem relates to range restriction, discussed briefly in Chapter 5, because an employer might not want to give jobs to less able people so that the later sample will tend to have mostly good performers. Ideally, employers need to engage everybody regardless of potential future competence or lack of it. Range restriction makes coefficients smaller, underestimating true validity unless a statistical correction is applied (Dobson, 1988). Another problem is sample attrition: the later sample is smaller just because some people leave or are not available. Even where a test is a good predictor, having high predictive validity, it may still not have sufficient validity. The test might not really measure performance but other factors associated with it. So determination of predictive validity is not as simple as it appears and, therefore, is rarely used.

In some psychological domains there may be no simple or obvious criterion measure available, for example it is difficult to provide evidence of predictive validity for many clinical tests or some aspects of personality (Kline, 2000). The Psychopathy Checklist – Revised (PCL–R), developed by Hare and colleagues (1990) and used by forensic psychologists, is said to possess predictive validity. Correlations have been based upon the scale scores of offenders and a variety of behavioural and laboratory measures.

Concurrent validity

Concurrent validation, another form of criterion-related validity, effectively gets rid of the problem of the time lag. If a new test is validated through correlation with a currently existing criterion, such as recent appraisal ratings, then it has concurrent validity. We would expect any new measure of neuroticism to correlate highly with the neuroticism scale of the NEO Personality Inventory (NEO-PIR). It might be thought that accountants have higher numerical ability and engineers higher mechanical aptitude than others, thus providing a basis for estimating concurrent validity. The quality of the 'benchmark' assessment is an important factor and, assuming measures have good reliability and sample size, correlations should be as high as possible. Those above 0.55 could be viewed as providing excellent support (Smith and Smith, 2005).

In occupational psychology the test-maker might test a sample of existing employees and obtain empirical evidence of a job performance criterion before correlating them. Employees need to represent a reasonable spread of scores, including poor, average and above average performers. However, for complex types of work a simple criterion might not exist. And concurrent validity does not necessarily imply that a test has predictive validity because the results can be confounded by other factors such as age, experience or knowledge of company culture, and the quality of the performance measure. Doing this provides some helpful evidence about the potential of a test for use in selection, but it does not determine its predictive validity.

The correlations gained are often referred to as validity coefficients. Equations can also be used to estimate predicted people's scores on the criterion based upon predictor scores. These calculate the Standard Error of the estimate (Sest), similar to the Standard Error of prediction in Chapter 5, and suggest that when a coefficient is low an individual's obtained score can vary widely from that predicted. We must also take care when interpreting predicted scores in cases when the correlation is moderate. Manuals should outline an analysis of the relationships between a new measure and the criterion on an empirical basis, such as correlations with measures and those relating to contrasting sample groups.

Concurrent validation is fine within the workplace, but again what about other areas of applied psychology? It all depends on the availability of benchmark assessments. They can exist in the field of intelligence, having the Wechsler scales and the Stanford-Binet assessment, although the picture is less clear elsewhere. Any benchmark will need to have acceptable validity and this is often not the case, meaning that new measures need to be correlated with others having doubtful validity or lacking unidimensionality. For these reasons concurrent validity rarely stands alone as a single piece of evidence and is mostly used in conjunction with other forms.

Construct Validity

Originally construct validity was thought to be a distinct form of validity after the term was introduced by Cronbach and Meehl (1955), although it has come to be viewed as an over-arching concept which encompasses all of the other forms. It is clearly the most significant aspect of thinking about validity because it is the common focus of evaluation

Table 6.1   *Evaluating construct validity through correlations*

Respondents (N)	Our Test (T scores)	Benchmark Test 1 (T scores)	Benchmark Test 2 (T scores)
Respondent 1	55	56	54
Respondent 2	43	42	44
Respondent 3	67	68	66
Respondent 4	49	46	51
Respondent 5	38	37	36
.	.	.	.
↓	↓	↓	↓
Respondent N	53	54	52
Correlation:	–	0.73	0.77

of test usefulness. It concerns the evidence which shows that the test really is a measure of what it claims to measure. Attributes are overwhelmingly abstract notions and do not exist in a physical sense. Therefore, we need to consider the underlying intention of any test and its interpretation and to base validation upon these. Some researchers have said that a construct is an idea of an attribute or characteristic inferred from research (Bechtoldt, 1959; Guion, 1965; Anastasi, 1988), although it might also be inferred from everyday observations. Yet we need concrete and operational measures of these things. So to claim construct validity we have to get to the heart of any assessment to evaluate what it is really measuring. This is why there is no easy way of generating this type of validity. You can't produce it like a rabbit out of a hat.

In statistical terms, construct validity represents the extent to which a measure's variance is linked with the variance of its underlying construct (Barrett et al., 1981; Guion and Cranny, 1982). There can be no single correlation for this. Validation requires review of a range of correlations and whether they match what would be expected, for example if a new scale of social anxiety correlates highly with other established measures of the same thing then it could be argued justifiably that it also measures this. An example would be the construct validation of the Gudjonsson Suggestibility Scale, used in forensic applications (Gudjonsson, 1997). Hypotheses were generated based upon predicted relationships between the suggestibility concept and personality constructs, including assertiveness and anxiety, as well as cognitive variables, and the Gudjonsson scale was then used to test out these hypotheses. This resulted in a range of findings which are linked by detailed reasoning.

Therefore, construct validity depends on all the evidence gathered to show that a test does relate to its construct. The simplest method is similar to the process required for concurrent validity, i.e. correlation of scores with other accepted measures of the same thing (Table 6.1), but this is only part of the story. A network of data has to be built up from a variety of sources including evidence of content validity, relationships with other tests, correlation with external criteria and evidence of subordinate or linked forms of validity (Cronbach and Meehl, 1955). Manuals then usually give patterns of correlations and conclude that the results support the measurement of a specific construct.

Subordinates

One type of subordinate validity is called convergent-discriminant validity which is based on the idea that a measure needs to correlate with others of the same thing but not with those measuring other constructs (Campbell and Fiske, 1959). Scores are said to 'converge' with similar measures and 'diverge' from dissimilar ones. Validation needs correlation with other measures, including some which are of constructs from similar, although different, domains. It is common, for example, for verbal ability test scores to be correlated with scores on other tests of the same kind, as well as with numerical test scores. All being well, correlations with numerical tests will be lower.

A related form is factorial validity. In this case scores are mixed with scores of other tests, both similar and dissimilar, and the data subjected to factor analysis. Factors derived should indicate that the scores match the pattern of similar ones and are distinct from those of different tests. Nominated group validity can be used when a construct is expected to predict that samples have different scores, such as a comparison of people diagnosed as having severe depression with others in the general population. Evidence of a difference indicates construct validity for the measurement of depression.

Incremental validity is another form of construct validity and determines any increase in validity, and whether this is significant, when an assessment is added to others. Imagine that you are using an interview, a personality assessment and a test of general mental reasoning to select IT employees. You then buy a more modern test of IT skills, say computer programming aptitude, but find that it doesn't improve the selection rate at all, having low incremental validity. The new material doesn't add much to what you were doing before and may involve some duplication, even with an interview. In this case more might be gained through the use of less expensive methods. Incremental validity can also be identified when a measure correlates weakly with the criterion variable but has no correlation with other tests used. Both this form of validity and a more obscure form – differential validity – are used in work psychology. Differential validity is found when correlations relating to different aspects of the criterion measurement also tend to have different values. Both incremental and differential versions are discussed by Vernon (1961).

The Multitrait-multimethod Approach

This approach provides a more consistent and elaborate form of convergent-discriminant validity, which can also be used to demonstrate true construct validity for a measure (Campbell and Fiske, 1959). It involves correlational matrices having mixtures of measures and methods of assessment. Each of the constructs needs to be measured in at least two different ways. A matrix is then created of correlations among the different constructs measured by different methods, for example the personality traits of emotional stability, impulsiveness and independence might be evaluated through the use of ratings by others, projective methods and questionnaires, resulting in a 9×9 matrix of coefficients. The matrix will identify convergent validity by identifying whether similar results are gained by alternative methods of measuring the construct. Significant correlations between the different methods will suggest that they are measuring the relevant construct.

Similarly, inspection should indicate whether tests hypothesized not to be associated are, in fact, not associated, as shown by their correlations. This will signify discriminant or divergent validity. A statistical process called structural equation modelling can also be used to identify evidence. Adaptation of the approach to construct validation of one measure only using the same and different methods of assessment has been suggested, although the methods used often appear to become more significant than the construct under consideration.

Summary

Validity is not a property which is possessed in any absolute sense. It concerns inferences made about the usefulness of a measure's scores and means we are seeking to identify those which are fit for purpose. Validation is a process of structured investigation which gathers empirical evidence involving validity coefficients. Content validity evaluates how well items represent a domain of all possible items. Criterion-related validity concerns a test's efficacy in making predictions and involves correlations with benchmark criteria. One form, predictive validity, is aimed at predicting behaviour, whilst concurrent validity evaluates whether a measure correlates significantly with relevant criteria. Construct validity has been seen as encompassing all of the other kinds of validity. It depends on all of the evidence gathered, and can also include convergent-discriminant, factorial, nominated group, incremental and differential validity.

 **Validation in Practice**

Giving Evidence

Test manuals should state the evidence in support of their validity. They should at least give an indication of the following:

- The size of samples used in studies
- When they were tested
- What criterion measures were used
- Whether studies were concurrent or predictive
- Whether correlations were corrected for range restriction
- Any other forms of correction applied

In practice, they often don't provide all of this information and there have been instances when statements have been misleading. One major example led to public criticism about the way in which some publishers present validity evidence. Johnson et al. (1988) said that scales were correlated with job performance and the correlations were statistically significant, although they were meaningless because the publishers had chosen the highest from a large number of possible correlations, which could not have been expected by experienced test users. This has since been referred to as the Blinkhorn effect. Effectively, publishers could sometimes be 'cherry-picking' high correlations and then ignoring or failing to report others.

There have long been arguments among researchers about construct validity (Jackson and Maraun, 1996a, b). These have included issues about subjective assertions based on a network of rationalizations, about substantial differences between inferences made and the behaviours of people, as well as about dependence upon correlational analysis. Mistakes can be made, for example through inaccurate association of a factor with its correlations, and subjective inferences are involved. Jackson and Maraun suggest that even in a detailed analysis some of the original hypotheses may not be supported and, therefore, there is an element of subjectivity. So construct validity involves a sum of all the findings for the purposes proposed at any one time and, in the positivist and hypothetico-deductive view of science of Popper (1972), can never be complete. It helps to know overall what should be required of a perfect validation process and Box 6.1 provides a summary.

Box 6.1   A Perfect Validation

Test manuals should provide:

- A definition or rationale for the construct measured, and identify relevant observable behaviours which define it in operational terms. Behaviours should be intercorrelated to show they are assessing the same construct.
- Evidence of content validity based upon analysis of judgements of experts.
- A pattern of relationships between the construct, its observable outcomes, and other constructs and behaviours, leading to hypothesized relationships among a network of variables.
- Evidence for reliability and internal consistency.
- Evidence of high correlations with established measures of the same construct (concurrent validity).
- Evidence of high correlations with established measures or events in the future (predictive validity).
- Evidence of high correlations with appropriate external criteria which are reliable and valid, e.g. academic achievement or other forms of assessment (construct validity).
- Evidence that scores discriminate significantly between relevant groups, as might be justifiably expected (construct validity).
- Evidence from a factor analysis suggesting that scores load highly on the factors of similar tests and not on those of dissimilar ones (construct validity).
- Interviews might also usefully be conducted of people who have completed the assessment to evaluate mental processes involved in responses.
- A conclusion which evaluates the evidence for the pattern of relationships proposed and those hypothesized and, therefore, indicates the soundness of the evidence for construct validity.

Validity's 'Faux Amis' (False Friends)

A number of other forms of validity have also been suggested unsuccessfully, because none of them relate to the empirical procedures we have discussed. If any new approach doesn't support the inferences made from scores or connect with validation processes, then it can't really be contributing to a discussion of validity. This is best shown by evaluating the two most common 'false friends'.

The first of these is face validity, which is better described as acceptability, and refers to the appearance of assessment materials. It is based upon what any respondent thinks is being assessed. One definition might be that a measure is face valid (or acceptable) if it appears to be measuring what it is claimed to measure. A measure having high face validity will look appropriate to the purpose to people taking it or associated with it. There is probably a link between the popularity of some tests and their acceptability. It is sometimes not a trivial matter because where test-takers don't take a test seriously the outcomes might be meaningless. Without it respondents may not cooperate. Armed forces personnel would obviously perceive reaction time tests as being more valid than a measure of customer service skills. Courts of law can also be misled by a superficial discussion of test content.

Items do, therefore, need to appear appropriate and interesting. Their style, words and phrasing are often scrutinized and should be suitable for the intended population. Basically, acceptability can be considered to be a form of spurious validity because any scrutiny of items provides no guarantee that a measure will assess what is being claimed. In fact, the presentational characteristics of a measure, whether it is dull or 'glossy,' may not have any relationship with the correctness of inferences from scores (Cattell and Warburton, 1967).

The other 'false friend' has been called faith validity. This has nothing to do with religious faith but refers to the beliefs of test users in the value of certain assessments and their attitudes towards them, and is probably related also to their acceptability. Inexperienced users may sometimes have substantial faith in a test, even when there is no evidence of validity. Naïve users also have a natural tendency to over-interpret test data. Faith validity is probably linked to anecdotal validity and the Pollyanna effect. The first bases justification on past assessments which have been remarkable and unforgettable, and thus are significant for someone. Success in identifying an important characteristic in a development scenario may influence someone's thinking for years. The Pollyanna effect is based on a fictional character who views the world in a positive, optimistic and enthusiastic light. People tend to agree that positive reports are more accurate and better descriptions of them (Sundberg, 1955; Thorne, 1961; Mosher, 1965). In addition, individuals who insist on the continual use of one measure in all situations, regardless of circumstances, are demonstrating poor quality use of tests. A questionnaire's popularity and the marketing efforts of publishers may play a role in this, rather than any issue of validity.

Evaluating Validity Coefficients

In Chapter 5 we looked at what might be acceptable values for reliability coefficients. This is less simple in the case of validity because of its different forms – coefficients for construct validity tend to be higher than those for criterion-related validity – and there may be some subjective element in any review. So there is less consistency over the criteria for

Table 6.2 *Evaluating validity coefficients*

Value Label	Percentage of Variance	Correlation
Evaluation of predictive and concurrent validities		
Inadequate	Under 4%	Under .2
Adequate	4–12%	.2–.34
Reasonable	13–15%	.35–.44
Good	16–29%	.45–.54
Excellent	Over 29%	.55 and above
Evaluation of construct validities		
Inadequate	Under 20%	Under .45
Adequate	20–29%	.45–.54
Reasonable	30–41%	.55–.64
Good	42–55%	.65–.74
Excellent	Over 55%	.75 and above

acceptability of coefficients and there are no clear rules. However, one system which provides some indicators would generally be helpful, such as those given in the *Review of Personality Assessments (Level B) for Use in Occupational Settings* (Lindley, 2001) and the *Review of Ability and Aptitude Tests (Level A) for Use in Occupational Settings* (Bartram, 1997). Their systems are given in Table 6.2.

It should be noted that this system was developed for use in the occupational field and the requirements may be different elsewhere. The late Paul Kline said the great majority of assessments used across many disciplines, including the 16PF and the MMPI, lack adequate evidence of validity (2000). He also criticized attempts to validate clinical scales on the weak evidential basis of *DSM* or other classifications of mental disorder. Although he found some tests, such as the Beck Depression Inventory, to have validity, others used in the field of therapy were said to have dubious validity, being founded simply on an appearance of consistency and having item content reflecting the needs of practitioners.

Another important issue in evaluating correlations concerns the probability of research findings occurring by chance. There is a likelihood of correlation coefficients being obtained by chance alone and test-makers should indicate the amount of chance existing in their findings. A common standard is to accept those having a less than five times in 100 probability of occurring by chance. When this happens the result is said to be statistically significant at a 5 per cent level. Research papers published in journals include statements such as '$r = 0.6$, $p < .05$' where r represents a correlation coefficient and p indicates probability. This suggests that the likelihood of the relationship occurring by chance alone is less than .05, which is the same as saying less than 5 per cent or less than 5 times in 100 (as explained in Chapter 5). In evaluating coefficients we should not only consider the strength of the relationship indicated by r, but also the likelihood of it occurring by chance, shown by the p value. For example:

$r = 0.32$, $p < .05$ means the chance level is less than 5 times in 100
$r = 0.44$, $p < .01$ means the chance level is less than 1 time in 100
$r = 0.60$, $p < .001$ means the chance level is less than 1 time in 1000

Table 6.3 *Validity data showing coefficients and probability indicators*

GROUP	N	VARIABLE	r
MBA students	243	Course results	.65**
Nursing students	105	Course results	.52*
High school students	97	Appraisal ratings	.48*
Technical staff	115	Appraisal ratings	ns
Clerical staff	82	Appraisal ratings	ns
Management staff	394	Appraisal ratings	.62**

Results are sometimes stated in tables, like Table 6.3 where N gives the sample size. An asterisked key is usually provided with such tables such as:

$$* = p < .05 \qquad ** = p < .01 \qquad ns = \text{not significant}$$

Lastly, it is always wise to evaluate the groups or populations and relevant situations for which a measure has been standardized and validated. Any new assessment should match the population and circumstances described in studies. More confidence can be placed upon outcomes where there is a greater match. Otherwise generalizability of the results could become difficult, as for example when forensic psychologists make use of assessments which have been standardized and validated on non-forensic populations.

Factors Affecting Coefficients

How much of the variance is truly shared between a measure and some other one may not be genuinely or accurately determined because of other factors which can interfere with correlations. The effect produced can reduce their value in some instances and enhance it in others. These factors, therefore, can be seen as sources of error affecting measures of validity. The common ones are:

(a) *Range restriction*

We have come across this before, including its effect on reliability. It is caused by the test-takers involved having similar scores, i.e. there is a lack of variability on one or both of the measures correlated. To get high coefficients there needs to be enough variation among scores on both measures. As the amount of restriction will vary from study to study, so the correlation obtained will also tend to vary. If people get roughly the same scores on the predictor variable, it will be difficult to distinguish between them on the other. Range restriction also occurs when a sample group is more homogeneous in terms of characteristics like age, sex and personality traits, called moderator variables, which can affect the correlation too by narrowing the range of scores. Many studies experience restriction of range and it is a particular problem for them.

(b) *Sample attrition*

We also met this problem briefly earlier when we discussed problems of reduced sample size in predictive validation (Schmidt, Hunter and Urry, 1976). It also enhances range restriction. All is not lost, however, as there are formulae and software programs which can calculate the value of the validity coefficient as if no range restriction or sample attrition existed. We can estimate what the validity would be for an original larger sample if we have a measure of the variance of test scores as well as that of the related smaller group.

(c) *Sample size*

Small samples have notoriously been used in many validation exercises. The smaller the sample of people involved, the larger the amount of error. Or, to put it another way, the bigger the sample, the smaller the standard error becomes. In the occupational field, studies need a criterion sample from one specific group doing one type of job, usually in one organization. A similar problem occurs with clinical samples where access to people having a specific disorder may also be limited. Small samples are said in statistical terms to be 'unstable' because two correlated samples of the same small size can sometimes generate remarkably different results. This is based on the fact that the laws of probability will sometimes give a correlation which is considerably lower than the true value for small samples. It has been possible to calculate what the sample size should be in certain circumstances.

(d) *Attenuation*

If the reliability of the criterion measure is poor it also can reduce validity coefficients. The correlation between two measures is said suffer from attenuation, i.e. reduction caused by their reliabilities. If the reliability of criterion measures used in different studies varies, then apparent validity coefficients will also vary (Schwab, Heneman and DeCottiss, 1975; Landy and Farr, 1980). The maximum validity is limited by the reliabilities. In fact, no test can have a validity coefficient which is higher than its reliability. The limitations caused by poor reliabilities will happen because it is never possible in practice to have perfect criteria available. Fortunately, statisticians have come to our rescue again with a correction formula to overcome this and it is possible to estimate true validity, provided we know the reliability of a criterion measure and the correlation between it and the predictor (Johnson and Ree, 1994).

(e) *Criterion contamination*

This involves bias in criterion scores and variations in the types of measures used as criteria, such as those of job performance or clinical interpretation. It, too, reduces coefficients. Validity will be greater when the impact of other factors unrelated to scores on the criterion is minimized (Mace, 1935; Thorndike, 1949; Smith, 1976). For example, people who have greater experience or more resources may have appraisal scores involving more bias. Or a clinical psychologist who is aware of a diagnosis of a specific disorder among patients may misinterpret their responses to a questionnaire.

(f) *Assumptions*

There is an assumption that to generate a validity coefficient the relationship between two variables used is linear. This being so, the predictor measure is able to predict both high and low scores accurately. Where it is not the case, the coefficient is once more reduced. Another assumption relates to the factor structure of tests. Different batteries of them sometimes measure similar but not identical attributes, for example different spatial reasoning tests will have different correlations with an underlying factor. These differences and their influence upon coefficients are difficult to quantify. Another assumption concerns test length because validity coefficients, like reliability, vary with this.

Summary

Estimations of test validity by lay people are frequently influenced by views of their acceptability, which occurs as forms of spurious validity such as face and faith validity. We have also looked at the guidance available on how to evaluate validity coefficients and how probability influences the occurrence of statistically significant findings. Lastly, we have considered factors which can interfere with the size of coefficients including range restriction, sample attrition, attenuation and criterion contamination.

What Have We Discovered About Validity?

This has been yet another important chapter relating to the evaluation of assessment instruments. Validity is crucial to evaluation of them and we should be in a position to carefully evaluate the evidence provided in any validation process. Like sleuths in any thriller, it is important to track down the evidence and to scrutinize it before coming to any decision. We have learned:

- About the significance of validity and its models, including content, construct and criterion-related validity, as well as about subordinate forms such as convergent-discriminant validity.
- About the main forms of spurious validity and their influences upon lay views of assessment.
- What validation means, what it should involve and how to evaluate any validation process.
- About evaluation of validity coefficients and different factors which can have an impact upon their values, including range restriction, sample size, attenuation and criterion contamination.

PART III

Applications of Psychological Assessment and Measurement

7

Measuring Intelligence and Ability

Learning Objectives

By the end of this chapter you should be able to:

- Discuss the concept of intelligence, how it might best be defined, and the differences between implicit and explicit theories.
- Give an account of the different approaches to understanding and measuring human intelligence, and the major outcomes of these.
- Outline the major issues concerning intelligence, including the nature–nurture debate, the problems raised by eugenics and the Flynn effect.
- Distinguish between intelligence, ability and aptitude, and give an account of modern ability testing.

What is This Chapter About?

It's about something which has been much used and abused. That frightens people, possibly more so than late-night horror films. Despite fascination with it, people will run a mile if they think their intelligence is going to be measured. It's nice to think we are highly intelligent but not so nice to discover we're not. People have their own pet ideas about it and want their children to be intelligent, seeming to prize it more than happiness. Intelligence may be a popular TV concept but has a lot to be blamed for. We saw the historical development of psychometrics in Chapter 1, much of it centred on intelligence. The history of psychometrics is linked with that of intelligence – so much that it is difficult to prise them apart. This chapter will discuss intelligence in more detail, beginning with a review of what it might actually be before diving into a tale of research, theorizing and debate, as well as of major developments in measurement. Then we evaluate the arguments so that you can discuss whether it really is all in our genes, whether it can be used to build a society of eggheads, and if you are superior to your forebears. Allied to this are the concepts of ability and aptitude, and we will also discuss their measurement and applications today.

Psychology's World Cup Winner – Intelligence

If it were possible to hold a world cup competition between all of the concepts investigated in psychology based on importance, then intelligence would surely be the winner. Even if we included such things as behaviour, memory, personality, psychopathology and attitudes, and many others, an overwhelming majority would probably say intelligence is the most fascinating and important issue. It has attracted interest and attention for a long time, so much debate and controversy, resulting in successes for some researchers and 'own goals' for others. It has been researched far more than any other concept and is seen as having far-reaching implications for everyone. No other aspect of human functioning explains so much of the differences in behaviour. It has fascinated great thinkers, even politicians and mass murderers, since time began. In the first half of the twentieth century many psychologists made a good living out of testing it. Although circumstances have changed, they continue to make much use of intelligence or cognitive assessment in a range of activities. Thinking about it influences people's perceptions, evaluations and decisions about themselves and others. It also impacts on social life, especially in relationships, in education and in the workplace. We all have theories about intelligence based on experiences, education, interests and preferences, using them to make judgements every day.

What is Intelligence?

Attempts to define it have been legion, causing much confusion. Few people will agree because it all depends on what they think is important or useful. Although it is basically an inferential construct, people's judgements tend to be pragmatic: in the developed world it might involve the use of IT, whilst in the third world it could involve survival factors like being able to recognize danger. One definition has been: 'Intelligence is what intelligence tests measure' (Boring, 1923). This is too simplistic and avoids answering the question through a circular definition. We need an exact understanding of what tests measure to use such a definition. Perhaps what matters most is that we have something which is worth measuring.

Implicit and Explicit Theories

Personal definitions of intelligence by ordinary people are called implicit theories. Studies around the world suggest these can be influenced by cultural factors. They have been investigated by, for example, Demetriou and Papadopoulous (2004), Baral and Das

Table 7.1 *National differences in conceptualizing intelligence*

Country	Example aspects of intelligence	References
India	Emotion Modesty & politeness Self-awareness Judging Thinking Decision-making Interest in others	Baral & Das (2004)
China	Empathy, compassion & politeness Learns quickly Self-knowledge Intellectual confidence Humility	Yang & Sternberg (1997)
Korea	Social skills Problem-solving skills Capable of learning skills Self-management Pragmatic & organized	Lim et al. (2002)
United States	Practical problem-solving Verbal ability Social skills Intellectual balance & integration Goal orientation Fluid & fast thinking	Sternberg (1985b); Sternberg et al. (1981)

(2004), Sternberg (2001), Sternberg et al. (1981) and Berry (1984), and Table 7.1 indicates some differences found. Western cultures emphasize mental processing speed and efficient management of information, whilst those in the East also include social and spiritual aspects, although some research indicates the two viewpoints are converging (Lim, Plucker and Im, 2002). Personal definitions also appear to change as we age. Sternberg (1985b) suggested that university professors differ when asked for definitions: those in different disciplines include attributes relevant to their own areas of study.

The trouble with implicit theories is that when people make judgements they do not communicate the underlying basis, being unable to understand their own complex reasoning, so that it is not transparent. In essence, the reasoning is personal, individual and subjective. The use of words such as 'sharp' or 'quick' in common definitions are too obscure and ambiguous to found a science of intelligence on. In psychology we need explicit theories, i.e. being understandable and having empirical and objective foundations. We need a definition encompassing mental processes linked to individual differences in many areas of life.

Ever since the first intelligence measures were developed, psychologists have struggled to agree. Binet suggested intelligence related to judgement, understanding and reasoning. Others thought that it depends on the number of connections, their complexity, and the organization of cells in the cerebral cortex (Jensen and Sinah, 1993), although this doesn't provide an adequate operational definition. After Binet, experience and judgement became factors, for example a suggestion that intelligence represents abstract thinking. Although abstract thinking was an important feature, it was not the only one. Another approach concerned definitions focussed on the way the word is used, linking intelligent ways of doing things and being innovative (Thorndike et al., 1921). Researchers working in the psychometric tradition adopted an empirical approach centred on hypotheses reflecting use of the term and the construction of theoretical models and tests. Galton, Pearson and Spearman were associated with this.

Spearman (1927) conducted the first factor analysis of abilities and said they could be explained in terms of a general factor called 'g' linked to specific factors. He referred to it as general intelligence, thought today to represent what is called fluid ability and helps people to solve problems. People having this general intelligence tend to do well on most tasks. It is always the most significant factor in any analysis of abilities. Spearman's 'g' has since been divided into two factors, crystallized ability and fluid ability. The fluid version is what intelligence tests measure, whilst the crystallized one reflects more culturally relevant skills. Although there appears to be a general factor, how well you cope in any environment is related also to specific cultural abilities. Other developments have also added new components to intelligence. Sternberg (1985a, 1988) focussed on an ability to adapt in a changing world and to motivate oneself, as well as tacit knowledge, defined as 'the practical know-how needed for success on the job'. Others, such as Das et al. (1994), have viewed intelligence as including attentiveness, information processing and planning, or even as a quality of mind which influences activities. Given the continuing lack of a comprehensively acceptable definition, some such as Vernon (1979) have gone to the extent of suggesting that the term should be discarded, replacing it with alternatives like general mental ability or scholastic aptitude.

So there is still no universally accepted answer to the question: 'What is intelligence?' Perhaps it is something that we can't ultimately define, but can recognize when we see it. The best definition is probably test related, in other words intelligence is what is assessed by intelligence tests. Therefore, it represents the basic reasoning ability which a person uses in different situations to solve problems.

An Intelligent History

The differences between many historical approaches to investigating intelligence are based on researchers' preferences about what was once a new statistical technique – factor analysis. In many instances they wanted the most parsimonious and practical ways of accounting for its results. Earlier theories differed in relation to 'g' – between insisting on its importance (as Spearman did), acknowledging it but saying it is not of central importance (Thurstone and Cattell), and rejecting its existence altogether (Guilford). Later development of hierarchical models linking abilities to 'g' also led to a difference between those who saw intelligence as a unitary capacity and others who preferred to consider it as constituting unrelated abilities. As time went on they came to what might be considered a consensus. But after that new ways of thinking about human cognition and information processing led to yet more views.

Although early work appeared to be in the UK, later parallel developments were undertaken in the US. Spearman (1904) was the first to investigate intelligence in terms of 'g' and the majority of modern tests still seek to measure it. He was among the first to attempt an empirical study and, in fact, developed factor analysis for this purpose. He correlated children's scores on a number of tests and factor-analysed the correlations. The correlations were all positive, suggesting that 'g' was at the root of them and that it represented the intelligence needed to do well on different tests, although he acknowledged that other factors might be involved. His findings suggested intelligence is a general ability, that people who are competent in one kind of problem tend also to be good at others. Although factor analysis has become more refined and complex since Spearman's time – his was quite primitive compared to methods today – the correlations between measures still include a similar general factor. It is the nature of this factor, 'g', which has been the source of differences between researchers.

At first Thorndike (Thorndike et al., 1921) went his own way. His theory – not based on factor analysis – proposed three kinds of intelligence including social, concrete and abstract forms. He saw them as a combination of differing abilities within the brain. But then in 1938 Thurstone used factor analysis and his conclusions were that intelligence is made up of seven group factors, including verbal comprehension, number, spatial visualization, perceptual speed, word fluency, memory and reasoning. Thurstone thought Spearman had merely showed that test scores correlated positively, although when he later factor analysed again he found a second-order factor which could be 'g'. He still disagreed about an overall factor; but thought that 'g' was the result of the primary abilities he had discovered. Thurstone had, in effect, invented the 'multifactor' approach to understanding intelligence and this was developed further by others, notably Guilford (1981).

Fluid and Crystallized Intelligence

A new development, seen as a compromise, came from Cattell who had got the idea that intelligence was not one single concept but was made up of two components (Cattell, 1987; Stankov, Boyle and Cattell, 1995). Using factor analysis, he confirmed Thurstone's discovery of primary abilities, but then went on to factor-analyse correlations between them. This led to the emergence of two second-order factors. Cattell acknowledged that general intelligence existed but said it was made up of two associated but distinct things: fluid and crystallized intelligence. Fluid intelligence was more genetically determined and, therefore, more culture free. It was, he thought, associated with how efficiently information could flow around the brain. He saw it as a primary reasoning ability, dealing with abstract problems and being more involved in adaptation. In contrast, crystallized intelligence evolved from the exercise of fluid intelligence within a certain environment. It represented acquired knowledge or skills, being made up of a store including vocabulary, comprehension and general knowledge. Cattell viewed the two forms as having a dynamic association: some aspects of crystallized intelligence would develop throughout life and reflect learning experiences. Fluid intelligence was considered to develop from birth and become fixed in adulthood. This suggests that disciplines needing abstract thinking, such as poetry or mathematics, might have their best achievements during early adulthood, whilst other fields like literature or philosophy need more developed knowledge and have their best works in later adulthood.

Guilford's Structure of Intellect

Disagreeing with the idea of 'g', Guilford suggested that cognitive performance could be better explained by evaluation of the type of mental process involved in tasks, the content operated on, and the subsequent product of a specific operation on a particular kind of test content. His basic abilities fell into three categories of operations, contents and products, with five in the first and second, and six in the last. He also identified an extra set of abilities including reasoning and problem-solving, decision-making and language skills. This led to his original model having 120 independent factors, being later revised to 150. Guilford's ideas were called the Structure of Intellect theory. Research failed to support the assumption of independence and it was criticized for not providing a hierarchical model having a general factor. However, his theory expanded the concept of intelligence and indicated that different aspects interweave to create specific abilities.

Vernon's Hierarchy

Increasing factor analysis of abilities led UK psychologists to view intelligence as a general factor which could be split into more specific abilities. The hierarchical perspective came into its own with the work of Vernon (1979), who unified the results of a range of factor analyses into a single theory and argued that no one had thought about group factors linking 'g' to specific abilities. This meant that intelligence was made up of sets of abilities depicted at differing levels. In 1950 he modified Spearman's approach to include two group factors: one concerning verbal and educational aspects and the other spatial factors in intelligence. In 1960 he proposed 'g' as being at the top of a branching tree, linked to two major factors called verbal-education (or v:ed) and practical-mechanical-spatial (k:m) at the next level. They were then broken down into minor group factors, which were then sub-divided at the bottom of the hierarchy into aspects of ability relevant to particular tests, shown in Figure 7.1. His v:ed included abilities such as verbal fluency and numerical ability, while k:m encompassed mechanical, spatial and psychomotor abilities. The model suggests that higher components represent a broader range of abilities and had a significant influence on development of the Wechsler intelligence scales.

An Integrative Model

The time was now ripe for someone to integrate more than 50 years of research. This was done by Carroll who related everything that had gone before from Spearman to Vernon. Taking an immense amount of data compiled between the 1920s and 1980s, Carroll subjected the lot to factor analysis and then suggested there were three hierarchical levels or 'stratums' to intelligence (Carroll, 1993). These were:

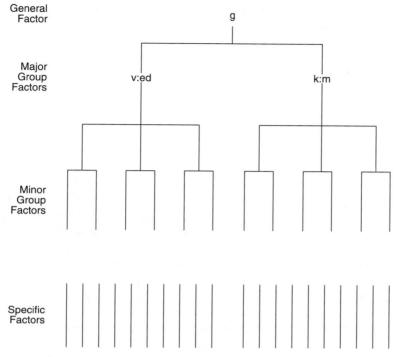

General
Factor

g

Major
Group
Factors

v:ed

k:m

Minor
Group
Factors

Specific
Factors

Figure 7.1   Vernon's hierarchical theory of intelligence

- Stratum I – made up of 69 specific kinds of intelligence or abilities.
- Stratum II – comprising eight broader factors emerging from the abilities at stratum I. These are:

  - Fluid intelligence
  - Crystallized intelligence
  - General memory and learning
  - Broad visual perception
  - Broad auditory perception
  - Broad retrieval ability
  - Broad cognitive pace
  - Processing speed

- Stratum III – representing a general level resembling 'g'.

The Theory of Cognitive Abilities

Carroll's publication of his analysis might suggest it was time to stop theorizing about intelligence. But that wasn't to happen. Horn had been working with Cattell on the fluid–crystallized intelligence approach in the 1980s. He had given up the idea of a 'g' factor and thought the research then available encouraged the view of seven more broad 'g' abilities to go with fluid and crystallized intelligence. These were:

- Short-term apprehension and retrieval abilities
- Visual processing
- Auditory processing
- Tertiary storage and retrieval
- Processing speed
- Correct decision speed
- Quantitative knowledge

Don't be surprised if you feel a little confused about the similarities between Carroll's work and Cattell and Horn's research. There are a number of them. Richard Woodcock thought so, too, and he got Horn and Carroll together to agree on an all-inclusive model. The result was the Cattell-Horn-Carroll theory of cognitive abilities (Flanagan, McGrew and Ortiz, 2000; Lohman, 2001). This now had a broad level, called stratum II, and a narrow level, stratum I, and the general factor was dropped altogether. The new model demonstrated further integration, but also appears to have been influenced by the needs of test-makers. Its emphasis was placed upon an understanding of cognitive abilities. It was less precise than earlier theories and had broadened to include aspects more of relevance to applied testing, yet also included less understood factors such as olfactory, tactile and kinaesthetic abilities.

Gardner and Sternberg

Two more approaches developed further the application of theory to applied settings and measurement. The first, by Gardner, was concerned about links with education and the effectiveness of factor analysis. His view is that Western education places emphasis on logical-mathematical and linguistic intelligences rather than aspects such as interpersonal intelligence. As a consequence, he says, educationalists show less interest in those who are weaker in the former but stronger in the latter. He performed a literature search to discover behaviours which changed together in regular patterns and suggested there were nine types of intelligence (Gardner et al., 1996; Gardner, 1983, 1998). These include musical, bodily kinaesthetic, interpersonal, intrapersonal (self-understanding), naturalist (being able to interact with nature) and existentialist (able to understand one's surroundings and place in a larger scheme) abilities.

Gardner defines intelligence as the ability to solve problems or to create products valued in cultural settings and challenges the notion of IQ, that there can be one number identifying intelligence. Rather, he says, every form of intelligence has its own index. Each relates to independent brain sections and there is no central function, although they can interact and cooperate. Every person has a distinct and unique collection of intelligences. In support of his view, he has referred to cross-cultural research indicating the role of cultural values in human abilities. Like Guilford's work, his theory provides a structure-of-intellect model which has been popular among educationalists. Sternberg (2000) says the theory needs more work to support it.

More opposition to the concept of IQ, because of its inherent suggestion that it represents a rigid measure of intelligence, has come from Sternberg. His 'triarchic theory' (1985a, 1988; Sternberg, Wagner, Williams and Horvath, 1995) identifies three forms of intelligence, each being underpinned by 'sub-theories'. The forms were labelled as the componential, experiential and contextual sub-theories, although the American Psychological Association has described them as analytical, creative and experiential reasoning. Analytical intelligence represents internal systems which underlie intelligent functioning. It has three metacomponents involved in problem recognition and solution and knowledge-acquisition, reflecting general mental ability. Individuals who are able to conduct them most rapidly are more intelligent. Creative intelligence concerns the different aspects of experience encountered and how external information interacts with the inner world, and the formulation of new ideas. The experiential aspect relates to practical application, including adaptation, generating new ways of thinking and making choices.

Sternberg conducted research using traditional intelligence tests and developed other measures to support his theory. Put simply, it seems to reflect the views of business people about intelligence. It confuses the concept of intelligence with success in life and work in the US in the late twentieth century and, in addition, combines the research traditions of personality and intelligence.

A Cognitive Psychology Model

Approaches to intelligence based upon factor-analytic research have come to be known as psychometric models. Growth of interest during the late twentieth century in information-processing models of the brain and behaviour from cognitive science has led to some applications of these to understanding intelligence. Developments in IT and artificial intelligence research have led to views of it in terms of information processing, attention and planning, i.e. aspects of cognition. This cognitive psychology model emphasizes biological and physiological processes (Schaie, 1983; Haier, 1991).

Research evidence has demonstrated that some measures of these processes, such as brain size, cognitive task efficiency, perceptual discrimination and response speeds, are likely to be effective in indicating the level of a person's intelligence. Studies have shown a significant correlation between brain size and IQ (Wilson, 1985; McDaniel, 2005). Elementary cognitive tasks, suggested by Jensen (1998), are simple exercises including stimuli discrimination, visual searching and information retrieval, and performance scores on these have also shown significant correlations with test scores. Aleksandr Luria, a Russian psychologist who was interested in neurological functioning, drew a distinction between simultaneous and sequential processing in the brain and suggested that tests could indicate both problems and improve performance in these (Luria, 1973). His ideas have led to new measures of IQ based upon the cognitive psychology model.

Summary

The significance of intelligence amongst ordinary people is reflected in implicit theories, which appear to be influenced by cultural factors. In contrast, researchers in the psychometric tradition have sought to establish explicit theories which are empirical and objective. Despite a long research tradition, there is still no universally accepted definition of intelligence, although a range of theories have been expounded about its nature. Much use has been made of factor analysis in investigation. Using this technique, early models focussed on the identification of general intelligence or 'g', culminating in hierarchical and multifactorial theories of abilities, although Cattell distinguished between fluid and crystallized forms. Attempts to integrate the different findings led to the Cattell-Horn-Carroll theory of cognitive abilities. Since then developments in understanding brain functioning have led to a cognitive psychology approach involving biological and psychophysiological models, whilst some dissatisfaction has resulted in alternative models from Gardner and Sternberg.

The Development of Intelligence Testing

Historically, the oldest assessments of human characteristics have included intelligence tests and they appear to have been used before other kinds of test. From a scientific point of view, intelligence testing relates to attempts to measure and quantify individual differences in cognitive ability through the use of standardized instruments. Now we know the theories about intelligence we may be better placed to understand how such measures came about.

We discussed measures of maximum performance in Chapter 1: they seek to identify the level of knowledge or ability which a person possesses. Most intelligence tests are knowledge or ability-based. The Wechsler Adult Intelligence Scales (WAIS), for example, includes sub-tests made up of knowledge-based items. This means they have item responses which are either correct or incorrect, increase in difficulty, often have time limits and can be totalled, providing unidimensional scales. In designing the scales psychometricians are using the items with a common aim: to identify individual differences derived from common experiences. They assume that, given similar experiences, people having higher intelligence will gain more from them than do others. Therefore, provided tests are reliably, validly and adequately constructed, differences in general mental ability should have a greater impact on scores rather than differences in experiences.

Despite this common aim, test design has not always been the same. Many provide time limits for responses, although some have untimed norms. In some the order of items is mixed, whilst others are grouped as sub-tests. Some have been designed for group administration, while others for individual administration. The aim of group testing has mostly been to predict job or academic performance in a less time-consuming way. Face-to-face administration with individuals usually takes more time and is often used for clinical, educational, forensic or neuropsychological diagnosis, and enables closer examination of characteristics. Some variations of tests have been constructed to assess young children, for example the Wechsler Preschool and Primary Scale of Intelligence, or for people having physical or learning disabilities. Total testing time for the fourth edition of the Stanford-Binet Intelligence Scale amounts to about 75 minutes depending on age and the number of tests administered. As we shall see, the Wechsler and the Stanford-Binet tests seem to have dominated the field.

Early Days

We looked at the life of Francis Galton, his ideas about intelligence and his discoveries in Chapter 1. Sometimes described as the forefather of intelligence testing, he thought that it could be measured directly using biological techniques based upon the senses. The first use of the term 'mental test' came when James McKeen Cattell developed Galton's methodology to include tactile and weight discrimination in his attempt to establish a quantitative approach. At the beginning of the twentieth century new attempts were developed by Binet and Simon with the aim of being able to predict differences in the performance of children. Binet thought that sound judgement, understanding and reasoning, representing higher mental processes, are important and developed measures involving coordination, verbal knowledge, recognition and execution of simple commands (Binet and Simon, 1916). The outcome was a standardized test (Terman and Merrill, 1960) designed to assess reasoning ability and judgement and included:

- Following a lighted match with the eyes
- Shaking hands
- Naming parts of the body
- Counting coins
- Naming objects in a picture
- Recalling digits after being shown a list
- Completing sentences having missing words

The test contained 30 brief tasks which were structured in increasing level of difficulty. The levels were meant to match a specific developmental stage for ages from three to 10 and were used to identify a child's 'mental age', as well as whether a child showed abilities more advanced or backward for the age. By determining the level typical for each age, Binet and Simon enabled age to be a criterion of intelligence, similar to the later evaluation of reading by reading age. Other tests were created for 12- to 15-year-olds and adults, and these were published in 1911. Their work has since been regarded as a milestone. Its adaptation in the US by Terman at Stanford is thought to have had a significant impact. Goddard translated it into English, enabling improvements in reliability and validation by Terman (1925), in addition to the development of the 'intelligence quotient' (IQ) by Stern. Binet found that by administering the test to a child he could compare answers given to those of others and decided on the average age of children having similar abilities, something he called mental age. He also found that a constant ratio was gained if mental age was divided by chronological age and he called this the 'intelligence quotient'. Stern (1965) constructed the IQ scale by multiplying this ratio by 100. Children of mental ages corresponding to their chronological ages, therefore,

Table 7.2   *Calculating IQ from mental and chronological ages*

Mental Age (MA)	Chronological Age (CA)	Ratio (MA ÷ CA)	IQ (Ratio × 100)
7	6	1.17	117
9	10	0.9	90
11	13	0.85	85
13	11	1.18	118
14	14	1.0	100

have IQs of 100. A child of 10 who was as good at the test as one of 12 would have an IQ of 120. It was later found that intelligence shows a normal distribution having a standard deviation of about 17. (See Table 7.2.)

The Stanford-Binet

Binet and Simon's test is widely recognized as the first psychometric assessment. Their tests and the development of it – the Stanford-Binet Intelligence Scale – were used worldwide for some 60 years. The fourth edition was constructed using modern techniques including Item Response Theory and, like the original, was designed to measure intelligence from age two to adulthood. The three categories of verbal reasoning, abstract/visual reasoning and quantitative reasoning, together with four short-term memory tests, make up a total of 15 sub-tests, predominantly measuring crystallized reasoning, apart from the abstract/visual reasoning section. It was standardized on a sample of 5013 people aged between two and 23. Raw scores on each sub-test can be converted to standard age scale scores having a mean of 50 and an SD of 8.0. Scores for the four areas can be combined and converted to a standard age score scale. The fifth edition now covers fluid reasoning, knowledge, quantitative reasoning, visual-spatial processing and working memory, and covers ages from two years upwards.

Alpha and Beta Tests

In 1917 the problems of existing tests were that they had to be given to individuals one at a time, making them time-consuming, and that they were unusable with adults because at age 18 intelligence wasn't linked any more with age. Therefore, candidates had to be assessed one at a time and couldn't be over 17. No one had planned for a big growth of interest in testing, especially by the US Army on entering World War I and having large numbers of adults to test. They wanted to evaluate the intellectual capabilities of soldiers to allocate appropriate tasks and ranks. A committee set up by the APA to help agreed to develop a test for administration to groups. Two were designed, called the Army Alpha and Army Beta tests. The Alpha version was developed for literate groups and the Beta for people who were either illiterate, low literates or could not speak English.

The Alpha test included timed assessment of a range of abilities, focussing on knowledge of both oral and written language, and included being able to follow oral directions correctly, solve arithmetic problems, demonstrate practical judgement, use synonyms and antonyms, complete number series and identify analogies. The Beta test was similar, although being unaffected by knowledge of English. Administration was conducted through the use of hand signals. Tasks included completion of maze and jigsaw-type problems, counting, matching numbers to symbols, and geometrical construction.

Both tests were piloted on a sample of 500 representing a wide range of backgrounds. Development was also based on criteria including the availability for group use, correlation with the Binet scales, ease of scoring, prevention of cheating and objectivity. Their construction led to one of the first mass programmes of testing, amounting to the assessment of 1.75 million people over a period of time, and included conscription into the US military. It all did a lot for public recognition of the benefits of testing, with high sales of what was called the National Intelligence Test after the war years, and boosted the number of people who could undergo assessment at the same time. They became the models for more tests and revisions of them are still used, for example the Beta-III, said by its publisher to be the result of more than 70 years of development (Harcourt Assessment, 2007). Based on a stratified sample of over 1200 people, it is described as a reliable indicator of a person's intellect when verbal skills may have a negative impact on scores.

Wechsler Scales

Binet's IQ scale and the Alpha and Beta scales were major influences upon David Wechsler, a student of Spearman, who created what has become probably the most important, well-known and widely used assessment of intelligence, the Wechsler Adult Intelligence Scale. Published originally in 1939 as the Wechsler-Bellevue Scale and in 1955 as the WAIS, it gradually replaced the Stanford version of Binet's test because it could be used with adults and was validated on large representative samples (Wechsler, 1958). A separate version, known as the Wechsler Intelligence Scale for Children (WISC), was developed for ages from five to 16. Like the Binet tests, they are administered on an individual basis.

Both have been through revisions, the most recent version of the WAIS including 14 sub-tests for different aspects of intelligence split into verbal and non-verbal (performance) scales, shown in Tables 7.3 and 7.4. Each scale includes questions covering all levels from being very easy to very hard. The inclusion of measures of comprehension, knowledge and vocabulary among the verbal sub-tests indicates that to some extent these measure crystallized intelligence. Performance on this scale appears, therefore, to be influenced by education and social class and scores correlate with academic and occupational success. Scores on the performance scale are associated with fluid ability and are less affected by other factors. Both scales, and that of the full-scale IQ, have high reliability coefficients.

Rather than using the IQ calculation developed by Stern, which involved the ages of children, Wechsler calculated IQ scores through the use of between-subject comparisons and the concept of deviation IQ. Standardization using stratified sampling enabled him to compare both individual and combined scores on the sub-tests with mean or typical scores for particular age groups throughout the life span from 16–17 up to those aged 85–89. Using the normal distribution, Wechsler calculated IQ scores on the basis

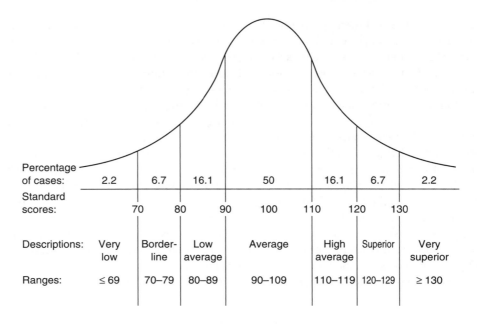

Percentage of cases:	2.2	6.7	16.1	50	16.1	6.7	2.2
Standard scores:		70	80	90 100 110	120	130	
Descriptions:	Very low	Border-line	Low average	Average	High average	Superior	Very superior
Ranges:	≤ 69	70–79	80–89	90–109	110–119	120–129	≥ 130

Figure 7.2   Wechsler's normal distribution

of the actual test score divided by the expected score for age groups and then multiplied the result by 100. This enabled him to transform scores to a standardized form which compared people to means rather than age. Mean scores for all age groups were transformed to an arbitrary value of 100 and all scores were then altered to be around this. Therefore, all final IQ scores depend upon their deviation from this, so the deviation IQ is defined as the extent to which they deviate from it. Using the properties of the normal curve described in Chapter 3, Wechsler had devised a scale having a mean of 100 and an SD of 15.0 so that 68 per cent of scores lie between one SD below the mean and one SD above, i.e. between 85 and 115. In addition, 95 per cent of scores lie within two SDs of the mean, between 70 and 130 on the scale. Use of the standard deviations like this enabled him to construct an effective benchmark for the comparison of people of all ages. The normal distribution for the WAIS-III is shown in Figure 7.2.

After standardized administration of the WAIS, raw scores are converted to standard scores for each sub-test and these are then combined to give index scores for verbal comprehension, perceptual organization, working memory and processing speed, as well as for verbal IQ, performance IQ and the full-scale IQ. These scores can be plotted graphically and subjected to analysis of discrepancies and in terms of strengths and weaknesses to support interpretation. They can also be converted to percentiles with 90 per cent or 95 per cent confidence limits. Its manual also provides qualitative descriptions of IQ score ranges, as shown in Table 7.5, and suggests that both qualitative and quantitative interpretation should take into account measurement error. Table 7.5 also indicates

Table 7.3   *Categorization of WAIS sub-tests*

Verbal	Performance
Vocabulary	Picture completion
Similarities	Digit symbol–coding
Arithmetic	Block design
Digit span	Matrix reasoning
Information	Picture arrangement
Comprehension	Symbol search
Letter–number sequencing	Object assembly

Table 7.4   *Descriptions of WAIS sub-tests*

Picture completion	Asks candidates to identify parts missing from pictures of incomplete objects
Vocabulary	Asks candidates to give definitions for words
Digit symbol–coding	Asks candidates to memorize specific symbols for different numbers and to complete a sequence using them
Similarities	Asks candidates to identify characteristics shared in common by two different objects or concepts
Block design	Assesses the ability to form patterns using cubes of different colours
Arithmetic	Presents candidates with arithmetic problems which they solve mentally and present orally
Matrix reasoning	Presents incomplete patterns which candidates complete by choosing from possible options
Digit span	Candidates repeat a sequence of digits read out by the assessor, both in normal and reverse order
Information	Candidates are asked to answer questions relating to knowledge of common events, objects, places and people
Picture arrangement	Asks candidates to place in logical story order a sequence of cards which have been mixed up
Comprehension	Candidates are asked to explain social rules, concepts or solutions for everyday problems
Symbol search	Candidates are presented with a series of target and search groups and are asked to identify whether either target symbol appears in the search group
Letter–number sequencing	Candidates are presented orally with sequences of letters and numbers which have to be repeated with the numbers in ascending order and the letters in alphabetical order
Object assembly	Asks candidates to assemble parts of common objects, rather like a jigsaw

the percentage included in each range within both the theoretical normal curve and that based upon the standardization sample of 2450. Good training is required for effective administration, scoring and interpretation.

Later additions to this assessment 'stable' have been the Wechsler Preschool and Primary Scale of Intelligence for children aged from two years six months to seven years three months; the Wechsler Abbreviated Scale of Intelligence which is a fast measure for

Table 7.5 *Qualitative descriptions of WAIS full-scale IQ scores*

IQ Score Range	Classification	Percentage included	
		Theoretical normal curve	Actual sample
130 and above	Very superior	2.2	2.1
120–129	Superior	6.7	8.3
110–119	High average	16.1	16.1
90–109	Average	50.0	50.3
80–89	Low average	16.1	14.8
70–79	Borderline	6.7	6.5
69 and below	Extremely low	2.2	1.9

ages six to 89; the Wechsler Individual Achievement Test, measuring language, numerical and reading abilities among children from four to 16 years 11 months; the Wechsler Test of Adult Reading; and the Wechsler Memory Scale. There is also the Wechsler Nonverbal Scale of Ability, for ages two to 21 years 11 months, said to be designed for culturally and linguistically diverse populations. This is designed to give a non-verbal measurement especially for those who are not proficient in English or have other language problems. The Wechsler 'stable' of tests has been revised regularly over the years.

Box 7.1 Assessing Intellectual Functioning

A person's level of intellectual functioning can impact upon behaviour in many ways. When this behaviour suggests difficulties in coping with everyday activities or social problems, the question then arises as to whether the person has a significant learning disability and needs support. This was the case for Mr Peter, a young man who was out of work and lived alone.

Like many other young men, Mr Peter (not his real name) would go out drinking with friends and it was this that led him into trouble through fighting with others. When he appeared before a local court the judge was concerned that he might have learning difficulties. A psychologist was commissioned to investigate his level of intellectual functioning.

The WAIS was used to determine his Full-Scale IQ and investigate aspects of his functioning. IQs 55 to 69 generally indicate a significant learning disability and those below 55 suggest severe learning disability. A person with an IQ of 70 lies at the 2nd percentile, which means that the individual has performed better than 2 per cent of the general population for the age level. Those with learning disabilities, therefore, tend to have IQs which fall in the lower 2 per cent of the population.

Emerson (2001) defines mental retardation as:

characterised by significantly sub-average intellectual functioning (IQ less than 75), existing concurrently with related limitations in two or more of the following applicable adaptive skill areas: communication, self-care, home living, social skills, community use, self-direction, health and safety, functional academics, leisure and work.

The results of the assessments made of Mr Peter were:

	IQ Score	IQ Range (95 per cent)
Verbal IQ	73	69–79
Performance IQ	63	58–72
Full-Scale IQ	66	63–71

The full-scale IQ for Mr Peter, therefore, was at a low level and he would be described as having a significant learning disability. Analysis of the profile of results in the different sub-tests indicated he had a deficit in performance capability, as well as in perceptual organization, working memory and cognitive processing speed. His verbal IQ was higher at 73 and his verbal comprehension index at 78. There were differences between his verbal comprehension and his working memory and processing speed at a .05 significance level, and these suggest he might be viewed as more intelligent than he actually was. Use of a word reading test also demonstrated that he had a reading age of approximately seven years.

These findings were consistent with his educational background. He had attended a language delay unit as a child and was statemented by educational psychologists at primary level. They were also consistent with medical reports.

Box 7.2   Working with Behavioural Problems

Fourteen-year-old Ralph was referred for assessment because he was experiencing a range of emotional and behavioural difficulties. His teachers became increasingly concerned and, following an incident, he was suspended from school. At the child clinic Ralph was assessed using standardized psychometric testing to identify any specific levels of difficulty which might help in planning for his continuing education and support.

He was assessed using the Wechsler Intelligence Scale for Children, which is based on the view that intelligence is not a single ability but an aggregate of a capacity to think, act and deal with events effectively. Its sub-tests are designed to identify different ability areas and these are grouped to identify Verbal or Performance abilities.

Verbal sub-tests assess knowledge about common events, objects and people, understanding of similarities, arithmetic, vocabulary, comprehension and memory. Performance ones include picture completion, linking shapes and numbers, picture arrangement, pattern construction using blocks, object assembly and understanding a maze.

The findings were:

Verbal sub-tests	Standard scores
Information	9
Comprehension	6

(Cont'd)

Arithmetic	8
Vocabulary	5
Similarities	5
Digit span	9

Performance sub-tests

Picture completion	8
Object assembly	6
Block design	8
Symbol search	10
Mazes	8
Coding	8
Picture arrangement	12

Verbal IQ	80
Performance IQ	88
Full Scale IQ	81
Verbal Comprehension (VC)	80
Perceptual Organisation (PO)	89
Freedom from Distractibility (FD)	91
Processing Speed (PS)	94

The results indicated that Ralph had a superior Performance IQ compared to his Verbal IQ, suggesting that he may sometimes appear to be competent although having some misunderstanding of statements and instructions. His highest score was in the picture arrangement sub-test, whilst his scores on similarities and vocabulary were much lower. Therefore verbal comprehension difficulties may have some impact upon his future academic attainment.

He was also tested using the Wechsler Objective Reading Dimensions, the Wechsler Objective Language Dimensions Test and the Wechsler Objective Numerical Dimensions. Ralph had good basic reading ability and an age appropriate level of spelling ability, although assessment indicated a low level of ability in listening and comprehending. His oral expression was also low for his age. His mathematical ability was sound, although absences from school were likely to have reduced this.

Overall, the findings suggested that it was important for Ralph's school attendance to improve so that he continued to improve his skills. His poor listening comprehension, verbal comprehension and oral expression could have a detrimental impact on his behaviour and emotional literacy, especially when he found it hard to understand complex situations involving verbal information, when he needed to understand instructions, or where he had to cope with difficult social interactions. A pressure to communicate effectively may have contributed to his emotional difficulties.

Ralph's teachers were advised to talk clearly and calmly to him, to avoid overloading him with instructions, information or complex emotional responses and to check that he understands situations.

The Problem of Culture

Wechsler provided a compromise between those who saw intelligence as a unified attribute of general intelligence, 'g', and other theorists who believed it was made up of many distinct abilities. However, one problem relates to the sub-tests of vocabulary and general knowledge where tasks are culturally dependent. Intelligence tests have for a long time been accused of having a cultural bias in favour of middle-class Western societies. Because of this a number of test-makers have tried to create tests which are 'culture-free', i.e. independent of cultural influences. But efforts to do this came to nothing and it was realized there could be no complete success in creating culture-free tests. As a result the aim was modified to the design of tests which are 'culture-fair'. This meant that items possessing particular characteristics of language or other culturally influenced aspects could not be included.

One of the first tests to meet the criteria was the Goodenough Harris Drawing Test (Goodenough, 1926; Harris, 1963) which asks individuals to complete the task of drawing a human figure. Ignoring any artistic merit, it is scored for body and clothing details, correct proportions among body parts, and other features. Being untimed, it has norms for children aged from three to 15 and scores can be converted to standard scores and percentiles.

Another culture-fair test is Raven's Progressive Matrices (Raven, 1965). This was developed by John Raven (1938), who sought to test the abstract ability inherent in Spearman's 'g' in a way which would be free from cultural influences and from language. He aimed to minimize both through a focus upon non-verbal tasks measuring abstract reasoning and it is, therefore, more a measure of fluid intelligence. This makes it useful in assessment of people having different backgrounds, although it is less predictive of academic success than a crystallized intelligence measure would be. Its advantage is that it may identify those whose attainments don't reflect true ability. The resulting test series – the Standard, Coloured and Advanced Progressive Matrices – can be used for ages from six to 80. The Coloured version was developed for use with children and older people, while parallel versions were designed to thwart attempts to memorize answers. The Advanced version caters for higher ability groups. A newer version, the Progressive Matrices Plus, provides more questions at the higher end of the standard ability range. The tests can be administered on either an individual or a group basis. They have a long history of use in the educational world, in clinical and other settings.

In the Matrices candidates are provided with a matrix of patterns in which one pattern is absent. Each item tests the ability to identify relationships among patterns and to reason by comparison of them, regardless of language. The patterns involve relationship rules and abstract reasoning is needed to identify them and choose a correct option. The total number of correct items is transformed to an overall IQ score based on the deviation from standardized norms. Normative data is available for both timed and untimed administrations. The result is what is generally regarded as a good, quick measure of 'g' (Jensen, 1998). The Mill Hill Vocabulary Scale, a measure of verbal ability, is often used alongside the Progressive Matrices.

The Alice Heim Series

Some tests have been designed especially for educational and occupational settings, often assessing general, verbal and spatial intelligence, for example the AH4 and AH5 Series developed by Alice Heim and colleagues at Cambridge (Heim, Watts and Simmonds, 1970). These relate well to the crystallized and fluid factors. The basic version is the AH4, designed for the general population, providing both verbal/numerical scores and abstract reasoning scores. The AH5 was designed on a similar basis although being aimed at a higher ability range. The AH6 is similar again, although being aimed at an even higher level. Another widely used example is the Watson-Glaser Critical Thinking Appraisal (Watson and Glaser, 1964). As a measure of crystallized ability, with a substantial verbal component, it is commonly used to assess ability to make sound judgements in higher-level work. An overall score is gained from performance on five sub-tests.

Later Developments

The influence of test publishers on the Cattell-Horn-Carroll theory of cognitive abilities and their involvement with Richard Woodcock led to a new suite of intelligence tests known as the Woodcock-Johnson Psychoeducational Battery (Woodcock and Johnson, 1978). This contains 21 separate measures and can be used to assess cognitive ability from two years onwards.

Sternberg thought traditional tests provided competent measures of abstract reasoning but that they did not adequately measure practical problem-solving and reasoning (Sternberg et al., 1995). He sought to assess his 'contextual subtheory' through the use of a concept which he called 'tacit knowledge'. This was defined as action-oriented knowledge, based upon understanding procedures rather than facts. Its assessment is related to organizational environments, such as in evaluating job performance, and is designed for understanding intelligence levels in specific areas of work. His approach, therefore, contrasts with other IQ tests which were designed for broader use across populations.

Cognitive and Clinical Approaches

Measures based upon the cognitive psychology approach involving biological and psychophysiological models have been developed by J.P. Das and colleagues (Das, Kirby and Jarman, 1979; Naglieri and Das, 1997), as well as by Alan and Naneen Kaufman (Kaufman and Kaufman, 2001). Das' work was inspired by the ideas of Luria (1973), resulting in the Cognitive Assessment System (CAS), designed for children and adolescents aged from five to 17. It assesses how knowledge is accessed and organized within a person's memory system and how a number of tasks are performed. An IQ score is derived from the 'PASS' system – planning, attention, simultaneous and successive – based on Luria's theory of the cognitive activity of the brain:

- Planning involves strategies used to solve a problem or reach a goal. It is evaluated by asking the individual to generate an approach to solving a particular task.

- Attention is associated with alertness or awareness. Tasks involve the person selecting one aspect and ignoring another relating to a stimulus.
- Simultaneous processes indicate an ability to perceive associations and to integrate information.
- Successive processes indicate the capability to place events in order.

The assessment system enables testers to identify discrepancies between ability and achievement and also to evaluate any potential attention deficits and hyperactivity disorders, learning disabilities, giftedness and brain injuries.

The Kaufmans took their ideas from both Luria and the Cattell-Horn-Carroll approach, combining both cognitive and neuropsychological research, to construct a range of ability tests. These include the Kaufman Assessment Battery for Children, the Kaufman Brief Intelligence Test, and the Kaufman Adolescent and Adult Intelligence Test. They assess three facets of intelligence, including simultaneous and sequential processing tasks, as in PASS, but also that of achievement through assessment of acquired knowledge, such as in reading and arithmetic. One of their aims has been to create tests which can help children through an understanding of their cognitive processes and which are not influenced by cultural factors related to learning.

In the clinical field tests have been developed to evaluate the cognitive abilities of adults with neurological impairments, such as the Cognitive Assessment of Minnesota. Other measures available for children include the Cognitive Abilities Test, which tests verbal, non-verbal and numerical reasoning from age 7 years 6 months to 17, and the British Ability Scales, evaluating cognitive functioning and crystallized intelligence from 2 years 6 months to 17 years 11 months (Elliot, 1983).

Thus it can be seen that although broader measures of intelligence are still available, there has been a progressive demand for some specialization over the years in more specific areas of applied psychology. While some people might deplore the commercialization of testing, a wide range of tests of general mental ability has probably enabled applied practitioners to conduct more effective assessments.

Summary

Attempts to measure intelligence originated with Galton and have expanded substantially since then. The first test was created by Binet and the concept of IQ was developed by Stern. Their work led to the Stanford-Binet Intelligence Scale and, following this, the US Army Alpha and Beta tests. Raven's non-verbal measure of 'g' – the Progressive Matrices – was published in 1938. In 1939 Wechsler published the first of his tests and went on to introduce the well-known Wechsler Adult Intelligence Scale and the Wechsler Intelligence Scale for Children. His efforts included a new method of calculating IQ through the use of standard deviations. Later tests acknowledged the work of Luria in understanding neurological functioning and include Das and Naglieri's Cognitive Assessment System, as well as the ability tests developed by the Kaufmans.

Issues about Intelligence

The Nature–Nurture Debate

The finding that some people perform better than others on IQ tests does not give us an answer to the question: Why are some people cleverer than others? There has been debate about whether the answer lies within our genes, i.e. that intelligence is biologically determined, or is linked to personal and environmental experiences. The first view is focussed on the genotype, which is our inherited genetic code made up of genes. Our genotype lays the foundation for our phenotype, its outward expression in physical appearance and traits, what we are and what we do. Some have said these are wholly determined by genes (our nature); others have said it is decided by environment and experiences (our nurture). Hence the term: the nature versus nurture debate.

Behavioural genetics is the study of their relationship and whether either plays a greater role in creating differences. There are about 30,000 genes providing three billion DNA letters in the human genome, making any understanding of it rather complex. Three main types of investigation have been used to analyse the relationship: family studies, twin studies and adoption studies (Plomin, 2004). Family studies have looked at the average IQ correlations between members of the same family (Neisser et al., 1996). This doesn't tell us much because children share an estimated average of 50 per cent of their genes with each parent and with each sibling, and because some similarities could be caused by environmental factors. It helps instead to investigate families which don't share genes like this. More important have been twin studies. When a mother's egg is fertilized and separates, forming two foetuses, they are referred to as monozygotic (MZ) twins. Their genetic make-up is identical. Dizygotic (DZ) twins are formed when two fertilized eggs develop at the same time. In this case they share an estimated average of 50 per cent of their genetic make-up. It is possible then to contrast non-twins and the two kinds of twins to investigate the relative impact of genes. Adoption studies have also been used. In this case there is no genetic inheritance from parents. The influence of genes and environment can be investigated when twins are reared apart. A review of both twin and adoption studies has been conducted (Ridley, 1999). (See Figure 7.3.)

Evaluation of genetic heritability can be made by examination of results from the three approaches using intelligence measures. This is determined by considering the difference between parents and children reflected in the percentage proportion of the shared variance of intelligence. When a parent and child are alike the proportion of shared variance is closer to 100 per cent; when they are different the proportion is closer to zero. Average heritability can be estimated for different populations and provides an estimate of the proportion of variance in intelligence accounted for by genetic factors. The heritability index (h^2) is defined as the ratio of test score variance due to heredity to score variance due to both heredity and environment.

The results of such studies have tended not to produce consistent results. Early work led to misinterpretation, for example when Eysenck made an estimation of heritability at about 69 per cent in the general population (Eysenck, 1979). Most estimates vary

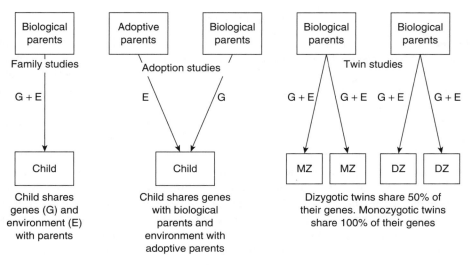

Figure 7.3 Differences between family, adoption and twin studies

from about 40 per cent to 80 per cent. Lowest correlations have been found between adoptive parents and children (.02). Those between MZ twins reared together have been as high as .85. Scores of MZ twins separated at birth and placed in different families, i.e. not having similar environments, give estimates of .76. Adopted-apart siblings, sharing half the number of genes compared to MZ twins, were a lot less similar (.24).

The picture involved is not clear, therefore, for example because some genes are dominant whilst others are recessive and they interact. There are also difficulties arising from how representative studies are. Other factors involve the parents. People find others who are similar to themselves, such as in intelligence, to be more attractive and are more likely to mate. This can have an impact on estimates of heritability, too (Mackintosh, 1998). Known as assortative mating, it indicates selection of partners on a non-random basis. What's more, considering that IQ is measured using IQ tests, it is likely that measurement factors need to be taken into account. What about the Standard Error of Measurement, for example, discussed in Chapter 5? A number of test error sources might be involved.

Any account of environmental influences could go on forever. Aspects of these vary enormously from the obvious, such as poverty, to the obscure, like the influence of TV. Any list includes the extent to which a child watches television and factors like birth weight, height, schooling, economic status and education – Bouchard and Segal (1985) provide a list. Such factors might broadly be categorized into biology, family, education and culture and some aspects of them are more difficult to recognize than others. We cannot be clear about their effects and interactions. What we can say is that no one has identified a specific gene for intelligence. Intelligence appears to be polygenic, i.e. linked to the interaction of many minor genes rather than a single major one. Genes play a significant role through our traits in determining and adapting environments and, therefore, it is difficult to separate nature and nurture.

Ideology and Intelligence

Development of methods of assessing intelligence has always been associated with eugenics. Eugenicists believe intelligence and moral superiority can be improved by selection. Galton supported their ideology and suggested that artificial methods could be used to increase intelligence in society (Galton, 1875). For one modern view of eugenics see Lynn (2001). During the early twentieth century a number of eugenicists sought to impose laws to enforce sterilization and people described as 'feeble-minded' were thought to constitute a large proportion of criminal offenders (Zeleny, 1933).

Galton's ideas were supported by Terman (1925) in the US, who said poor intelligence existed among some ethnic groups and that this was inherited. A Bill there was proposed in 1922 by H. H. Laughlin to enforce sterilization among people of low intelligence, the insane, the criminal, the epileptic, the blind, deformed and the dependent, such as homeless people and orphans. Together with some other countries, the US instigated a programme encompassing methods to encourage varying birth rates among different groups using birth control, enforced sterilization, marriage regulations and immigration controls. IQ tests such as the Alpha and Beta tests were used to identify people having low intelligence. With the rise to power of the Nazis eugenics became the centre of attention in Germany. In 1933 they enacted a law founded upon Laughlin's proposal, leading to sterilization of 'mentally retarded' people. The Holocaust was then designed to exterminate groups including Jews, Communists, homosexuals, the mentally ill and disabled, as well as political activists, members of the clergy and criminals.

It's not surprising, therefore, that after World War II there was wide condemnation of the movement and countries disbanded their programmes. The intelligence testing movement and psychometrics were also criticized, being seen by some people as having provided a basis for events. But interest in eugenics did not disappear. In 1960 it was reported that, on a group basis, white people were superior to those who are black in a number of ways, including intelligence. Some psychologists, including Jensen (1973) and Eysenck (1973), said differences were due to genetics, though others attributed them to cultural variations. A debate ensued in which people, led by Kamin (1974), criticized Jensen and Eysenck's studies and the ideology of intelligence testing. The row led to court cases in the US over the issue of bias in testing.

Psychometrics fell into disrepute, although the issue of racial differences did not disappear. In 1994 two US authors, Herrnstein and Murray, published a book – *The Bell Curve: Intelligence and Class Structure in American Life* – based upon a frequency distribution of IQ test scores, in which they predicted the formation of a class system with people having higher IQs at the apex. Intelligence, they said, was more important than socioeconomic status. They claimed that white Americans had a mean score on the WAIS which was 15 points higher than those who were black. On the Stanford-Binet the gap was greater, at 18 points. Their conclusions implied that groups having lower levels of intelligence were potentially lowering average IQ and causing social problems. The book got a lot of supportive publicity, as well as criticism that its conclusions were wrong. The APA accepted there were differences but the gaps, they said, could be a result of cultural differences.

Substantial criticisms of Herrnstein and Murray's book followed. These are reviewed thoroughly in Maltby, Day and Macaskill (2007), although aspects concerning measurement are important here. Its authors were said to have assumed there is such a thing as a general factor of intelligence on which human beings differ. This is debatable, as we have seen. They also assumed that IQ tests measure it accurately, which is also arguable. They were said to base their arguments on psychometric IQ test scores, although measures can be distinguished in terms of differing approaches, not all of which are psychometric. Other assumptions included statements that IQ scores are stable over time and are heritable. Kamin's criticisms (1995; Kamin and Goldberger, 2002) focussed on statistical thinking and research evidence, and a major point he raised is that they misuse correlation. For example, he says, they consider both IQ scores and socioeconomic status as causal variables of future economic and social welfare among groups. They had combined flawed statistical thinking with impaired evidence from a number of sources.

The Flynn Effect

One of the most striking events in the history of intelligence has been the discovery of the Flynn effect. This suggests intelligence increases in each generation. The key questions are: How did the discovery come about? Is it true? If it is, what is the cause? The story began about 1987 when James Flynn reported his findings (Flynn, 1999). Scores on tests can fluctuate, but they suggested there is a regular fluctuation over time worldwide. If intelligence is rising it poses a problem for eugenicists who say it is at risk of declining because lower IQ people have more children, making higher intelligence rarer.

There are two possible sources for the discovery. One is that large organizations regularly assess the mental capabilities of job applicants. Another is that publishers need to update their norms, especially when they construct newer versions of a test. In 1981 Flynn began looking at manuals of tests like the WAIS and the Stanford-Binet and spotted that often when a group was given both a revised test and the older version they always obtained higher scores on the new one (Flynn, 1987). For example, he found that if a group got an average IQ of 100 on the 1972 version of the WISC, they averaged 108 on the 1947/48 version. This means that, although being average on the later test, they were above average compared to others in 1947/48. The group was establishing higher standards for the average over time.

Flynn found that, based on 1932–1978 results, the population of white Americans had gained 14 points, averaging .3 points a year. His report included data from 14 countries, combining large sets from military organizations. In 1994 he included data from 20 countries (Flynn, 1994). He demonstrated that IQ scores showed generational rises of about 15 points every 50 years and were rising every year in a number of countries. Highest increases were in non-verbal performance, measuring fluid intelligence, and the lowest were linked to crystallized intelligence. More research confirmed this, with Flynn concluding that fluid intelligence rises about 15 points per generation on average, and crystallized tests about nine points per generation.

Why it should happen is complex, with a range of views leading to more research. Improvements in education and access to knowledge may have caused it, although these are partially cultural and do not explain a worldwide increase. Flynn discounted the idea that generations are becoming more intelligent on the grounds that this would mean a lot more geniuses. Rather than intelligence, he thought abstract ability was increasing and environmental factors were enhancing scores (Flynn, 1994, 1999). A number of hypotheses link environmental issues to the effect (Neisser, 1998). These include length of time at school, test sophistication and early mental stimulation, although they don't provide adequate explanation (McKey et al., 1985). The cognitive stimulation hypothesis links the effect to visual media and IT, but there is no research evidence to support this. Lynn (1990) suggests it is related to nutrition and some studies support this view, especially in relation to breast-feeding and vitamin/mineral supplements (Smith, Durkin, Hinton, Bellinger and Kuhn, 2003; Oddy et al., 2004). Others have disagreed (Crombie et al., 1990; Schoenthaler, Bier, Young, Nichols and Jansenns, 2000). Nutrition forms just one part of a supportive environment.

Two studies suggest the effect could be at an end or in reverse. One was in Norway where scores were discovered to have stopped increasing (Sundet, Barlaug and Torjussen, 2004) and the other in Denmark (Teasdale and Owen, 2005). So there is no firm conclusion. Some researchers are convinced the Flynn effect exists, others are doubtful. And there is no clear evidence of what causes it. There is much more research to be done.

Summary

Behavioural genetics is the study of the role of nature and nurture in creating individual differences. The extent to which intelligence is genetically inherited on average across the population is referred to as its heritability. Evaluation of this has included family, twin and adoption studies and estimates vary considerably. It has been found difficult to separate the influence of nature and nurture on human intelligence. The field of eugenics has emphasized the influence of genetic heritability and is concerned with a selection process for humankind intended to create children of superior intelligence. Debate about this was generated by Herrnstein and Murray's 1994 book in which they discussed the relationship between race and IQ in pessimistic terms. Debate has also arisen over the Flynn effect which suggests there is a sustained annual increase in intelligence throughout the world. Potential explanations have included education, test sophistication, parental practices and nutrition as causal factors.

Measurement of Abilities and Aptitudes

As a result of the debates about IQ it has often been unfashionable. This might explain why the terms ability or aptitude have been more socially acceptable. A person's abilities, originating in hierarchical models of intelligence, seem to be of more practical use. More specific abilities may be of greater importance, especially in applied areas of

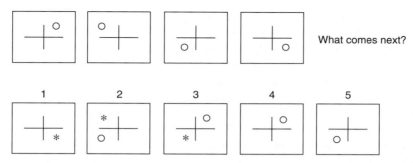

Figure 7.4   An abstract reasoning test item

practice. It is more acceptable to think of a profile of abilities in which any one individual can score highly on some whilst doing less well on others: every person will have strengths and weaknesses. Higher-level abilities can be seen as abstractions from more specific underlying abilities and aptitudes. Fleishman separated abilities into four categories: cognitive, psychomotor, perceptual and physical (Fleishman and Quaintance, 1984; Fleishman and Reilly, 1991) and most research has revolved around cognitive ability tests because of their stronger relationship with performance. The nature of psychomotor ability has been subject to much debate (Carretta and Ree, 1997, 2000).

Ability tests are used to measure a person's potential and to predict future performance. In contrast, attainment tests assess present performance, focussing on capability at the time of testing. The distinction with aptitude tests is not always clear and can be arguable. Ability is often assumed to underlie aptitude, describing the degree to which a person can carry out a mental operation, the general reasoning involved. Aptitude tests, having a narrower focus, determine the likelihood that a person can learn a specific skill and often involve the name of a type of work, such as clerical filing, technical checking or manual dexterity. But ability and aptitude test scores are occasionally linked to educational attainment, for example a person will need to have sufficient skills to read tests. The exception is an abstract/spatial reasoning test where there may be little or no reading. (See Figure 7.4.)

To obtain an overall picture of a person's abilities, we need to assess a range of them as well as, depending on the type of performance involved, the level of general intelligence. The overlap with this can be quite high, for example tests of numerical reasoning tend also to be good measures of it. To understand the range of tests available today, it helps to see abilities as part of a continuous spectrum representing Cattell's separation of general mental ability (Cattell, 1987; Stankov et al., 1995):

CRYSTALLIZED ABILITY ◄·····················► **FLUID ABILITY**

(Most dependent on direct
experience and learning)

(Reflects a more general
ability to adapt or
transfer experience to
new problems)

As with intelligence, both culture and background appear to have an influence in determining which abilities are important. Different cultures will emphasize different types, as we saw earlier. The quality of crystallized ability is also a function of an individual's fluid ability. Because of its nature, a high level of fluid ability will have a more direct impact on abstract reasoning scores. Tests of abstract reasoning often involve making decisions about shapes or configurations of lines, as in IQ tests. There is an emphasis, therefore, upon reasoning and we often speak of verbal reasoning and numerical reasoning.

In general terms ability tests range from abstract concepts, such as verbal fluency, spatial orientation and numerical reasoning, to the practical, such as clerical speed or computer programming. They are usually timed so that response speed is involved. They can be defined in terms of:

- An ability domain – this represents the 'language' used, for example in terms of spatial, numerical or verbal thinking;
- A set of mental operations – the manipulations or tasks set for candidates;
- The level of difficulty, i.e. the degree of ability required.

General ability tests are broader and will sample from more than one domain, usually verbal and numerical, often spatial as well, whilst specific tests will sample items from a single domain, often from a restricted area, for example in higher level numerical and verbal critical reasoning tests. Critical reasoning tests will often present candidates with a passage of information or data, and then ask questions about it. There exists quite a wide range of these as they are a standard product for the selection of graduates or managers. Some researchers think that most measure more than a single ability and, therefore, are not unidimensional (Ree and Carretta, 1997, 1998).

A range of different approaches is also available in ability testing, including:

- 'Paper-and-pencil' testing (the most common approach),
- Apparatus tests (such as for speed of movement or precision), and
- Computerized tests (increasingly offered by publishers).

Work-sample tests are often also used in occupational assessment and simulate an important part of a job. These are basically attainment tests which sample aspects of a job, being often based upon experience, for example in a test of typing skills. The popular in-tray exercise is a work-sample test. Similarly, job simulation exercises are used in assessment centres where they simulate the demands of a job. They are designed to quantify part of the job in an objective way.

Ability testing can often be considered in terms of how we might want to take a picture of a person with a camera. A wide angle view will provide a general impression, giving a broad global understanding. Or we can zoom in to gain more detail, although losing sight of the complete picture. General ability tests such as the Alice Heim Series or Raven's Matrices give bigger views, allowing us to have a lot more information. Specific ability tests, such as those which combine to make up the General Ability

Tests (GAT), provide a close-up set of pictures. GAT includes tests of verbal, spatial, abstract and numerical reasoning. Other general ability tests are the General Reasoning Test (GRT) or the Graduate and Managerial Assessment (GMA) test. They can be used separately to look at specific abilities or in combination to give a bigger picture.

Multiple aptitude batteries, reflecting the hierarchical structures of Burt (1949) and Vernon (1950, 1969), have been popular. Cattell (1971) and Horn (1978) also proposed hierarchical models, although they didn't put 'g' at the top. But most of the variance of a battery is due to 'g' (Jensen, 1998) and the largest proportion of variance accounted for by a single ability is about 8 per cent (Ree and Carretta, 1994; Carretta and Ree, 1996). Schmidt, Ones and Hunter (1992) suggest that evidence for the incremental validity of specific abilities over the GMA is poor. Examples of batteries are the General Aptitude Test Battery, which includes tests of general ability, clerical perception, motor coordination and manual dexterity, and the Differential Aptitude Test Battery.

Utility Analysis

There has been a progressive recognition of testing in commerce and industry since World War II and tests are now widely used, with a large and competitive market for them. Their value lies in the fact that, used appropriately, they provide an objective assessment and can compare people on the same basis. Evidence is clear that a good test provides a better predictor of performance than other methods such as interviews.

Being able to estimate their quantitative financial value in selection can boost their advantages in the eyes of business (Boudreau, 1989) and there are a number of ways of doing this. One of the simplest is given by the equation:

Average Gain = validity (r) × average test score (z) × SDy

Where r = the validity coefficient of the test; Average test score = the average standard (z) score of candidates; and SDy = the standard deviation of employees' annual job performance in £'s.

For example where r = .6, z = 2 and SDy = 90 000 sterling, then:
The average gain = .6 × 2 × 90,000 = 108,000 (sterling) per candidate

The equation helps us to understand the factors involved in identifying the advantages of using selection tests. Obviously, the validity coefficient is important because it shows the extent to which performance on a test is linked to that in a job.

Summary

Abilities and aptitudes originated in hierarchical models of intelligence. They can be used to measure a person's potential and predict performance. Ability describes the degree to which a person can carry out a mental operation, the general reasoning skills involved, whilst aptitude tests measure mental operations affecting the likelihood of a person being able to learn a skill. Together, they can provide an overall picture of a person's capabilities. Ability can be defined in terms of a domain – the form of reasoning applied – as well as mental operations and the level of difficulty. Utility analysis can be used to evaluate the benefits of testing in the workplace.

What Have We Discovered About Measuring Intelligence and Ability?

In this chapter we have looked at intelligence, how psychologists have tried to define it and how they have theorized, researched and disagreed about it. The outcomes have had an impact on measures of intelligence. We have also reviewed the issues arising, including the nature–nurture debate, the controversies about eugenics, and the Flynn effect. We have looked at ability and aptitude testing, what these measure, how they differ and are used in the modern world. We have learned:

- About the difficulties involved in trying to define intelligence and the differences between implicit and explicit views.
- The origins of intelligence and IQ testing, and the different theories, including the theory of 'g', hierarchical and psychometric theories, multifactor and cognitive theories, the theory of multiple intelligences and triarchic theory.
- About major attempts to measure intelligence which continue to be widely used, such as the Wechsler tests, Raven's Matrices and the Cognitive Assessment System, and their important features.
- About important issues, such as the genetic heritability of intelligence, eugenics and the Flynn effect.
- About abilities and aptitudes, what they are and how they are used.

8

The Assessment and Measurement of Personality

Learning Objectives

By the end of this chapter you should be able to:

- Distinguish between subjective and scientific views of personality, as well as between situational and dispositional approaches.
- Describe how psychologists have sought to define personality and how it is distinguished from other attributes, such as attitudes, interests, values and motivation.
- Describe and evaluate differing theoretical approaches to understanding human personality and how these link with assessment.
- Evaluate critically the use of personality questionnaires, the issues involved and their limitations.

What is This Chapter About?

Whatever you call it, it's about power and money. It has been known by a number of aliases such as nature, temperament, disposition, character and even charisma. Here we call it personality. Knowing about it well gives power over others through being able to predict or manipulate their behaviour. That power might lead to wealth, especially by selling such knowledge to others who want to use it, too, for their own ends. This explains the proliferation of books about it. Construct a popular questionnaire and this, too, might make you rich. As with intelligence, any science of personality needs to be clear about what we mean by it, how it is distinguished from other constructs, and how we might assess it. We also need to be clear about the theories underlying assessment methods. Theory and assessment always work hand-in-hand. We will lastly consider the use of questionnaires to describe personality characteristics, the issues involved and their limitations.

The Concept of Personality

We all have a natural curiosity about why people behave as they do. Differences in behaviour have always grabbed attention and have led to many attempts to model it, some more scientific than others. Perceptions of specific behaviours thought to be consistent have led to a vast accumulation of words representing characteristics, as any dictionary will demonstrate. So psychology doesn't really own the phenomenon of personality, for example famous writers have been rewarded for their ability to create characters in a psychologically meaningful way. Thinking and theorizing have gone on for a long time and appear to be natural tendencies amongst just about everyone. Consequently, there have been many different approaches among both psychologists and non-psychologists.

Personality is a concept used in daily life because of the judgements we form, consciously or not, about others. Often, when the word 'personality' is used by people, it refers to a global implicit judgement made up of all the impressions and feelings created by someone. When people tend to react to situations in a fairly consistent manner, this will be observed by the typical non-psychologist. But any everyday assessment is bound to be subjective and associated with personal meanings and impressions. People often tend to muddle up different aspects, like affiliation with others and self-confidence. As with intelligence, the 'pet' theories people have are called implicit personality theories (Bruner and Tagiuri, 1954). They proliferate because everyone has got one and are overwhelmingly based on superficial, casual and chance observations. Because of this there is often a focus upon the most noticeable characteristics. People talk of someone having 'lots of personality' or 'no personality' or 'a strong personality', referring probably to social competence and popularity. Someone might be 'a personality' or even 'a big personality'. People use broad generalizations and stereotypes.

Once again, we need to be scientific, to use empirical methods and to be explicit. Research into personality focuses on objective descriptions. To understand a person we need to know more, for example, about behavioural style, intellectual functioning, motives, attitudes, beliefs and values, as well as how these are organized. Personality combines with them all to construct the outward manifestation of someone. Any scientific approach needs to be both more comprehensive and precise.

As we saw in Chapter 1, there is a distinction between relatively enduring or more stable characteristics – known as traits – which can predict behaviour (McCrae and Costa, 1990) and other more transient emotional responses or moods called states (McConville and Cooper, 1992). A sudden experience of fear will pass with time, being a state. But if it persists it can become a trait, as with a timid person. The distinction isn't absolute, though traits are always long term, making them difficult to change. They represent

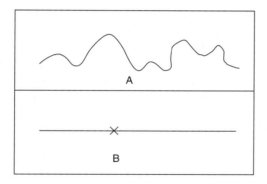

Figure 8.1   The situational view (A) sees personality as being inconsistent, while the dispositional approach (B) sees it as being consistent and unchanging on a trait continuum

implied associations between observed behaviour and inner tendencies to act in certain ways. In psychometrics the focus is upon precise, objective measurement. Traits like emotional stability or impulsiveness can be measured in populations and their mean levels calculated, enabling normative assessment on reliable and valid scales.

Situational and Dispositional Approaches

Some social psychologists have argued that personality doesn't exist. They say people change their behaviour across situations and over time, demonstrating no consistency, an approach called situationalism (Mischel, 1968, 2004; Wright and Mischel, 1987). The counter-argument suggests there is behavioural change, but that this can be accommodated in the way we measure characteristics. Change will depend on events, for example there are 'strong' situations having a big impact, whilst there are 'weak' ones having little effect. People adapt their behaviour to fit. Strong situations generally occur less often than weak ones. Even in occasional highly structured situations where behaviour is constrained, people still demonstrate some aspect of their personality, even if only in a cautious way such as a sly 'wink'.

Studies show people do behave consistently across different events, with most correlations being above 0.7 and others above 0.3 (Small, Zeldin and Savin-Williams, 1983). A number of characteristics have also been shown to remain largely invariable after the age of 30. So the evidence is that personality does exist. This counter-argument is sometimes called the dispositional approach, and it views personality through consistent and unchanging dispositions, regardless of circumstances. (See Figure 8.1.)

How Do We Define Personality?

With difficulty! Trouble is that there has been a multitude of definitions. It was once said there are as many definitions as there are theorists, which makes for a lot. So there is no easily identifiable common approach. From ancient times thinkers have attempted to identify the main factors by which people differ and to create some form of classification, and yet there is still no agreement. Perhaps the problem is that personality is a concept which is broad and nebulous, making it difficult to define succinctly. What doesn't help either is that definitions are mostly based on differing theories. The fact remains that how we define a concept plays a crucial role in how we investigate it, making this an important matter. A simple definition might be 'personality is something which makes everyone either similar or different to others'. But this could equally be said of other traits such as intelligence and doesn't explain enough to make it satisfactory.

Gordon Allport defined personality in 1937 as 'the dynamic organization within the individual of those psychophysical systems that determine a unique adjustment to the environment'. In 1961 he again defined it, this time as 'the dynamic organization inside the person of psychophysical systems that determine the person's characteristic patterns of behaviour and thought'. His definitions have been the most quoted. There are a multitude of other attempts, too, and the most common references are to:

- A style or mode of behaviour
- Relatively stable or enduring characteristics enabling prediction
- Uniqueness
- Adaptation or adjustment to the environment
- Characteristic patterns of behaviour, thinking and feelings

There has often been reference to personality as arising from a combination of relatively enduring dimensions of individual differences, which means that other characteristics, such as intelligence and cognitive abilities, motives, values and attitudes, also have to be considered (Carver and Scheier, 2000). The reason for this is that some theorists have tried to study it from a holistic point of view. Personality thus becomes a unique combination of cognitive and affective characteristics which make up a relatively consistent behavioural pattern. However they define it, theorists generally say that any significant behaviour should distinguish one person from others and be consistent over situations and time. Most would probably subscribe to the following as a broad definition:

> The characteristic, stable patterns of behaviour and modes of thinking and feeling that determine a person's unique way of adjusting to the environment

The only problem is that we might include within this definition some other aspects which we want to assess. So how do we distinguish between personality and other attributes, such as attitudes, values and motivation?

Making Distinctions

(a) Attitudes
We looked at attitudes in Chapter 2. Allport's definition of an attitude was quoted there: 'An attitude is a mental and neural state of readiness, organized through experience, exerting a directive or dynamic influence upon the individual's response to all objects and

situations with which it is related' (Allport, 1937, 1961). So it's a learned disposition to respond positively or negatively to any person, object, issue or event. Some psychologists have viewed it in terms of a tendency to evaluate a stimulus with a degree of favour or disfavour, and this tendency may be reflected in thoughts, feelings or behaviour (Ajzen and Fishbein, 2000). The common view is that it is a predisposition to behave in a particular way.

(b) Interests

These are thought to be a sub-set of a person's attitudes relating to the evaluation of personal beliefs. If we have a particular belief and feel positive about it, then we are more likely to want to do more or think more about that belief.

(c) Values

Values relate to the usefulness, importance or worth we attach to either activities or objects and to how people should behave, and can be linked to our interests and attitudes. We define values as the ultimately desirable goals or end states, called terminal values, about which we have strong feelings (Locke, 1976). We are thought to strive towards our values and to use them as a means of judging our actions and those of others.

(d) Motivation

Motivation is a characteristic made up of our needs, interests and aspirations. This focuses upon what drives us to do some things but not others, i.e. our driving force, its direction and our persistence.

Summary

Despite the views of 'situationalist' psychologists, who see personality as being ever-changing, researchers in psychometrics have taken a dispositional approach which views it as being made up of consistent trait-based internal characteristics. Many attempts have been made to define personality, most notably Allport, and the most common aspects refer to relatively stable characteristics involving patterns of behaviour, thoughts and feelings. It has also been distinguished from other related attributes such as attitudes, values and motivation.

Theories of Personality

There have been a number of contrasting approaches to understanding this elusive concept. Not all theories embrace the same subject matter, viewing it instead in widely disparate ways, and this has had a big impact on assessment measures. Personality is a complex concept and can be conceptualized in many ways. It is not fixed and is influenced by factors both internal and external to any individual. Unsurprisingly, therefore, different ways of modelling and theorizing about it have emerged. No one single theory encompasses everything. Methods of investigation have also varied widely, too.

Another important reason for the differences relates to how individuals or schools of thought have been limited by knowledge and understanding at the time of their thinking. Therefore, theories have their origins in different paradigms, i.e. alternative assumptions and patterns of thinking relevant at the time. There is a common aim, however, to develop a model providing a systematic account of the unique personality structure shared by people. Through this, theorists hope to generate a way of understanding individuals. Some theories have a greater focus on assessment than others, for example psychometric and type approaches have used questionnaires, while social and behavioural ones use rating scales.

As usual, it helps to classify theories, but some issues make this difficult. We could classify them in terms of whether a scientific approach has been used, whether they make use of personality 'types' or not, or whether they link personality to biology or other aspects of the body. Alternatively, we could distinguish them on the basis of how they see people, either as unique individuals or from an individual differences viewpoint. This means that, before discussing theories, we need firstly to clarify two issues:

(a) Types versus Traits

It has always been natural for people to think about personality 'types' and to stereotype others. Doing this makes it easier to cope with a complex social world through labelling, like the 'bookish' or 'bossy' types. Being a 'leader' or 'charismatic' are also types. The simplest appears to have arisen in modern times: that which distinguishes 'winners' from 'losers'. Most non-psychologists are type rather than trait theorists.

Types can be seen as categories or clusters of traits. An appropriate definition might be that types represent distinct groups of people characterized by a unique configuration of features. They are the oldest and simplest way of thinking about people, and this has made them popular. In the nineteenth century Lombroso characterized all criminals as having 'enormous jaws, high cheek bones and prominently arched eyebrows'. In the days before modern science, therefore, it was not unusual to attempt to distinguish between people, often on the basis of differences in personality or bodily appearance, and this has persisted. Some questionnaires are based on type theory. Typologies fail to recognize that characteristics are normally distributed and that it isn't really possible to divide people into a few categories. They also use rigid labels, which can be misleading. Type theories could be grouped together, but can also be separated because of having their origins in different paradigms.

Traits have their own limitations, for example there is a great number of them. Allport and Odbert (1936) identified 18,000. The use of factor analysis and their separation into different forms have helped to reduce the number considerably. They are more straightforward than types, and are capable of measurement. They form a normally distributed continuum on a scale, having a mean score at the centre. The first assessment of extraversion found that it is distributed like this. (See Figure 8.2.)

(b) Idiographic versus Nomothetic Approaches

To develop a theory about people depends on what kind of a theory you want and what you want it to achieve. You might take a holistic view, believing in unique individuals

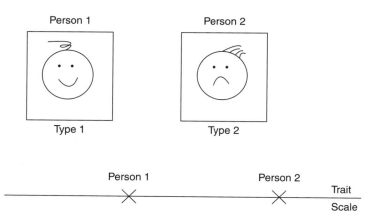

Figure 8.2   Types distinguish between people using categories, while traits distinguish them using scores on scales

and that to understand personality you need to evaluate as much of their mental processes as possible (Magnusson and Torestad, 1993). You might think the differences between people outweigh similarities. On this basis, data collection will involve qualitative methods such as interviews and observations. Assessments might include the Rorschach Ink-Blot or the Repertory Grid technique. This approach focuses on the individual and results in a potentially infinite number of descriptions. It is referred to as an idiographic approach, derived from the ancient Greek word *idios*, meaning 'private' or 'personal'. Researchers who use it prefer to investigate people only on an individual basis, for example in a therapeutic environment. Freud used it to create his theory. The idiographic paradigm, therefore, is based on an assumption that people have unique characteristics and cannot be described in identical terms. Although it provides a richer understanding of individuals, it is difficult to generalize findings to others.

An alternative method would be to identify some attribute which you think is an important aspect of personality and to measure it within a large group, possibly using standardized questionnaires. By doing this you can identify individual differences in the extent of the trait. The focus this time is on similarities, with the view that each person can be represented in terms of different degrees of the same thing. This is called the nomothetic approach, the term being derived again from an ancient Greek word for 'law'. It assumes the existence of a finite number of variables which account for differences and that these can be described, explained and predicted. Trait-based theories do this, and the psychometric approach links traits and measurement (see Table 8.1). The benefit is that they enable predictions to be made of behaviour.

Despite this distinction, psychologists using the nomothetic approach have argued that they do still accept and can work with uniqueness (Carver and Scheier, 2000). The uniqueness comes from a person's particular combination of personality variables, the degrees to which they exhibit them and their interactions. Combinations and interactions make each one unique. Those working within the idiographic paradigm also often evaluate case studies to find common themes, create theories and make predictions. So the differences may not be so clear cut.

Table 8.1   *Comparing idiographic and nomothetic approaches*

	Idiographic	Nomothetic
Approach	Sees individuals as unique	Sees common themes in the ways people behave
Aim	To understand each person	To identify traits which best describe all personality
Research approach	Qualitative	Quantitative
Data collection	Interviews, diaries, clinical/therapeutic data	Scores on self-report questionnaire scales
Advantages	Deeper understanding of the person	Comparison between individuals and ability to make predictions
Disadvantages	Problems in trying to make generalizations	Purely descriptive profiles which are more superficial

We can now review the principal theories of personality and its assessment. The literature abounds with different taxonomies and labels, so I have preferred to use the term 'paradigm' as this enables us to group together theories which relate to similar patterns of thinking. Some theories will not be accommodated easily into just one paradigm and may be placed in others, too. We will consider assessment issues, too, especially reliability and validity.

The Physiological Paradigm

Approaches to personality here view it as being associated with physiological characteristics of people. They range from simple descriptions of behaviour through to suggestions that characteristics are the result of different kinds of physiology. Theories which link personality to wider aspects of biological functioning are more complex and so don't belong to this category. Here we meet classical and constitutional theories which take a type approach.

Classical typology

A classical typology comes from our old friends, the Greeks, who theorized about types and 'humours'. The physician Hippocrates made what is probably the first attempt at a formal theory to account for differences between people around 400 BCE, and his ideas were popularized by Galen in the second century CE. Hippocrates suggested that temperament is determined by relative amounts of certain bodily fluids, resulting in four kinds of temperaments. He distinguished between them, depending on whether the predominant fluid is blood, black bile, yellow bile or mucous, as indicated in Table 8.2. The terms he gave to these types – sanguine, melancholic, choleric and phlegmatic – are still widely used today and influenced the work of Eysenck. It wasn't considered possible for these types to combine in any way and they were thought to be inherited. They have been linked with the effects of endocrine activity on temperament.

The problem with this approach is that it assumes people have to drop into one of the categories, rather than being made up of mixtures or combinations. It's perfectly possible in real life for many people to demonstrate something of more than one, possibly of

Table 8.2   *The four temperaments of Hippocrates*

Predominant body fluid	Type label	Temperament characteristics
Blood	Sanguine	Optimistic, cheerful, easy-going
Black Bile	Melancholic	Depressive, gloomy, slow to respond, sad
Yellow Bile	Choleric	Quick to anger, vehement, irascible
Phlegm and Mucous	Phlegmatic	Apathetic, listless, reticent

three types, for example someone who is depressed, apathetic and easy to anger. This is often a problem where people are dropped into boxes.

Constitutional typology

In the twentieth century other theorists sought to link personality with individual physique, an approach described as presenting a constitutional typology. Kretschmer (1925) began by stating, incorrectly as it happens, that schizophrenia is associated with tall, thin people, while short, fat people are more prone to manic-depressive psychoses. An alternative was devised by W. H. Sheldon in the 1940s. He classified body build into three somatotypes based on 'endomorphy', 'mesomorphy' and 'ectomorphy' components after studying thousands of photographs of male bodies (Sheldon, 1970). Endomorphy related to the digestive system and level of fatness observed, mesomorphy to the muscles and amount of musculature, and ectomorphy to the nervous system and brain and thus the body's leanness or fragility. These resulted in three somatotypes known as endomorphs, mesomorphs and ectomorphs, whose differing types of physique are described in Table 8.3. Sheldon used correlational studies to show that each type is associated with temperament. Accumulating data on 45,000 participants, he also constructed tables of male body types using a grading scale to match individuals against the extremes.

Sheldon's work led to debate and other studies of the relationship between personality and biology. He reported strong statistical relationships between body structure and personality, although he did not take account of measurement error. He was convinced scientific studies would eventually support his hypotheses, although this has not been the case. However, he was an early pioneer in applying the concepts of psychometrics, for example in conducting surveys, using questionnaires and in trying to conduct correlational analyses.

The Psychodynamic Paradigm

Psychodynamic theories are concerned with dynamic interactions between conscious and unconscious psychological drives. They originated with Sigmund Freud (1856–1939), whose theory of psychoanalysis was both a form of therapy and a system of psychology. Freud began his pioneering work in the nineteenth century as a medical doctor dealing with psychiatric problems and became interested in the role of the unconscious as a driving force. Based on his observations Freud saw personality as being like an iceberg – little exists in the conscious mind, while most lies submerged in the unconscious. To understand any individual we need to understand the structure and content of the unconscious mind (Freud, 1940/1969).

Table 8.3   *Sheldon's somatotypes*

Physique label	Physique description	Personality characteristics
ECTOMORPH	Skinny, fragile	High physiological arousal, social restraint, need for solitude
MESOMORPH	Athletic, trim	Energetic, forceful, tough-minded
ENDOMORPH	Flabby, plum	Sociable, relaxed, high need for affection, love of comfort

Personality was made up of three parts: the 'id', 'ego' and 'superego'. The id contains the primitive, raw, inherited passions and desires of the personality and provides energy to drive the organism. Freud (1901/1965, 1923/1960) considered sexual and aggressive impulses to be the most powerful forces. It seeks immediate gratification of its primitive drives. The ego represents the executive component which attempts to channel the id's drives into realistic processes. While the id is irrational and impractical, the ego is rational and practical. The superego adds a moral component. It can be considered as the conscience and seeks to counter the impulses of the id and to persuade the ego to consider moral and other rules in deciding how to satisfy impulses. Conflicts between these systems lead to anxiety. The ego copes by using defence mechanisms to distort reality so that people change the way they think about the anxiety. These mechanisms include denial, rationalisation, repression and projection. People differ in the balance between the components and also in the mechanisms they use. Freud also believed that personality develops through a series of psychosexual stages.

Rather than being a single theory, like psychoanalysis, psychodynamics represents a group of associated theories which were developed from Freud's work by different thinkers, including Adler, Jung, Lacan, Horney, Fromm, Erikson and McDougall. The term 'neo-Freudian' is sometimes used. In some instances they have adapted or rejected parts of Freud's ideas, although the underlying assumptions of psychoanalysis remain.

The major contribution of psychodynamics lies in its recognition that behaviour is motivated by unconscious needs and conflicts. Freud did seek to consider the complexity of human behaviour and his model has been thought to possess face validity in terms of the conflict often experienced in making choices and the anxiety involved. Defence mechanisms, too, appear to provide good explanations of common behaviour. The psychodynamic approach is still influential in many ways and has made a major contribution to literary theory. Although psychoanalysis played a significant role in the development of more humane treatment of mental patients, there has been much debate about its therapeutic value.

From an assessment point of view, psychodynamic theories lack scientific rigour and methods. It is difficult to design objective experiments to test Freud's hypotheses, which were based on his interpretations of observations. His theory is also not conducive to prediction because different behaviours could be indicators of the same underlying impulse. Psychoanalytic practice began with free association and dream interpretation, moving on later to influence the development of projective assessments. Chapter 9 includes a more detailed discussion of them.

Jungian type theory

Initially Carl Jung worked with Freud although they later fell out and Jung developed his own system of thinking, which was related to psychoanalysis. His 'analytical psychology' was influenced by a combination of philosophy and mythology. Like Freud, Jung saw personality or 'psyche' as being made up of interacting components such as the ego. This, he said, is the conscious part of the mind which faces conflict from both a personal and a collective unconscious, including repressed individual and collective human experiences. The collective form contains aspects of experience which have been passed down through generations and are shared by all humans, enabling him to account for behavioural similarities. An outline of Jung's work is provided by Bennett (1983).

Jung's conception of personality is based upon the view that individual differences are the result of a few basic observable disparities in functioning. The first involves his distinction between extraversion and introversion, people having a preference either for being extravert (E) or introvert (I). He viewed the two orientations or 'attitudes' as being distinct categories. The extrovert is interested in the outer world and seeks external stimulation, whilst the introvert is oriented towards the inner world, needing internal stimulation. Further categorizations were made according to fundamental functions by means of which a person sees the world and makes choices. These are:

(i) *Sensing (S) or Intuition (N)*

Does a person perceive by means of the five senses using empirical observation or go beyond what is present to focus upon associations between what is perceived and make use of inner judgement? Sensing concerns realistic representations of the world, whilst intuition is an unconscious process focussed on the basic essence of reality. Intuition is represented by the letter N because I has already been used for introversion.

(ii) *Thinking (T) or Feeling (F)*

Are a person's decisions made objectively or subjectively? The Thinking function tends to be more intellectual and bases perceptions on fact and logic, while Feeling centres evaluations in the emotions, having an emphasis on attitudes, beliefs and values.

Jung combined these differing orientations by considering that people have preferences between E and I, S and N, and T and F. The preferred pole in each case makes up one personality attribute and these are then combined. One of the preferred functions, that used in the preferred attitude (E or I), is referred to as the dominant function and the other is the auxiliary function. For the introvert the dominant is used in the inner world and the auxiliary in the outer world; for the extravert the dominant is in the outer world and the auxiliary in the inner. His theory was developed by Isabel Myers and Katherine Briggs, who added another dimension to help identify dominant and auxiliary functions. This was:

(iii) *Judging (J) or Perceiving (P)*

Does a person become fixed when a decision is made or remain open to more information? Is there a preference for an organized lifestyle or for spontaneity and improvization? If Judging is chosen, either Thinking or Feeling is used mostly in the outer world. If Perceiving is chosen, either Sensing or Intuition is used mostly in the outer world. The dominant function will vary for extraverts and introverts.

Myers and Briggs constructed a questionnaire known as the Myers-Briggs Type Indicator (MBTI). Individuals who complete the questionnaire are assigned to one side of each dimension and are allotted a four-letter type code, for example ENTP, out of 16 possible types. They acknowledged that it is possible for a person to be balanced in the middle of any dimension. The instrument has been extensively used worldwide, having a strong following (Myers and McCaulley, 1985). Some modern versions have been constructed, the most notable being the Jung Type Indicator, which was constructed using modern test theory, and the Type Dynamics Indicator, which can compare how people see themselves and how they would prefer to be.

Opinions on the MBTI are divided. Supporters say Jung's types have been operationalized successfully and that it is useful in selection and development assessments (DeVito, 1985). But it comes from psychoanalysis and is, therefore, speculative in origin (Kline, 2000). Like Freud's work, it lacks scientific foundation, making any rigid application of the types insupportable. The 16 outcomes appear to represent 'pure' types and it is unlikely people will be purely one of them. People can be extroverted in some situations and introverted at others; they may be capable of both objective and subjective thought. On these grounds, the approach could be too general to make sensitive discriminations. Another issue is that the MBTI doesn't include any assessment of test-takers' attitudes, so conclusions can be distorted. Any true typology is expected to be bimodal, i.e. having two score distributions centred upon the extremes (see Chapter 4), although this is not the case with the MBTI. The picture is even more difficult regarding validity (Stricker and Ross, 1964; Carlyn, 1977). Evidence for this is based upon correlational studies (Chapter 6), yet the MBTI is partially ipsative and, therefore, they are difficult to do. So there is inadequate evidence for its validity. Its use is best confined to development, team or counselling activities.

The Cognitive-behavioural Paradigm

Social learning theory grew out of classical learning theories like those of Pavlov (1906, 1927, 1928), Watson and Skinner, which disagreed fundamentally with psychoanalysis and demanded rigorous scientific methods. These behaviourists laid the foundation for a more scientific approach and led to the work of Dollard and Miller (1941, 1950), who saw the value of thinking in terms of 'cognitive processing'. They also stressed the importance of observational learning because the performance of role models could be observed and imitated by others. From this basis social learning theorists see personality in behavioural terms, suggesting that our behaviour defines our personalities.

Miller and Dollard redefined psychoanalytic concepts in terms of stimulus-response relationships which result in learning to behave in certain ways. Therefore personality is shaped through the development of habits and the influence of rewards and punishment. Early views focussed on observable behaviour and saw learning almost as a reflex action. Later perspectives, of Rotter, Bandura and Mischel, incorporated cognitive and social factors. In their view behaviour patterns are still seen in relation to external conditions, but greater emphasis is given to internal variables.

Importance was also given to the interpretation of any situation by individuals, including intellectuality, thinking style and sociocultural influences. Bandura (1977, 1995, 1999,

2002) demonstrated the use of self-reinforcement. Rotter referred to the expectancies applied in situations as locus of control (1966, 1982). At the Internal end of this dimension are people who view behaviour and events as being under personal control. At the other extreme are Externals who perceive their behaviour to be influenced by events out of their control and subject to luck, more powerful others, and fate. Rotter's measure of this dimension is still used in research, clinical and occupational work.

Social learning has not had much impact in terms of the wider assessment of personality. Its focus has been more upon assessments involving individuals and situational variables, making use of observations, diaries and interviews. But it has had an impact in encouraging improvements in assessment and the measurement of locus of control has been popular. Modern cognitive psychology, which tries to scientifically investigate inner mental constructs, may also be an outcome.

The Phenomenological Paradigm

The phenomenological approach came from philosophers who focussed upon direct personal and subjective experiences, and is linked to the twentieth century existentialist movement. People working in this tradition believe unique individuals can only be understood in terms of inner experiences and that psychology should focus on them. Any separation of personality into its elements is thought to do an injustice to it. They form a diverse group but are united by the view that personality can only be understood in terms of immediate and unanalysed experiences. Individuals are seen as responding to the world through perceptions which create personal experiences and meanings. The core position of this approach is, therefore, one of subjectivity.

The humanistic viewpoint

The most prominent contributors to the 'humanistic' school were Carl Rogers (1902–87) and Abraham Maslow (1908–70). According to them, the element of the environment which has meaning for an individual is the phenomenal field and the self is one element of this. The sum of all the attributions made about the self by a person is the self-concept. In growing up people discover they are the objects of conditional positive regard, which means they are accepted by others provided they live up to certain standards of attitude and behaviour, or conditions of worth. As adults, therefore, they are unable to achieve fully functioning capacity unless others provide unconditional positive regard, which amounts to a warm, genuine acceptance of their worth. Free will and individual uniqueness are core aspects.

Rogers, a clinical psychologist, thought personality problems were a result of patients experiencing a gap between what they were (their real selves) and what they would ideally like to be (their ideal selves) and how they tried to cope with this gap (1956, 1961, 1977). To evaluate it he thought the patient's subjective experiences provided the most useful data. He became the founder of person-centred therapy, which was designed to provide a supportive environment for treatment. The aim was to help individuals create positive change, while the therapist supported them.

Humanistic thinkers believe that, basically, people are generally well-intentioned and have a need to develop their potential. They place emphasis upon the positive

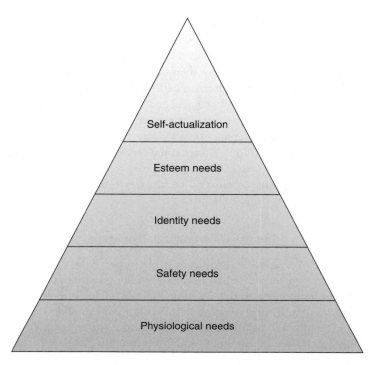

Figure 8.3   Maslow's hierarchy of needs

characteristics of growth, self-expression and self-fulfilment. Maslow, for example, is well known for saying that everyone strives to reach a state of self-actualization, which represents an idealistic harmony between real and ideal selves. Self-actualization was seen as a major force in development of personality; it was also key to mental health, and thus people play an active role in determining their own personalities. (See Figure 8.3.)

One benefit of humanism is that it brought into focus cross-cultural differences in assessment. However, although some people still cling to Maslow's hierarchy of needs – including physiological and safety needs, the need for belonging and love, and esteem needs – it has not stood up to scientific validation. His work and that of Rogers are littered with ill-defined concepts based on little evidence; they are idiographic, lacking objective methods. Assessments tend to be focussed on interviews and case studies. Some techniques for evaluating feelings and attitudes have been developed, including Stephenson's Q-sort (1953), and some self-concept scales and self-esteem inventories. The Q-sort provides cards having statements on them, such as 'I worry about what people think of me', which participants sort into piles ranging from most relevant to the least relevant. This is repeated so that changes can be monitored. It provides a quantifiable measure of a person's feelings over time (Rogers and Dymond, 1954; Block, 1961), although there are issues concerning distortion and identification of real sources of change. Self-esteem inventories tend to have poor validity.

Personal constructs and the Repertory Grid

Like social learning theorists, George Kelly (1905–66) believed people could be understood only in terms of personal experiences. Kelly (1955, 1958, 1963) thought that internal models – which he called 'constructs' – were formed by individuals because they behave like scientists. People wanted to understand events and to make predictions about them. So they create internal construct systems through continually formulating hypotheses about the world and then testing them out. In this way we develop personal systems which determine behaviour and personality. Those systems which do not properly reflect the world result in psychological ill-health. Kelly's Personal Construct Theory has been important in the development of assessment techniques.

The Role Construct Repertory Grid, known commonly as the Rep Grid Test although Kelly insisted it was not a test, was designed to elicit and investigate constructs. It is based on an assumption that everyone interprets events differently. The rep grid focusses upon 'elements' in the life of a person, which could be the self, other people, objects and even events. The question then is: How does the individual construe such elements and what are their relationships? A person may list or be presented with a list of people, whose names are given in groups of three and the individual is asked to indicate how two of the three are similar and the third different from the others. For example, someone might say that two are generous whilst the third is mean. Effectively, the participant sorts people into categories of personal relevance. This is repeated for different groups of three people from the list, enabling the constructs used to organize information to emerge.

In many instances constructs are represented by two terms or phrases which have opposing meanings, such as decisive/indecisive or friendly/unfriendly. Participants are encouraged to provide distinct psychological attributions rather than physical or other descriptions. Gradually, a matrix can be built up through this process, having the elements across the top and the constructs elicited listed down the sides, as shown in Table 8.4. After a sufficient number has been recorded (usually about 12), the participant can be asked to rate each element on a scale such as 1 to 5 or 1 to 7 in terms of each construct. Examination of the matrix indicates which dimensions are important.

Although there is no standard method of scoring, a wide range of analyses are possible, ranging from simple evaluation of similarities to factor analysis. Analysis can focus on the number of constructs elicited, their nature, which attributes of others are most emphasized and any differences between elements. High correlations between two or more constructs may indicate an underlying core component. It has been suggested, therefore, that the method can assess the cognitive complexity of individuals (Bieri, 1955).

Kelly saw the therapist's role in helping people to become more aware of faulty constructs and the need to change them. Studies were significant in finding differences between the personal construct systems of patients suffering from schizophrenia and those experiencing depression, neuroses and mild organic disorders, and with a healthy control sample. The technique has been adapted to other applications, for example, becoming an objective method of conducting job analysis in organizations. (See Table 8.4.)

Kelly's method can provide a useful awareness of the ways in which people perceive their world, how they organize attitudes and beliefs, how emotional responses are

Table 8.4   Kelly's Repertory Grid

	Sister	Brother	Friend	Father	Mother	
Generous	3	1	3	4	2	Mean
Decisive	4	2	2	3	1	Indecisive
Friendly	5	1	5	4	3	Unfriendly
Intelligent	3	3	5	3	3	Dim
Gentle	1	5	2	1	5	Violent
Caring	4	1	3	3	5	Uncaring
etc.						etc.

generated and their influences on behaviour. It focuses on uniqueness whilst also viewing everyone within the same conceptual framework and is adaptable to situations. For these reasons it has been popular with therapists, counsellors, psychologists and Human Resources professionals. A good introduction to its use is Fransella (2003).

The process of undertaking it, however, is complex, especially if factor analysis is used, needing expertise and being time-consuming. It tends also to focus too much on thought processes at the expense of other aspects of personality and could be seen as mechanistic. Effective use depends on expertise in interpreting outcomes and no systematic interpretation is provided, introducing some subjectivity. There may also be the problem of whether participant and assessor have a mutual understanding of constructs elicited. Being idiographic in nature, there can never be any standardization or possibility of comparing a person with others. A new version needs to be constructed each time, meaning that reliability and validity have to be re-checked. For these reasons, the rep grid is not truly an objective measure of personality. Basically, it is simply a structured way of obtaining personal information.

Murray's theory of needs

We all have needs and they are an important driving force in constructing personalities, according to H. A. Murray (1938). The concept of needs has a long history and Murray was prominent among thinkers, suggesting that they arise in parts of the brain. Older theories said that whenever a gap arises between a person's state and the equilibrium required for survival, the experience produced is felt as tension and a need arises to overcome it. Feeling hungry, for example, creates a need for food. Murray focussed on psychological needs which would also reduce tension.

In his theory personality is a result of the relative amounts of each need and the ways in which they are organized. He identified a long list of them, more than 30. Some have stood the test of time and are still researched, for example the need for achievement, or 'achievement motivation' (McClelland, 1976; Koestner and McClelland, 1990). This has been defined as the need to accomplish something significant and surpass others. Two other interesting needs are the need for affiliation, linked to trust, affection and empathy, and the need for power.

Murray developed the first assessment of needs, the Thematic Apperception Test (TAT), seeing it as a tool for understanding personality. A projective assessment (see Chapter 9), it consists of a series of unstructured pictures which were designed to be open to different interpretations. Some examples are:

- A young boy looks at a violin on a table.
- A young woman stands with her face in her hands, her left arm against a door.
- A small girl climbs a winding staircase.
- Strange clouds overhang a snow-covered cabin.

Designed to be sufficiently ambiguous to elicit differing stories from people, the pictures are used to encourage participants to create stories about their perceptions. They may be asked to say what is happening, who the people are, what has happened before and what could be the outcome, although there has been much variation in the administration, scoring and interpretation of responses, as well as in which sub-set of cards is administered. Responses are analysed using a strict scoring system to identify recurring themes, as well as potential 'projections'. The manual provides a range of needs and emotions which can be identified. Many theories of personality can be applied to interpret responses, especially the psychoanalytic approach.

Originally the technique was popular and highly regarded. How interpretation is conducted is of importance and different interpreters should be expected to obtain similar conclusions about participants, i.e. their findings should correlate. This type of correlation was called inter-rater reliability in Chapter 5. Having a clear guide for scoring suggests there is a satisfactory level of reliability and a figure of 0.9 has been claimed. But the issue of other forms of reliability is more complex and subject to debate. Murray emphasized the need for well-trained and 'gifted' testers, although how these are identified is a problem. Used well, therefore, the TAT could provide good information about personality, but its pictures have been described as old-fashioned, are not seen as relevant to applied settings and take a long time to score. The approach is purely idiographic, being adopted by clinicians who place emphasis on the depth of understanding gained. From a psychometric view, there are problems relating to administration, lack of objectivity and standardization, meaning there can be no comparison of individuals, and therefore use of the TAT has declined. Study of the need for achievement by McClelland has attracted more attention.

The Biological Paradigm

Links between biology and psychology make sense. When you're hungry or tired the chances are that you get bad-tempered. The brain is at the centre of all this. Being enormously complex, it is connected throughout the body and can transmit messages rapidly. It manages both unconscious body systems, such as digestion, and conscious processes including thinking which links to behaviour. If you suffer brain damage there is a chance you may suffer changes in your personality, too. Neuropsychology is concerned with these links and seeks to use scientific methods in understanding them. It's not surprising, therefore, that attempts have been made to develop biological models of personality.

Eysenck's theory
The most well-known is that of Hans Eysenck (1967, 1990, 1994), who was one of the first to devise a biological model. According to Eysenck, the brain contains two sets of

neural operations, one excitatory and the other inhibitory. The first tries to keep us active and awake, whilst the other is focussed on inactivity. We try to maintain a balance. Sitting at the base of the brain is the ascending reticular activating system (ARAS) which controls the arousal level of the cortex above, effectively acting as a kind of 'dimmer switch'. Eysenck's theory suggests that the systems of extraverts and introverts work at different levels, with the introvert's cortex being more aroused. Most people prefer a moderate arousal level and any very high or low level is perceived as unpleasant. Therefore, in situations where external stimulation is present introverts experience greater arousal and will try to escape from it. So they need more effort to adapt, whilst extraverts, having a need for more arousal, are more comfortable. Because of their natural arousability levels, introverts try to avoid intense stimuli while extraverts search for them.

Eysenck also referred to a second brain process involving a part known as the limbic system which, he said, accounted for individual differences in neuroticism. This is defined as being made up of traits such as anxiety, worrying and moodiness, although Eysenck viewed it in terms of emotionality – highly neurotic people tending to experience more extreme emotional responses. It was associated with the arousability of the limbic system. It is connected in turn to the autonomic nervous system (ANS), which regulates involuntary processes like the activity of muscles, heart rate and sweat glands. The ANS is also known as the peripheral system because it functions mostly outside of the brain and spinal column. Part of this, the sympathetic nervous system (SNS), appears to be over-active in anxious people, whilst the associated parasympathetic nervous system (PNS) opposes it and is calming, being stronger in more unemotional people. Neurotic individuals possess a hyper-arousable limbic system and are more likely to experience emotional reactions. Eysenck also suggested that individual differences in psychoticism might be linked to a chemical messenger in the brain.

Gray's theory

A similar approach came from Jeffrey Gray, who studied under Eysenck. His reinforcement sensitivity theory (Gray, 1970, 1981, 1987) suggests that personality is connected with the interaction between two brain systems: the Behavioural Approach System (BAS) and the Behavioural Inhibition System (BIS). The BAS centres on motivations to approach the environment, causing people to be sensitive to rewards and to look for them; whilst the BIS focusses on motivations to avoid, causing people to be sensitive towards dangers. These were associated with the characteristics of impulsivity and anxiety, with individuals high on approach being more impulsive and those high on inhibition more anxious. A questionnaire based on the two scales was developed in the US.

Cloninger's theory

A third model was proposed by C. Robert Cloninger, who combined findings from psychological, social and medical sciences. His theory is related to seven personality domains, including 'temperament' domains of novelty-seeking, harm avoidance, reward dependence and persistence, and 'character' domains of self-directedness, cooperativeness and self-transcendence (Cloninger, 1987; Cloninger, Svrakic and Przybeck, 1993). Self-directedness relates to a person's level of autonomy, cooperativeness to links with society, and self-transcendence to beliefs about mystical experiences. Cloninger linked these to neurotransmitters in the brain, as well as to learning through rewards and punishments. His work is linked to the Eysenck and Gray models, for example reward dependence reflects Gray's BAS system.

The evidence for these biological theories is inconsistent and contradictory despite much research (Matthews and Gilliland, 1999) and evidence linking physiology to personality is still needed. Some findings support Eysenck's thinking in terms of arousal, as well as the approach/inhibition systems of Gray, although others do not support them and suggest a weak relationship. A link between neuroticism and arousal is not generally supported. However, it seems that characteristics are associated with physiological activities such as heart rate, skin conductance and brain activity. Given that the brain is a complex organism with substantial interconnections, it is possible that each theory represents an oversimplification and that some combination is needed to establish a connection with personality.

They have contributed to assessment, including the questionnaire developed for Gray's scales and Cloninger's Tri-dimensional Personality Questionnaire, revised as the Temperament and Character Inventory, based on his biological factors and used to assess personality disorder. The Cloninger inventory may be a variation on Eysenck's model. Most notable, however, are the interconnections between the theories and the fact that Eysenck's is linked to his factor-analytic studies of personality and to his development of a psychometric trait-based measure.

The Trait Paradigm

Forget all the theorizing about personality for a moment and let's ask some basic questions. Is personality just one thing itself? Can it be taken apart? If so, what do the parts look like? Is it like a Lego model made up a lot of bits joined together? Historical approaches might answer that it can't be pulled apart, that it is something to be understood purely as a whole. This is an idiographic view. But it makes sense to compare people with other people: someone may be depressed, but just how depressed is depressed? Logic indicates that we need to compare people who are mildly, moderately or severely depressed. If personality is one thing then we can't do that and we need to take it apart. We might separate it into types. The alternative, however, is to take a hammer to it and look at what we get.

Doing this goes back to Allport in 1937 and the demolition work has been continued by others such as Eysenck, Cattell, and Costa and McCrae since. They have suggested that personality is made up of components called traits. Measured perfectly on them, people's scores are spread along a continuum, probably looking like a normal distribution curve, having most people around the average and fewer at the extremes, as Figure 8.4 shows.

We defined traits in Chapter 1 as relatively enduring characteristics (Cattell, 1973). Being abstractions, they are independent of any stimulus external to a person. They are also thought to be non-situational, although may sometimes be modified depending on events. They can be any characteristic, whether emotional, cognitive or behavioural, which influences how personality is demonstrated. Examples of traits might be how outgoing,

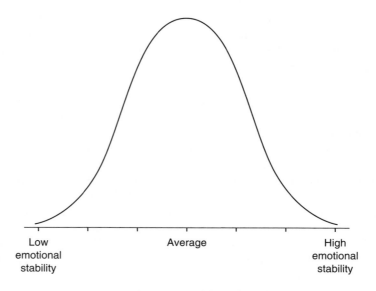

Low
emotional
stability   Average   High
emotional
stability

Figure 8.4   A normal distribution of people on the trait of emotional stability

assertive or caring we are. If these are the elements of personality, then you might ask: 'What are they made out of?' The answer is that they represent single dimensions containing related components. Thus the fundamental trait of neuroticism includes behaviours and cognitions associated with guilt, low self-esteem, depression and anxiety.

This approach describes personality in terms of continuous scales and an inventory is made up of any number of them. Someone may be at the centre of a scale measuring intelligence, towards the low end of a scale of anxiety, towards the high end for impulsiveness, and so on, until an overall picture is gained. In everyday life we come closest to the trait approach in making comments such as 'shy,' 'quite dominant' or 'not very confident'. Thousands of words might be considered as traits and psychologists have attempted to construct a short list of the most important. The trait paradigm assumes that:

1   Our thoughts, feelings and behaviours vary in a number of ways.
2   These variations can be measured.
3   When they are measured, they are normally distributed like other characteristics.

On this basis, there is no such thing as trait theory: it's not a theory. It's about what the parts of personality might be, not about the aspects of a typical theory such as how it develops and whether it can be changed. All we have developed is a system for specifying the components and measuring them. It provides a means of describing what any personality is like and does not explain how it developed. For this reason some people say we are just labelling and quantifying personality. Maybe that's so, but then along any dimension there are places for different people and when we look at one individual's positions on dimensions we can combine them in a unique description. Having a normal distribution enables us to do parametric stats and because of this the trait approach has made an important contribution to the study of personality.

That recurring technique called factor analysis has enabled researchers to identify the underlying basic dimensions or 'factors' from many trait labels. A few can be found to underpin hundreds of traits; for example labels such as friendly, cooperative and good-natured might all be found under the heading of 'agreeableness'. This is sometimes called the 'lexical hypothesis', going back to Galton (1884), and the approach was developed by a number of theorists, including Eysenck and Cattell. Basing his work on empirical observations and large-scale analyses, Eysenck (1967) suggested there are three dimensions along which personality varies:

- Introversion – Extraversion
- Neuroticism – Stability
- Psychoticism – Normality

These major dimensions resulted from correlations between groups of traits. For example, extraversion derives from traits including sensation-seeking, assertiveness, activity, liveliness, sociability and others all found to correlate with each other. His neuroticism includes tension, guilt, depression, anxiety and moodiness. Eysenck described his third dimension as representing the degree to which a person is tough-minded, and called it 'psychoticism' following observations that psychotics score highly on it. They are impulsive, impersonal, egocentric, cold, aggressive, anti-social and lack empathy. They are also creative which, according to Eysenck, was consistent with the theory that genius and madness are linked. Overall, the dimensions are concerned with 21 traits. Eysenck's theory resulted in his development of questionnaires – the Maudsley Personality Inventory (MPI), the Eysenck Personality Inventory (EPI) and the Eysenck Personality Questionnaire (EPQ).

Cattell identified 16 important dimensions or 'source traits,' some of which correspond to Eysenck's findings (Cattell et al., 1970). He collected an enormous number of trait names used in everyday language to describe behaviour before eliminating synonyms. People were rated on the remaining descriptions, revealing some 40–50 dimensions which were factor analysed down to 12 factors. A questionnaire was developed and the outcomes again analysed, leading to four more, making a total of 16. These form the basis of the 16 Personality Factor inventory (16PF). He called them primary factors, although they are source traits and represent enduring aspects of behaviour, accounting for the variation in more observable surface traits (Cattell, 1950). What we see on a daily basis are the surface ones corresponding to common generalizations and are less stable. Source traits are fundamental units which govern behaviour whilst interacting together and with other characteristics. When analysis was conducted again, they revealed second-order factors, including Eysenck's extraversion and anxiety.

The original 16PF has gone through a number of revisions and there are also today equivalent questionnaires which measure much the same factors, such as the 15 Factor Questionnaire and the 15FQPlus. In contrast, some inventories appear to measure more of the original surface traits, such as the Occupational Personality Questionnaire (OPQ). Cattell's 16 factors are shown in Table 8.5. Looking at them you might ask: why are there no D, K or J factors and why are there Q1 to Q4 factors? The answer is that some factors did not prove to be replicable in adults – D, J

Table 8.5   *Cattell's 16 source traits*

Factor	Scale label	Low score description	High score description
A	Warmth	Reserved	Warm
B	Reasoning	Concrete	Abstract
C	Emotional stability	Reactive	Emotionally stable
E	Dominance	Deferential	Dominant
F	Liveliness	Serious	Lively
G	Rule-conscious	Expedient	Rule-conscious
H	Social boldness	Shy	Socially bold
I	Sensitivity	Utilitarian	Sensitive, aesthetic
L	Vigilance	Trusting	Vigilant
M	Abstractedness	Grounded, practical	Abstracted
N	Privateness	Forthright	Private
O	Apprehension	Self-assured	Apprehensive
Q1	Openness to change	Traditional	Open to change
Q2	Self-reliance	Group-oriented	Self-reliant
Q3	Perfectionism	Tolerates disorder	Perfectionistic
Q4	Tension	Relaxed	Tense

and K – and were removed. Four others were found only in questionnaires and not in the analysis of language, but they seemed important and Cattell felt they should be included. He distinguished these as factors Q1 to Q4. There have been debates about Cattell's work and its outcomes, and arguments over scale reliabilities, although these were improved later.

Box 8.1   Personality and Management Development

Development centres provide one of the most useful tools for accurately identifying the gaps between an individual's abilities and those needed for jobs. They give information on individual abilities and provide a mechanism for empowering people to develop themselves and to improve organizational performance. Psychometric assessments can make a major contribution to outcomes and are most effectively used as one element in a range of procedures (Coaley and Hogg, 1994; Lee and Beard, 1994).

Mrs Greene took part in a development programme provided by an international company. This was designed to enhance organizational performance through the identification of potential and to encourage self-development. In taking part Mrs Greene completed the 16PF. The outcomes of this, discussed during feedback, revealed that she was ambitious to progress in management.

The analysis suggested Mrs Greene was able to cope with most social situations, although she did not always choose to socialize. She was reasonably expressive and warm towards others, at times liking to be sociable and at others preferring non-social activities. She tended towards being precise and exact in her work and could be assertive, although she would defer to others wherever appropriate.

Mrs Greene was not easily intimidated and did not often experience anxiety. She was confident in interactions with others and was comfortable speaking to groups. She was communicative and self-disclosing to a typical level, although tended to lack concern for maintaining a socially approved image, and overall maintained a balance between being dependent upon others and high independence.

In thinking style Mrs Greene suggested she took an objective approach to her work and was able to adjust to the facts of situations. She was open to change, but did not have any need for excessive variety. In general, she preferred to think things through before committing herself to action and would take issues seriously and anticipate difficulties. She would be guided by rules to a typical extent and had a realistic level of scepticism. In evaluating information, she could shift flexibly between focussing on the practical and being oriented towards ideas, balancing operational and strategic needs.

In work style, she was confident and thoughtful. She preferred to work in a team, and was likely to be tactful and diplomatic. Preferring to be organized and to plan ahead to meet goals, Mrs Greene experienced typical levels of tension. She was able to cope with life's demands and to tolerate frustration as much as others. She did not experience self-doubt to any great extent, and could remain relatively calm in difficult situations.

Following the programme Mrs Greene undertook an MBA and is now a senior manager.

Essentially, all personality can be reduced to five components. Tupes, Chrystal and Goldberg were the first to do this, with a review by Goldberg (1981). Costa and McCrae (1985, 1992) also factor analysed a number of broad-based questionnaires and their work has become the most well-known. Despite using different terms the research has produced five main factors, said to describe all of personality 'space' and making up the modern dominant model of personality. Labels for the traits found differ among theorists and from questionnaire to questionnaire, although the ideas making up scale contents are the same. Known as the 'Big Five', the most common terms appear to be:

- Extraversion
- Emotional stability/Neuroticism
- Agreeableness
- Conscientiousness
- Openness to experience

As a result it should be possible to summarize any profile on the basis of these factors alone. Many theorists now agree that when the data are summarized in this way the same five constructs emerge. The simplicity of the 'Big Five' makes them appealing. Costa and McRae (1992) developed a measure based upon these findings known as the NEO as an acronym for the five traits. The second-order factors arising from many questionnaires can often be aligned with them, for example, those of the 15FQ and the 16PF can be aligned with the model, as shown in Table 8.6.

Extraversion represents a predisposition to experience positive emotional states, having more social confidence and feeling good about oneself and the world in general. People with higher levels are more socially outgoing.

Neuroticism represents a tendency to experience negative emotional states and negative views of oneself, such as anxiety, self-consciousness and vulnerability. People with higher levels experience more negative moods and stress.

Table 8.6 *Matching 15FQ and 16PF global factors with the Big Five*

The Big Five	15FQ	16PF
Extraversion	Introversion–Extraversion	Introversion–Extraversion
Neuroticism	Anxiety	Anxiety
Agreeableness	Independence	Independence
Conscientiousness	Control	Self-control
Openness to experience	Pragmatism	Tough poise/Tough-minded

Agreeableness represents a tendency to get along well with others, as well as a desire to get things done. This links personality to responsiveness in many situations.

Conscientiousness represents a tendency to be careful, meticulous, organized and structured in behaviour. It also includes how much individuals internalize moral values and rules.

Openness to experience represents a tendency to be open to a variety of experiences, to be creative and tolerant. Someone high on this is likely to be more open to change.

Overall, the appeal of the trait approach is that it can be operationalized through the construction of objective measures and is empirical. It has been linked with development of a number of research-based questionnaires; Eysenck developed his through trait research and Cattell's work led to the 16PF. These questionnaires can usefully be administered to groups. The approach, however, takes too little account of situational influences on behaviour and provides no clues to the development of personality or how it may change.

Summary

Theory and practice are necessarily linked. We have reviewed a range of personality theories and their relationships with assessment methods, from classical typology to trait theory. Psychodynamic theories have resulted in projective assessments such as the Rorschach and the Myers-Briggs Type Indicator, whilst cognitive-behavioural thinking led to a few scales, most notably locus of control. The phenomenological perspective provided the humanists' Q-sort technique, the repertory grids of Kelly, and the Thematic Apperception Test. A biological view also prompted development of some questionnaires. Eysenck and Cattell used the trait approach to develop a number of questionnaires. The benefits and limitations of differing assessments have been discussed and we have also distinguished between type and trait models and idiographic and nomothetic views.

Questionnaire-based Personality Assessment

The psychometric model focuses on traits relevant to how individuals adjust to the environment and to differences between people. It involves a normative process with the placing of scores on rating scales and use of statistical methods. To do this questionnaires are generated. Even where the psychometric model isn't used, as with type approaches, self-report questionnaires are often developed. These have both advantages and limitations:

Self-report Data

In completing questionnaires, people answer questions about themselves. The accuracy of the data gained will, therefore, depend on personal insight. This is variable: it's possibly linked to age, maturity and intelligence, although we cannot be sure. Interpretation should be conducted with caution and include discussion with the individual concerned in a feedback interview.

Distortion of Responses

In some instances people will distort or 'fake' responses to questions as a result of their expectations or mind set, especially where an inventory is used in decision-making. They may portray themselves in an unrealistically positive light and as being socially likeable, indicating higher 'social desirability' (Paulhus, 1984; Rees, 1999). This tendency can be reduced by standardized administration procedures which offer feedback and confidentiality. Social desirability might also be seen as another aspect of personality itself, representing a desire to be accepted by others.

The problem is often less serious than claimed because many participants are involved in situations where they realize that accurate results will contribute best to their welfare. Where time is taken during administration to ensure that they understand the importance of truthful responses, the outcomes are likely to be more accurate. Developments in questionnaire methods and technology have also resulted in improvements, such as in the calculation of measures of a person's test-taking style. Many include a measure of socially desirable responding which can be scored, based on the inclusion of items designed to determine whether people are presenting themselves in an unrealistically positive light.

Random Responding

This is a problem when respondents have little motivation in completing a questionnaire or have been strongly encouraged or coerced to do so. There is a risk they may select responses at random and are unlikely to read items. Random responses can be identified by the inclusion of an infrequency scale, consisting of items which have only one correct answer but, unlike those used in reasoning tests, the answer is obvious, for example 'Babies generally walk before they can crawl'. A random-responder is unlikely to notice that this is factually incorrect. The problem is that they tend to be obvious to people who are reading carefully and can then be a distraction. Some inventories come with software using an infrequency scale which identifies responses having a low endorsement rate.

Central Tendency

This is the name given to the style of people who constantly choose the middle option for items, having a response set to do this. People might be defensive and don't want to

Table 8.7   *An example of a correlation matrix*

						Personality scales									
	A	B	C	D	E	F	G	H	I	J	K	L	M	N	O
Appraisal evaluation	ns	ns	ns	ns	ns	ns	ns	.33	ns	ns	ns	ns	ns	ns	ns
Qualification level	ns	.47	ns	ns	ns	ns	−.4	.57	.42	ns	ns	ns	ns	ns	ns
Attendance	ns	ns	ns	ns	ns	ns	−.5	.61	ns	ns	ns	ns	ns	.44	ns
Punctuality	ns	ns	ns	ns	ns	ns	ns	ns	ns	.4	ns	ns	ns	ns	ns
Customer ratings	ns	ns	ns	ns	ns	ns	ns	ns	ns	ns	ns	.4	ns	ns	ns
Length of experience	ns	ns	ns	ns	ns	ns	−.4	.48	ns	ns	ns	ns	ns	ns	ns

reveal much information about themselves or are young people who lack certainty. There is also a chance that someone has moderate views compared to others. Careful wording of items can minimize the effect and it may be measured through the use of software (Rust, 1996; Huba, 1987). If scores are high on a central tendency scale, then the profile may not validly represent the person. An interview could help determine whether it is genuine.

Measurement Error

Scales used in inventories are subject to measurement error, as Chapter 5 shows. There can be no 100 per cent accuracy and rating scales should be reliable. Reputable inventories usually have carefully researched items designed to ensure a consistent assessment of traits. Even with the best, there is a margin of error and this means scores can't be seen in any rigid way: they should be considered as guides to how individuals might behave in many circumstances. Having said this, it is still a better guide than the subjective views of an interviewer.

Correlational Approaches to Validation

In Chapter 6 we discussed validation. We saw that in many processes designed to provide evidence for construct validity publishers will correlate scores with those on other measures. High correlations then suggest they are measuring the same thing. However, in the case of assessing the validity of scales within a personality inventory, the use of correlations raises a problem. It is caused to some extent by the fact that there are often more scales within an inventory – from just three in the case of the EPI to 16 in the 16PF and to 30 for the OPQ. If scores on a number of scales are correlated with scores on other measures we can end up with cross-correlational matrices. Imagine I develop a personality inventory having 15 scales, called factor A to factor O, and that I then correlate the scores of a large sample of employees with their scores on six measures of performance. The correlation matrix produced is shown in Table 8.7.

The matrix shows 15 x 6, i.e. 90 correlations. Of these, 12 are given as being statistically significant, the others having 'ns' recorded as being not significant. The publisher might, on this basis, state that there is good evidence for the validity of factors G and H, whilst there is some support, albeit lower, for factors B, I, J, L and N. But there is a problem here arising from probability theory which says that if lists of random numbers are continually recorded one of them will eventually correlate reasonably well with one of the criteria, suggesting that the random numbers are valid. If the sample size is small a set of random numbers giving a high correlation will rapidly become clear. In contrast, if sample size is large then it will take a longer time before a set of higher correlations becomes available. Therefore, 'spurious' correlations can occur purely by chance depending on sample size. The word 'spurious' signifies that they appear to be statistically significant when they may not, in fact, be so.

Usually tests of statistical significance will take sample size into account in any research process and deal with it. There are corrections which can be applied. But it is often not considered in the case of validation studies having large matrices. In the case of statistical tests the probability of a significant correlation occurring by chance is less than 5 per cent or 1 in 20. If a matrix of 20 correlations is constructed using random numbers, then one of them has a high probability of being significant purely by chance. When the matrix has 100 correlations, by the laws of probability we can expect that at least five of them will be significant by chance alone. A publisher might take advantage of this and publish the five correlations, indicating them as evidence of validity and hoping you don't know about the effect. But now you do. This provides a word of warning for anyone buying a personality inventory.

So our matrix includes 90 coefficients, 12 of them given as significant. For each 20 coefficients one could be significant by chance, suggesting that 4.5 per cent could occur among the total. We can't have half a correlation, so we will round this up to 5. The number of significant coefficients needs to be greater than this to have some which are potentially genuine, and this is the case. Obviously, the spurious ones occur at random and, therefore, do not appear as a pattern. In our example the factors which appear most valid would be H and G, although it is worth saying that the matrix is provided only as a simplified example and many more significant coefficients would normally be generated. A statistical correction can eliminate the effect.

Summary

The use of self-report questionnaires to assess personality characteristics continues to grow. Issues concerning their use, such as those relating to response styles, including distortion, central and random responding, as well as measurement error, have been largely met by developments in technology and the application of codes of good practice for their administration, data management and feedback interviews to individuals.

What Have We Discovered About the Assessment and Measurement of Personality?

In this chapter we have looked at personality and its assessment. This area has been much debated over a long time and there are no simple solutions on how it should be assessed, although scientific practice suggests the need for objective and empirical methods. Most assessments have been linked to theories which reflect different historical periods and each has its benefits and limitations. Our choice depends upon whether we take a more holistic view, as in therapeutic settings, or whether we are seeking to make comparisons between people.

We have learned about:

- The distinction between subjective and objective models, and contrasting views relating to the nature of personality.
- How attempts have been made to define and distinguish it from other characteristics.
- How thinkers and scientists have evolved different models and processes of assessment.
- How inventories have evolved, why they are useful, and their benefits, issues and limitations.

9

Alternative Perspectives on Assessment

Learning Objectives

By the end of this chapter you should be able to:

• Explain the influence of subjectivity, stereotyping and the Barnum effect on common forms of assessment, and the dangers of these.
• Discuss a range of non-psychometric forms of assessment in general use, including interview, projective, behavioural and objective test methods, and their advantages and limitations.
• Give an account of the theories and measures used to assess motivation, values and interests.

What is This Chapter About?

We have come a long way in learning about psychological assessment and psychometrics. However, not everything fits neatly into our almost linear comprehensive view. Some methods do not fit into any simple model or classification. We need to now look at the most common of these and to apply our evaluation skills to a mixed bag including pseudoscientific models, generally accepted approaches such as interview, projective and behavioural techniques, as well as assessment of other characteristics.

Alternative Approaches to Assessment

Human judgement is fallible, according to *The Oxford Companion to the Mind* (Gregory, 1987). People are poor judges of others, despite claims often that they can 'sum up' someone accurately. Such statements usually demonstrate that the claimants are complacent about their own abilities rather than being good judges of others. But there are, in fairness, many instances where objective measures are not available and many characteristics, such as the likeableness of people, cannot be measured directly. We make judgements of this kind every day.

In psychology our aim is to make assessments which have reliability and validity. This is particularly important where they provide a basis for decision-making. Yet there has been a long history of different approaches. We all have some understanding, too, of the personalities of people we encounter and we have referred to our unstated theories as implicit theories which are influenced by subjective feelings.

Implicit theories are found to extend beyond the information suggested by behaviour, especially through stereotyping which suggests that traits tend to be related within individuals. Stereotypes are shared beliefs about the enduring characteristics and behaviour of people and are mostly attached to general social roles, relating for example to age, body size, gender, family or work roles. Assessments of other people can be influenced unknowingly by assumed stereotypes. Archer and Lloyd (2002) and Leyens, Yzerbyt and Schadron (1994) provide good overviews of stereotyping processes.

Attribution Processes

When one person makes statements about another, these are referred to as attributions. Most information about others is derived from their overt behaviour and the settings in which it occurs. So the basic data for making inferences relate to actions. But actions alone cannot provide us with much information unless we know what caused them. Determination of the causes of action is called the attribution process and the study of this is part of attribution theory (Heider, 1958; Jones and Davis, 1965). Theorists have shown that people demonstrate a tendency to relate events to the internal personality of others, rather than to other causes, and this is known as the fundamental attribution error. It has consequences for how we evaluate assessments made by people about other people. Attribution theory suggests that what we should really be looking at when one person makes an attribution is its originator and what significance it has for that person rather than for the target. This means people can make assessments of each other, but their judgements are often misguided. (See Figure 9.1.)

Spurious Validity

The ability to make generalized statements, based often upon personal impressions and stereotyping, is called the Barnum Effect. The name derives from Colonel Phineas Barnum, variously described as a once-famous nineteenth century US showman, rodeo and circus entertainer, who made people feel he had an extraordinary ability to assess their personalities (Forer, 1949; Meehl, 1956; Snyder, Shenkel and Lowery, 1977). The effect uses common ideas, global and generalized terms, and stereotypical information, for example a person's appearance, gender, age or race, as a basis for judgement. Barnum statements are likely to be accepted when they are generalized, apply to many people, are

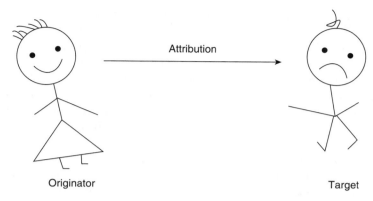

Figure 9.1   The attribution process

favourably worded and made by higher-status people. Notice the use of the title 'Colonel'. An example might be the statement: 'You are someone who tries hard to overcome difficulties'. Another word for it is 'gullibility'. The effect occurs when people accept interpretations based on vague statements having a high base-rate occurrence in the population. Barnum also notoriously said 'There is a fool born every minute'.

Individuals assessed by an astrologer or palmist often say, too, that it appears to be convincing, although this is a belief which has no connection with its validity. Just because they like it doesn't mean it is accurate. What it does have is called 'spurious validity,' mentioned in Chapter 6. There exists a range of approaches to assessment, some of them using the effect and possessing this kind of validity.

Graphology

Handwriting analysis was widely practised in the past in France, although it has declined considerably. Rather than evaluating the quality of handwriting, graphologists link its style to many characteristics, especially personality, although sometimes including intelligence, sexuality and job performance. But the research evidence is not good (McKenzie, Davey and Harris, 1982). Investigation indicates that different graphologists fail to agree about individuals, suggesting poor validity. When challenged about this by Jeffrey Gray at a conference, a graphologist admitted that 'it all depends on which school of graphology you go to' (I was there). Reviewing studies, Klimoski and Rafaeli (1983) state that it is not a viable assessment method. Graphologists do not analyse copied text, but ask people to write pen pictures of themselves. This means assessments are based often on people's perceptions of themselves and suggests they interpret what people write rather than how they write it (McLeod, 1968; Neter and Ben-Shakhar, 1989). The profiles may also depend on the Barnum effect.

Polygraphy

Used worldwide by police forces, this form of assessment uses tests based on physiological reactions to questions and is the result of an old idea that telling lies is linked to physiology.

The polygraph is, actually, an accurate device which can depict valid pictures of different body reactions through ink pens writing on charts or the use of computer monitors. It amplifies signals detected by sensors attached to a suspect under interrogation. Most common assessments are of sweating, blood pressure, heart rate or breathing rate and any changes are regarded as indicators of emotional arousal (Bull, 1988; Ben-Shakhar and Furedy, 1990).

However, there is little evidence to support its use, and its reliability and validity have been much debated. A joint US/UK investigation concluded that the methods used are not standardized satisfactorily in psychometric terms and highlighted a lack of checks on procedures used by different polygraphers. These procedures include misleading the individual about its effectiveness and the induction of anxiety to increase compliance (Report of the Working Group, 1986). Crucially, its key assumption lies in the relationship between emotional arousal and deception. Deception is supposed to cause stress or anxiety and this is translated into recorded physiological reactions. Therefore, the device should not be described as a 'lie detector'.

The evidence is that no typical emotional change exists for lying, although some distinct emotions can all result in similar reactions, including anger, fear, shame or guilt. Anyone frightened or angry could have reactions indicating they are lying. Two procedures of questioning have been devised, the Control Question Test (CQT) and the Guilty Knowledge Test (GKT), although studies indicate that both make mistakes. The CQT involves misleading suspects, which is thought unethical, and the GKT has limited applicability. Similar attempts to identify deception have been through the use of voice stress analysis and pupil dilation. These assume that an unsteady voice or enlargement of the pupils provides evidence of lying. A balanced overview of arguments is available from Hants and Quick (1995), Lykken (1988) and Hants (1994).

Other Pseudosciences

Before the Enlightenment and the scientific revolution there were many beliefs labelled as 'sciences', some involving assessments. A few pseudoscientific doctrines have survived and still continue to attract adherents. Astrology and numerology make assessments based on time and place of birth. Palmistry relates to line patterns on the palm of the hand, which is still apparently being used in personnel selection in some countries. Tarot readings provide assessment focussed on patterns of cards. Another, physiognomy, attempted to determine aspects of personality from external body features, especially facial ones. Its use can still be seen when employers ask for photographs of candidates for jobs. Lastly, phrenology, the study of 'bumps' on the head, had a big influence in the nineteenth century and was taken seriously by many until about 1950 in the UK. This associated abilities, personality characteristics and problems with development of areas of the brain and suggested assessment could be conducted through the touching of the outside of a skull by an expert. Protuberances could be identified.

The dangers
Potentially extensive dangers could ensue through using such methods as psychological assessments. They lack explicit or recognized inference rules and are unable to make

accurate, reliable or valid predictions. They mostly do not have any theoretical or empirical justification, provide no testable theories, and there is little, if any, evidence supporting predictions. Historical or cultural traditions are represented by them, and for this reason they still generate feelings of spurious validity among some people. Outcomes can lead to poor quality of guidance or development, ineffective decision-making and even distress, as well as poor selection or promotion decisions by employers.

More Accepted Forms of Assessment

Methods which have a scientific approach to measurement, such as tests and question-naires, have been emphasized. However, there are other widely used techniques which, in some instances, can provide good information about a person. Psychologists and HR professionals have been rather creative in developing methods, especially concerning personality. In fact, duplication of inferences by differing methods can help to provide extra support in decision-making. The more varied the assessments are of an individual, the more we learn and, therefore, the more effective conclusions are. On this basis alternative methods can be helpful.

Situational Assessments

These are based upon observations and inferences in specific situations, for example case studies or interviews. Interviewing is one of the most widely used assessments, being specific about a person, although it is often difficult to generalize behaviour and disposition to other situations. Distortion occurs mostly when people 'act out' an attitude or behaviour purely for the occasion and might be reduced through confidentiality, offering feedback, and use of structured questioning. Informal, unstructured interviews will be more influenced by distortion. Bias occurs when it is done informally and without training.

Interviews can be used for a range of purposes. In research contexts they help acquire qualitative information; in clinical settings they can collect case history information, as well as help make diagnoses (sometimes called diagnostic interviewing) and for patient in-take information (Levinson, Darrow, Klein, Levinson and McKee, 1978). Clinical practice includes interviewing, often as a preliminary for diagnostic formulation and the reliability and validity of this is unknown (McCrae and Costa, 1990; Lindsay and Powell, 1994). In some instances interviewing is used to determine a disorder based on classification criteria provided in the *Diagnostic and Statistical Manual of Mental Disorders (DSM)* or the *International Classification of Diseases (ICD)* which were discussed in Chapter 1. Techniques used may vary depending on an interviewer's theoretical inclination.

In the occupational field a selection or development interview is an attempt to systematically gather information about someone's background, knowledge and personality. This is often structured, using approaches such as competency-based or behavioural questioning techniques. Whatever its purpose, an interview is a complex interpersonal skill and is subject to the influence of the interviewer's own characteristics (Herriott, 1989, 2002; Thornton, 1993). Potential bias includes:

- *Self-delusion* when interviewers think themselves to be brilliant at interviewing and making judgements about others.
- *The 'halo' effect* whenever we judge others in terms of our own characteristics. People usually like others who are similar to themselves.
- *The fundamental attribution error* when we attribute a person's reactions or behaviour to personality rather than to other factors.
- *Early impressions* which are gained quickly and have a big impact on decision-making.
- *Subjectivity* when we make a judgement based on our own meanings, values, interests or preferences.
- *Stereotyping* when we make judgements based on shared beliefs.
- *Value judgements*, which are based on our own values, desires or goals, often involving strong feelings.
- *Negative information*, which is gained early on and can be difficult to change. This encourages people to decide too soon and then look for evidence in support.
- *Generalizations*, which seek to draw broad conclusions from a specific attribute or a single behaviour.
- *Impression formation* when judgements are based on a few or superficial aspects of someone.
- *Non-verbal cues* which have an influence, especially eye contact, smiling or appearing energetic to impress.
- *Paralinguistic cues*, which influence verbal fluency, speaking also with a standard dialect and rapid speech to impress the interviewer.
- *Contrast effects* when an average candidate follows three poor ones and gets rated highly, while one who comes after three good candidates gets rated down.

The effectiveness of interviews has been researched extensively. Despite its popularity, inter-rater reliability is often evaluated at about 0.3 and typical validity coefficients are around 0.15. Untrained interviewers demonstrate poor predictive validity, whilst those trained to use a structured approach can improve this to 0.5 (Robertson and Smith, 2001). The trouble is that interviewers vary in approach, style, characteristics and behaviour, as well as in aims and methods. For these reasons the interview is over-rated. Standard job interviews also correlate highly with ability tests, suggesting they can provide only a minimal incremental validity (see Chapter 6). Lengthy clinical interviews can cover a wide range of information including background experience, personal problems and relationships with others, gaining a deeper understanding. But they remain subjective and depend on personal judgement.

Reports by Others

These involve the giving of feedback by others, for example through use of 360-degree instruments which give a 'holistic' view of someone. They collect ratings from others, who have had contact with a target individual, which are often represented graphically to give an overall profile. Ratings might be given by combinations of managers, colleagues, subordinates and customers. They can be placed on behaviourally anchored scales, which provide a standardized format and are quicker to use, with descriptions being attached to specific values. The outcomes can then be reported to the individual concerned in feedback. Compared to self-ratings, ratings provided by others have higher validity for predicting job criteria (Mount, Barrick and Strauss, 1994; Nilsen, 1995).

But there are problems, for example the perceptions of others are subjective. Distortion can also be caused and unwarranted inferences made. Managers may spend little time observing a person and have limited actual knowledge and impression management can influence perceptions. Colleague or 'peer' ratings may be linked to friendship, popularity contests or aspects of competition. Racial bias has also been suggested to occur (Lewin and Zwany, 1976). Subordinates and customers often lack insight about the person or knowledge of the job involved. Lastly, it is possible that where attributions are made by six or fewer observers, the target person may be able to identify those who gave certain ratings.

Projective Instruments

Any method which can avoid the problems we saw with questionnaires in Chapter 8 is likely to be valued highly. Projective techniques, like the Rorschach ink-blot, have been widely used because their methods are indirect – respondents don't know how they are being evaluated. The term 'projective technique' is said to have been given to assessments where respondents are asked to project 'their drives, emotions, sentiments, complexes and conflicts' on to obscure stimuli. Ambiguity is the central feature, although there are a few tests which lack this, for example sentence completion tests and those using objects and models with children.

Supporters argue that when people are asked to describe something which isn't clear then their descriptions will reflect something personal. Stimuli are often vague, unstructured or open-ended materials, pictures or word tasks which respondents describe, complete or tell a story about. The lack of awareness means the method is less subject to response sets or deception. People are able to respond freely and their responses arise from within themselves. Someone may focus on a complete stimulus or just one aspect of it, or even suggest some kind of movement in it. To report that you are looking at an inkblot might be classified as being defensive or even pathological. Responses are interpreted to gain understanding of the person's mental state.

The Rorschach ink-blot test (Rorschach, 1921) is joined here by the Thematic Apperception Test (TAT) (Murray, 1938), discussed in Chapter 8. Responses on the Rorschach are scored by considering factors such as content, the part which produces them, and response time. The TAT was originally designed to assess motives like the need to achieve. Those developed for children may use pictures of animals rather than humans, as in Blum's Blacky Pictures (Blum, 1949). Another option consists of multiple-choice projective tests in which respondents select responses from a list, while attributes are understood through interpretation of consistencies and unusual features among responses. Extensive training is needed. Supporters of the method believe it opens the door to deeper layers of personality which a person may not be aware of and may be unconscious (Carstairs, 1957), linking it with psychodynamic theories.

These techniques have difficulties in terms of reliability and the validity of inferences, as well as in their theoretical basis. Research has demonstrated poor reliability and validity (Eysenck, 1959; Anastasi, 1988). Responses can vary widely, being situation-specific and depending also on the characteristics of administrators (Vernon, 1963). Distortion can occur when different raters make contrasting judgements about the same person, suggesting little consensus about the meaning of responses and resulting in poor inter-rater reliability.

Eysenck (1959) criticized these techniques on the grounds they provide no coherent theoretical account of the nature of the projection involved, although Semeonoff's projective test theory (1971, 1981) suggests that people identify with stimuli and project feelings on to them. Claims by manuals that they can measure many disparate characteristics make it difficult to accept that they have a scientific basis. Holtzman's newer version of the Rorschach (Holtzman, 1981), using short answer questions, is more psychometrically sound but gains less information.

Observations of Behaviour

How a person behaves is linked to internal characteristics, including ability, personality, motivation, state and mood, as well as environmental factors and situations. This assumption is key to the psychometric model of behaviour. Systematic observations, including behavioural antecedents and consequences where appropriate, have been widely used. In the clinical field the aim is often to assess problems and develop intervention programmes. A psychologist might wish, for example, to observe a team of carers in order to suggest how they can improve or expand their repertoire of reactions relating to people in their care. With individuals, a person experiencing social phobia might be observed in a social setting to assess factors associated with anxiety and the outcomes of responses in situations provoking it. There might be the need for observation of both individuals and groups, as in seeking to understand the challenging behaviour of someone having learning disability and its relationship with the activities of carers (Emerson, 2001).

Applied behaviour analysis has been used in a range of clinical areas, such as care settings, to teach skilled behaviour, to enhance competence and motivation, as well as in reducing challenging behaviour (Tate and Baroff, 1966; Baer, Wolf and Risley, 1968, 1987; Bailey and Meyerson, 1969). Psychologists may want to identify target behaviours, possible alternatives and causal factors relating to a patient, and intervention strategies. Procedures include recording the frequency and duration of behaviours, and can involve others, for example parents, nurses or carers.

Box 9.1   Using Behavioural Analysis

Functional behaviour analysis is designed to identify the discriminative stimuli and reinforcements which are linked to the behaviours of individuals (Bijou and Baer, 1961; Bijou, Peterson and Ault, 1968; Carr, 1988; Horner, Sprague, O'Brien and Heathfield, 1990). Through structured interviews and observational records, it can identify the processes responsible for someone's behavioural repertoire, including causal, precipitating and maintenance factors.

It was applied when Miss P, a 41-year-old Down's syndrome woman, was referred to the Psychology Service following reports of challenging behaviour. The service was asked to see her and to advise care staff who had difficulties in managing her when she became attached and dependent and had outbursts. She demonstrated aggression towards new staff and placed a strain on relationships with persistent aggressive and destructive behaviour. She also experienced mood swings.

Investigation using the Functional Analysis Interview Form (O'Neill et al., 1997) showed that Miss P demonstrated a range of challenging behaviours including:

- Physically attacking staff, such as snatching and breaking spectacles, pushing and hitting, punching or pulling hair;
- Throwing objects such as a fire extinguisher, items of furniture, cutlery or cooking utensils.

Behavioural analysis based on observation and interviews also at day care activities showed that she was more likely to demonstrate challenging behaviours when she experienced stress, fatigue or frustration or when she was not gaining attention. One tutor said 'Without reassurance she has been known to get upset and to react with physical violence.'

Observations suggested Miss P had an outgoing temperament, preferring often to be with others, especially care staff, desiring warm and close relationships to the point of becoming demanding when they did not pay attention to her or provide affection. Problem behaviours were hypothesized to be precipitated by her perceived lack of close relationships and her feelings of being unwanted. She needed frequent positive reinforcement and might become moody whenever this was not available.

A care plan was developed providing counselling sessions using a combination of symbols and cartoon narratives to address anger management issues and provide relaxation techniques. Guidance was also given to staff with regard to managing behaviours, for example in encouraging Miss P to use deep breathing or other relaxation exercises. Staff could reinforce interventions and were encouraged to interact more frequently with her. Progress was monitored by a weekly check of the number of incidents and a wall chart was constructed to provide a simple record. When there was no challenging behaviour a large star was displayed for the day. Despite an occasional setback, a gradual reduction was found in the number recorded during the overall period of intervention and in its last six weeks no incidents were reported.

In occupational use observations consist of recorded attributions made by assessors of the behaviour of individuals in assessment or development centres where group or role-play exercises are conducted. Such exercises range from leaderless discussion to more complex tasks involving, for example, decision-making in unusual scenarios. A group might run a company and adopt the roles of decision-makers, sometimes with an element of competition, or even conduct a practical exercise in a rural setting, for example in building a bridge. Observations here are best linked to job-related competencies or skills. Their advantage is that they provide a direct assessment of real behaviour and whether an individual is capable of doing something, and can also evaluate social skills. They can be objective when clear assessment criteria are used. But such events are time-consuming in construction and management, including assessor training to ensure good inter-rater reliability. It may also be difficult to generalize from observed performance to workplace behaviour because people may adapt to fit the occasion. Group dynamics are never simple, making it difficult to evaluate the abilities of any one person.

Educational psychologists, too, make observations of children in situations, either for understanding behaviours prior to intervention or for research. Observation in the playground is uncontrolled, sometimes referred to as 'naturalistic' observation. This doesn't mean, however, that they are unsystematic because a careful record can be made. Time sampling can also be used in which observations are made over a short period on a daily basis (Emerson, 2001). Controlled observations have been made in 'environmental assessment' (Moos and Moos, 1994) where, for example, children have been placed in a specific situation designed to elicit responses.

Objective Tests

Like projective assessment, objective tests are immune to the 'faking' of responses. They involve behaviour which can be objectively recorded or scored, usually through motor responses or perceptions, and are focussed on responses in specific situations. Objective scoring should give high reliability. A simple example might be to measure reaction times in response to words in order to identify emotional problems. In many instances responses are associated with aspects of personality. Where they involve the manipulation of objects they are called performance tests. Schmidt (1988) suggests that in the clinical field these are better than other assessments in the diagnosis of disorders. Examples are:

(i) *The rod and frame test*
This was designed to assess field dependency, the degree to which anyone is influenced by situational variables and the ability to resist them (Witkin and Goodenough, 1977). It is conducted in a darkened room so that participants have no clues about true horizontal or vertical alignments. Being seated, each is asked to adjust a rod placed within a perpendicular frame, both illuminated. The rod can be moved so that it is upright. Eventually the frame is twisted so that it is no longer perpendicular and the person asked to make the rod upright again. The question then is whether the rod's background, the frame, influences perception (called field dependency) or if other factors are involved. The influence of cues in the perceptual field may predominate and this is extrapolated to social settings where the attitudes of others could be more influential. In this way performance may link to behaviour elsewhere, for example of suggestibility or compliance.

(ii) *The embedded figures test*
Attributed to Witkin, Oltman, Raskin and Karp (1971), in this test the person is shown a figure and asked to find it in a more complex and confusing pattern. It was designed as another measure of field dependency and to identify how much performance is influenced by other factors. Overall scores are objective and have good test-retest reliability. They correlate with some aspects of personality, such as degree

of participation with others in learning situations. One of the performance sub-tests in the WAIS-III is based on this process.

(iii) *The lemon drop test*

The distinction between extraverts and introverts was important in Eysenck's person-ality theory (1955), discussed in Chapter 8, and he attempted to find direct experi-mental ways of distinguishing between them. In the theory introverts have a higher level of cortical arousal than extraverts and will be sensitive, therefore, to even more sensory stimulation. So if a standard number of drops of lemon juice are dropped on to the tongues of introverts they will salivate more than extraverts do.

There have been a lot of similar tests – Cattell and Warburton (1967) listed 688. They include chairs which sway in a development of the rod-and-frame test, the Fidgetometer which measures movements, the Slow Line Drawing test, pictures which change to identify adaptability in cognitive processing, measurement of tap-ping speed linked to assertiveness, copying of drawings to assess perfectionism, and pictorial designs for identifying creativity. Some assess anxiety or aspects of person-ality, whilst others are physiological. Test batteries also exist, such as the Objective Analytic Battery. The Morrisby tests assess a range of variables including innovative-ness, commitment and tenacity.

Such ingenious tests have advantages, although they are used mostly by specialists. Their outcomes are objective, unambiguous and difficult to fake, and can also be used in different cultures. However, some are time-consuming, expensive and need to be conducted in a laboratory. Some may be difficult to administer compared to ques-tionnaires; whilst people may also see them as silly and unappealing. They often lack normative data and there are low correlations with questionnaire scores, suggesting no empirical evidence of validity. Despite these problems, however, they appear to be useful in diagnosing mental illness. The consensus is that more research is needed.

Honesty and Integrity Questionnaires

If you are last to leave an office at the end of the day and found £20 on the floor, what would you do? Would you (a) hand it to security, (b) give to your manager on return-ing or (c) pocket it? That is the kind of item sometimes found in honesty questionnaires. You might think it is transparent: it's possible for someone who would pocket the note to choose either of (a) or (b) rather than admit being dishonest. These kinds of test have been used to identify people more likely to commit counterproductive behaviours, such as theft, in organizations.

Two descriptive terms apply to them – 'honesty' and 'integrity' – which seem to be used sometimes interchangeably. There are two kinds – 'overt' ones having items like the one above and others described as 'personality-oriented'. Overt tests often contain items con-cerning beliefs about the frequency and extent of theft, thoughts about theft and assess-ments of honesty, as well as asking for a confession of previous episodes of stealing. They contain direct questions and biographical items. Examples are the Employee Attitude Inventory, the Stanton Survey and the Trustworthiness Attitude Survey.

The second type is similar to personality questionnaires, although being broader and not confined to the issue of theft. These include items relating to reliability at work and dependability, conscientiousness and attitudes towards authority which are less transparent. As with questionnaires, they provide evidence of reliability and validity. Examples are the Hogan Development Survey (HDS) and Giotto. Hogan's measure identifies potentially disruptive or counterproductive behaviour in the workplace, known as the 'Dark Side' of the individual, whilst Giotto is based on the theory of a Renaissance artist who described virtues and vices as being made up of a number of contrasting attributes.

Such tests have been popular, especially considering high levels of theft by employees and its impact on the finances of US companies. A meta-analysis of 665 honesty/integrity test studies concerning validity based on 500,000 people suggested that they identify dishonesty quite well with a predictive correlation of 0.39 and can also predict job performance (Ones, Viswesvaran and Schmidt, 1993). Relationships were also shown with other forms of counterproductive behaviour. The attribute of conscientiousness was found to provide the single largest source of variance.

However, Sackett and colleagues have conducted extensive studies of these measures (Sackett and Dekker, 1979; Sackett and Harris, 1984; Sackett and Wanek, 1996; Sackett, Burris and Callahan, 1989). They suggest that methodological differences between studies involved in the meta-analysis have a large influence on the findings, for example higher validity coefficients appear when concurrent rather than predictive approaches are used. Other criticisms have also indicated that the mean correlation for theft criteria is low at 0.09. This suggests the tests do not validly predict theft, which is what they were designed to do. A separate analysis of personality-based measures (Salgado, 2000) found that conscientiousness and agreeableness are associated with counterproductive behaviour. The evidence, therefore, provides more support for these. But the major criticism is that there is no one single theory of honesty or integrity and so we cannot be certain what is being measured, particularly in using overt tests. Camara and Schneider (1994) say there is little agreement on the behaviours involved and insufficient evidence.

Summary

We have seen that human judgement is fallible in trying to make assessments of people, being influenced by subjectivity, stereotyping and the fundamental attribution error. A number of popular assessments make use of the Barnum Effect and common belief is said to give them spurious validity. We have also discussed more traditional methods including graphology, polygraphy, astrology, numerology, palmistry, physiognomy and phrenology, and problems relating to their use as forms of assessment. Others have included situational assessment, such as interviewing, reports by others, projective instruments, behavioural observations, objective tests and honesty/integrity questionnaires. We have looked at examples of these, as well as their advantages and limitations.

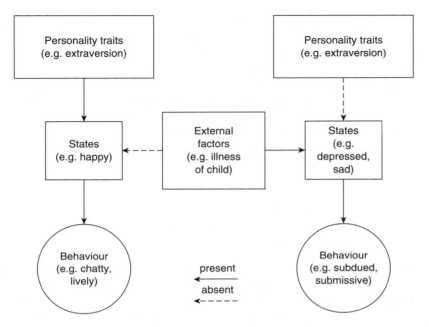

Figure 9.2   Traits, states and behaviour

Measuring Motives, Values and Interests

Measuring Motives

Intelligence, abilities and personality together can't account for all human behaviour, much as we would like them to. Imagine someone waking up after a late party the night before and having to go to work. Whilst one person would prefer to take the day off on the sick, another might still go to work. This suggests our behaviour is influenced by attributes which are not abilities or personality traits. Something else might make a difference, such as moods or motivation. These are affected by traits and situational variables.

Discussed in Chapter 8, motivation appears to relate to things like needs, interests and aspirations. It focuses on our driving force, its direction and persistence. A number of theories have sought to explain it, including drive theories, arousal theories and hedonistic theories, and it has been well researched. Whilst traits are stable over time, characteristics like motivation are more affected by mood states and situational factors, and are thus more changeable. The relationship between traits and behaviour may be mediated by states, whilst that between traits and states could be moderated by situational factors (Rusting, 1998), as shown in Figure 9.2. In short, traits cannot always account for behaviour.

The complexity of motivation has made it difficult to define. Early theories bridged the gap between biological and psychological needs (Murray, 1938; Maslow, 1954), while later ones include Herzberg's two-factor approach involving satisfaction and dissatisfaction, McClelland's needs theory linking needs for achievement, affiliation and power, and two-process theories, such as that of Adams (1963, 1965), which associate economics and psychology. The central theme has been a distinction between psychological and physiological motives. Furnham (2005) said: 'One of the oldest and most difficult topics in psychology is the fundamental problem of why people are motivated to do anything at all, and if they do something, why that and not something else'. Recent attempts to define motivation have centred more upon the question of why people act the way they do (Beck, 1990; Franken, 1993). Key to many has been a focus on aspects of behaviour:

- It drives people into action
- A direction of behaviour and energy towards satisfaction of needs and drives
- The amount of energy/effort put in and its persistence
- It can involve a range of goals

Although there have been many attempts to measure motivation and its underlying drive, the most significant is that of Cattell (Cattell, 1957; Cattell and Child, 1975). He identified a number of factors of motivational strength, indicating that it is a multidimensional concept and that some elements are unconscious. These drives/goals were classified as either basic or culturally formed, referred to respectively as 'ergs' and 'sentiments'. Ergs are sometimes biological drives that are pleasurable to satisfy, such as sex or eating food; while sentiments reflect drives which are more culturally determined. Some of these are shown in Table 9.1.

Cattell and his colleagues developed adult and child versions of a Motivational Analysis Test, having 208 items distributed within four sub-tests to assess the extent of an individual's ergs and sentiments. Each sub-test was designed to be a questionnaire-based objective test so that people completing them couldn't identify what was being measured. An alpha coefficient of 0.45 was reported, suggesting unsatisfactory reliability, and investigations by Cooper and Kline (1982) indicate little evidence for the validity of the adult version. The only thing that can be said in its favour is that, having norms based on US samples, it is one of the few objective tests to have been standardized.

Table 9.1 *Cattell's motivational factors*

Ergs (basic drives)	Sentiments (culturally determined drives)
Mating	Self-sentiment
Hunger	Conscience
Assertiveness	Career/profession
Fear	Having a spouse or partner
Narcissism (comfort-seeking)	Parental home
Pugnacity	Sporting
Acquisitiveness	Money

Other tests have been developed to measure specific aspects of motivation, although they may measure personality traits instead, reflecting the difficulty of distinguishing between the two. In fact, most self-report 'motivation' questionnaires are likely to reflect personality rather than motivational drives. Cattell constructed an objective questionnaire because he thought people would lack self-awareness and that, therefore, a self-report questionnaire wasn't appropriate. But occupational interest has been strong so that some personality questionnaires include dimensions for measuring achievement motivation.

The result has been a plethora of motivational questionnaires which, generally, suggest that motivated people will be more productive. ASE's Occupational Motivation Questionnaire, for example, measures seven different types of work-related motivation. SHL's Motivation Questionnaire has 18 dimensions, classified into energy and dynamism, synergy, intrinsic and extrinsic motivations. PSL's assessment range includes another MQ, this time measuring eight dimensions. The Motivation and Culture Fit Questionnaire of Criterion Partnership assesses motivation among other factors such as job satisfaction, fulfilment and morale. The construct is sometimes linked to values, as in the Values and Motives Inventory of Psytech International. This is said to profile the motivating forces likely to determine the amount of energy or effort an individual will expend. So, despite its complexity and difficulties in its measurement, motivation is big business. Inevitably, it has been linked to factors such as values and interests.

Measuring Values

If we are motivated by something, whether a hobby or a sport, reading or hang-gliding, then we must value it. Our values reflect how much we rate the merit or importance of something, its worth and usefulness, and are inevitably associated with our actions. Not only are they linked to motives, they are also associated with interests and attitudes although not being the same. Measures of values, interests and attitudes have similar item content. Once again, there have been varying definitions. The most quoted was given by Rokeach (1973, 1979), who conducted comprehensive research into values. He defined any value as: '…an enduring belief that a specific mode of conduct or end-state of existence is personally or socially preferable to an opposite or converse mode of conduct or end-state of existence' (1973, p. 5).

Rokeach thought that values are stable over time and are associated with ethical or moral choices, what we think is acceptable or unacceptable. Other definitions have focussed on evaluations associated with personal standards (Rand, 1964; Locke, 1976). There are two types of value, according to Rokeach: those applying to modes of conduct (instrumental values) and those applying to end states (terminal values). Instrumental values are subdivided into moral values and competence values; terminal ones are split into personal and social values. Moral values relate to interpersonal conduct, competence ones to inner feelings of social adequacy; personal values are concerned with inner states like peace and tranquillity; whilst values such as interpersonal respect, equality and world peace are socially centred (Figure 9.3).

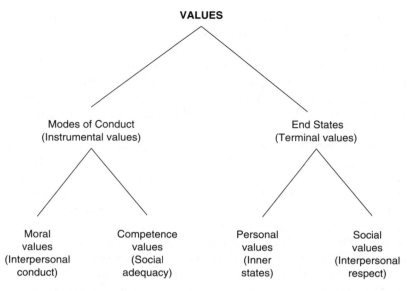

Figure 9.3   Rokeach's model of values

The evidence is that values have a significant role in vocational choice and thus play a role in career guidance. When people's values are being met by a job they are happier at work and have higher job satisfaction (Watts, Super and Kidd, 1981). Different cultures may also value such things as individualism and masculinity to different degrees. As a result measures of values have been included within some vocational counselling and motivational assessments.

The most well-known measures are the Study of Values (Allport, Vernon and Lindzey, 1960) and the Rokeach Value Survey (Brookhart, 1995). The third edition of the Allport method, designed in 1931, is old-fashioned, although scores have been related to vocational choice. It assesses six basic variables: theoretical, economic, aesthetic, social, political and religious. Being self-referenced, it asks respondents to rank order statements according to different criteria. Both split-half and test-retest reliabilities are high at above 0.8, although its norms and validity are questionable. In contrast, Rokeach's measure has been popular because it assesses a lot of values and is easy to score. It consists of a series of lists, each having 18 instrumental and 18 terminal value descriptors, and respondents are asked to place the items in each list in rank order based on personal importance. Having levels of reliability between 0.6 and 0.8 for the scales, reviews by, for example, Braithwaite and Scott (1991) have supported its use in research. It is also an ipsative measure.

Super's Work Values Inventory (1970) has been found more useful in the work setting, especially with younger adults. Super thought that needs, values and interests differ essentially in their breadth and levels of abstraction, with interests being the least abstract. He placed needs at the most abstract level and defined values and interests as lower-order concepts arising from needs. Values were defined as the objectives sought to satisfy needs, while interests were the specific activities and objects through which an individual strives towards values and the satisfaction of needs. The inventory assesses 15 values, including security, pay, intellectual stimulation, creativity, prestige and independence, using Likert scales (Chapter 2). Respondents indicate the degree of importance they give to the value reflected by each item. Each scale has percentile norms based on US samples, good test-retest reliability coefficients and evidence of content, concurrent and construct validity.

Aspects of both the Value Survey and the Work Values Inventory were later combined to create the Values Scale measuring 21 values. The aim was to understand the values individuals hope for in differing life roles and the importance of work roles as part of these. All of the scales provided in the second edition have good psychometric properties.

Some other instruments measuring values in the workplace include FIRO-B, which is sold for personal, team and leadership development, and was designed by Schutz (1989). It assesses the extent to which individuals value inclusion, control and affection in relation to others. There are also Gordon's Survey of Personal Values (SPV) and Survey of Interpersonal Values (SIV). The SPV measures values placed on activities including practical mindedness, achievement, variety, decisiveness, orderliness and goal orientation; while the SIV assesses those concerning personal, social, marital and occupational adjustment (Gordon, 1993). The Values and Motives Inventory, from Psytech, measures values identified as being important to work behaviour.

Measuring Interests

Assessment of interests has been important in the occupational and vocational fields, and research has grown. Much of the literature has been devoted to understanding individual differences and their role in supporting occupational choices. But, as we have seen, it is difficult to distinguish between interests, values and especially motives, which is why some seek to mix them, as in the Motives Values Preferences Inventory (Hogan and Hogan, 1987). There must also be links with personality, so interests could be seen as consisting of a combination of aspects of personality, values and motivation.

Definitions of interests have focussed on a person's 'preferences' or 'likes' and 'dislikes'. Carlson (2002) suggests they could be seen as a kind of 'desire', especially for what people want to understand and do. On this basis, interests indicate what people enjoy and do not enjoy doing. This could account for Super's view (1970) that they are less abstract and, therefore, more practical in nature. There have been a number of theories about them and are classified most effectively by Furnham (1992), as shown in Table 9.2.

The Strong Vocational Interest Blank
Some interest inventories were designed to support career guidance and development, the earliest being by Edward Strong in 1919 and later revised (Strong, Campbell, Berdie and Clerk, 1971). Construction of measures using criterion keying was discussed in Chapter 3

Table 9.2   *Theoretical approaches to vocational interests*

Approach	Key themes
Psychodynamic	• Relates to influence of internal processes on career decisions • Considers the impact of unconscious motives and interactions with others
Developmental	• Places emphasis on lifespan development and change • Considers environmental influences and the concept of 'effort'
Sociological	• Relates to political and socioeconomic influences • Views education and opportunities as more significant than characteristics such as ability and personality
Motivational	• Approaches based on theories of needs • Relates to individual needs and their satisfaction in the workplace
Existential	• Based upon humanistic approach to personality • Emphasizes self-actualization through achievement of goals
Decision-making	• Focuses on factors determining decision-making, such as valuations, perceptions and attributions

and Strong used an adaptation of this, referred to as 'occupational keying', to make the Strong Vocational Interest Blank. After developing items which asked about preferences for a variety of activities, objects or people, he asked those working within a range of occupations, for example farmers, architects and scientists, to also complete them. He was then able to identify which items distinguished between the occupational groups. Any person then completing the inventory could be matched against groups to see which one best reflected responses. The most recent version provides scales relating to occupational themes, basic interests, relevant occupations and the individual's personal style.

Test-retest reliabilities are reported to be over 0.9, although longer-term ones lie in the range 0.6–0.7. But the inventory's validity is more questionable. The fact that it was constructed by criterion-keying, that it may not reflect changes in many occupations and that it asks for an expressed interest in any particular occupation (Katz, 1972) have been major criticisms. Responses have been developed for more occupations and Strong's approach has encouraged the design of other inventories.

The Kuder interest tests

More recent versions of the Strong inventory have been adapted to scoring based on interest themes or areas of interest following the work of Kuder (1954). Kuder developed the notion of general themes of relevance to many types of occupation, including:

- Outdoor
- Mechanical
- Computational

- Scientific
- Persuasive
- Artistic
- Literary
- Musical
- Social Service
- Clerical

He constructed scales for each of these themes to create the Kuder Preference Record, which was revised to become the Kuder General Interest Survey (1970a) and also the Kuder Occupational Interest Survey (1970b). In these tests respondents are presented with items made up of groups of three activities and are asked to identify the most liked or disliked. A score for each theme is determined and the highest are combined to establish relevant occupations. For example, someone with high scores on computational and artistic scales might be directed towards graphic or media design. Another with high scores on outdoor and persuasive scales will be guided towards becoming a travelling sales executive.

Like the Strong, the Kuder test is a criterion-keyed inventory with similar problems. Its response process is also ipsative and again creates difficulties, especially with regard to evidence for construct validity and construction of norms, although the tests have been widely researched and used in the US. His theme-based approach has influenced the development of other measures such as SHL's Managerial Interest Inventory (1989), Harcourt's Career Interest Inventory and Psytech's Occupational Interest Profile, which combines occupational interests and work needs. Other examples include the Rothwell-Miller Interest Inventory (Miller, Rothwell and Tyler, 1994) and the Jackson Vocational Interest Survey (Jackson, 1977).

Holland's inventories

Holland's research, theory and interest inventories have also been influential and are based on the view that interests, and therefore occupations, are related to personality characteristics (1966, 1985, 1996). A key aspect is that any match between interests and work activities will result in enhanced job satisfaction. Holland used factor analysis to identify six occupational categories which were related through a hexagonal model of interests, as shown in Figure 9.4, rather than on a random basis as before. The categories are: realistic, investigative, artistic, social, enterprising and conventional, abbreviated to RIASEC.

Using his Self-Directed Search (SDS) – Form R assessment, respondents can identify their three highest scores among the categories and, in many instances, are placed closer together around the outside of the hexagon. For example, if the order of someone's scores was Enterprising, Social and Conventional then the person would be classified as an ESC type. Holland thought that occupations could be classified in a similar way, according to the kind of work. So to find matching careers, the person's three-letter code would then be entered into an 'Occupations Finder' to generate related job titles.

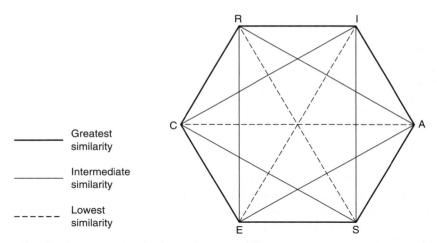

Figure 9.4 Holland's hexagonal model of interests

Participants can also make use of the Vocational Preference Inventory. This involves ratings of like/dislike to a range of occupations and the scoring of responses on 11 scales, including the six RIASEC interest scales and five others reflecting personality characteristics of self-control, status, masculinity–femininity, infrequency and acquiescence. The RIASEC code is again used with the finder to identify relevant jobs. Data on this suggest moderate–good reliabilities and evidence is available also of validity, particularly concurrent and predictive validity.

But there have been criticisms of the item set, of the number of themes, of their arrangement and correlations between them (Gati, 1991). Prediger suggests the model could be shrunk to a three-factor version having two bipolar dimensions of 'ideas–data' and 'people–things', and another reflecting response bias (Prediger, 1976; Prediger and Vansickle, 1992a, b). 'Things' concern interests and occupations having low interpersonal contact, whilst 'data' concerns concreteness and practicality, and 'ideas' reflect thinking, creativity and knowledge. There has been much empirical support for this view (Prediger, 1982).

Summary

There are a number of attributes which can have an impact on behaviour, but are difficult to define. They appear to be interrelated and associated also with personality, resulting in some combined measures. Motivation is linked to mood states and situational factors, and a number of motivational assessments are available. Measures have also been developed of values. Interests have been viewed as more practical in nature and different models have resulted in vocational inventories.

What Have We Discovered About Alternative Perspectives on Assessment?

Understanding and knowledge gained earlier has been much in evidence in this chapter. We have evaluated a range of alternative perspectives, definitions, theories, models and their applications. They have ranged from assessments made by people about others and their key characteristics, such as subjectivity and stereotyping, through to those of motivation and values. We have looked at the Barnum Effect and spurious validity and their influence upon popular forms of assessment. The benefits and limitations of other methods have been considered, such as interviews, 360-degree instruments, objective and projective measures, observational methods and honesty/integrity questionnaires. Lastly, we have looked at complex characteristics which do not fit easily within the trait-based paradigm but which enable us to better understand behaviour. In sum, we have learned about:

- The influence of subjectivity, stereotyping and the Barnum effect on common forms of assessment.
- Non-psychometric forms of assessment in general use, including interviews, projective, behavioural and objective test methods.
- Theories and principal measures used to assess motivation, values and interests.

PART IV

Ethical and Professional Issues

10

Best Practice in Assessment and Testing

Learning Objectives

By the end of this chapter you should be able to:

- Explain the need for ethical codes relating to psychological assessment, linking them to relevant legislation and to issues such as informed consent, confidentiality, data protection and test security.
- Understand the need for professional standards relating to administration, scoring, interpretation of outcomes and giving feedback.
- Appreciate the key principles of computer-based assessment and likely future developments in testing.

What is This Chapter About?

No matter how well any assessment is constructed, how accurate or valid it is, the results are worthless unless it is administered, scored and interpreted fairly and accurately. That is the focus of this chapter. Central to criticisms of the testing movement have been concerns about fairness, privacy and confidentiality. Psychologists have become increasingly concerned about the availability of tests and their ethical and sensitive use. The dangers of misuse or incompetent use are considerable and it is generally accepted that tests should be used only by qualified practitioners. In this chapter we will consider codes of practice and the legislation which impacts upon test-users, for example regarding fairness and confidentiality. We will consider best practice in administration, scoring, interpretation and feedback to test-takers and in written reports. We will also look at potential future developments.

Ethics, Fairness and Assessment

Psychological assessments are potent tools. Misused or used negligently, they can cause unhappiness, distress and discrimination. They can cause bad decisions to be made, which might disrupt their family life, cause them to lose their partners, children, homes or jobs, or to act in ways which have negative impacts on themselves or others. Poor decisions could also result in litigation against the person responsible for assessment.

Whatever the domain of psychology involved, it is important to handle measures in fair and ethical ways. The modern view is that users must be licensed or qualified (see Box 10.3). This is why professional bodies have ethical codes of practice, often including specific codes, and anyone making assessments should be familiar with the relevant code of practice. That of the American Psychological Association, for example, deals extensively with issues across the discipline of psychology and provides supplementary guidance on testing. The British Psychological Society (BPS), too, provides a *Code of Ethics and Conduct* (2006), as well as *Generic Professional Practice Guidelines* (2008) for psychologists having a section on assessment, and a *Code of Practice for Psychological Testing* (2003). A summary of the generic guidelines relating to assessment is shown in Box 10.1, and the content of the psychological testing code in Box 10.2. In the event of any ethical dilemma the rights of respondents should always remain paramount and practitioners should seek advice from a supervisor or their professional body, or even request expert guidance provided by professional liability insurers.

Box 10.1   Generic Professional Practice Guidelines

The following extract is taken from the guidelines published by the British Psychological Society on the society's website at www.bps.org.uk.

Assessment Materials

Psychologists should be mindful at all times of the confidential nature of assessment materials. Many assessment measures are invalidated by prior knowledge of their specific content and objectives. Psychologists who use these materials are required to respect their confidentiality and to avoid their release into the public domain (unless this is explicitly allowed in the nature of the instrument and by the test publisher).

Psychologists should, therefore, take reasonable steps to prevent misuse of test data and materials by others. Misuse includes release of such data and materials to unqualified individuals, which may result in harm to the client.

For these reasons, psychologists should not include raw data from psychometric assessment in the shared part of records, as this would mean allowing detailed information on the content and nature of tests to be released to non-psychologists, who may not have the training or expertise to be able to interpret the information they contain. The results of psychometric assessment should be incorporated into reports which explain their context and appropriate interpretation and which are included in the shared institutional record.

Such psychometric test data should be kept in areas of records with controlled access. The use of 'sealed envelopes' is recommended both for paper and electronic records. This information should only be released to those with legitimate authority and who are qualified to use and interpret them.

Box 10.2   Code of Good Practice in Psychological Testing

People who use psychological tests are expected to:

Responsibility for Competence

1   Take steps to ensure that they are able to meet all of the standards of competence defined by the Society for the relevant Certificate(s) of Competence in Testing, and to endeavour, where possible, to develop and enhance their competence as test-users.
2   Monitor the limits of their competence in psychometric testing and not to offer services which lie outside their competence nor encourage or cause others to do so.
3   Ensure that they have undertaken any mandatory training and that they have the specific knowledge and skills required for each of the instruments they use.

Procedures and Techniques

4   Use tests, in conjunction with other assessment methods, only when their use can be supported by the available technical information.
5   Administer, score and interpret tests in accordance with the instructions provided by the test distributor and to the standards defined by the Society.
6   Store test materials securely and to ensure that no unqualified person has access to them.
7   Keep test results securely, in a form suitable for developing norms, validation and monitoring for bias.

Client Welfare

8   Obtain the informed consent of potential test-takers, making sure that they understand why the tests will be used, what will be done with their results and who will be provided with access to them.
9   Ensure that all test-takers are well informed and well prepared for the test session, and that all have had access to practice or familiarisation materials where appropriate.
10 Give due consideration to factors such as gender, ethnicity, age, disability and special needs, educational background and level of ability in using and interpreting the results of tests.
11 Provide the test-taker and other authorised persons with feedback about the results in a form which makes clear the implications of the results, is clear and in a style appropriate to their level of understanding.
12 Ensure test results are stored securely, are not accessible to unauthorised or unqualified persons and are not used for any other purposes other than those agreed with the test-taker.

Fairness in Testing

Considering that many early tests were standardized on samples of white people, it's not surprising that questions arose about their validity in the assessment of others and whether they discriminated against different groups. Everyone will accept today that all people should be considered fairly. This is a fundamental right, regardless of gender, race, religion, colour, ethnic origin or background, age, sexual orientation or disability.

As the use of psychometric testing has become more widespread there have been worries that not all groups get equal treatment when compared to others doing the same tests. This might occur because of intentional attempts to discriminate, although it happens, too, when tests are poorly constructed. Legislation is in place in the UK, US, Europe and many other countries to ensure people do not suffer any discrimination. In some countries there is no such legislation. But most of these have national groups based on ethnic, religious or cultural differences, and practitioners will appreciate the need to treat them all on a fair basis. This will ensure that they maintain and enhance respect for themselves as testers, for the measures used and for their employers.

There are two major types of discrimination recognized by the law in the US and the UK – direct and indirect discrimination. The difference is reflected in the concepts of disparate treatment – which may have resulted from direct discrimination – and adverse or disparate impact – which results from indirect discrimination. Adverse impact happens when a requirement is applied to all individuals but has a disproportionately unfavourable effect on one group. It can arise from the use of assessments, especially when they are used to make decisions about people. Discrimination could potentially occur, for example, when they are used to make decisions about treatment or placements or for job selection. If a test systematically under-predicts the true performance of one group compared to others, it is likely to be less valid for the group and, therefore, a source of discrimination. This could be caused by a number of factors relating to items, including levels of difficulty based upon needing special knowledge, where they have little or no meaning for some groups, where responses might be influenced by a test-taker's attitude, and where, having poor validity, they under-predict true performance.

Adverse impact is most relevant in relation to assessment for employment. In UK law a complainant does not have to show any discriminatory intent on the part of the decision-maker. The case is based on the argument that there is something the decision-maker does or fails to do which results in discrimination and that this is evidenced by the disproportionate numbers of people affected from one or more groups. Direct discrimination requires complainants to show they were intentionally treated differently and to establish it four questions need to be answered:

- Has a rule or condition been applied to all participants, regardless of gender, race, religion, colour, ethnic origin or background, age, sexual orientation and disability?
- Does that rule exclude disproportionately more people from one group than people not from that group?
- Is it to the disadvantage of people from the group to be excluded in this way?
- Can the decision-maker show that the need for the rule overrides the adverse effect?

Legislation in the UK includes the following:

1 The Sex Discrimination Act (1975). The Equal Opportunities Commission issued its Code of Practice in 1985.
2 The Race Relations Act (1976). The Commission for Racial Equality issued its Code of Practice in 1984. In the employment field the CRE Code stressed the need to clarify requirements for English and qualifications at a level appropriate for jobs. The two organizations were later integrated within the Equality and Human Rights Commission.
3 The Disability Discrimination Act (1995) makes it unlawful for an employer to treat disabled people less favourably than others because of their disability, unless there is good reason.

The UK became a signatory to European Human Rights legislation in 2000 and age discrimination legislation was introduced in 2006. The US also has legislation banning discrimination on the grounds of race, gender, age, disability and religion, while the cities of Boston and San Francisco banned discrimination on the grounds of 'heightism' and 'weightism'. The legislation requires that decisions should be made on merit, not on the basis of, for example, race or sex. It is not unlawful to try to correct an imbalance of the sexes in a work force or group by seeking to operate a quota system, although this should be used only where people are of equal merit. Codes of Practice stipulate that any assessment should be based on a job analysis procedure to define the knowledge, skills and abilities normally required for effective performance in jobs.

The broad objective concerning disability is to ensure that people with disabilities have equal access to opportunities and, to this end, decision-makers are subject to a positive duty to make reasonable adjustments to environments, equipment and/or practices to accommodate someone having a disability. People with disabilities can only be treated less favourably if the difference can be justified, taking into account a duty to make reasonable adjustments.

At the core of this legislation is the definition of disability. A person will have protection under the law through having 'a physical or mental impairment which has a substantial and long-term adverse effect on the ability to carry out normal day-to-day activities'. This, therefore, includes mental illness. With no cap on the damages which may be awarded, possibly including damages for injury to feelings, there is every incentive for decision-makers to comply and to review their practices to remove areas of vulnerability. This will include removing unjustifiable barriers affecting people having disabilities. In the case of tests, discrimination is more likely to occur when items are more difficult for one group compared to another, where an item is less reliable for its members or where people having disability cannot perform effectively because of some obstacle. The practical implications of this for testing are:

• Tests need to meet a set of quality criteria, like those of Chapter 1.
• Testers should ensure they accommodate people having disabilities. The legislation refers to 'reasonable adjustment' and this means, for example, that individuals having visual impairments are supported by the use of large type or Braille materials. In the case of

measures not having time limits, such as questionnaires, people having visual disabilities may be able to dictate responses. Those having hearing disabilities should benefit from written instructions; otherwise a signing interpreter might be employed. Someone who uses a wheelchair will need a writing surface placed at an appropriate height.

• What is meant by 'disability' and 'reasonable adjustment' are open to debate and even back pain has been accepted as a disability. It helps to ask in advance how a particular disability might affect test performance and what support the individual thinks would be best given.

• It helps to prepare by sending out letters of invitation before assessment asking people whether they have any special needs, so that they can provide information in advance and enable testers to prepare adequately.

• The most difficult issues concern norms and time limits, and these often arise in relation to dyslexia. Schools and universities provide extra time for participants in this case, although publishers' norms are mostly based on set time limits and are, therefore, inapplicable if the time is extended. If in doubt, testers should check with a publisher. Few tests have norms without time limits. Rare examples include Raven's Progressive Matrices and the Watson-Glaser Critical Thinking Appraisal, which has untimed norms, for example, for graduate banking applicants in the UK. More untimed tests are needed.

• In some cases it can be difficult to determine the appropriate kind of adjustments needed and it might then be wise to contact relevant charities or the publishers. In all cases it is wise to be clearly willing to offer assistance.

• It helps to have a short conversation with each participant before assessment to identify whether there is anyone whose original language is not English. If so, they might be asked whether they feel at a disadvantage. Experience suggests that anyone who learned English as a second language after childhood could be disadvantaged and, if this is the case, a record made. It is possible also to offer to administer instead a test of abstract reasoning which normally has little verbal content, such as the Progressive Matrices, with the help of an interpreter if necessary. Some publishers have tests available in a range of languages.

Checking bias and using cut-offs

Ability tests are designed to discriminate between people although on a fair basis, i.e. between those who perform well and those who don't. The existence of bias suggests that items are too difficult for some people for reasons not connected with the ability under investigation, for example because a test assumes a form of cultural knowledge which they do not possess. Whenever tests are used as part of any decision-making process, it is important to ensure that they exhibit few group differences. Bias may occur when differences exist between the mean scores of different groups. A mixed-model analysis of variance (ANOVA) can demonstrate the significance of any group × item interaction to indicate whether items are easier for members of one group compared to those of another, although it is only effective using large samples and generally does not identify items responsible. A range of techniques has been developed for detecting bias (Osterling, 1983; Reynolds, 1995).

Box 10.3   Qualifications Needed for Assessment Measures

Publishers generally restrict test sales to those who have appropriate qualifications. These come in four groups depending on the level of skill required:

1   A basic level relates to measures which are unlikely to lead to dire consequences should anything go wrong. They need a minimum level of knowledge or skills, and are not designed to be used for any major decision-making, being aimed at supporting training, development or counselling activities. Questionnaires which promote discussion about self-awareness might fit in here, for example team style inventories. They are mostly sold to teachers, lecturers or trainers.

2   The Certificate of Competence in Occupational Testing (Test Administration) is offered by the British Psychological Society's Psychological Testing Centre. This recognizes that competent test administration and scoring are critical to successful use of tests, that poor practice will invalidate a test and impact on the experience of participants. This qualification sets minimum standards for those using tests at a basic level.

3   The Level A certificate forms a second level, covering the underlying knowledge of measurement and practical skills and focussing on tests of maximum performance. It enables purchasers to have access primarily to tests of ability and aptitude which are simpler to administer and score. Training is competency-based and covers test construction, reliability, validity, administration, interpretation and scoring, and provision of feedback.

4   Level B extends learning to include measures of typical performance, mainly those needing interpretation in terms of theories or models. It builds on Level A, which is a pre-requisite. It involves more complex measures, such as of personality, interests, motivation and values, which need thoughtful interpretation. Level B is currently divided into three levels:

- Level B (Intermediate) is designed to provide people with sufficient expertise in the use of one instrument. Candidates learn theories and methods of assessment, as well as administration, scoring, interpretation skills and how to write reports.
- Level B (Intermediate Plus) is a qualification for people seeking expertise in the use of an additional instrument. Candidates provide evidence of competence for this, which should be 'sufficiently different' from the one learned in the previous stage.
- Level B (Full) represents a level of general competence which is significantly broader. Emphasis is placed on experience of testing in a range of contexts, including computerized administration and report generating systems.

We discussed cut-off scores and error in Chapter 5. Use of a cut-off for decision-making will illustrate what happens when there is bias. A test which discriminates between two groups will have two score distributions, one with a lower mean representing the group discriminated against. This is shown in Figure 10.1. The shaded area represents scores of those potentially being discriminated against. So where there is test bias, it can be seen that using the same cut-off to different groups of people will be unfair to any group having a lower mean score as it under-predicts their performance and over-predicts that of a higher-scoring group. The use of a group-related cut-off would be fairer.

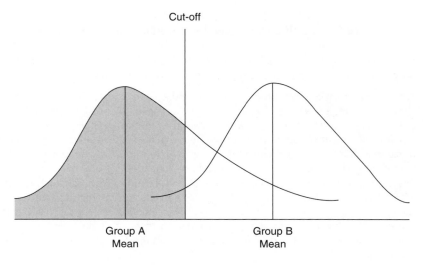

Figure 10.1   The impact of using a cut-off score when there is test bias

Data Protection

Many countries have laws to protect personal information and professionals should be aware of data protection legislation established in the countries in which they are working. Regulation in the UK comprehensively covers personal data, including note-books in which people are identified, application forms and other records. The law gives the right to test-takers to have access to information held on them and states that those holding it should be registered with data protection authorities. 'Sensitive' data could include a person's:

- Ethnic origin
- Beliefs and opinions, for example on religion or politics
- Disabilities
- State of physical or mental health
- Sexual orientation
- Any convictions, offences committed or legal proceedings

The law distinguishes between individuals on whom information is possessed (called data subjects) and those who keep and process information (data controllers). Controllers need to register the data acquired and their uses, and others involved must comply with their responsibilities under the law. To knowingly misuse or disclose per-sonal information is a criminal offence. The main principles of the legislation say that personal information must:

- Be processed fairly and lawfully
- Be used for limited, stated purposes

- Be adequate, relevant and not excessive
- Be accurate
- Be secure
- Not be stored for longer than is required
- Not infringe the rights of data subjects
- Not be transferred to countries which do not have adequate data protection

Confidentiality and Security

The unwarranted disclosure of tests, the items in them, and identifiable data relating to people who have completed them is a prime concern for practitioners. There are three reasons for this. First, any form of assessment is a personal process, meaning that it is improper to communicate results to others who do not have any worthwhile reason to know them. Given the nature of assessment in some fields, such as clinical, forensic or educational settings, the outcomes become more complex, for example in integrating results with personal background information, other data and observations, into a combined description of a person. This means that overall results need greater skills in interpretation.

Secondly, there is always a chance that test outcomes can be misused or abused. Anyone lacking technical competence could risk invalidating the process. Outcomes should always be focussed on the relevant purposes involved and it is unwise, therefore, to release technical information, raw scores or unexplained standardized scores. Because of their nature, percentiles are best interpreted in a verbal way, such as 'at an average level', 'above average' or 'below average'. Court reports, for example, ought not to state raw scores. Competent use at all times needs a good working knowledge of the specific technical characteristics of measures and of appropriate standards for their use.

Lastly, by getting into the wrong hands, assessment results can be inappropriately or wrongly interpreted by untrained people. They will not know, for example, that all outcomes are subject to error. Test booklets and response materials will be viewed by people who might take them at a later date and this, too, can invalidate testing. Supervised administration under standard conditions is necessary for most assessments because it ensures respondents are adequately briefed, complete the tests on their own and have not previously copied them.

It is vital that materials and data are stored in locked units to which only qualified users have access. The same is true for access to electronic files containing data. Decision-makers, who are often unqualified, might be allowed access to the outcomes of assessment only under the supervision of those having recognized training. In the case of research, it is wise to make data anonymous through the use of identification codes which are stored separately, whether on computer or in paper files.

Security relates to all assessment materials, not just to test booklets. Damaged or out-of-date materials must be shredded. In addition, it is considered unwise to send materials by post to individuals. Where people want information on testing in advance it is best to provide published practice leaflets or refer them to books on how to do tests.

Reasonable efforts should be made to maintain the security of information and to dispose of relevant paperwork after an appropriate time.

Informed Consent

Before individuals undergo assessment they should give their consent and, whatever the purpose, have a right to withdraw it. They have a right to know what is about to happen, why it is needed, and understand the implications of information given. Agreement needs to be based on people understanding the assessment, the uses made of outcomes, who will 'own' the information gained, and the qualifications of the tester. Explicit consent has to be given, although this does not have to be written provided it is clearly stated. It is important to indicate who will see any report and that the person assessed has a right to a copy. They also have a right to know their scores and what they mean; therefore, it is unethical not to offer personal feedback in many instances. Where testing is for job selection those involved should be sent an advance letter informing them of it, what the outcomes will be used for and who will know them. A sample consent form is shown in Figure 10.2.

The BPS Professional Practice Guidelines recognize the difficulties which may be encountered in gaining consent in some situations, for example in assessing young children or people having learning disabilities. Anyone likely to be involved in these situations would be wise to read the section on informed consent in the guidelines, which may be accessed via the website www.bps.org.uk. The question at issue is whether the person concerned is able to understand the information provided and its implications. Sometimes it may be necessary to gain consent from a parent, custodian or someone having appropriate responsibility.

Summary

Psychological assessment needs to be conducted in a fair and ethical manner, in accordance with relevant equal opportunities legislation and professional codes of practice. Legislation distinguishes between direct and indirect discrimination. Direct discrimination results in disparate treatment of individuals, whilst indirect discrimination leads to adverse impact, having a disproportionately unfavourable effect on a group of people. Measures are biased when they systematically under-predict the true performance of one group compared to others. Fair assessment needs an understanding of data protection legislation, with a commitment to confidentiality and security for both materials and data. It is also important to be aware of informed consent, that the permission of people is needed before testing.

Professional Issues in Testing

Test Administration

Approaches to administration can vary widely and there is no regulation of publishers on how they go about it. It will depend on what kind of assessment

USE OF TEST RESULTS

Name: _____

Date: _____

I agree to my test results on..
....
....
being used for the purpose of:-

(Please tick where you agree to your test results being used)

Selection for a job   ❑

Selection for promotion   ❑

Selection for training   ❑

Identifying training needs   ❑

Identifying development needs   ❑

Counselling   ❑

Culture audit   ❑

Equal opportunities analysis   ❑

Developing comparison groups (Norms)   ❑

Identifying the effectiveness of the test (Validation)   ❑

Signature _____ **Date** _____

Figure 10.2   A sample consent form

is being used, as well as factors relating to test-takers such as their age, background and mental condition. Whatever the format, it should never be forgotten that a test's reliability depends on how it is administered and scored. The skills of the administrator and the testing situation itself will also play a part in how good the results are.

The objective is to ensure that a test is administered and scored in the same way for everyone who takes it and in the same way that it was administered during original standardization. So it is crucially important to conduct administration correctly and to a high standard. Therefore, good training is needed, ensuring an administrator is familiarized with the correct materials and procedure. The best way to become familiar with any test's admin is to get someone who is an expert on it to administer it to you.

Done well, administration ensures good reliability because it reduces the possibility of unusual or random events, such as interruptions. In the unlikely event of these happening they can be recorded and taken into account in interpretation of the outcomes. Correct admin will ensure the results have sound validity by encouraging participants to respond naturally and honestly, as well as good public relations for assessment practice, for the administrator concerned and for any organization involved. The danger of saying this is that many beginners adopt a rigid and formal approach, although this, too, can influence performance because participants get more anxious. A clear and relaxed tone generally works best, with a level of rapport designed to motivate people and minimize sabotage in using questionnaires.

Choose any testing room carefully. There should be no possibility of interruptions – if necessary with a sign on the door to deter intruders. The room should be well lit and ventilated, the temperature comfortable, having no sources of distraction such as noise or poor ventilation. It is wise to place participants at clearly allocated places, having plenty of room to work. The administrator needs to check the physical environment is appropriate before beginning and that all correct materials are available, including question booklets and response sheets (see Box 10.4). For ability testing participants need two sharp pencils and an eraser each, and it is often sensible to take extra supplies. Materials should include a specially designed document, sometimes referred to as a 'Test Log' or 'Assessment Record,' which can record:

- The name of the administrator and date of assessment
- The number of participants
- Details of measures used
- Start and end times for each test
- Names or identification codes for participants
- Any personal problems
- Details of unusual events or disturbances which occur
- Any loss of or damage to materials, and subsequent action taken

Box 10.4   A Checklist for Testing

The materials needed for testing are:

- Signs saying 'NO ENTRY – TEST IN PROGRESS'
- Administration instructions or a test manual containing these
- A stopwatch or clock
- Unmarked test booklets
- Answer/response sheets
- A Test Log or Record Document
- Consent forms
- Spare/rough paper
- Sharpened pencils (minimum two per person)
- Erasers
- Spare pencils, erasers and a sharpener

Introducing assessment

Good practice begins with an introduction to ensure participants are told about what will happen and why and so that they experience less anxiety, provide useful information about themselves and gain a good impression of events. This will depend to some extent on the situation involved and its objectives. But there are some common guidelines. For example, it should enable administrators to introduce themselves and anyone else present, to describe the purpose of assessment and to ensure people give informed consent.

An introduction generally includes a brief description of tests and how long the session will last. In ability testing it helps to say there is no pass or fail on the tests and that they play only one part in a larger process of information-gathering. In the circumstances of clinical assessment where individuals are asked for right or wrong responses, such as in intelligence or memory testing, it helps to say that few people get everything correct and to reassure them not to worry unduly but to do their best. Reference should be made to confidentiality and feedback on the results. It is often wise, too, to check that people are comfortable and are not being distracted, whether they can hear clearly and see documentation adequately or whether they need and have available a hearing aid or spectacles. They should be asked whether they have any questions or problems before beginning. It helps, too, to check by observation and questioning the levels of anxiety experienced and to give appropriate reassurance. Unless participants have been notified previously not to bring mobile phones or watches having alarms to the session, it is important to ensure these are turned off.

In the case of personality questionnaires, it is important to emphasize that they should respond honestly and provide genuine information. If they do not do so, then the resulting profile will provide false information. It helps to tell them about the nature of any social desirability scale, indicating whether they have sought to portray themselves in too good a light. Simply mentioning the existence of a distortion measure can reduce this effect

(Kline, 1993). Where testing is administered by computer a check should be conducted of people's familiarity with them and they need to have a preliminary practice session.

Using administration scripts

Despite the many responsibilities involved in their use, standardized administration scripts are not 'rocket science'. With ability tests, for example, they usually begin with an introductory preamble, followed by some practice questions and their answers given before final instructions. Sometimes a script is provided on specially designed cards; on other occasions – especially with clinical assessments – it is contained in the publisher's manual. In many cases, too, different font sizes or colours will distinguish between what the administrator should do (when to distribute booklets or response sheets) from what to say to participants. Although this seems easy enough, it is vital not to depart from the instructions in any way.

Instructions need to be read clearly and at a moderate pace without any unnatural emphasis. Remember: if the instructions are not identical to those administered to the sample of people used for standardization the results will not possess the same significance or interpretation. Instructions, time limits, item presentation and response procedure should be identical.

Modifications might be made occasionally in clinical assessment, although this should be only after careful reflection and consultation on the circumstances and an appropriate professional judgement. It is more likely in assessment of people having learning or other disabilities, who have a mental health problem, or who are very young or older. Untimed norms could be used where they are available and it helps to provide more time for practice items, to record any undue anxiety or other problems for consideration during interpretation, and to provide some extra encouragement in the introductory phase. In using the WAIS, for example, the administrator can encourage individuals when they give correct responses during some sub-tests so that they are not demotivated by mistakes.

People taking ability or objective tests should not be hurried, especially over practice questions, and should be watched to ensure they are marking responses in the right way and that they do not turn over pages of booklets until instructed. Guidance is often given on how to deal with those who have difficulty with the practice component. A timer should be started when the instruction to begin is given and the test ended at the exact time set. Most ability tests and some clinical assessments are timed, so a stopwatch or stop-clock is needed. After assessment people should always be thanked for taking part and given advice on what happens next.

Scoring Tests

Scoring systems, too, can come in a number of formats and, just as with administration, it is important to follow instructions carefully and accurately. Being also standardized, scoring needs a methodical and meticulous approach. Computerized scoring has become increasingly available, although manual methods remain widely used and occasionally both are possible. In some cases computerized scoring is the only option. Accuracy is important because bad scoring increases error variance.

Manual scoring comes in two formats. The first involves marking keys, which have also been called marking cards, templates or acetates. Basically, they consist of plastic, cardboard or hard sheets containing holes or clear spots in the shape of circles, squares or rectangles which, when placed over a completed response sheet, identify the number of the items and whether responses are correct. Most are simple to use, provided they are correctly aligned and publishers give guidance on this.

Correct items can be counted to give a total score in some cases, whilst in many personality inventories they are totalled for different scales. Clinical assessments will often simply ask the user to count up or to add response scores without keys. This sounds simpler, although it is always wise to get an experienced colleague to check results. A disadvantage with some marking keys is that it is impossible for the scorer to identify irregularities, such as when someone has marked more than one item response where only one is needed.

A second approach uses 'self-scoring' forms. These have a backing sheet which is sealed beneath the response sheet and can be accessed only by tearing the two apart as if it were a pay slip. This is based on a pressure-sensitive process which transfers marks on the response sheet to the backing one. When torn apart a grid is revealed. If responses fall within the areas of circles, squares or even triangles they can be counted and totalled. For some questionnaires the responses which fall within different bands of colour or shading are totalled to provide raw scores for scales. The 16PF5 and 15FQ+ use this process. The disadvantage is that often people do not apply enough pressure to transfer their marks and it is important to mention this to them before administration.

Interpretation

To put it bluntly, the raw scores obtained by scoring are meaningless. They don't tell you what people can or can't do, what they are or are not like. To give them meaning begins with conversion to norm-referenced or criterion-referenced scores, as we saw in Chapter 3. The simplest process is to convert them to percentiles or one of the other standard scores outlined in Chapter 4, such as z scores, T scores, stens or stanines. These give us scores having significance through comparison with the mean score of a representative sample of people called the 'norm group'. Standardized scores enable us to make interpretations and comparisons and to calculate averages or differences, which are all based on understanding the technical properties of scales. Normative data enable us to compare someone's score with those of others and to take account of factors such as age, gender or other aspects of background. So raw scores are just a beginning and, being meaningless, should never be communicated to untrained people. When we looked at percentiles in Chapter 3 we considered different systems, such as grades A to E or below average to above average, which can interpret percentiles in a commonsense way to others.

Some manuals will direct the user to an appropriate norm group, while others provide a more extensive choice of norms, like the Watson Glaser Critical Thinking Appraisal. The norm group which best matches the person and the purposes of assessment should always be chosen, for example in a selection procedure the job description should be the guide. In the case of questionnaires the outcomes of the norming result in a 'profile' which portrays normative scores, often sten scores, for the scales. People generally like profiles because they are more understandable and attractive in a pictorial format. An example of a 15FQ+ profile is shown in Figure 10.3. Suitable training, such as that for the current BPS certificates outlined in Box 10.3, will ensure users understand norm tables and know how to interpret scores appropriately.

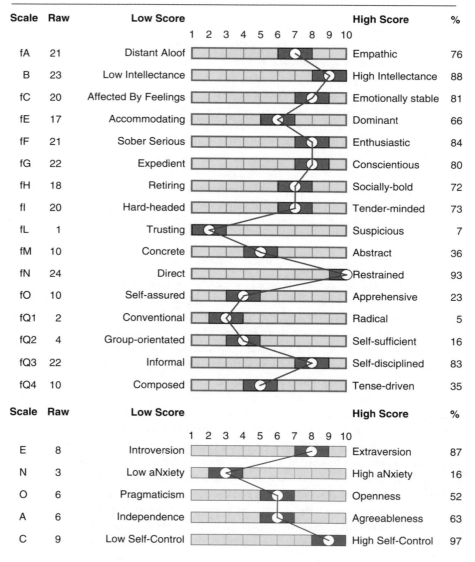

15FQ + Profile

Scale	Raw	Low Score	1 2 3 4 5 6 7 8 9 10	High Score	%
fA	21	Distant Aloof		Empathic	76
B	23	Low Intellectance		High Intellectance	88
fC	20	Affected By Feelings		Emotionally stable	81
fE	17	Accommodating		Dominant	66
fF	21	Sober Serious		Enthusiastic	84
fG	22	Expedient		Conscientious	80
fH	18	Retiring		Socially-bold	72
fI	20	Hard-headed		Tender-minded	73
fL	1	Trusting		Suspicious	7
fM	10	Concrete		Abstract	36
fN	24	Direct		Restrained	93
fO	10	Self-assured		Apprehensive	23
fQ1	2	Conventional		Radical	5
fQ2	4	Group-orientated		Self-sufficient	16
fQ3	22	Informal		Self-disciplined	83
fQ4	10	Composed		Tense-driven	35

Scale	Raw	Low Score	1 2 3 4 5 6 7 8 9 10	High Score	%
E	8	Introversion		Extraversion	87
N	3	Low aNxiety		High aNxiety	16
O	6	Pragmaticism		Openness	52
A	6	Independence		Agreeableness	63
C	9	Low Self-Control		High Self-Control	97

Figure 10.3 A sample personality profile from the 15FQ+
Reproduced by special permission of the publisher, Psytech International Ltd.

Giving Feedback

After assessment people should be given feedback which tells them about the outcomes in an understandable way. Whatever approach is taken, the most important factors concern issues of responsibility towards the person, towards others having responsibility for someone, and to broader ethical issues. Feedback should always be done sensitively and carefully. Given well, it can generate positive feelings among people about testing, about those involved, and about themselves. Done badly, it can cause distress, leading to a poor image of the process and to bad decision-making. A structured approach, without being personally evaluative, always works best. The trouble with being so strict about this is that sometimes people adopt a style which is overwhelmingly positive about the person and so becomes meaningless, reflecting the Barnum Effect discussed in Chapter 9. Once again, good training is invaluable.

The contexts of doing feedback can vary widely, although basic principles will almost always apply. Problems can occur in clinical diagnosis when a score or combination of them is seen as representing a disorder. Similarly, problems can occur in intelligence testing when people get upset because of having low scores. Some personality characteristics, such as emotional stability, also cause difficulty, although people low on this tend to be overwhelmingly aware of it. In all cases the best interests of the person should take precedence and any discussion needs to be handled with sensitivity and expertise. An emotional stability factor occurs in a number of inventories and feedback needs good rapport and a good discussion focussing on the positives rather than negatives. Emphasizing confidentiality can help. Sometimes it is possible to give feedback face-to-face directly after completion of assessment, but mostly this is not possible and other methods have to be found. Overall, there are a number of possibilities:

- *Telephone feedback*, for example where people have done ability tests.
- *Face-to-face feedback* at a later stage, for example where people have completed personality or other questionnaires.
- *Written reports*, such as for developmental, coaching, clinical or counselling purposes.
- *Written reports to third parties* such as law courts, schools, employers or to GPs who have referred someone for assessment.

Telephone feedback

This is probably the most common approach in dealing with ability or aptitude tests in the occupational domain, because the main aim will be to communicate the results. A major problem in using the phone, of course, is the lack of non-verbal cues; in other words it is impossible to see the impact of what is said. Lack of knowledge about reactions means it is unwise to use the telephone when quite personal feedback is given, for example when dealing with personality. But it does have the advantage of being suitable for giving highly confidential information, provided you check the identity of the person beforehand. A structured process for giving feedback over the phone is outlined in Box 10.5.

> ## Box 10.5   A Structured Process for Telephone Feedback
>
> You should avoid being personally evaluative in any way and aim to leave test-takers feeling positive about themselves. The following helps to provide a structured process:
>
> Step 1:   Put the person at ease and establish a level of rapport by asking about the experience of being tested.
>
> Step 2:   Ascertain the individual's level of knowledge about testing and pitch discussion at that level.
>
> Step 3:   Provide relevant information about the tests (validity and reliability) expressed in suitable terms and without using technical jargon.
>
> Step 4:   Describe the norm group(s) with which the candidate is being compared.
>
> Step 5:   Place information in the context of other information gained about the person
>
> Step 6:   Give opportunity to ask questions.
>
> Step 7:   Make the feedback developmental for the person.

Face-to-face feedback

Giving feedback on the outcomes of complex assessments is more difficult and demanding. In these cases recognition of how they are being received is an important part. The main aim is usually to communicate and explore a person's preferences and styles of behaviour, and to elicit supportive evidence for these. No assessment can be 100 per cent accurate, so we do need to discuss it with the individual concerned. But anyone giving feedback needs to master the intricacies of the instrument, as well as to manage the social encounter. The types of context in which it is appropriate to feed back results include selection, developmental, coaching, clinical or counselling scenarios and the most common purpose is to help individuals learn more about themselves. This contributes to their ability to make informed personal choices in the future.

Good preparation is essential, especially in ensuring a private and uninterrupted setting, as well as in planning how to communicate outcomes. It should also take place as soon after the original assessment as possible. Time is an important factor and up to 2–3 hours needs to be available, ensuring sufficient discussion. The process involves not only exploring the implications of results, but also of the personal background and issues which might be raised. The role of the feedback giver should be focussed mainly on helping to clarify differences between what people feel and know about themselves and what the new information suggests.

A relatively open, natural and informal approach works best. The event must be a positive experience with no over-emphasis on negative descriptions of dimensions. There are no rights or wrongs about many psychological attributes and descriptors of scales have both positive and negative aspects depending on the context. In fact, scale descriptions provided by publishers are not usually understandable to untrained people, so appropriate language should be used which the person can understand without feeling patronized.

A good introduction would repeat statements made during administration, including a reminder of confidentiality, an explanation of dimensions and, where appropriate, of how scores are compared to a reference group which acts as a benchmark. It also helps to explain that any profile cannot be 100 per cent accurate and, therefore, can only be used to make suggestions which need validation by them. Rapport is best developed by asking about the experience and feelings about being assessed. Following this different structured approaches are possible, including:

(a) Describing a factor, asking individuals where they feel they have scored on it and then explaining the result. This enables exploration of the validity of a score through the use of their experiences, impressions and personal understanding. A difficulty of this is that it tends to be time-consuming and may not help in understanding patterns formed from combinations of factors. It needs substantial notes and preparation, but is especially useful in counselling, coaching, developmental or clinical settings where there are specific issues needing attention.

(b) Through the use of a profile sheet, allowing people to take notes if they wish or by promising a written feedback report. It is not appropriate to give someone a complete profile to keep since the descriptions used may confuse them in the future. In addition, providing a complete profile immediately may mean that people become absorbed in things of most interest to them. It is better to discuss one factor at a time, with a brief description for each end. Covering the profile with a blank sheet means that the first factor can be explained. Then the cover is drawn down to reveal factors one at a time for separate discussion. As the process progresses it becomes possible to discuss combinations of scores.

The conclusion of any feedback should be focussed on the implications and thoughts which have arisen and with emphasis on the positives. This will be clear in a vocational guidance feedback or a range of other contexts. Plans for the future could then be jointly constructed. It helps to provide a written report afterwards which summarizes the main points and conclusions.

Written reports

Reports provide another way in which results might be communicated. A carefully considered and well-constructed written report can provide a helpful outcome. It will have a structure based on an explanation of the assessment conducted, although some reports, perhaps for coaching or training purposes, need to leave the reader with options for future development or actions to take. The purpose of the report and the needs of its recipient will make for the difference. It is wise to present any interpretation or comments in non-technical terms.

Reports should be logically structured and standardized methods of presentation often work best because they provide a focus. For example, the structure could be based on:

- A cover page, stating on whom and for whom the report is written, together with a confidentiality statement.
- An introduction outlining the purposes and date of assessment and background context.
- A section detailing the nature of the assessment(s) conducted and brief details of them, including norm groups used. It is wise to add a comment about the limitations of assessment and the error range likely.
- A results section outlining the findings.
- In some instances a section could list areas for further investigation if this is relevant.
- A brief summary of key conclusions.

This format can be adapted to a range of purposes, although reports written for courts of law need more special treatment and it is recommended that anyone wishing to write them attends a suitable course. In the occupational field a personality report can be structured in terms of competencies such as interpersonal style, approach to working, decision-making, problem-solving, management style, etc. With experience, the writer can decide upon the dimensions and then frame reports around them.

Tact and sensitivity need to be applied in large doses, though this doesn't mean the Barnum effect has to be adopted. It means that positive statements come before negative ones. Negatives need to be approached in constructive and developmental ways, with sensitively written phrasing. For example, rather than referring to 'low emotional stability', the author could comment 'You tend to be more aware of your feelings and of those of other people'. Care should be taken over terms used and categorical statements or value judgements avoided. To do this phrases such as '… may be…', '… could be…', '… likely to be…', '… appears to be…', '… suggests s/he is…' are recommended, along with others of a similar kind. Developmental reports will be written in the second person, i.e. using 'you' as the recipient, whilst organizational reports for managers are in the third person, using 'she' or 'he'. In the latter case the need for sensitivity remains because it may be shown to the respondent at some stage or a manager may later disclose parts of it. For example, you can't use words like 'weakness' or 'unacceptable' for obvious reasons, and have to find acceptable alternatives.

Computerized reports

Computer-generated reports have become increasingly widely used. Assessments having software-based scoring and reporting available include the Dyscalculia Screener and the British Ability Scales in the educational field, the Adolescent Psychopathology Scale and the Connors scales of general psychopathology in child mental health, as well as the Wechsler Memory Scale and Wechsler Adult Intelligence Scale-III. Reports are designed to interpret scores, summarize performance, and provide appropriate tables or graphs to make the job of assessment easier. In the occupational or vocational fields many measures come with software which will generate reports, both for the person assessed and for a manager.

Reports are usually designed to look like those written manually. However, it can all look rather obvious when you compare outputs for different people because shared attributes result in a repetition of the same words and phrases. This is because any specific score on a scale will link to a certain formula of words. Rolls (1993) says this occurs where computers possess a structured set of rules which guide objective ways of choosing the text given within a database. Essentially, there are a set of rules and a collection of phrases and sentences. The rules decide on the descriptions and the phrases or sentences come from different sources, for example experienced writers of reports, research and the test manual. The reports have the big advantage of being less time-consuming to produce. They can be lengthy, especially if a measure contains a number of dimensions and a substantial paragraph is available for each. But they are more consistent because the same data will always generate the same report. This has a benefit in the clinical field, being more valid than traditional reports (Hoffman, 1962; Ben-Porath and Butcher, 1986), and they are usually well structured.

However, there has been criticism. Descriptive reports for third parties often appear to be harsh about a person because they are less tactful and sensitive than a human interpreter would be. They are also less focussed on the purpose for which an assessment was made, resulting in a generalized narrative. Lastly, the user is at the mercy of its authors, being dependent on the phrasing, grammar, spelling, punctuation and writing style used. For these reasons it is best to check through any computer-generated report and to adapt it to the purpose and preferred style.

Lanyon (1987) says some reports are unethical because they present unvalidated accounts and are likely to be used by non-professionals who don't know their limitations. Developers have also been criticized on the basis that they encourage users to implement them largely on faith (Harris, 1987). There are considerable dangers in their use by untrained people who do not understand them and access should be restricted (Matarazzo, 1983, 1986; Bartram, 1995b). Perhaps because of such concerns, the British Psychological Society has published guidelines for the development and use of computerized reports (1999).

Testing in the Twenty-first Century

It could be argued, as Blinkhorn (1998) did, that there was little change in test theory over the last half of the twentieth century. Developments related principally to the growing use of computer technology and to more complex statistical methods of test construction. There has been, and continues to be, an increasing number of assessment materials of all kinds, many offering substantial improvement over existing ones, although in some areas emphasis is still placed on tests constructed some time ago, perhaps reflecting inadequate development in theory. Kline (2000) saw a need for new advances in terms of both theoretical and measurement issues.

A major area for the future involves computerized testing. Computers have played a growing role in item evaluation and construction, as well as in administration, scoring and interpretation of tests, and in providing reports, like the 15FQ+ questionnaire. Use of software to input responses directly has made scoring easier and more accurate, and the overall administration is less time-consuming. Mental health patients have expressed a preference for this (Klinger, Johnson and Williams, 1976). Delivery of tests over the internet supports the view that technology can provide standardized administration and scoring (Nunnally and Bernstein, 1994). A good example of a computerized assessment making effective use of technology is the Type Dynamics Indicator which, drawing on the traditional approach of the MBTI, expands it to a more innovative understanding of the person.

There have been some concerns, however, for example about raised levels of anxiety and diminished attitudes towards testing compared to traditional procedures (Hedl, O'Neil and Hansen, 1973), whether computerized items have the same interpretation as identical ones in booklets (Mazzeo and Harvey, 1988), and the impact of technology on social desirability scores (Evan and Miller, 1969; O'Brien and Dugdale, 1978; Davis and Cowles, 1989; Richman, Kiesler, Weisband and Drasgow, 1999). Other problems lie in people's familiarity with IT, the ease with which they can change responses and progress through testing, and the stability of any system online. If an assessment has been forwarded via the internet a major difficulty concerns 'authenticity' – i.e. how sure an administrator can be about who has completed it. Checks on this have involved re-testing under supervision. It is likely, therefore, that shorter-term advances may try to make further improvement in such areas.

Apart from technological advance, there is a need for more innovation focussed on new theories and assessment methods. These present more difficult challenges. As we have seen, major developments have taken place in the assessment of intelligence, abilities and in personality. There has been a tendency by some theorists to revisit and refashion assessment, for example the emotional intelligence movement (Goleman, 1995). Genuine innovation is needed and this means new theoretical understandings because, as we have seen, theory and assessment are inevitably linked. Related developments are also needed in measurement techniques.

Potential future developments in the personality domain have included conditional reasoning based on scale development (James, 1998), as well as virtual reality assessment using computerized interactive simulation (Hough and Ones, 2001), genetic testing (Plomin and Crabbe, 2000; Cook and Cripps, 2005) and neurological testing involving psychobiology (Depue, Lucianna, Arbisi, Collins and Leon, 1994). Biodata scales have been said to measure both personality characteristics and cognitive abilities (Mumford, Costanza, Connelly and Johnson, 1996). Legal issues may be raised by some of these and future changes in the law affecting testing will also need to be taken into account. More complex modelling of 'g', as well as other factors of intelligence and specific abilities are likely, making use of developments in technology, as well as innovations in more specialized areas, such as leadership and creativity. Hopefully we will see improvements in clinical assessment, too, resulting in more diagnostic measures having sound construction and validity.

Predicting the future is, therefore, difficult in what has become a more complex and technical discipline. Overall, it appears fair to say that its future will need some initial consolidation in computer-based assessment to resolve current concerns, as well as to improve professional practice. By the time this has been achieved, there may be sufficient foundations for theoretical progress and, therefore, other avenues of assessment in a range of applications. A priority should be more effective methods for construction and measurement, making more reliable and valid tests available.

Summary

Professional issues in assessment include administration, scoring, interpretation and the provision of feedback. Good preparation is essential to standardized test administration. Because of the concerns people have about testing, it is important to ensure that it is conducted well and to maintain the reliability and validity of measures used. Scoring methods include the use of scoring keys, self-scoring response sheets and computer-based scoring. Processes exist for both telephone and face-to-face feedback, which need good preparation. Report writing can also be conducted manually or through use of computer-generated reports. We have also looked at future developments in testing.

 ## What Have We Discovered About Ethical and Professional
Issues in Testing?

Fairness, privacy and confidentiality are important issues in testing. Codes of practice have been established because of concerns about potential bias and data management. We have looked at legislation which impacts on professional practice in a number of ways. We have also discussed best practice in administration, the scoring of responses, in interpreting scores, and in giving feedback. It has been clear that good training is important for all who wish to conduct assessment of others. We have learned about:

- The application of ethical codes and best practice to assessment.
- Discrimination legislation and how this affects practice.
- The significance of confidentiality, data protection and security, and informed consent.
- How standardized administration, scoring and interpretation should be conducted.
- The importance of good feedback methods.
- The key principles of computer-based assessment and how these will influence future developments in testing.

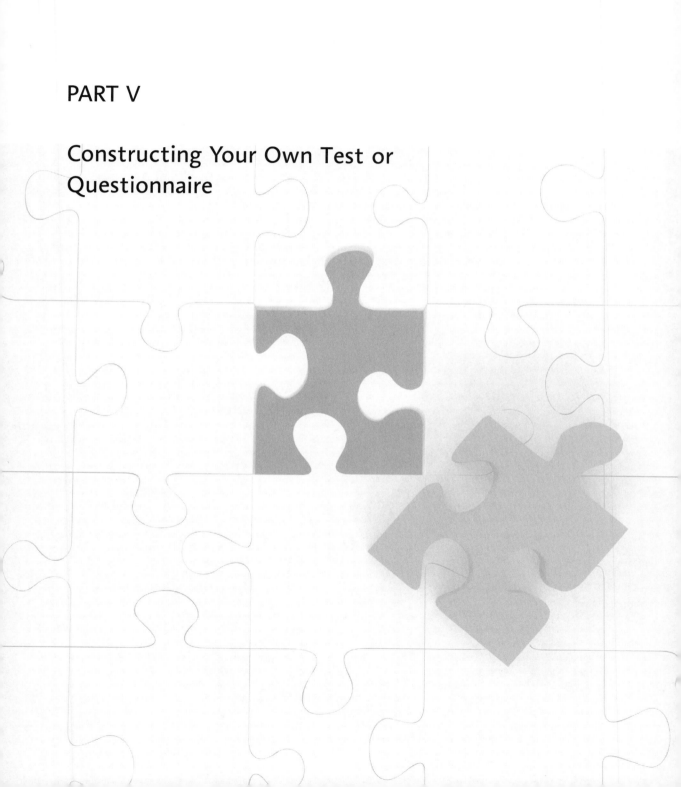

PART V

Constructing Your Own Test or Questionnaire

11

How to Make Your Own Test or Questionnaire

Learning Objectives

By the end of this chapter you should be able to set about constructing your own test or questionnaire measure.

What is This Chapter About?

In Chapters 2 and 3 of this book (if you can remember that far back) we learned about how publishers make tests. Here we are going to walk the well-trampled path of trying to make one of our own. Not that it is necessarily a good idea – it's a long and arduous route and we have no certainty of getting there in the end. There is much work involved in developing any measure, but undertaking it will give you a better understanding of tests and how they are made. It should go along with understanding of the statistical methods involved and, therefore, I recommend that you combine the process here with the advice given in Field (2005). We will draw on Field's book occasionally and assume that you have available the Statistical Package for the Social Sciences (SPSS) to undertake some of the statistical procedures needed. Other useful sources are Thorndike and Hagen (1977) and Kline (1986, 1998). Firstly, it is a good idea for you to review Chapters 2 and 3 and perhaps also Chapters 5 and 6, so that you can evaluate the reliability and validity of your questionnaire. Depending on how thorough the approach is, the outcome will be a questionnaire you can usefully administer to people. Whatever kind of measure you want to construct, this chapter will guide you through the main stages needed.

Constructing your Measure

Step 1: Set Clear Aims

Choosing an attribute or construct for measurement is the basic thing to do. It helps to find something which you are interested in, to think about what access you have to people who will be your participants, and the number of them. If your measure is likely to be used for research, you could also think in advance about what your hypotheses might be. We begin by providing specific answers to the following questions. Without clear answers to them your measure may not be useful:

- What precisely will this measure?
- What is the intended target group?
- What will be its purpose and what will it be used for?

Step 2: Define the Attribute(s)

Failure to clarify exactly what is to be measured could mean that you end up with an assessment which is muddled. It might result in measurement of associated attributes rather than the one really intended. Having a good understanding of relevant psychological theory and research can help, too, enabling you to identify what items should or should not be included. A detailed description will help also in fixing the nature of the measure and its items. A literature review will help so that you have a sound basic understanding of the attribute and other research involving it. You might also be able to identify other existing measures and to consider, therefore, what kinds of items are needed, what your questionnaire might look like and how it will differ from them.

Step 3: Write a Plan

Based upon the outcomes of steps 1 and 2, a detailed plan now needs to be written for the way ahead. An outline project plan helps because this will clarify deadlines for completion of items, preparation of the completed questionnaire, piloting it, checking reliability and validity, and for deciding on scoring. Firstly, think about how you will go about determining the following:

(a) *Test content* – What should be covered by this and what will it look like? Look at other measures, either of the same attribute or related ones. How do they compare to what you want to achieve? A structured way of thinking about this is given by Rust and Golombok (1999). They use a grid-style blueprint for determining content areas and how these are potentially manifest by people. Alternatively, Field's (2005) advice is to get a small group to 'brainstorm' a list of as many facets of your construct as possible. He also suggests you include people who might be at the extremes of your construct so that you can identify item content which reflects the entire spectrum.

(b) *Target population* – When everything is completed, who will this questionnaire be aimed at? This will be related to your original purpose in designing it.

(c) *The kinds of items needed and their number* – We reviewed the different kinds of items used in different measures such as ability tests, person-based or personality question-naires and attitudes in Chapter 2. This will help you decide on the basic format. In many instances a 5 or 7-point Likert response scale having the standard Agree–Disagree ordinal categories works best because this has a neutral point for people who have no view either way. Think about the different kinds of item needed, for example what would you think of a numerical reasoning test which contains only multiplication items? In other words, we need to reflect all relevant aspects of the attribute. For a rel-atively simple measure, it would be wise to aim for at least 40 items and these could then be reduced to about 30 when you evaluate them.

(d) *Administration instructions* – The best advice here is, again, that you look at some existing measures and their instructions. This will give you an idea of how yours should be structured and phrased. Figure 11.1 illustrates those provided for a personality questionnaire.

INSTRUCTIONS

This is a questionnaire about your interests, preferences, thoughts and feelings about a number of things relating to your work. Please focus upon yourself at work as you complete the question-naire. There is no time limit.

You should be provided with an answer sheet, a pencil and an eraser, together with the questionnaire.

Before you begin, please print your name in the space provided at the top of your answer sheet, together with the date.

You are asked to rate yourself on a scale from 1 to 5 on a total of 120 phrases or statements. When you have made your choice, mark your rating (1, 2, 3, 4 or 5) by circling the appropriate number for that question on your answer sheet.

For example:

1	2	3	4	5
STRONGLY DISAGREE	DISAGREE	IN-BETWEEN	AGREE	STRONGLY AGREE

1. I enjoy playing sports

A person who strongly agrees with this statement would clearly circle the number 5 against question 1 on the answer sheet.

Please try to remember:

• Be as truthful and as honest as you can. Please don't give a rating which seems to be the right thing to say or how you might like to be.
• The choice may appear to be fine in some cases, but don't spend too much time pondering the answer to each question. You should work as quickly as you can, rather than spending too much time analysing each statement in depth.
• Try to avoid the middle or in-between answer wherever possible.
• Please ensure that you complete all questions.
• If you wish to change an answer, erase it and mark your new answer.

Please turn over and begin......

Figure 11.1   Instructions for participants

(e) *Any time limits or the time required for completion* – This depends on the kind of measure. Ability tests are timed, for example, whilst person-based or personality questionnaires are not. Obviously, you don't want to construct something which takes too long to do (which will make your friends avoid you if they are busy); but neither do you want it to be too short because then it is unlikely to include all relevant items.

(f) *How scores should be calculated and interpreted* – If you are sufficiently sophisticated, you could put the measure on computer and design a software programme to do the scoring. The simplest process might be to sum responses, though if you write some items which are negatively phrased compared to others you will need to reverse their scores before totalling.

Step 4: Writing Items

The next step is to write items and to consider the most appropriate response format, resulting in what is commonly called an answer sheet. For ability tests and long personality questionnaires items come in a separate booklet from the answer sheet, although with shorter questionnaires using Likert-type attitude or attribute scales the items and responses go together on the same sheet (see Figure 11.2). For our purposes you need an initial 40–50 items and a final 30 plus, and so the Likert format is probably most appropriate.

1 STRONGLY DISAGREE	2 DISAGREE	3 IN-BETWEEN	4 AGREE	5 STRONGLY AGREE

Figure 11.2   Response options for a personality questionnaire

Having generated suggestions by research and/or the methods given in 3(a), you need to construct items to match the chosen rating scale. Any suggestions should be rephrased to fit. Guidance on writing them is given in Chapter 2, for example any which are basically asking the same thing need to be eliminated. Each should be written clearly and simply, avoiding double negatives and being as short as possible. It can help to ask someone else to read them. Items in a person-based questionnaire need similar properties and should aim for specific rather than general behaviours. To reduce response bias, where someone tends to give the same answer to every item, reverse-phrase some of them. They need to be scored in reverse afterwards before any analysis.

Once items are written you will need to consider your format for presenting them to people in a clear and understandable way. There should be space (or a page) at the beginning for a heading/title and appropriate biographical information depending on any potential future analysis, such as name, age, sex and date of administration. Instructions will need to be clear and unambiguous, letting people know how to select a response and record this. A statement that 'All information will be treated in the strictest confidence' could be included in the instructions for a questionnaire which is used in a research exercise.

Layout of items should be simple and straightforward, and enable respondents to easily connect responses with the different options. Consider some of the questionnaires you have seen or are available for inspection and think about your preferred format. For example, you could set out the options at the top of the response page, as indicated by Figure 11.2. Person-based measures frequently have items and response options on the same layout, as suggested by Figure 11.3. Use the most appropriate format for your purpose, print the outcome and make sufficient copies to give to your chosen group.

	SD	D		A	SA
1. ————————————————	1	2	3	4	5
2. ———————————————	1	2	3	4	5
3. ——————————	1	2	3	4	5
4. —————————————	1	2	3	4	5
5. —————————	1	2	3	4	5

Figure 11.3   Items and response options for a person-based questionnaire

Step 5: Selecting Items

You now need to administer the items to a trial sample of people. A time limit may not be imposed at this stage, even when it is intended to impose one after development. In this case participants might be asked to indicate where they have reached among items after different time intervals. The data gained from this process, including participant feedback, then undergo analysis to create an accurate and valid measure of one or more attributes. This analysis will be based upon the following techniques.

To begin with enter your data into SPSS, ensuring that the columns represent items and the rows across the spreadsheet represent data from each individual for each item. Effectively, a person's response to each item is entered into the column for that item. To do this your response scale should be converted into numbers indicating the strength of the response, for example strongly disagree = 1; disagree = 2; uncertain, neutral, no opinion or neither agree nor disagree = 3; agree = 4 and strongly agree = 5. This means that the person who disagrees with an item statement gains two points, whilst one who strongly agrees gains five. Don't forget to reverse score any reverse phrased items, so that in the case of my items 1 = 5, 2 = 4, 3 = 3, 4 = 2 and 5 = 1.

We are now ready to begin an analysis of the items, with the aim of identifying and eliminating those which do not do their job adequately. It is wise to begin by looking at descriptive statistics and Chapter 2 of Field (2005) will help with this. Look at the outputs:

(a) *Item range and mean*

Evaluate the range of each item. For them to be satisfactory they need to make full use of the scale. Any item which doesn't make use of all of the points on the scale (like 1 through to 5) has a limited range and needs to be discarded. Look also at the mean score. This shows how much individuals agree or disagree with your items. Ideally, the mean should be about value 3. If it is lower than 2 or higher than 4, this means that responses have predominantly been at the ends of the scale, when you want them to be spread out. Point your finger at them and say: 'You're fired.'

(b) *Skewness*

Evaluate the distribution of responses for each item. In Chapter 4 we investigated the properties of the normal distribution and learned that many distributions are skewed. This distribution should ideally be normally distributed, too, having the mean score at its centre, and we don't want to use items demonstrating significant skew. This can be checked by identifying the skewness value and the Standard Error of skewness (SEskew) in the SPSS output. Dividing the skewness by its standard error for each item gives the value of a z score (also mentioned in Chapter 4) and if this is greater than 1.96, being more than two standard deviations above the mean, then the item distribution is significantly skewed. Once again, get rid of it.

(c) *Standard deviation*

Similarly, look at the standard deviations. These indicate the extent of differences in responses to each item. Values at zero mean that respondents have given identical answers to the item, for example everyone may have said they strongly disagree with it. Consequently, it is not indicating any differences between people and needs to go. Poorly understood item content might have caused everyone to respond in the same way.

(d) *Item-total correlations*

Items should only be chosen if they measure the same attribute as other items in the questionnaire. Discrimination reflects this ability, ensuring that individuals who possess the attribute should respond to all of the items in a certain way. It is determined by correlating scores on each item with the total score for the questionnaire. Higher correlation coefficients signify that items are more discriminating. Any which are negative or have zero value must be eliminated. The Pearson product-moment correlation coefficient is mostly used for this. In SPSS a corrected item-total correlation can be calculated which multiplies the coefficient by the standard deviation for the item, although its value is dependent on sample size. There is no set minimum value, although Field (2005) recommends a value of about 0.3 so that items having coefficients above this can be retained.

(e) *Inter-item correlations*

To understand the items which make up the questionnaire, it helps to construct what is called an R-matrix. This is simply a cross-correlation of all of the items as separate variables (Field, 2005: 620–1), and gives the correlation coefficients for each pair of items. By displaying those which are statistically significant, it illustrates any clusters of inter-relating items. If all items in your questionnaire inter-correlate at a significant level then they are assessing aspects of the same attribute. Items which do not correlate at a 5 per cent or 1 per cent level are, once again, candidates for the bin.

(f) *Factor analysis*

Having by now eliminated a number of items, we come to an evaluation and interpretation of the structure of those remaining using factor analysis. As mentioned in Chapter 3, this has been used for the construction of many questionnaires. It tells us which items go together and which don't, and a factor is a construct determined by the correlations of variables (known as their loadings). The analysis will check whether items relate to a factor, indicating a common theme. A unidimensional scale will need only one factor to describe it and high loadings will suggest that one alone is needed to explain data. If other factors exist they are described as the second, third, fourth, etc.. A first factor having low loadings will indicate there is no common factor, while moderate loadings suggest others can be extracted.

The procedure begins by correlating every variable with every other one to generate a matrix, as in (e) above. Our aim is to examine the remaining items to clarify the number of distinct dimensions, which items relate to particular factors where more than one is involved, and which need to be eliminated. So you will determine which factors you wish to keep, the items loading on to them and what these factors represent in terms of your attribute. Chapter 15 of Field (2005) will tell you how to go about the procedure using SPSS. Hopefully, you will have about 20–30 items left for your questionnaire.

(g) *Reliability*

We need to assess the reliability of our questionnaire. High reliability is an important property of any measure, as Chapter 5 suggests. The easiest way of doing this is to let SPSS determine the Cronbach alpha reliability coefficient for your items. It is important to remember, though, that the people whose scores are used to compute it should be similar to those you intend to assess afterwards. In SPSS use the reliability analysis box to select the items and the default option will give Cronbach's alpha.

One of the options marked 'Scale if item deleted' is useful because this tells us what the alpha value would be if each particular item is deleted. If it goes up substantially when an item is deleted, then it means the item is having a detrimental impact on overall reliability and should be removed. The message is that if you take out the item reliability will increase, which can only be good. If your questionnaire and items have been constructed well, the value of the overall reliability of the measure should be 0.8 or higher.

(h) *Validation*

Validation is a difficult and time-consuming aspect of construction, as indicated in Chapter 6. Questionnaires constructed for special purposes, for example as part of a research project, are unlikely to need full-scale validation. Content analysis can be supported on the basis by which you generated items and eliminated inappropriate ones. Did you sample them adequately initially and are they now truly representative of the construct under investigation? If so, remaining ones must then relate to the attribute being measured. Acceptability, or face validity, can be evaluated by asking people to assess whether your questionnaire looks relevant and reasonable.

Factorial validity relates to your interpretation of the factor structure of the questionnaire and whether this makes sense in general terms. The question is whether the items you have linked to factors, thus clustering into relevant groups, are appropriate in the eyes of others. Construct validity seeks to establish whether the questionnaire is really measuring what it is claimed to measure and needs a larger process of validation, as discussed in Chapter 6. At its simplest, it means that item scores should link to observable behaviours, for example you could compare scores on an extraversion scale with the number of friends people say they have. Items need, therefore, to make sense in an external context.

Step 6: Standardization

Standardization, discussed in Chapter 3, allows you to interpret scores by creating norms. These consist of mean scores for specific samples of people belonging to your target population. The process is only useful if you need to interpret scores by comparison with a benchmark group and if your questionnaire is being developed for research purposes only there will be no need to do this. Otherwise very large samples are required for standardization.

Step 7: Final Preparation

Any final amendments can now be made. There will be the need to ensure instructions and answer/response sheets are satisfactory, that scoring procedures work effectively and the ensuing scores of individuals can be effectively interpreted. In the case of personality questionnaires some form of profile sheet is often needed to illustrate the different scores on scales. All is now complete – Good luck!

Appendix A
A Table of Areas Under the Normal Curve

z	.00	.01	.02	.03	.04	.05	.06	.07	.08	.09
−3.0	.0013	.0013	.0013	.0012	.0012	.0011	.0011	.0011	.0010	.0010
−2.9	.0019	.0018	.0018	.0017	.0016	.0016	.0015	.0015	.0014	.0014
−2.8	.0026	.0025	.0024	.0023	.0023	.0022	.0021	.0021	.0020	.0019
−2.7	.0035	.0034	.0033	.0032	.0031	.0030	.0029	.0028	.0027	.0026
−2.6	.0047	.0045	.0044	.0043	.0041	.0040	.0039	.0038	.0037	.0036
−2.5	.0062	.0060	.0059	.0057	.0055	.0054	.0052	.0051	.0049	.0048
−2.4	.0082	.0080	.0078	.0075	.0073	.0071	.0069	.0068	.0066	.0064
−2.3	.0107	.0104	.0102	.0099	.0096	.0094	.0091	.0089	.0087	.0084
−2.2	.0139	.0136	.0132	.0129	.0125	.0122	.0119	.0116	.0113	.0110
−2.1	.0179	.0174	.0170	.0166	.0162	.0158	.0154	.0150	.0146	.0143
−2.0	.0228	.0222	.0217	.0212	.0207	.0202	.0197	.0192	.0188	.0183
−1.9	.0287	.0281	.0274	.0268	.0262	.0256	.0250	.0244	.0239	.0233
−1.8	.0359	.0351	.0344	.0336	.0329	.0322	.0314	.0307	.0301	.0294
−1.7	.0446	.0436	.0427	.0418	.0409	.0401	.0392	.0384	.0375	.0367
−1.6	.0548	.0537	.0526	.0516	.0505	.0495	.0485	.0475	.0465	.0455
−1.5	.0668	.0655	.0643	.0630	.0618	.0606	.0594	.0582	.0571	.0559
−1.4	.0808	.0793	.0778	.0764	.0749	.0735	.0721	.0708	.0694	.0681
−1.3	.0968	.0951	.0934	.0918	.0901	.0885	.0869	.0853	.0838	.0823
−1.2	.1151	.1131	.1112	.1093	.1075	.1056	.1038	.1020	.1003	.0985
−1.1	.1357	.1335	.1314	.1292	.1271	.1251	.1230	.1210	.1190	.1170
−1.0	.1587	.1562	.1539	.1515	.1492	.1469	.1446	.1423	.1401	.1379
−0.9	.1841	.1814	.1788	.1762	.1736	.1711	.1685	.1660	.1635	.1611
−0.8	.2119	.2090	.2061	.2033	.2005	.1977	.1949	.1922	.1894	.1867
−0.7	.2420	.2389	.2358	.2327	.2296	.2266	.2236	.2206	.2177	.2148
−0.6	.2743	.2709	.2676	.2643	.2611	.2578	.2546	.2514	.2483	.2451
−0.5	.3085	.3050	.3015	.2981	.2946	.2912	.2877	.2843	.2810	.2776
−0.4	.3446	.3409	.3372	.3336	.3300	.3264	.3228	.3192	.3156	.3121
−0.3	.3821	.3783	.3745	.3707	.3669	.3632	.3594	.3557	.3520	.3483
−0.2	.4207	.4168	.4129	.4090	.4052	.4013	.3974	.3936	.3897	.3859

(Cont'd)

z	.00	.01	.02	.03	.04	.05	.06	.07	.08	.09
−0.1	.4602	.4562	.4522	.4483	.4443	.4404	.4364	.4325	.4286	.4247
−0.0	.5000	.4960	.4920	.4880	.4840	.4801	.4761	.4721	.4681	.4641
0.0	.5000	.5040	.5080	.5120	.5160	.5199	.5239	.5279	.5319	.5359
0.1	.5398	.5438	.5478	.5517	.5557	.5596	.5636	.5675	.5714	.5753
0.2	.5793	.5832	.5871	.5910	.5948	.5987	.6026	.6064	.6103	.6140
0.3	.6179	.6217	.6255	.6293	.6331	.6368	.6406	.6443	.6480	.6517
0.4	.6554	.6591	.6628	.6664	.6700	.6736	.6772	.6808	.6844	.6879
0.5	.6915	.6950	.6985	.7019	.7054	.7088	.7123	.7157	.7190	.7224
0.6	.7257	.7291	.7324	.7357	.7389	.7422	.7454	.7486	.7517	.7549
0.7	.7580	.7611	.7642	.7673	.7704	.7734	.7764	.7794	.7823	.7852
0.8	.7881	.7910	.7939	.7967	.7995	.8023	.8051	.8078	.8106	.8133
0.9	.8159	.8186	.8212	.8238	.8264	.8289	.8315	.8340	.8365	.8389
1.0	.8413	.8438	.8461	.8485	.8508	.8531	.8554	.8577	.8599	.8621
1.1	.8643	.8665	.8686	.8708	.8729	.8749	.8770	.8790	.8810	.8830
1.2	.8849	.8869	.8888	.8907	.8925	.8944	.8962	.8980	.8997	.9015
1.3	.9032	.9049	.9066	.9082	.9099	.9115	.9131	.9147	.9162	.9177
1.4	.9192	.9207	.9222	.9236	.9251	.9265	.9279	.9292	.9306	.9319
1.5	.9332	.9345	.9357	.9370	.9382	.9394	.9406	.9418	.9429	.9441
1.6	.9452	.9463	.9474	.9484	.9495	.9505	.9515	.9525	.9535	.9545
1.7	.9554	.9564	.9573	.9582	.9591	.9599	.9608	.9616	.9625	.9633
1.8	.9641	.9649	.9656	.9664	.9671	.9678	.9686	.9693	.9699	.9706
1.9	.9713	.9719	.9726	.9732	.9738	.9744	.9750	.9756	.9761	.9767
2.0	.9772	.9778	.9783	.9788	.9793	.9798	.9803	.9808	.9812	.9817
2.1	.9821	.9826	.9830	.9834	.9838	.9842	.9846	.9850	.9854	.9857
2.2	.9861	.9864	.9868	.9871	.9875	.9878	.9881	.9884	.9887	.9890
2.3	.9893	.9896	.9898	.9901	.9904	.9906	.9909	.9911	.9913	.9916
2.4	.9918	.9920	.9922	.9925	.9927	.9929	.9931	.9932	.9934	.9936
2.5	.9938	.9940	.9941	.9943	.9945	.9946	.9948	.9949	.9951	.9952
2.6	.9953	.9955	.9956	.9957	.9959	.9960	.9961	.9962	.9963	.9964
2.7	.9965	.9966	.9967	.9968	.9969	.9970	.9971	.9972	.9973	.9974
2.8	.9974	.9975	.9976	.9977	.9977	.9978	.9979	.9979	.9980	.9981
2.9	.9981	.9982	.9982	.9983	.9984	.9984	.9985	.9985	.9986	.9986
3.0	.9987	.9987	.9987	.9988	.9988	.9989	.9989	.9989	.9990	.9990

References

Adams, J. S. (1963). Toward an understanding of inequity. *Journal of Abnormal and Social Psychology, 67*, 422–436.

Adams, J. S. (1965). Inequity in social exchange. In L. Berowitz (ed.), *Advances in experimental psychology*, vol. 2. New York: Academic Press.

Aguinis, H. (1993). Action research and scientific method: Presumed discrepancies and actual similarities. *Journal of Applied Behavioral Science, 29*, 416–431.

Aguinis, H., Henle, C. A. & Ostroff, C. (2001). Measurement in work and oragnizational psychology. In N. Anderson, D. S. Ones, H. K. Sinangil & C. Viswesvaran (eds.), *Handbook of Industrial, Work & Organizational Psychology*, vol. 1, 27–47. London: Sage.

Ajzen, I. & Fishbein, M. (2000). Attitudes and the attitude-behaviour relation: reasoned and automatic processes. In W. Strobe & M. Hewstone (eds.), *European Review of Social Psychology*. Chichester: Wiley.

Allport, G. W. (1937). *Personality: A psychological interpretation.* New York: Holt.

Allport, G. W. (1961). *Pattern and growth in personality.* New York: Holt, Rinehart & Winston.

Allport, G. W. & Odbert, H. (1936). Trait names: A psycho-lexical study, *Psychological Monographs, 47*, 1–171.

Allport, G. W., Vernon, P. E. & Lindzey, G. (1960). *Study of values manual.* Chicago: Riverside.

American Psychiatric Association (1994). *Diagnostic and statistical manual of mental disorders.* Washington, DC: American Psychiatric Association.

Anastasi, A. (1988). *Psychological Testing.* New York: Macmillan.

Anastasi, A. & Urbina, S. (1997). *Psychological Testing* (7th ed.). Upper Saddle River, NJ: Prentice Hall.

Angoff, W. H. (1971). Norms, scales and equivalent scores. In R. L. Thorndike (ed.), *Educational Measurement* (2nd ed.). Washington, DC: American Council on Education.

Archer, J. & Lloyd, B. (2002). *Sex and gender.* Cambridge: University of Cambridge Press.

Baer, D. M., Wolf, M. M. & Risley, T. R. (1968). Some current dimensions of applied behaviour analysis. *Journal of Applied Behavior Analysis, 1*, 91–97.

Baer, D. M., Wolf, M. M. & Risley, T. R. (1987). Some still-current dimensions of applied behavior analysis. *Journal of Applied Behavior Analysis, 20*, 313–327.

Bailey, J. S. & Meyerson, L. (1969). Vibration as a reinforcer with a profoundly retarded child. *Journal of Applied Behavior Analysis, 2*, 135–137.

Baker, L. D. & Daniels, D. (1990). Nonshared environmental influences and personality differences in adult twins. *Journal of Personality and Social Psychology, 58*, 103–110.

Bandura, A. (1977). *Social learning theory.* Englewood Cliffs, NJ: Prentice Hall.

Bandura, A. (ed.) (1995). *Self-efficacy in changing societies.* New York: Cambridge University Press.

Bandura, A. (1999). Social cognitive theory of personality. In L. Pervin & O. John (eds.), *Handbook of personality* (2nd ed.). New York: Guilford.

Bandura, A. (2002). Swimming against the mainstream: The early years from chilly tributary to transformative mainstream. *Behaviour Research and Therapy, 42*, 613–630.

Baral, B. & Das, J. P. (2004). Intelligence: What is indigeneous to India and what is shared? In R. J. Sternberg (ed.), *International handbook of intelligence* (270–301). Cambridge: Cambridge University Press.

Barrett, G. V., Phillips, J. S. & Alexander, R. A. (1981). Concurrent and predictive validity designs. *Journal of Applied Psychology, 66*, 1–6.

Barrett, P. & Kline, P. (1981). A comparison between Rasch analysis and factor analysis of items in the EPQ. *Journal of Personality and Group Behaviour, 1*, 1–21.

Bartram, D. (1995a). *Review of Personality Assessment Instruments (level B).* Leicester: British Psychological Society.

Bartram, D. (1995b). The role of computer-based test interpretation (CBTI) in occupational assessment. *International Journal of Selection and Assessment, 3*(3), 178–185.

Bartram, D. (ed.) (1997). *Review of Ability and Aptitude Tests (Level A) for Use in Occupational Settings.* Leicester: British Psychological Society.

Bartram, D. & Lindley, P. (1994). *Test Interpretation: Level A Open Learning Programme.* Leicester: British Psychological Society.

Bechtoldt, H. P. (1959). Construct validity: a critique. *American Psychologist*, 619–629.

Beck, R. C. (1990). *Motivation: Theories and principles* (2nd ed.). Englewood Cliffs, NJ: Prentice-Hall.

Bennett, E. A. (1983). *What Jung really said.* New York: Schocken Books.

Ben-Porath, W. S. & Butcher, J. N. (1986). Computers in personality assessment: A brief past, ebullient present and an expanding future. *Computers in Human Behaviour, 2*, 167–182.

Ben-Shakhar, G. & Furedy, J. J. (1990). *Theories and applications in the detection of deception.* New York: Springer-Verlag.

Berry, J. W. (1984). Towards a universal psychology of cognitive competence. In P. S. Fry (ed.), *Changing conceptions of intelligence and intellectual functioning*, 35–61. Amsterdam: North Holland.

Bethell-Fox, C. E. (1989). Psychological testing. In P. Herriott (ed.), *Assessment and selection in organisations.* Chichester: Wiley.

Bieri, J. (1955). Cognitive complexity-simplicity and predictive behaviour. *Journal of Abnormal and Social Psychology, 51*, 263–268.

Bijou, S. & Baer, D. M. (1961). *Child Development, vol. 1. A systematic and empirical theory.* New York: Appleton-Century-Crofts.

Bijou, S., Peterson, R. F. & Ault, M. H. (1968). A method to integrate descriptive and experimental field studies at the level of data and empirical concepts. *Journal of Applied Behavior Analysis 1*, 175–91.

Binet, A. & Simon, T. (1916). *The development of intelligence in children.* Baltimore, MD: Williams & Wilkins. (reprinted 1973, New York: Arno Press; reprinted 1983, Salem, NH: Ayer).

Binet, A. (1916). New methods for the diagnosis of the intellectual level of subnormals. In E. S. Kite (Trans.), *The development of intelligence in children.* Vineland, NJ: Publications of the training school at Vineland. (Originally published in 1905 in *L'Annee Psychologique, 12*, 191–244.

Binet, A. & Simon, T. (1911). *La mesure du développement de l'intelligence chez les jeunes enfants*. Paris: A. Coneslant.

Birnbaum, A. (1968). Some latent trait models and their use in inferring an examinee's ability. In F. M. Lord and M. R. Novick (eds.), *Statistical theories of mental test scores*. Reading, MA: Addison-Wesley.

Blinkhorn, S. E. (1998). Past imperfect, future conditional: Fifty years of test theory. *British Journal of Mathematical and Statistical Psychology, 50*, 175–185.

Block, J. (1961). *The Q-sort methodology in personality assessment and psychiatric research*. Springfield, Ill: Charles C. Thomas.

Blum, G. S. (1949).A study of psychoanalytic theory of psychosexual development. *Genetic Psychology Monograph, 39*, 3–99.

Boring, E. G. (1923). Intelligence as the tests test it. *New Republic, 34*, 34–37.

Bouchard, T. J. & Segal, N. L. (1985). Environment and IQ. In B. B. Wolman (ed.), *Handbook of intelligence: Theories, measurements and applications*. New York: Wiley.

Boudreau, J. W. (1989). Selection utility analysis: A review and agenda for future research. In M. Smith & I. T. Robertson (eds.), *Advances in selection and assessment*. Chichester: Wiley.

Bowman, M. L. (1989). Testing individual differences in Ancient China. *American Psychologist, 44*, 576–578.

Braithwaite, V. A. & Scott, W. A. (1991). In J. P. Robinson, P. R. Shaver & L. S. Wrightsman (eds.) *Measures of personality and social psychological attitudes*. New York: Academic Press.

British Psychological Society (1999). *Guidelines for the development and use of computer-based assessment*. Leicester: British Psychological Society.

British Psychological Society (2003). *Psychological testing: A user's guide*. Leicester: British Psychological Society.

British Psychological Society (2006). *Code of ethics and conduct*. Leicester: British Psychological Society.

British Psychological Society (2008). *Generic professional practice guidelines*. Leicester: British Psychological Society.

Brookhart, S. M. (1995). Review of the Rokeach value survey. *Twelfth Mental Measurements Yearbook*, 878–879.

Bruner, J. S. & Tagiuri, R. (1954). The perception of people. In G. Lindzey (ed.), *Handbook of social psychology*. Cambridge, MA: Addison-Wesley.

Bruvold, W. H. (1975). Judgmental bias in the rating of attitude statements. *Educational and Psychological Measurement, 45*, 605–611.

Bull, R. (1988). What is the lie-detection test? In A. Gale (ed.) *The polygraph test: Lies, truth and science*. London: Sage.

Burt, C. (1949). The structure of the mind: A review of the results of factor analysis. *British Journal of Educational Psychology, 19*, 100–111, 176–199.

Camara, W. J. & Schneider, D. L. (1994). Integrity tests: Facts and unresolved issues. *American Psychologist, 50*, 459–460.

Campbell, D. T. & Fiske, D. W. (1959). Convergent and discriminant validation by the multitrait-multimethod matrix. *Psychological Bulletin, 56*, 81–105.

Carlson, A. (2002). *Interests*. Online at vocationalpsychology.com/term-interests.htm.

Carlyn, M. (1977). An assessment of the Myers-Briggs Type Indicator. *Journal of Personality Assessment, 41*, 461–473.

Carr, E. G. (1988). Functional equivalence as a mechanism of response generalization. In R. H. Horner, G. Dunlap & R. L. Koegel (eds.) *Generalization and maintenance life-style changes in applied settings*. Baltimore: P. H. Brookes.

Carretta, T. R. & Ree, M. J. (1996). Factor structure of the air force officer qualifying test: Analysis and comparison. *Military Psychology, 8*, 29–42.

Carretta, T. R. & Ree, M. J. (1997). Negligible sex differences in the relation of cognitive and psychomotor abilities. *Personality and Individual Differences, 22*, 165–172.

Carretta, T. R. & Ree, M. J. (2000). General and specific cognitive and psychomotor abilities in personnel selection. The prediction of training and job performance. *International Journal of Selection and Assessment, 8*, 227–236.

Carroll, J. B. (1993). *Human cognitive abilities: A survey of factor-analytic studies*. New York: Cambridge University Press.

Carstairs, G. (1957). *The twice-born: A study of a community of high caste Hindus*. London: Hogarth Press.

Carver, C. S. & Scheier, M. F. (2000). *Perspective on personality* (4th ed.). Boston: Allyn & Bacon.

Cattell, R. B. (1950). *Personality: A systematic, theoretical and factual study*. New York: McGraw-Hill.

Cattell, R. B. (1957). *Personality and motivation structure and measurement*. Yonkers: New World.

Cattell, R. B. (1965). *The scientific analysis of personality*. Baltimore, MD: Penguin.

Cattell, R. B. (1971). *Abilities: Their structure, growth and action*. Boston: Houghton Mifflin.

Cattell, R. B. (1973). *Personality and mood by questionnaire*. New York: Jossey-Bass.

Cattell, R. B. (1978). *The scientific use of factor analysis*. New York: Plenum.

Cattell, R. B. (1986). *Handbook for the 16 Personality Factor Questionnaire*. Champaign, IL: Institute for Personality and Ability Testing.

Cattell, R. B. (1987). *Intelligence: Its structure, growth and action*. (Revised and reprinted version of *Abilities: Their structure, growth and action*.) New York: Springer.

Cattell, R. B., Eber, H. W. & Tatsuoka, M. M. (1970). *Handbook for the sixteen-personality factor questionnaire*. Champaign, IL: Institute for Personality and Ability Testing.

Cattell, R. B. & Child, D. (1975). *Motivation and dynamic structure*. New York: Wiley.

Cattell, R. B. & Warburton, F. W. (1967). *Objective personality and motivation tests*. Urbana: University of Illinois Press.

Child, D. (1991). *The essentials of factor analysis* (2nd ed.). London: Cassell.

Cloninger, C. R. (1987). A systematic method for clinical description and classification of personality variants. *Archives of General Psychiatry, 44*, 573–578.

Cloninger, C. R., Svrakic, D. M. & Przybeck, T. R. (1993). A psychobiological model of temperament and character. *Archives of General Psychiatry, 50*, 975–990.

Coaley, K. & Hogg, B. (1994). The use of psychometric tests. In Lee, G. & Beard, D. (1994) *Development centres: Realising the potential of your employees through assessment and development*. London: McGraw-Hill.

Cook, M. & Cripps, B. (2005). *Psychological assessment in the workplace: A manager's guide*. Chichester: Wiley.

Cooper, C. (1983). Correlation measures in item analysis. *British Journal of Mathematical and Statistical Psychology, 32*, 102–105.

Cooper, C. & Kline, P. (1982). The internal structure of the motivation analysis test. *British Journal of Educational Psychology, 52*, 228–233.

Costa, P. T. & McCrae, R. R. (1985). *NEO personality inventory manual*. Odessa: Psychological Assessment Resources.

Costa, P. T. & McCrae, R. R. (1992). *Revised NEO personality inventory (NEO-PI-R) and NEO five-factor inventory (NEO-FFI): Professional manual.* Odessa: Psychological Assessment Resources.

Crawford, J. R. (2004). Psychometric foundations of neuropsychological assessment. In L. H. Goldstein & J. E. McNeil (eds.), *Clinical neuropsychology: A practical guide to assessment and management for clincians.* Chichester: Wiley.

Crombie, I. K., Todman, J., McNeill, G., Florey, C. D., Menzies, I. & Kennedy, R. A. (1990). Effect of vitamin and mineral supplementation on verbal and non-verbal reasoning of schoolchildren. *Lancet, 335,* 1158–1160.

Cronbach, L. J. (1946). Response sets and test validity. *Educational and Psychological Measurement, 6,* 475–494.

Cronbach, L. J. (1951). Coefficient alpha and the internal structure of tests. *Psychometrika, 12,* 297–334.

Cronbach, L. J. (1976). *Essentials of psychological testing* (3rd ed.). New York: Harper & Row.

Cronbach, L. J. (1994). *Essentials of psychological testing* (5th ed.). New York, NY: Harper-Collins.

Cronbach, L. J., Gleser, G. C., Nanda, H. & Rajaratnan, N. (1972). *The dependability of behavioral measurements: Theory and generalizability for scores and profiles.* New York: Wiley.

Cronbach, L. J. & Meehl, P. E. (1955). Construct validity in psychological tests. *Psychological Bulletin, 52,* 281–302.

Crowley, A. D. (1981). The content of interest inventories: Job titles or job activities. *Journal of Occupational Psychology, 54,* 135–140.

Dagnan, D. Trower, P. & Smith, R. (1998). Care staff responses to people with learning disabilities and challenging behaviour: A cognitive-emotional analysis. *British Journal of Clinical Psychology, 37,* 59–68.

Das, J. P., Kirby, J. & Jarman, R. F. (1979). *Simultaneous and successive cognitive processes.* New York: Academic Press.

Das, J. P., Naglieri, J. A. & Kirby, J. P. (1994). *Assessment of cognitive processes: The PASS theory of intelligence.* Boston: Allyn & Bacon.

Davis, C. & Cowles, M. (1989). Automated psychological testing: Method of administration, need for approval, and measures of anxiety. *Educational and Psychological Measurement, 49,* 311–337.

Demetriou, A. & Papadopoulous, T. (2004). Human intelligence: From local models to universal theory. In R. J. Sternberg (ed.), *International handbook of intelligence,* 445–474. Cambridge: Cambridge University Press.

Depue, R. A., Lucianna, M., Arbisi, P., Collins, P. & Leon, A. (1994). Dopamine and the structure of personality: Relation of agonist-induced dopamine activity to positive emotionality. *Journal of Personality and Social Psychology, 67,* 485–498.

DeVito, A. J. (1985). Review of the Myers-Briggs Type Indicator. In J. V. Mitchell (ed.), *The Ninth Mental Measurement Yearbook.* Lincoln, NE: Buros Institute of Mental Measurement.

Dobson, P. (1988). The correction of correlation coefficients for restriction of range when restriction results from the truncation of a normally distributed variable. *British Journal of Mathematical and Statistical Psychology,41,* 227–234.

Dollard, J. & Miller, N. (1941). *Social learning and imitation.* New Haven, CT: Yale University Press.

Dollard, J. & Miller, N. (1950). *Personality and psychotherapy: An analysis in terms of learning, thinking, and culture.* New York: McGraw-Hill.

Doyle, K. O. (1974). Theory and practice of ability testing in Ancient Greece. *Journal of the History of the Behavioural Sciences, 10,* 202–212.

Edwards, A. L. (1957). *The social desirability variable in personality research*. New York: Dryden Press.

Elliott, C. (1983). *The British ability scales*. Windsor: NFER.

Emerson, E. (2001). *Challenging behaviour: Analysis and intervention in people with severe intellectual disabilities*. Cambridge: Cambridge University Press.

Evan, W. M. & Miller, J. R. (1969). Differential effects on response bias of computer vs. conventional administration of a social science questionnaire: An exploratory, methodological experiment. *Behavioural Science, 14*, 216–227.

Eysenck, H. J. (1955). Cortical inhibition, figural after-effects and theory of personality. *Journal of Abnormal and Social Psychology, 51*, 94–106.

Eysenck, H. J. (1959). The Rorschach. In O. K. Buros (ed.), *The vth mental measurement yearbook*. Highland Park: Gryphon Press.

Eysenck, H. J. (1960). *The Structure of Human Personality*. London: Routledge & Keegan Paul.

Eysenck, H. J. (1967). *The biological basis of personality*. Springfield, IL: Charles C. Thomas.

Eysenck, H. J. (1973). *The inequality of man*. London: Maurice Temple-Smith.

Eysenck, H. J. (1979). *The structure and measurement of intelligence*. New York: Springer-Verlag.

Eysenck, H. J. (1990). Biological dimensions of personality. In L. A. Pervin (ed.), *Handbook of personality: Theory and Research*, 244–276. New York: Guilford.

Eysenck, H. J. (1994). Personality: Biological foundations. In P. E. Vernon (ed.), *The neuropsychology of individual differences*. London: Academic Press.

Eysenck, H. J. & Eysenck, S. B. J. (1975). *Manual of the Eysenck Personality Questionnaire*. London: Hodder & Stoughton.

Eysenck, H. J. & Eysenck, M. W (1985). *Personality and individual differences: A natural science approach*. New York: Plenum.

Fan, X. (1998). Item response theory and classical test theory: An empirical comparison of their item/person statistics. *Educational and Psychological Measurement, 58*(3), 357–374.

Ferguson, G. A. (1981). *Statistical analysis in psychology and education* (4th ed.). New York: McGraw-Hill.

Field, A. (2005). *Discovering statistics using SPSS* (2nd ed.). London: Sage.

Flanagan, D. P., McGrew, K. S. & Ortiz, S. (2000). *The Wechsler intelligence scales and Gf-Gc theory: A contemporary approach to interpretation*. Needham Heights, MA: Allyn & Bacon.

Fleishman, E. A. & Quaintance, M. K. (1984). *Taxonomies of human performance: The description of human tasks*. New York: Academic Press.

Fleishman, E. A. & Reilly, M. E. (1991). *Human abilities: Their definition, measurement and job task requirement*. Palo Alto, CA: Consulting Psychologists Press.

Flynn, J. R. (1987). Massive IQ gains in 14 nations: What IQ tests really measure. *Psychological Bulletin, 101*, 171–191.

Flynn, J. R. (1994). IQ gains over time. In R. J. Sternberg (ed.), *Encyclopedia of human intelligence*, pp. 617–623. New York: Macmillan.

Flynn, J. R. (1999). Searching for justice: The discovery of IQ gains over time. *American Psychologist, 54*, 5–20.

Fopma-Loy, J.L. (1991). *Predictors of caregiving behaviours of formal caregivers of institutionalised people with dementing illnesses*. Unpublished doctoral dissertation, University School of Nursing, Indiana.

Forer, B. R. (1949). The fallacy of personal validation: A classroom demonstration of gullibility. *Journal of Abnormal and Social Psychology, 44*, 118–123.

Foucault, M. (2001). *Madness and civilization*. London: Routledge.

Franken, R. E. (1993). *Human motivation* (3rd ed.). Pacific Grove, CA: Brooks Cole.

Fransella, F. (2003). *International handbook of personal construct psychology.* London: Wiley.

Freud, S. (1901/1965). *The psychopathology of everyday life.* London: Hogarth Press.

Freud, S. (1923/1960). *The ego and the id.* New York: Norton.

Freud, S. (1940/1969). *An outline of psychoanalysis.* New York: Norton.

Furnham, A. (1992). *Personality at work: The role of individual differences in the workplace.* London: Routledge.

Furnham, A. (2005). *The psychology of behaviour at work* (2nd ed.). London: Psychology Press.

Gahagan, D. (1987). Attitudes. In J. Radford & E. Govier (eds.), *A textbook of psychology.* London: Sheldon Press.

Galton, F. (1865). Hereditary talent and character. *Macmillan's Magazine, 12,* 157–166, 318–327.

Galton, F. (1869). *Hereditary genius: An inquiry into its laws and consequences.* London: Macmillan.

Galton, F. (1874). *English men of science: Their nature and nurture.* New York: Appleton.

Galton, F. (1875). The history of twins, as a criterion of the relative powers of nature and nurture. *Fraser's Magazine, 92,* 566–576.

Galton, F. (1884). Measurement of character. *Fortnightly Review* 42.

Gardner, H. (1983). *Frames of mind: The theory of multiple intelligences.* New York: Basic Books.

Gardner, H. (1993). *Multiple intelligences: The theory in practice.* New York: Basic Books.

Gardner, H. (1998). Are there additional intelligences? The case for naturalist, spiritual and existential intelligences. In J. Kane (ed.), *Education, information and transformation,* 111–132. Englewood Cliffs, NJ: Prentice Hall.

Gardner, H., Kornhaber, M. & Wake, W. (1996). *Intelligence: Multiple perspectives.* Fort Worth, TX: Harcourt Brace.

Gati, L. (1991). The structure of vocational interests. *Psychological Bulletin, 109,* 209–224.

Gibbs, J. C., Basinger, K. S. & Fuller, D. (1992). *Moral maturity: Measuring the development of sociomoral reflection.* Hillsdale, NJ: Lawrence Erlbaum.

Goldberg, L. R. (1981). Language and individual differences: The search for universals in personality lexicons. In L. Wheeler (ed.), *Review of personality and social psychology,* 2, 141–165. Beverley Hills, CA: Sage.

Goleman, D. P. (1995). *Emotional intelligence: Why it can matter more than IQ for character, health and life-long achievement.* New York: Bantam.

Goodenough, F. L. (1926). *Measurement of intelligence by drawings.* New York: Harcourt Brace.

Gordon, L. V. (1993). *Survey of interpersonal values (SIV).* Maidenhead: McGraw-Hill.

Gough, H. G. (1975). *The Californian Psychological Inventory.* Palo Alto: Consulting Psychologists Press.

Gray, J. A. (1970). The psychophysiological basis of introversion-extraversion. *Behavior Research and Therapy, 8,* 249–266.

Gray, J. A. (1981). A critique of Eysenck's theory of personality. In H. J. Eysenck (ed.), *A model for personality,* 246–276. New York: Springer.

Gray, J. A. (1987). *The psychology of fear and stress* (2nd ed.). Cambridge: Cambridge University Press.

Gregory, R. L. (ed.) (1987). *The Oxford companion to the mind.* Oxford: Oxford University Press.

Gudjonsson, G. H. (1989). Theoretical and empirical aspects of interrogative suggestibility. In V. A. Gheorghiu, P. Netter, H. J. Eysenck & R. Rosenthal (eds.), *Suggestion and suggestibility: Theory and research.* Berlin: Springer-Verlag.

Gudjonsson, G. H. (1997). *The Gudjonsson Suggestibility Scales Manual.* Sussex: Psychology Press.

Guilford, J. P. (1981). Higher-order structure-of-intellect abilities. *Multivariate Behavioural Research, 16,* 411–435.

Guilford, J. P. & Fruchter, B. (1978). *Fundamental Statistics in Psychology and Education.* New York: McGraw-Hill.

Guion, R. M. (1965). *Personnel testing.* New York: McGraw-Hill.

Guion, R. M. (1998). *Assessment, measurement and prediction for personnel decisions.* Mahwah, NJ: Lawrence Erlbaum.

Guion, R. M. & Cranny, C. J. (1982). A method of concurrent and predictive designs: a critical reanalysis. *Journal of Applied Psychology, 67,* 239–244.

Guttman, L. (1944). A basis for scaling quantitative data. *American Sociological Review, 9,* 139–150.

Haier, R. J. (1991). Cerebral glucose metabolism and intelligence. In. P. Vernon (ed.), *Biologic approaches to the study of human intelligence.* Norwood, NJ: Ablex.

Hambleton, R. K. & Swaminathan, H. (1985). *Item response theory: Principles and applications.* Boston: Kluwer-Nijhoff.

Hants, C. R. (1994). Assessing children's credibility: Scientific and legal issues in 1994. *North Dakota Law Review, 70(4),* 879–903.

Hants, C. R. & Quick, D. D. (1995). The polygraph in 1995: Progress in science and the law. *North Dakota Law Review, 71,* 987–1020.

Harcourt Assessment (2007). *Occupational assessment catalogue.* London: Harcourt.

Hare, R. D., Harpur, T. J., Hakstian, A. R., Forth, A. E., Hart, S. D. & Newman, J. P. (1990). The revised Psychopathy Checklist: Reliability and factor structure. *Psychological Assessment: A Journal of Consulting and Clinical Psychology, 2,* 338–341.

Harris, D. B. (1963). *Children's drawings as measures of intellectual maturity: A revision and extension of the Goodenough Draw-A-Man test.* New York: Harcourt Brace.

Harris, W. G. (1987). Computer-based test interpretations: Some development and application issues. *Applied Psychology: An International Review, 36(3/4),* 237–247.

Hathaway, S. R. & McKinley, J. C. (1951). *The Minnesota Multiphasic Personality Inventory Manual (Revised).* New York: Psychological Corporation.

Hattie, J. (1985). Methodology review: Assessing unidimensionality of tests and items. *Applied Psychological Measurement, 9,* 139–164.

Hedl, J. J., O'Neil, H. F. & Hansen, D. N. (1973). Affective reactions to computer based intelligence testing. *Journal of Consulting and Clinical Psychology, 40,* 217–222.

Heider, F. (1958). *The psychology of interpersonal relations.* New York: Wiley.

Heim, A. W., Watts, K. P. & Simmonds, V. (1970). *AH4, AH5 and AH6 tests.* Windsor: NFER.

Herriott, P. (1989). Selection as a social process. In J. M. Smith & I. T. Robertson (eds.), *Advances in selection and assessment.* Chichester: Wiley.

Herriott, P. (2002). Selection and self: Selection as a social process. *European Journal of Work and Organisational Psychology, 11(4),* 385–402.

Herrnstein, R. & Murray, C. (1994). *The Bell Curve: Intelligence and class structure in American life.* New York: Free Press.

Hodgkinson, G. P., Daley, N. & Payne, P. L. (1996). Knowledge of, and attitudes towards, the demographic time bomb. *International Journal of Manpower, 16,* 59–76.

Hoffman, B. (1962). *The tyranny of testing.* New York: Crowell-Collier.

Hogan, R. & Hogan, J. (1987). *Motives, Values, Preferences Inventory (MVPI).* Tunbridge Wells: Psychological Consultancy Ltd.

Holland, J. L. (1966). *The psychology of vocational choice.* Waltham: Blaisdell.

Holland, J. L. (1985). *Self-directed search: Professional manual.* Odessa, FL: Psychological Assessment Resources.

Holland, J. L. (1996). Exploring careers with a typology: What we have learned and some new directions. *American Psychologist, 51,* 397–406.

Holtzman, W. H. (1981). Holtzman inkblot technique. In A. I. Rabin (ed.), *Assessment with projective techniques.* New York: Springer.

Horn, J. L. (1978). Human ability *systems.* In P. B. Baltes (ed.), *Life-span development and behaviour, 1,* 211–256.

Horner, R. H., Sprague, J. R., O'Brien, M. & Heathfield, L. T. (1990). The role of response efficiency in the reduction of problem behaviors through functional equivalence training: A case study. *Journal of the Associations for Persons with Severe Handicaps 15,* 91–7.

Hough, L. M. & Ones, D. S. (2001). The structure, measurement, validity, and use of personality variables in industrial, work and organizational psychology. In Anderson, N., Ones, D. S., Sinangil, H. K. & Viswesvaran, C. *Handbook of Industrial, Work & Organizational Psychology.* London: Sage.

Huba, G. J. (1987). On probabilistic computer-based test interpretations and other expert systems. *Applied Psychology: An international review, 36, (3),* 357–73.

Hughes, D. & Tate, L. (2007). To cheat or not to cheat: Candidates' perceptions and experiences of unsupervised computer-based testing. *Selection & Development Review, 23*(2), 2007.

Jackson, D. N. (1977). *Jackson Vocational Interest Survey Manual.* Port Huron, MI: Research Psychologists Press.

Jackson, J. S. H. & Maraun, M. (1996a). The conceptual validity of empirical scale construction: The case of the sensation seeking scale. *Personality and Individual Differences, 21,* 103–110.

Jackson, J. S. H. & Maraun, M. (1996b). Whereof one cannot speak, thereof one must remain silent. *Personality and Individual Differences, 21,* 115–118.

James, L. R. (1998). Measurement of personality via conditional reasoning. *Organizational Research Methods, 1(2),* 131–63.

Jensen, A. R. (1998). *The g factor: The science of mental ability.* Wesport, CT: Praeger.

Jensen, A. R. (1973). *Educability and group differences.* London: Methuen.

Jensen, A. R. (1980). *Bias in Mental Testing.* New York: Free Press.

Jensen, A. R. & Sinah, S. N. (1993). Physical correlates of human intelligence. In P. A. Vernon (ed.) *Biological approaches to the study of human intelligence.* Norwood, NJ: Ablex.

Johnson, J. T. & Ree, M. J. (1994). RANGEJ: A Pascal program to compute the multivariate correction for range restriction. *Educational and Psychological Measurement, 54,* 693–695.

Johnson, C. E., Wood, R. & Blinkhorn, S. F. (1988). Spuriouser and spuriouser: the use of ipsative personality tests. *Journal of Occupational Psychology, 61*(2), 153–162.

Jones, E. E. & Davis, K. E. (1965). From acts to dispositions: The attribution process in person perception. In L. Berkowitz (ed.) *Advances in experimental social psychology,* vol. 2. New York: Academic Press.

Jung, C. G. (1921). Psychological Types, Vol. 6. *The Collected Works of C. G. Jung.* London: RKP.

Kamin, L. J. & Goldberger, A. S. (2002). Twin studies in behavioural research: A sceptical view. *Theoretical Population Biology, 61,* 83–95.

Kamin, L. J. (1974). *The science and politics of IQ.* New York: Wiley.

Kamin, L. J. (1995). Lies, damned lies, and statistics. In R. Jacoby & N. Glauberman (eds.), *The Bell Curve debate: History, documents, opinions,* 81–105. New York: Times/Random House.

Katz, M. R. (1972). The Strong Vocational Interest Blank. In O. K. Buros (ed.) *The VIth Mental Measurement Yearbook*. Highland Park: Gryphon Press.

Kaufman, A. S. & Kaufman, N. L. (2001). *Specific learning disabilities and difficulties in children and adolescents: Psychological assessment and evaluation*. Cambridge: Cambridge University Press.

Kelly, G. A. (1955). *The psychology of personal constructs* (vols 1 & 2). New York: Norton.

Kelly, G. A. (1958). Man's construction of his alternatives. In G. Lindzey (ed.), *Assessment of human motives*. New York: Rinehart & Winston.

Kelly, G. A. (1963). A theory of personality: *The psychology of personal constructs*. New York: Norton.

Klimoski, R. J. & Rafaeli, A. (1983). Inferring personal qualities through handwriting analysis. *Journal of Occupational Psychology, 56*, 191–202.

Kline, P. (1986). *Handbook of test construction*. London: Routledge and Kegan Paul.

Kline, P. (1988). *Psychology exposed*. London: Routledge.

Kline, P. (1992). *The handbook of psychological testing*. London: Routledge.

Kline, P. (1993). *Personality: The psychometric view*. London: Routledge.

Kline, P. (1994). *An easy guide to factor analysis*. London: Routledge.

Kline, P. (1998). *The new psychometrics*. London: Routledge.

Kline, P. (2000). *Handbook of psychological testing*. London: Routledge.

Klinger, D. E., Johnson, J. H. & Williams, T. A. (1976). Stragies in the evaluation of an online computer-assisted unit for intake assessment of mental health patients. *Behavior Research Methods and Instrumentation, 8*, 95–100.

Koestner, R. & McClelland, D. C. (1990). Perspecives on competence motivation. In L. A. Pervin (ed.), *Handbook of personality: Theory and research*. New York: Guilford Press.

Kozlowski, S. W. J. & Klein, K. J. (2000). A multilevel approach to theory and research in organizations: Contextual, temporal and emergent processes. In K. J. Klein & S. W. J. Kozlowski (eds.) *Multilevel theory, research and methods in organizations* (512–553). San Francisco: Jossey-Bass.

Kretschmer, E. (1925). *Physique and character*. New York: Harcourt Brace Jovanovich.

Kuder, G. F. (1954). Expected developments in interest and personality inventories. *Psychometrica, 2*, 151–160.

Kuder, G. F. (1970a). *Kuder General Interest Survey*. Chicago: Science Research Associates.

Kuder, G. F. (1970b). *Kuder Occupational Interests Survey*. Chicago: Science Research Associates.

Kutchins, H. & Kirk, S. A. (1997). *Making us crazy: The psychiatric Bible and the creation of mental disorders*. New York: Free Press.

Landy, F. J. (1980). Stamp collecting vs science. *American Psychologist*, November, 1183–1192.

Landy, F. J. & Farr, J. L. (1980). Performance rating. *Psychological Bulletin, 87*, 72–107.

Lanyon, R. I. (1987). Personality assessment. *Annual Review of Psychology, 35*, 667–707.

Lee, G. & Beard, D. (1994). *Development centres: Realising the potential of your employees through assessment and development*. London: McGraw-Hill.

Levinson, D. J., Darrow, C. N., Klein, E. B., Levinson, M. L. & McKee, B. (1978). *The season's of man's life*. New York: Knopf.

Levy, P. (1973). On the relation of test theory and psychology. In P. Kline (ed.), *New approaches in psychological measurement*. Chichester: Wiley.

Lewin, A. Y. & Zwany, A. (1976). Peer nominations: A model, literature critique and a paradigm for research. *Personnel Psychology, 29*, 423–447.

Leyens, J. P., Yzerbyt, V. & Schadron, G. (1994). *Stereotypes and social cognition*. London: Sage.

Likert, R. A. (1932). A technique for the measurement of attitudes. *Archives of Psychology, 140.*

Lim, W., Plucker, J. A. & Im, K. (2002). We are more alike than we think we are: Implicit theories of intelligence with a Korean sample. *Intelligence, 30,* 185–208.

Lindley, P. (ed.) (2001). *Review of personality instruments (level B) for use in occupational settings* (2nd ed.). Leicester: British Psychological Society.

Lindsay, S. J. E. & Powell, G. E. (1994). Practical issues of investigation. In S. J. E. Lindsay & G. E. Powell (eds.), *The handbook of clinical adult psychology,* (2nd edition). London: Routledge.

Locke, A. E. (1976). The nature and causes of job satisfaction. In M. D. Dunnette (ed.), *Handbook of industrial and organizational psychology.* Chicago: Rand McNally.

Lohman, D. F. (2001). Issues in the definition and measurement of abilities. In J. M. Collis & S. J. Messick (eds.), *Intelligence and personality: Bridging the gap in theory and measurement,* 79–98. Mahwah NJ: Erlbaum.

Lord, F. M. (1974). *Individualised testing and item characteristic curve theory.* Princeton: ETS.

Lord, F. M. (1980). *Applications of item response theory to practical testing problems.* Hillsdale: Erlbaum.

Luria, A. R. (1973). *The working brain: An introduction to neuropsychology* (B. Haigh, Trans.). New York: Basic Books.

Lykken, D. T. (1988). The case against polygraph testing. In A. Gale (ed.), *The polygraph test: Lies, truth and science,* 111–125. London: Sage.

Lynn, R. (1990). The role of nutrition in secular increases of intelligence. *Personality and Individual Differences, 11,* 273–286.

Lynn, R. (2001). *Eugenics: A reassessment.* Westport, CT: Praeger.

Mace, C. A. (1935). *Incentives: Some experimental studies* (Report 72). London: Industrial Health Research Board.

Mackintosh, N. J. (1998). *IQ and human intelligence.* Oxford: Oxford University Press.

Magnusson, D. & Torestad, B. (1993). Individual differences in anxiety and the restriction of working memory capacity. *Personality and Individual Differences, 15,* 163–173.

Maltby, J., Day, L. & Macaskill, A. (2007). *Personality, individual differences and intelligence.* Essex, UK: Pearson.

Maslow, A. H. (1954). *Motivation and personality.* New York: Harper.

Matarazzo, J. D. (1983). Editorial on computerised psychological testing. *Science,* 22 July, 221, 223.

Matarazzo, J. D. (1986). Computerised clinical psychological test interpretations: Plus all and no sigma. *American Psychologist, 41*(1), 1424.

Matthews, G. & Gilliland, K. (1999). The personality theories of H. J. Eysenck and J. A. Gray: A comparative review. *Personality and Individual Differences, 26,* 583–626.

Mazzeo, J. & Harvey, A. L. (1988). *The equivalence of scores from automated and conventional educational and psychological tests: A review of the literature* (College Board Report 88–8). Princeton, NJ: Educational Testing Service.

McClelland, D. C. (1976). *The achieving society.* New York: Irvington Publishers.

McConville, C. & Cooper, C. (1992). The structure of moods. *Personality and Individual Differences, 13,* 909–919.

McCrae, R. R. & Costa, P. T. (1990). *Personality in adulthood.* New York: Guilford Press.

McDaniel, M. A. (2005). Big-brained people are smarter: A meta-analysis of the relationship between in vivo brain volume and intelligence. *Intelligence, 33,* 337–346.

McKenzie, D. & Harris, M. (1982). *Judging people.* London: McGraw-Hill.

McKey, R. H., Condelli, L., Granson, H. Barrett, B., McConkey, C. & Plantz, M., (1985). *The impact of Head Start on children, families and communities.* Washington, DC: CSR.

McLeod, E. M. (1968). A Ripper handwriting analysis. *The Criminologist,* Summer.

Meehl, P. E. (1956). Wanted – A good cookbook. *American Psychologist, 11,* 262–272.

Messick, S. (1975). The standard problem: meaning of values in measurements and evaluation. *American Psychologist, 30,* 955–966.

Messick, S. (1980). Test validity and the ethics of assessment. *American Psychologist, 35,* 1012–1027.

Messick, S. (1989). Validity. In Linn, R. L. (ed.), *Educational Measurement.* Washington, DC: American Council on Education, 13–103.

Michell, J. (1990). *An introduction to the logic of psychological measurement.* Hillsdale, NJ: Erlbaum.

Miller, K. M., Rothwell, J. W. & Tyler, B. (1994). *Rothwell-Miller Interest Blank.* London: Miller & Tyler.

Mischel, W. (1968). *Personality and assessment.* New York: Wiley.

Mischel, W. (2004). Toward an integrative science of the person. *Annual Review of Psychology, 55,* 1–22.

Mislevy, R. J. (1982). Adaptive EAP estimation of ability in a microcomputer environment. *Applied Psychological Measurement, 6*(4), 431–444.

Mitchell, G. & Hastings, R.P. (1998). Learning disability care staffs' emotional reactions to challenging behaviours: Development of a measurement tool. *British Journal of Clinical Psychology, 37*(4), 441–449.

Moos, R. H. & Moos, B. S. (1994). *Family environment scale manual: Development, applications, research* (3rd ed.). Palo Alto, CA: Consulting Psychologists Press.

Mosher, D. L. (1965). Approval motive and acceptance of 'fake' personality test interpretations which differ in favorability. *Psychological Reports, 17,* 395–402.

Mount, M. K., Barrick, M. R. & Strauss, P. P. (1994). Validity of observer ratings of the Big Five personality factors. *Journal of Applied Psychology, 79,* 272–280.

Mumford, M. D., Costanza, D. P., Connelly, M. S. & Johnson, J. F. (1996). Item generation procedures and background data scales: Implications for construct and criterion-related validity. *Personnel Psychology, 49,* 361–398.

Murphy, K. R. & Davidshofer, C. O. (1998). *Psychological testing* (4th ed.). Upper Saddle River, NJ: Prentice Hall.

Murray, H.A. (1938). *Explorations in Personality.* New York: Oxford University Press.

Myers, I. B. (1962). *Manual for the Myers-Briggs Type Indicator.* Palo Alto, CA: Consulting Psychologists Press.

Myers, I. B. & McCaulley, M. H. (1985). *Manual: A guide to the development and use of the Myers-Briggs Type Indicator.* Palo Alto, CA: Consulting Psychologists Press.

Naglieri, J. A.& Das, J. P. (1997). *Cognitive assessment system: Interpretive handbook.* Itasca, IL: Riverside.

Neisser, U. (1998). Introduction: Rising test scores and what they mean. In U. Neisser (ed.), *The rising curve: Long-term gains in IQ and related measures.* Washington, DC: Americal Psychological Association.

Neisser, U., Boodoo, O., Bouchard, T. J., Boykin, A., Brody, N. & Ceci, S. J. et al. (1996). Intelligence: Knowns and unknowns. *American Psychologist, 51,* 77–101.

Neter, E. & Ben-Shakhar, G. (1989). Predictive validity of graphological inferences: A meta-analytic approach. *Personality and Individual Differences, 10,* 737–745.

Nicholson, T., White, J. & Duncan, D. (1998). Drugnet: A pilot study of adult recreational drug use via the WWW. *Substance Abuse, 19,* 109–21.

Nilsen, D. (1995). Investigation of the relationship between personality and leadership performance. Unpublished doctoral dissertation, University of Minnesota. In L. M. Hough & D. S. Ones (2001).

Nunnally, J. O. (1978). *Psychometric Theory.* New York: McGraw-Hill.

Nunnally, J. O. & Bernstein, I. H. (1994). *Psychometric theory* (3rd ed.). New York: McGraw-Hill.

O'Brien, T. & Dugdale, V. (1978). Questionnaire administration by computer. *Journal of the Market Research Society, 20,* 228–237.

Oddy, W. H., Sherriff, J. L., de Klerk, N. L., Kendall, G. E., Sly, P. D. & Beilin, L. J. (2004). The relation of breastfeeding and body mass index to asthma and atopy in children: A prospective cohort study to age 6 years. *American Journal of Public Health, 94,* 1531–1537.

O'Neill, R. E., Horner, R. H., Albin, R. W., Storey, K. & Sprague, J. R. (1997). *Functional Analysis and Program Development for Problem Behavior.* Pacific Grove, CA: Brooks/Cole.

Ones, D. S., Viswesvaran, C. & Schmidt, F. L. (1993). Comprehensive meta-analysis of integrity test validities: Findings and implications for personnel selection and theories of job performance. *Journal of Applied Psychology, 78,* 670–703.

Osgood, C. E., Suci, G. J. & Tannenbaum, P. H. (1957). *The measurement of meaning.* Urbana: University of Illinois Press.

Osterling, S. J (1983). Test item bias. In J. L. Sullivan & R. G. Niemi (eds.), *Quantitative applications in the social sciences, 30.* Beverly Hills, CA: Sage.

Paulhus, D. L. (1984). Two-component models of social desirable responding. *Journal of Personality and Social Psychology, 46,* 598–609.

Pavlov, I. P. (1906). The scientific investigations of the psychical faculties or processes in the higher animals. *Science, 24,* 613–619.

Pavlov, I. P. (1927). *Conditioned reflexes.* London: Oxford.

Pavlov, I. P. (1928). *Lectures on conditioned reflexes.* New York: International Publishers.

Pedhazur, E.J. & Pedhazur Schmelkin, L. (1991). *Measurement, design and analysis.* Hillsdale, NJ: Lawrence Erlbaum.

Plomin, R. (2004). *Nature and nurture: An introduction to human behavioural genetics.* London: Wadsworth.

Plomin, R. & Crabbe, J. (2000). DNA. *Psychological Bulletin, 126,* 806–828.

Popper, K. R. (1972). *The logic of scientific discovery.* Tiptree: Anchor Press.

Prediger, D. J. (1976). A world-of-work map for career exploration. *Vocational Guidance Quarterly, 24,* 198–208.

Prediger, D. J. (1982). Dimensional underlying Holland's hexagon: The missing link between interests and occupations? *Journal of Vocational Behavior, 21,* 259–287.

Prediger, D. J. & Vansickle, T. R. (1992a). Locating occupations on Holland's hexagon: Beyond RIASEC. *Journal of Vocational Behavior, 40,* 111–128.

Prediger, D. J. & Vansickle, T. R. (1992b). Who claims Holland's hexagon is perfect? *Journal of Vocational Behavior, 40,* 210–219.

Rand, A. (1964). *The virtue of selfishness.* New York: Signet.

Rasch, G. (1960). *Probabilistic models for some intelligence and attainment tests.* Copenhagen: Denmark Institute of Education.

Rasch, G. (1966). An item analysis which takes individual differences into account. *British Journal of Mathematical and Statistical Psychology, 19,* 49–57.

Rasch, G. (1980). *Probabilistic models for intelligence and attainment testing.* Chicago: University of Chicago Press.

Raven, J. C. (1938). *Progressive matrices: A perceptual test of intelligence.* London: Lewis.

Raven, J. C. (1965). *Progressive matrices.* London: H. K. Lewis.

Ree, M. J. (1995). Nine rules for doing ability research wrong. *The Industrial-Organizational Psychologist, 32,* 64068.

Ree, M. J. & Carretta, T. R. (1994). Factor analysis of the ASVAB: Confirming a Vernon-like structure. *Educational and Psychological Measurement, 54,* 459–463.

Ree, M. J. & Carretta, T. R. (1997). What makes an aptitude test valid? In R. Dillon (ed.), *Handbook of testing*, 65–81. Westport, CT: Greenwood Press.

Ree, M. J. & Carretta, T. R. (1998). General cognitive ability and occupational performance. In C. L. Cooper & I. T. Robertson (eds.), *International review of industrial and organizational psychology, 13*, 159–184. London: Wiley.

Rees, C. J. (1999). *Investigations in the faking good of personality questionnaire results in the occupational context*. Unpublished PhD thesis, UMIST, Manchester.

Report of the Working Group on the use of the polygraph in criminal investigation and personnel screening (1986). *Bulletin of the British Psychological Society, 39*, 81–94.

Reynolds, C. R. (1995). Test bias and the assessment of intelligence and personality. In D. H. Saklofske & M. Zeidner (eds.), *International handbook of personality and intelligence*. New York: Plenum.

Richman, W. L., Kiesler, S., Weisband, S. & Drasgow, F. (1999). A meta-analytic study of social desirability distortion in computer-administered questionnaires, traditional questionnaires and interviews. *Journal of Applied Psychology, 84*, 754–775.

Ridley, M. (1999). *Genome: The autobiography of a species in 23 chapters*. London: Fourth Estate.

Robertson, I. T. & Smith, J. M. (2001). Personnel selection. *Journal of Occupational and Organisational Psychology, 74(4)*, 441–472.

Rogers, C. R. (1956). What it means to become a person. In C. E. Moustakas, *The self: Explorations in personal growth*, pp. 195–211. New York: Harper.

Rogers, C. R. (1961). *On becoming a person: A therapist's view of psychotherapy*. Boston: Houghton Mifflin.

Rogers, C. R. (1977). *Carl Rogers on personal power*. New York: Delacorte Press.

Rogers, C. R. & Dymond, R. F. (eds.) (1954). *Psychotherapy and personality change*. Chicago: University of Chicago Press.

Rokeach, M. (1973). *The nature of human values*. New York: Free Press.

Rokeach, M. (1979). *Understanding human values*. Palo Alto, CA: Consulting Psychologists Press.

Rolls, S. R. (1993). *The validity and utility of computer-based test interpretations (CBTIs) in staff selection decision situations*. Unpublished PhD thesis, Cranfield Institute of Technology.

Rorschach, H. (1921). *Psychodiagnostics*. Berne: Hans Huber.

Roskam, E. E. (1985). Current issues in item-response theory: Beyond psychometrics. In Roskam, E. E. (ed.) *Measurement and personality assessment*. Amsterdam: Elsevier.

Rotter, J. B. (1966). Generalized expectancies for internal versus external control of reinforcement. *Psychological Monographs, 80*, 609.

Rotter, J. B. (1982). *The development and application of social learning theory: Selected papers*. New York: Praeger.

Runco, M. A. (2004). Creativity. *Annual Review of Psychology, 55*, 657–687.

Rust, J. (1996). *Orpheus user manual*. London: Psychological Corporation.

Rust, J. & Golombok, S. (1999). Modern Psychometrics: The science of psychological assessment (2nd edn.). London: Routledge.

Rusting, C. L. (1998). Personality, mood and cognitive processing of emotional information: Three conceptual frameworks. *Psychological Bulletin, 124*, 165–196.

Sackett, P. R., Burris, L. R. & Callahan, C. (1989). Integrity testing for personnel selection: An update. *Personnel Psychology, 42*, 491–529.

Sackett, P. R. & Dekker, P. J. (1979). Detection of deception in the employment context: A review and critique. *Personnel Psychology, 32*, 487–506.

Sackett, P. R. & Harris, M. M. (1984). Honesty testing for personnel selection: A review and critique. *Personnel Psychology, 37*, 221–245.

Sackett, P. R. & Wanek, J. E. (1996). New developments in the use of measures of honesty, integrity, conscientiousness, dependability, trustworthiness and reliability for personnel selection. *Personnel Psychology, 49*, 787–829.

Salgado, J. F. (2000). *The big five personality dimensions as predictors of alternative criteria.* Paper presented at the 15th annual conference of the Society for Industrial and Organizational Psychology, New Orleans, LA.

Schaie, K. W. (1983). The Seattle longitudinal study: A twenty-one year exploration of psychometric intelligence in adulthood. In K. W. Schaie (ed.), *Longitudinal studies of adult psychological development*, 64–135. New York: Guilford Press.

Schmidt, F. L. (1988). Objective personality tests – some clinical applications. In K. M. Miller (ed.), *The analysis of personality and research*. London: Independent Assessment and Research Centre.

Schmidt, F. L., Hunter, J. E. & Urry, V. W. (1976). Statistical power in criterion related validation studies. *Journal of Applied Psychology, 61*(4), 473–485.

Schmidt, F. L., Ones, D. S. & Hunter, J. E. (1992). Personnel selection. *Annual Review of Psychology, 43*, 671–710.

Schoenthaler, S. J., Bier, I. D., Young, K., Nichols, D. & Jansenns, S. (2000). The effects of vitamin-mineral supplementation on the intelligence of American schoolchildren: A randomized double-blind placebo-controlled trial. *Journal of Alternative and Complementary Medicine, 6*, 19–29.

Schutz, W. (1989). *Fundamental interpersonal relations orientation-behaviour (FIRO-B)*. Palo Alto, CA: Consulting Psychologists Press.

Schwab, D. P., Heneman, H. G. & DeCottiss, T. A. (1975). Behaviourally anchored rating scales: a review of the literature. *Personnel Psychology, 28*, 549–562.

Selltiz, C., Wrightsman, L. S. & Cook, S. W. (1976). *Research methods in social relations* (3rd ed.). New York: Holt, Rinehart and Winston.

Semeonoff, B. (1971). *Projective tests*. Chichester: Wiley.

Semeonoff, B. (1981). Projective techniques. In F. Fransella, *Personality*. London: Methuen.

Sharrock, R., Day, A., Qazi, F. & Brewin, C. R. (1990). Explanations by professional care staff, optimism and helping behaviour: An application of attribution theory. *Psychological Medicine, 20*, 849–855.

Sheldon, W. (1970). *Atlas of men*. New York: Macmillan.

Shirley, L. (2003). *Validating an attributional questionnaire with British nurses and care staff for people with dementia*. Unpublished doctoral thesis, University of Teesside.

Shirley, L. (2005). The development of a tool to measure attributional processes in dementia care settings. *Clinical Psychology Forum*, 154.

Small, S. A., Zeldin, R. S & Savin-Williams, R. C. (1983). In search of personality traits: A multimethod analysis of naturally occurring prosocial and dominance behaviour. *Journal of Personality, 51*, 1–16.

Smith, M., Durkin, M. S.,Hinton, V., Bellinger, D. & Kuhn, L. (2003). Influence of breast-feeding on cognitive outcomes at age 6–8 years: Follow-up of very low birth weight infants. *American Journal of Epidemiology, 158*, 1075–1082.

Smith, M. & Robertson, I. T. (1993). *The theory and practice of systematic personnel selection*. London: Macmillan.

Smith, M. & Smith, P. (2005). *Testing people at work: Competencies in psychometric testing*. Oxford: BPS Blackwell.

Smith, P. C. (1976). Behavior, results and organizational effectiveness: The problem of criteria. In M. D. Dunnette (ed.), *Handbook of Industrial and Organisational Psychology*, 745–775. Chicago: Rand McNally.

Snyder, C. R., Shenkel, R. J. & Lowery, C. R. (1977). The acceptance of personality interpretations: The Barnum effect and beyond. *Journal of Consulting and Clinical Psychology*, 45(1), 104–114.

Spearman, C. E. (1904). 'General intelligence,' objectively determined and measured. *American Journal of Psychology, 15*, 201–293.

Spearman, C. E. (1927). *The abilities of man: Their nature and measurement*. New York: Macmillan.

Stankov, L., Boyle, G. J. & Cattell, R. J. (1995). Models and paradigms in personality and intelligence research. In D. Saklofské & M. Zeidner (eds.), *International handbook of personality and intelligence: Perspectives on individual differences*, 15–43. New York: Plenum Press.

Stanley, B. & Standen, P.J. (2000). Carers' attributions for challenging behaviour. *British Journal of Clinical Psychology, 39*, 157–168.

Stanton, J. M. (1998). An empirical assessment of data collection using the Internet. *Personnel Psychology, 51*, 709–725.

Stephenson, W. (1953). *The study of behaviour*. Chicago: University of Chicago Press.

Stern, W. (1912). *Die Psychologische Methoden der IntelligenzPruifung*. Barth: Leipzig.

Stern, W. (1965). The psychological methods for testing intelligence. In R. J. Herrenstien & E. G. Boring (eds.), *A source book in the history of psychology*. Cambridge, Mass.: Harvard University Press.

Sternberg, R. J. (1985a). *Beyond IQ: A triarchic theory of human intelligence*. New York: Cambridge University Press.

Sternberg, R. J. (1985b). Implicit theories of intelligence, creativity and wisdom. *Journal of Personality and Social Psychology, 49*, 607–627.

Sternberg, R. J. (1988). *The triarchic mind: A new theory of human intelligence*. New York: Cambridge University Press.

Sternberg, R. J. (ed.) (2000). *Handbook of intelligence*. Cambridge: Cambridge University Press.

Sternberg, R. J. (2001). The concept of intelligence. In R. J. Sternberg (ed.), *International handbook of intelligence*, 3–15. Cambridge: Cambridge University Press.

Sternberg, R. J., Conway, B. E., Ketron, J. L. & Bernstein, M. (1981). People's conceptions of intelligence. *Journal of Personality and Social Psychology, 41*, 37–55.

Sternberg, R. J., Wagner, R. K., Williams, M. W. &Horvath, J. A. (1995). Testing common sense. *American Psychologist, 50*, 912–927.

Stevens, S. S. (1946). On the theory of scales of measurement. *Science, 103*, 667–80.

Stevens, S. S. (1968). Measurement, statistics and the schemapiric view. *Science, 161*, 849–56.

Stinglhamber, F., Vandebberghe, C. & Brancart, S. (1999). Les reactions des candidats envers les techniques de selection du personnel: une etude dans un contexte francophone. *Travail Humain, 62*, 347–361.

Stricker, L. J. & Ross, R. (1964). An assessment of some structural properties of the Jungian personality typology. *Journal of Abnormal and Social Psychology, 68*, 62–71.

Strong, E. K., Campbell, D. P., Berdie, R. E. & Clerk, K. E. (1971). *Strong vocational interest blank*. Stanford: Stanford University Press.

Sundberg, N. D. (1955). The acceptability of 'fake' versus 'bona fide' personality test interpretations. *Journal of Abnormal and Social Psychology, 50*, 145–7.

Sundet, J. M., Barlaug, D. G. & Torjussen, T. M. (2004). The end of the Flynn effect? A study of secular trends in mean intelligence test scores of Norwegian conscripts during half a century. *Intelligence, 32*, 349–362.

Super, D. E. (1970). *Work values inventory: Manual.* Chicago: Riverside.

Szasz, T. S. (1970). *The manufacture of madness.* New York: Dell.

Tate, B. G. & Baroff, G. S (1966). Aversive control of self-injurious behaviour in a psychotic boy. *Behavior Research and Therapy, 4,* 281–287.

Teasdale, T. W. & Owen, D. R. (2005). A long-term rise and recent decline in intelligence test performance: The Flynn effect in reverse. *Personality and Individual Differences, 39,* 837–843.

Terman, L. M. (1916). *The measurement of intelligence.* Boston: Houghton Mifflin.

Terman, L. M. (1917). The intelligence quotient of Francis Galton in childhood. *American Journal of Psychology, 28,* 209–215.

Terman, L. M. (1925). *Genetic studies of genius,* vol.1. *Mental and physical traits of a thousand gifted children.* Stanford, CA: Stanford University Press.

Terman, L. M. & Merrill, M. A. (1960). *Stanford-Binet intelligence scale.* New York: Houghton Mifflin.

Thompson, B. (1994). Guidelines for authors. *Educational and psychological measurements yearbook, 54,* 837–847.

Thorndike, R. L. (1949). *Personnel selection.* New York: Wiley.

Thorndike, R. L. & Hagen, E. P. (1977). *Measurement and evaluation in psychology and education* (4th ed.). New York: Wiley.

Thorndike, E. L., Terman, L. M., Freeman, F. N., Calvin, S. S., Pentler, R., Ruml, B. & Pressey, S. L. (1921). Intelligence and its measurement: A symposium. *Journal of Educational Psychology, 12,* 123–147.

Thorne, F. C. (1961). Clinical judgement: a study of clinical errors. *Journal of Clinical Psychology,* xxiii, 1342 pp.

Thornton, G. C. (1993). The effect of selection practices on applicants' perceptions of organisational characteristics. In H. Schuler, J. L. Farr & M. Smith (eds.), *Personnel selection and assessment: Individual and organisational perspectives.* Hillsdale, NJ: Lawrence Erlbaum.

Thurstone, L. L. (1919). *Intelligence tests for college students.* Pittsburgh: Carnegie Institute of Technology.

Thurstone, L. L. (1938). Primary mental abilities. *Psychometric Monographs,* 1.

Thurstone, L. L. (1953). *Examiner manual for Thurstone Temperament Schedule.* Chicago: Science Research Associates.

Thurstone, L. L. & Chave, E. J. (1929). *The measurement of attitude.* Chicago: University of Chicago Press.

Vernon, P. E. (1950). *The structure of human abilities.* New York: Wiley.

Vernon, P. E. (1960). *Intelligence and attainment tests.* London: University of London Press.

Vernon, P. E. (1961). *The measurement of abilities.* London: University of London Press.

Vernon, P. E. (1963). *Personality assessment.* London: Methuen.

Vernon, P. E. (1969). *Intelligence and cultural environment.* London: Methuen.

Vernon, P. E. (1979). Intelligence testing and the nature/nurture debate, 1928–1978: What next? *British Journal of Educational Psychology, 49,* 1–14.

Watson, G. & Glaser, E. M. (1964). *Critical thinking appraisal.* New York: Harcourt Brace Jovanovich.

Watts, A. G., Super, D. E. & Kidd, J. M. (eds.) (1981). *Career development in Britain.* Cambridge: Hobson's Press.

Wechsler, D. (1958). *The measurement and appraisal of adult intelligence* (4th ed.). Baltimore: Williams & Wilkins.

Weiner, B. (1980). A cognitive (attribution) – emotion-action model of helping behaviour: An analysis of judgments of help giving. *Journal of Personality and Social Psychology, 39,* 186–200.

Weiss, D. J. & Yoes, M. E. (1991). Item response theory. In. R. K. Hambleton & J. N. Zaal (eds.), *Advances in educational and psychological testing: Theory and applications*, 69–95. Boston, Kluwer.

Widiger, T. A. & Costa, P. Y. (1994). Personality and personality disorders. *Journal of Abnormal Psychology, 103*, 78–91.

Wilson, R. S. (1985). Risk and resilience in early mental development. *Developmental Psychology, 21*, 795–805.

Witkin, A. & Goodenough, D. R. (1977). Field dependence and personal behaviour. *Psychological Bulletin, 84*, 661–689.

Witkin, A., Oltman, P. K., Raskin, E. & Karp, S. A. (1971). *Manual to the embedded figures tests*. Palo Alto, CA: Consulting Psychologists Press.

Wood, R. (1976). Trait measurement and item banks. In D. N. M. de Gruijter & L. J. T. van der Kamp, *Advances in psychological and educational measurement*. Chichester: Wiley.

Wood, R. (1978). Fitting the Rasch model: A heady tale. *British Journal of Mathematical and Statistical Psychology, 31*, 27–32.

Woodcock, R. W. & Johnson, M. B. (1978). *Woodcock-Johnson Psycho-Educational Battery*. Hingham, MA: Teaching Resources.

World Health Organization (2004). *The international classification of diseases and health related problems, ICD-10* (2nd ed.). Geneva: WHO.

Wright, J. C. & Mischel, W. (1987). A conditional approach to dispositional constructs: The local predictability of social behaviour. *Journal of Personality and Social Psychology, 53*, 14–29.

Yang, S. & Sternberg, R. J. (1997). Taiwanese Chinese people's conceptions of intelligence. *Intelligence, 25*, 21–36.

Zeleny, L. (1933). Feeblemindedness and criminal conduct. *American Journal of Sociology, 38*, 564–576.

Author Index

Subject Index

Assessment, Measures and Tests Index

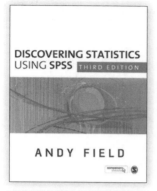
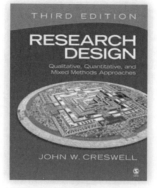

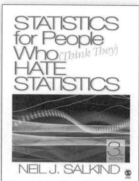

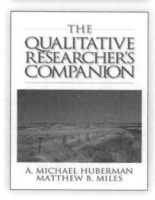

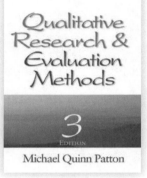
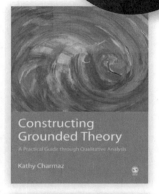
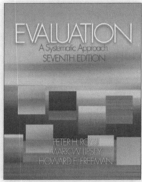
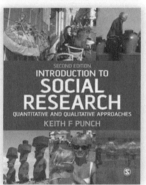
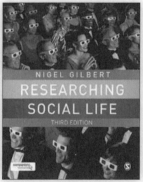
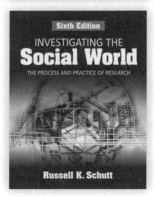